WRITTEN TO BE HEARD

WRITTEN TO BE HEARD

Recovering the Messages of the Gospels

Paul Borgman and Kelly James Clark

WILLIAM B. EERDMANS PUBLISHING COMPANY
GRAND RAPIDS, MICHIGAN

Wm. B. Eerdmans Publishing Co.
4035 Park East Court SE, Grand Rapids, Michigan 49546
www.eerdmans.com

25 24 23 22 21 20 19   1 2 3 4 5 6 7

ISBN 978-0-8028-7704-8

Library of Congress Cataloging-in-Publication Data

A catalog record for this book is available from the Library of Congress.

Contents

CONTENTS

Foreword

You and I, literate citizens of the modern world, typically engage the New Testament gospels in the same way we engage most narratives: we read them; we don't listen to them read aloud. And in our reading, we naturally employ the habits and skills we have acquired for reading and interpreting modern narratives, historical or fictional. We read the gospels *as if* they were modern narratives.

Some of us listen to passages from the gospels read aloud in church. But the printed liturgy for the day usually includes the text of the passage, inviting us to follow along by reading. And even if we don't follow along, our listening is no different, in essentials, from reading the passage for ourselves.

Almost always our reading of the gospels consists of reading snatches. Few of us have ever read a gospel straight through, and, almost certainly, none of us has ever listened to a gospel read aloud straight through. We don't have time. In our liturgies, our group Bible studies, our private devotions, we content ourselves with snatches.

In our interpretation of what we read, we typically treat each gospel as part of that larger composition which is the Gospels, or the New Testament. And we employ theological lenses—the lens of Pauline theology, the lens of the theology of the book of Hebrews, or some alternative. We interpret what one of the gospels says about salvation, about sin, about righteousness, about Christ's crucifixion, in the light of what the other gospels say about those matters and through the lens of our theology.

After developing the point that the gospels were written to be listened to by people who had the listening skills and habits of antiquity, the authors of *Written to Be Heard* analyze each gospel in detail to answer the question, What would ancient listeners have heard as the message of the gospel when they listened to it read in its entirety rather than in snatches, and when it was presented as a unified whole rather than as part of that larger entity which is the Gospels, or the New Testament? What cues would they have picked up as to the structure of the gospel and hence its message? What would they have heard as the message when they did not interpret it in the light of the theology of the New Testament epistles?

In their introductory discussion of ancient compositional and listening practices, the authors place special emphasis on two points. Authors in the ancient world who created compositions for listening typically made heavy use of repetitions to structure their composition: repetitions of words, of turns of phrase, of types of episodes, of images. Listeners grasped the structure of the composition, and hence its meaning, by being attentive to those repetitions. Repetition is seldom a structuring device in modern narratives, with the result that we are not attuned to taking note of repetitions. And even if we were, the fact that we read and listen to the gospels in snatches results in our seldom being aware of the repetitions and of their structuring function.

Authors in the ancient world were also fond of using so-called chiastic structures. In a chiastic structure, the main point of the passage is in the center. What immediately follows the center (call it A') mirrors what immediately preceded the center (call it A); what follows A' mirrors what preceded A; and so forth. Modern authors do not use chiastic structures, and so, of course, we are not attuned to taking note of them when we read ancient literature. We fail to catch the main point of a chiastically structured passage.

The detailed reading of the four gospels plus the book of Acts that *Written to Be Heard* presents is a literary reading. But it's a literary reading of a very different sort from most so-called literary readings. Most literary readings of the gospels treat them as texts meant to be read rather than listened to, and they employ modern skills and habits of interpretation. They do not invite and enable us to become first-century listeners.

The experience of many readers will be, as was mine, that of scales falling from one's eyes. So *that's* the message of Matthew, of Mark, of Luke-Acts, of John! I had never noticed those repetitions, or those chiastic structures. Nothing in my training as a reader led me to notice them. So I missed the cues to the structure of each gospel, and hence its main message. And even if I had been trained to notice repetitions, the fact that I engage the gospels in snatches means that I miss most of them. As for interpretation, I had always interpreted each gospel as part of that larger composition which is the Gospels, and through the lens of Pauline theology.

Why didn't someone write *Written to Be Heard* long ago?

NICHOLAS WOLTERSTORFF

Preface

As we were working on this volume, I (Kelly Clark) was repeatedly re-minded of the Simon and Garfunkel song "The Sounds of Silence." This refrain kept welling up insensibly in my mind:

> People talking without speaking
> People hearing without listening
> People writing songs that voices never share.

It wasn't all directly relevant, of course; insensible mental wellings-up typ-ically aren't. But it was just close enough that with one teeny tiny change it fit:

> People *reading* without hearing
> People hearing without listening
> People writing songs that voices never share.

That's it. Now it's nearly perfect not only for our book but also for the gospels themselves.

The gospels—Mark, Matthew, Luke-Acts, and John—we've come to learn were never intended to be read. In days long before public libraries, the internet, Amazon, and free public education, the gospels were spoken, performed, even sung to their mostly preliterate audiences. Their mean-ings, then, were transported in hearing cues and delivered to ears. Sadly, in our considerably more literate era, we can't hear the songs that voices never share. When read, the profound messages of the gospels go unheard in texts crafted for the listener's ear, not the reader's eye. For most readers, then, the hearing cues that make up those patterns are silenced. As a result, the meaning of the gospels has been lost.

This book assists the reader in uncovering what N. T. Wright calls the lost meaning of the gospels by carefully guiding him or her through the hearing process. Engaging each gospel as an orally derived text enables the recovery of Jesus's explosive messages and the meanings of his life, death, and resurrection—messages that disturbed and compelled their original, listening audiences.

Guiding our readers through a hearing of each gospel, perhaps for the first time, we hope for hearts fired by each gospel's radical vision of, for example, Jesus as Lord of God's kingdom come to earth, a kingdom of superior righteousness and communal flourishing (*shalom*), or of John's other-worldly peace that comes from abiding in Jesus who abides in the Father.

Most importantly, we hope for hearts fired by the gospels' radical visions of how to live abundantly within communities ruled by a new and challenging law of love—even for enemies—a love expressed as communal inclusion, peace, and harmony.

Acknowledgments

We are grateful to Trevor Thompson of Eerdmans Publishing and his team of editors for wise counsel and enthusiastic support.

Paul is grateful to his former students who, beyond the classroom, became serious readers and editors of his work. These include (and I apologize for any inevitable lapses in memory): former students Shawn Fisher, Joanna Greenlee Kline, Maria Constantine, Megan Good Larissa, Joel Nolette, and Paul Fey; fellow professors and scholars Harold Heie, Steve Hunt, David Moessner, Clifton Black, Graeme Bird, Warren Carter, David Mathewson, Mark Matson, Joel Green, Ruth-Anne Reese, and Craig A. Evans; from the clergy, Manny Faria, Charles Moore, and brother Dean Borgman. Each of these gifted readers has provided invaluable feedback without which this project would not have been completed.

INTRODUCTION

CHAPTER 1

Reading What Was Written to Be Heard: The Lost Gospels

The Lost Message of the Gospels

"We have forgotten what the four gospels are about," claims renowned scholar N. T. Wright in *How God Became King: The Forgotten Story of the Gospels*. While we are familiar with how the gospels begin (miraculous births and marvelous beginnings) and end (tragic death and glorious resurrection), says Wright, we ignore their "missing middles"—precisely where we learn what the life and death of Jesus *mean*.[1] The main body of each gospel, which tells us what it is about, has been lost.

Our aim in this guide is to recover the lost messages of Mark, Matthew, Luke-Acts, and John.[2] We take Matthew, Mark, and Luke-Acts (the so-called Synoptic Gospels) as fairly unified in their views but with remarkably distinct emphases. (Since the author of Luke was also the author of Acts, we take Luke-Acts as the entire gospel according to Luke, to be read as a unified whole.) John, on the other hand, has a very different message. To recover the messages of the gospels, messages that account for Wright's concern for their missing middles, we must learn *how to read what was made to be heard—how to read as if hearing!* That is the purpose of this book.

To get an idea of how "lost" the central messages have become, try answering these basic questions:

- What is the gospel, the "good news"?
- What does it mean to be "saved"?
- What is the role of Jesus in this salvation?

Raised in environments reflecting Western cultural values and Protestant evangelicalism, the responses of your authors to these three questions would have been off-base for the early part of our adult years. We are not clairvoyant about your answers, of course, but we can offer a guess that is informed by typical answers by hundreds of college students over a combined span of seventy years. The wrongheaded responses of most of these students, many from devout Christian homes, have confirmed our sense of how this book can help our readers to learn how to read what was made to be heard.

Consider these answers in the light of the gospels read-as-if-heard:

What Is the Gospel, the "Good News"?
- That God's kingdom has come on earth as the fulfillment of God's covenant with Israel, and through Israel to all people (the Synoptic Gospels).[3]
- That if you believe in the union of God and Jesus, you are immediately transformed into an eternal child of God (John's Gospel).[4]

What Does It Mean to Be "Saved"?
- Entrance into God's earthly kingdom, requiring repentance (transformation) and belief (trust) in the good news (Synoptic Gospels).[5]
- Abiding forever in Jesus, who abides in the Father, through belief in the union of Jesus and the Father (John's Gospel).

What Is the Role of Jesus in This Salvation?
- To proclaim and demonstrate the good news of God's covenant kingdom come to earth (Synoptic Gospels).[6]
- To perform "signs" (miracles) in order to generate belief in his union with the Father, which brings eternal life; to conquer sin as "Lamb of God."[7]

If you are surprised by these answers, this guide will help you read what was made to be heard—the lost messages of the gospels.

Written to Be Heard: Three Principles

Imagine a preliterate but precocious three-year-old listening to a recitation of a fairy tale:

"Oh, grandmother, what big ears you have!"
"All the better to hear you with," said the wolf.
"Oh, grandmother, what big eyes you have!"
"All the better to see you with."
"Oh, grandmother, what big hands you have!"
"All the better to grab you with!"
"Oh, grandmother, what a horribly big head you have!"

"No, no!" the young one might protest. "*Mouth*, not *head*!" The storyteller corrects the error, bemused.

"Oh, grandmother, what a horribly big mouth you have!"
"All the better to eat you with!"

The child is content and wants more.

Three-year-olds often unwittingly memorize tales they have repeatedly heard word for word. Their listening-learning skills are not unlike those of the preliterate, oral culture that constituted the intended audience of the gospels. As many scholars have pointed out, ancient storytellers such as the gospel writers used sophisticated patterns of repetition, heard by those with excellent mnemonic capacities, to structure their work.[8] They did so because the gospels were made to be heard. Emerging from their oral culture, these texts were designed for listeners' ears, not readers' eyes. In order to more fully hear each of the gospels, we will keep secondary references and footnotes to a minimum.

First Principle: Read to "Hear" the Distinctive Shape of Each Gospel Crafted through Repeated Hearing Cues

What most preliterate, oral-culture listeners would have found easy to understand is for modern readers very difficult. Written-culture readers need to learn how to "hear" the oral cues and patterns that shape each gospel. Even the most earnest and thorough reading of each gospel misses the medium, the literary construction of each text as oral performance. And, missing the medium, we miss the message. The writers of what came to be called "the Gospels" could rely on the tried and true narrative techniques of ancient writers because their audience, hearing thousands of stories (and reading no books), had acquired muscular memory systems that would assist them through the intricate world of literature spoken by a trained reader. In this book we provide "hearing aids" that highlight the oral cues running through each gospel text.

The shaping of texts for oral performances, which would have been obvious to ancient listeners, is lost on even the best contemporary reader. Even if we were to *listen* carefully to an audio recording or hear a dramatic reading of a gospel, we would still miss much of its meaning because of our diminished listening skills. As literary scholar Robert Alter notes in his study of narrative artistry in the Bible, we miss a structure that is almost musical in nature, "the measured repetition that matches the inner rhythm of the text, or rather, that wells up from it." This shaping, he claims, "is one of the most powerful means for conveying meaning without expressing it."[9] *Measured repetition* and *rhythm*, musical terms that typically apply to poetry, are necessary for understanding biblical narratives as well. In these pages we recapture some of this experience by focusing on the "measured repetition" and "inner rhythm of the text."

N. T. Wright argues that we can recover the lost meaning of each gospel by reading each gospel as a unified whole. While we mostly agree with him, we question his claim that *reading* is the solution to the problem. While repeated readings of each gospel in its entirety would be helpful, it would not rectify the problem. We miss the meaning partly *because we read.* The meaning of the gospels is in the *hearing*, as their first audiences heard. We will need to read-as-if-hearing, with pointers provided by this guide.

And yet Wright is right—we must preserve the integrity of each gospel by taking it as a unified and coherent whole. Each gospel, we will argue, has its own "voice," its unique theological perspective. Literary approaches to theological discovery of the sort we commend assume the unity and coherence of the gospels within their sociohistorical setting.

Second Principle: Listen to Each Gospel as a Unified Whole within Its Own Textual and Cultural Context

When we take Mark, for example, as an integrated unity of literary elements speaking in its own voice, one informed by ancient Jewish culture, Mark's distinctive theological perspective slowly emerges. Our approach rejects assumed and articulated approaches that interpret one biblical text in the light of others. To hear each gospel voice, we ignore the voice of any other gospel or epistle. We don't, for example, read Mark in the light of John, or Luke in the light of Paul. We seek what Mark meant by *repentance* or what Matthew meant by *righteousness*. We seek to listen carefully to the unique voice of each of the gospel writers for their distinctive theological visions.

Our literary approach to the gospels, while sensitive to sociohistorical context, differs from a historical approach.[10] While historical approaches carefully examine each part, we seek the text's interconnected unity. Only then can we "uncover" the meaning that is embedded within its structure. As Robert Alter notes, "What we find in biblical narrative is an elaborately integrated system of repetitions, some dependent on the actual recurrence of individual phonemes, words, or short phrases, others linked instead to . . . actions, images, and ideas."[11] Uncovering and understanding these overall patterns of hearing cues—repeated words, dramatic scenes, images, metaphors, and themes—will help the reader recover the unified and distinctive message of each gospel.[12]

Finally, we miss the meaning of the gospels because we read them through the distorting lenses of our own culturally influenced religious beliefs and traditions. In short, we fail to grasp their meanings because we think we know them already. But our inherited theologies and beliefs can prevent us from hearing each gospel in its own voice and context.

Third Principle: Be Aware of and Set Aside Prior Religious Beliefs and Commitments That Can Distort the Voice of Each Gospel

We need to sink—without bias—into the world portrayed in the text to hear its singular voice. Our journey into this world, of course, is never over—we can never completely divest ourselves of our biases, and we can never completely give our undivided attention to the text. So, if we want a life inspired and informed by each gospel's narrative vision, we must enter its narrative world and then exit to reenter again and again. We exit with an expanded sense of the possible and probable, and reenter with increasingly chastised assumptions—our starting points.

What unfolds in this guide, then, is an attempt at as bias-free a literary exploration as possible, an investigation checked for objectivity by examining the orally derived shape and meaning of each individual gospel narrative considered as a whole, in its own voice, on its own literary terms, and within its own cultural and historical contexts.

We offer a recovery of what's been lost—the unique message of each gospel—through a careful analysis of what each text says, heard in its own ancient voice and on its own ancient literary terms. Without slowing down to "hear," we miss each gospel's narrative logic. The discipline of literary hearing/reading can help recover the radical message(s) of each gospel heard whole. While we cannot cover all of the oral patterns heard by their ancient audiences, we will provide some tools for contemporary readers to hear how each gospel understands the mission and accomplishment of Jesus. Without attending carefully to each author's patterns of hearing cues and overarching oral structure, we miss the message of each gospel as a whole. The challenge of recovering our forgotten or lost gospels requires learning *how to read as if hearing* and *how to hear each gospel as a whole* and *how to hear with a minimum of distorting biases.*

Hearing the Gospels: Two Examples

Unlike most contemporary narratives, the gospels proceed forward while circling backward, like a symphony. Successive patterns overlap and interconnect with each other to build their compelling messages. The stories spiral forward while harkening backward. Such orchestration echoes something prior while moving forward. Consider the Gospel of Matthew. The phrase "blessed are you" is repeated ten times early in the first of five discourses, the "sermon on the mount" (chaps. 5–7). It is echoed, negatively, in the last discourse (chaps. 23–25): "woe to you" is heard seven times in rapid succession. The audience comes to understand the meaning of *blessed* in the light of *woe*, just as the cause and consequences of *woe* are more compellingly understood in the light of what it means to be *blessed*. By carefully attending to such cues, the audience hears that the blessed are saved while the wicked are lost. But this is just a start. We will step back and view the details of blessing and woe and their respective discourses within the literary context of each whole gospel.

Matthew's narrative orchestration brings to mind the early four notes of Beethoven's Fifth Symphony, *ta-ta-ta-dum*, and then, repeated immediately but a note lower, the same **ta-ta-ta-dum**. The first audiences would hear of salvation throughout Matthew—life in the flourishing kingdom among those of superior righteousness (*ta-ta-ta-dum*) as opposed to the impoverished lost life among the unrighteous (**ta-ta-ta-dum**). And they would hear of hypocrites, phonies who only appear righteous (**ta-ta-ta-**

dum), and of the genuinely righteous who feed the hungry, clothe the poor, and care for "the little ones" (*ta-ta-ta-dum*). In this dramatic hearing, one better understands the blessing, the communal flourishing, that characterizes God's kingdom (*ta-ta-ta-dum*). And one appreciates more keenly the horror of self-seeking religious pride (***ta-ta-ta-dum***).

Matthew's message of the superior righteousness required for kingdom entrance (5:20) is embedded within his structure of successive and overlapping patterns of hearing cues. We will help your eye to see what ancient ears heard, the major message embedded in the narrative's basic structuring. As N. T. Wright argues, by focusing on the beginnings and the endings of Matthew-Mark-Luke, we have lost the middle: in the case of Matthew, the law updated and clarified (*fulfilled* is the word used by Jesus) that forms the covenantal basis of God's kingdom on earth, a salvation that is membership in a new way of living, in a kingdom like none other.

Moreover, by focusing on salvation in the afterlife achieved through Jesus's death on the cross, we miss out on the teaching of Jesus about *this life*; by focusing on salvation as the gaining of heaven above, we lose sight of Jesus's teaching about God's kingdom *on earth*; by believing that faith alone saves, we lose Jesus's demanding call to *superior righteousness*; by focusing on our own salvation, we lose Jesus's shocking call *to deny ourselves, to be a servant, and to take up our crosses* on behalf of others; by making our relationship with God entirely personal, we lose the understanding of salvation as *communal flourishing*; and finally, by focusing on the benefits that we gain from God, we lose Jesus's *challenge of radical inclusion* of the outcast, the little ones, and the suffering. In short, we lose the gospel, at least according to Matthew.

John, to take a second and revealing example, is very different. His majestic otherworldly vision is more Bach's angelic chorus than Beethoven's human choir. John's stratospheric voice sings of the believer's transportation into God's glorious, eternal, and heavenly family. It is a heavenly chorus about a divine life above that begins on earth below. John's narrative also includes antiphonal and sinister dirges of darkness opposing light, of death opposing life, and of conspiracies to destroy God's only and loving Son. John's ethereal, other-world theology of the believer being raised above to dwell in God's heavenly kingdom is all the more conspicuous when placed in juxtaposition to Matthew's more earthy voice of God's kingdom come down to earth.

Conclusion: Recovering the Message of Each Gospel

From the time of Jesus's departure in the fourth decade of the first century up through the fall of Jerusalem and the destruction of its temple (70 CE), word was spreading about the great news brought by Jesus of God's reign on earth, in fulfillment of God's ancient covenant with Israel. Jesus's authority to explain and manifest the good news was dramatically affirmed by his astounding miracles, healings, and teachings. People would hear Jesus's pithy sayings, extended teachings, and mysterious parables tightly wound around the proclamation of "the gospel," *the good news of the arrival of God's kingdom now, here, on earth.* They would hear of how entrance to God's kingdom requires repentance, a radical turnaround from ordinary selfishness and parochialism to extraordinary concern for others.

For the primarily Jewish listeners, it was a fresh, shocking, but strangely compelling vision. God's radically inclusive kingdom was marked by the extraordinary self-giving and compassion of its grateful members. These communities would hear of those whose lives had been completely turned around by Jesus. They were known by their love, which expanded outward to embrace the diseased and the destitute as neighbors. Jesus's demonstration of a new kind of love for overlooked children and hemorrhaging women was both challenging and compelling. Such communities of listeners, taking Jesus to heart, held their possessions in common and shared with everyone according to need; they opened their doors widely even to their enemies. All around Judea up through Samaria and Galilee, stories of the kingdom of God could be heard in the many sighs of relief, in the singings of praises, in the exclamations of gratitude, and in the footsteps of those beating a path to learn and to be a part of it all. After Jesus died, in confirmation of God's ancient covenant, word of his rising from death galvanized believers, who were empowered to spread the gospel, thus expanding God's inclusive and compassionate kingdom from Israel out to the entire world.

Those who gathered around the storytellers would come to hear a version of what we now call Matthew, Mark, or Luke-Acts—maybe more than just one. And their children would hear, too, that the kingdom had come on earth and was growing.

Another group of listeners heard of astonishing miracles accompanied by marvelous explanations of what each miracle signified: sharing in the divine life of Jesus with his Father above. With the eloquence of prophets past, John reflects the divine revelation about the transformation from death to life, from darkness to light, from ordinary existence and its disappointments below to eternal life above in the divine family. We hear, at the heart of John's Gospel, repeated declarations that Jesus and the Father above are intimately related from before time and creation, and that to believe in this intimacy is to attain an abundant and eternal life here and now. More than the other gospel visions, John's vision of Jesus, mixed in with some texts from St. Paul, would become the dominant thinking of the church.[13]

Biblical literature, like most classic world literature, seeks to express a vision of the world that answers the most pressing question of humankind: What is ultimately meaningful in a world experienced as precarious but precious, a world of deepest longing and desire, of exquisite pleasure and demoralizing loss? The soaring majesty of language creations, for people of the Book, embodies this world of deepest longing and desire, of fear and dread, clothed in grand narrative dress from Genesis through the gospels. Here is the story of salvation's blessing, of the coming to fruition of God's divine plan of rescue and delight. The writers and authors of what become biblical texts hold their work to be sacred—that is, fundamentally about the main character, God, entering into relationship with human characters within human space and time in order to illlumine the Way of salvation's blessing.

For both readers of great literature and followers of Jesus, we offer the keys to the recovery of the radical and relevant messages of the forgotten gospels. We offer, in short, the keys to the kingdom.

PART ONE

The Gospel of Mark

CHAPTER 2

"The Kingdom of God Has Come Near; Repent" (Mark 1:1–4:34)

The Message of Mark

Mark's simple and stark message is easily obscured if read through an inherited Christmas-Easter lens, a lens of God's triumphal entry into human history and glorious exit into eternity. For example, Mark omits entirely the birth of Jesus, beginning instead with John's baptism of the adult Jesus. And Mark's mention of the resurrection, in a single sentence, serves as prelude to the shock of an ending emphasizing disciple failure (16:6–8a). Mark's narrative does not end with triumphal words of Jesus's victory over sin, death, and the devil; instead it ends in fear and unbelief: the disciples, having deserted Jesus, do not get to hear of the resurrection.

Mark's story begins with a joyous declaration: "The beginning of the good news of Jesus Christ [Messiah, the Anointed One], the Son of God" (1:1). The good news that Jesus brings is, we hear, the good news from God: "Jesus came to Galilee, proclaiming the good news of God, and saying, 'The time is fulfilled, and the kingdom of God has come near; repent, and believe in the good news'" (1:14–15). The original listening audiences would have anticipated this good news in a way modern audiences may not. Steeped in the scriptures, they, like a character in Mark, would have been "waiting expectantly for the kingdom of God" (15:43). For them, Israel's history converges on the redemption and deliverance of Israel.

Initially, the astounding inauguration of God's kingdom on earth is matched by astonishingly favorable responses. John the baptizer's preparation for Jesus and his kingdom is met with eager anticipation: "People from the whole Judean countryside and all the people of Jerusalem were going out to him, and were baptized by him in the river Jordan, confessing their sins" (1:5). But the celebratory tone of Mark's fifteen-verse preface serves as an antiphonal "setup" for a story of increasingly dismal and even tragic responses of all the major characters to the authoritative power and teachings of Jesus. The narrative's initial joy and promise are dramatically eclipsed by its concluding gloom. At the end of Mark, we hear that three women at Jesus's empty tomb are told to inform the disciples, who have deserted the Messiah and fled the scene, that Jesus has been raised from the dead. Out of fear they don't: "They went out and fled from the tomb, for terror and amazement had seized them; and they said nothing to anyone, for they were afraid" (16:8a). End of story.[1]

What are we to make of Mark's sudden and apparently inexplicable ending? The disciples' faithlessness is highlighted in this sudden ending: because of the women's fearful disobedience and the disciples' fearful faithlessness, the scattered disciples don't hear of the glorious news of the resurrection; because of the women's fear, "they said nothing to anyone" (16:8a). Absent at his crucifixion, the disciples are, after denial and desertion, absent at his resurrection. They don't get to hear the news.

While Mark surely believes in Jesus's triumphal resurrection, his narrative underplays it, focusing instead on the tragic unbelief of his closest followers. A Hollywood publicity firm might summarize Mark this way: "Exciting announcement of God's good news, with impressive endorsements, is greeted with initial but superficial enthusiasm. As pressures increase, enthusiasm decreases, attended by denial and desertion by the disciples and death for Jesus. Although death is defeated, no one remains to carry on the good news."

Mark's audiences, several decades after the departure of Jesus, know, of course, that this gospel of God's kingdom did not end dismally. His audiences know that the disciples repented after all and spearheaded the kingdom mission to Israel and beyond. Some have witnessed this repentance firsthand as strangers and outcasts welcomed by the disciples into their emerging kingdom. Mark, then, is writing for and to this later audience, would-be disciples who may be wavering.

Mark's central message is one of both warning and promise. Mark's repeated warnings (8:15; 12:38; 13:5, 9, 33) come with the promise that "the one who endures to the end will be saved" (13:13). Mark drives home his message in four sections, each organized around increasingly complex patterns of authority-response.

The Good News and Its Authoritative Proclaimer (Mark 1:1–15)

Between the preface's opening (the good news brought by Jesus [1:1]) and its conclusion (the good news of God's kingdom [1:14–15]), we hear five powerful witnesses to the authoritative power of Jesus as God's Anointed One, the Christ (1:1):

- *Mark the author*, who declares Jesus as Messiah, God's Son (1:1)
- *The prophet Isaiah*, who foretold the prophet-messenger (1:2)
- *John the Baptist*, of whom Isaiah spoke, who prepares the way for Jesus (1:3–8)
- *God*, who states, "You are my Son, the Beloved; with you I am well pleased" (1:11)
- *Satan*, God's adversary, who fails to tempt Jesus away from his calling (1:12–13)

This simple repetition of five highly credited witnesses attests to the authoritative power of Jesus. According to Mark, acceptance of the gospel is grounded in the authority of Jesus, which is confirmed by Scripture (divine words), fulfilled prophecy, an authoritative teacher (John the Baptist), and finally God himself. Even Satan, who cannot pry Jesus from his calling, must concede Jesus's preeminence.

As Mark's story proceeds, Jesus's authority as God's bringer of the good news is further confirmed by both his teaching and deeds. The shape of the preface suggests as much: *the good news of Jesus Christ* at the beginning (1:1) is echoed at the end by the hearing cue *the good news of God* (1:14). "The good news of Jesus Christ, the Son of God" (1:1) is also "the good news of God" (1:14–15). God, who is bringing his kingdom to earth, has committed the good news from on high to Jesus.

With the full authority to proclaim and demonstrate the good news, then, Jesus challenges his listeners with the proper response: turn your life around (repent) and embrace the good news (believe). Mark's story moves ahead in overlapping circles of authority and response, a narrative dynamic that increasingly generates an implied question for the listener: *How do you respond to the good news of Jesus?*

Authority-Response, the Beginning:
Twelve Successive Episodes (Mark 1:16–3:6)

Mark begins with a dizzying succession of twelve brief episodes that illustrate characteristic responses to the authoritative power of Jesus. Mark's quick pace accentuates the *authority-response* pattern that orchestrates all that follows in the story as a whole. There is no plot as such: if not recognized as a pattern connected by the repeated hearing cue of authority and response, these three chapters might appear choppy, one isolated incident following another with no better rationale than "this happened here, then that happened there." But if one leans in and listens carefully, one will hear a tightly ordered pattern of authority and response. The pattern holds it all together; intrigue builds according to ways in which various responses from differing quarters play out.

In very rapid progression we hear:

1. *Authority of Jesus*: Jesus challenges four fishermen to follow him.
   Response: They do (1:16–20).
2. *Authority of Jesus*: Jesus enters a synagogue, teaching.
   Response: They "were astounded at his teaching, for he taught them as one having authority, and not as the scribes" (1:21–22).
3. *Authority of Jesus*: A demon-possessed man responds with horror at the presence of Jesus, whom he calls "the Holy One of God"; Jesus casts out the evil spirit.
   Response: All those gathered respond with amazement at such teaching accompanied by "authority" (1:23–28).
4. *Authority of Jesus*: Jesus heals Simon's mother-in-law of fever.
   Response: She responds by serving him and his friends (1:29–31).
5. *Authority of Jesus*: "The whole city was gathered around the door. And he cured many who were sick with various diseases, and cast out many demons; and he would not permit the demons to speak, because they knew him."
   Response: The overpowered demons are not permitted to respond with speech (1:32–34).[2]
6. *Authority of Jesus*: After prayer, Jesus returns to teaching and healing. He cures a leper, warning him to say nothing.
   Response: The cured man's joy cannot be contained, and he "began to proclaim it freely, and to spread the word, so that Jesus could no longer

go into a town openly, but stayed out in the country; and people came to him from every quarter" (1:35–45).

7. *Authority of Jesus (a)*: Jesus forgives a paralytic man his sins.
   Response (a): The religious leaders charge him with blasphemy.
   Authority of Jesus (b): "So that you may know that the Son of Man has authority on earth to forgive sins," Jesus says to the paralytic, "I say to you, stand up, take your mat and go to your home."
   Response (b): "They [the crowd] were all amazed and glorified God, saying, 'We have never seen anything like this!'" (2:1–12).

8. *Authority of Jesus*: Jesus asks a man to leave his despised vocation—collecting taxes for the Roman Empire—and follow him.
   Response: "And he got up and followed him" (2:13–14).

9. *Response*: Religious leaders scoffingly complain of Jesus's fraternization with "tax collectors and sinners."
   Authority of Jesus: Jesus replies, "I have come to call not the righteous but sinners" (2:15–17).

10. *Response*: Religious leaders complain that Jesus and his disciples do not fast, and pick grain on the Sabbath (they can't recognize and won't respect the authority of Jesus).
    Authority of Jesus: Jesus tells them that he is like the bridegroom with his wedding guests and that now is no time for fasting (2:18–28).

11. *Authority of Jesus*: Jesus heals a man's withered hand on the Sabbath.
    Response: "The Pharisees went out and immediately conspired with the Herodians against him, how to destroy him" (3:1–6).

12. *Response*: "When his family heard it [that Jesus had returned home, with crowds tightly packed around him], they went out to restrain him, for people were saying, 'He has gone out of his mind.'" (The religious leaders chime in with the thought that perhaps Jesus is in league with Satan.) The crowd says, "Your mother and your brothers and sisters are outside, asking for you."
    Authority of Jesus: "And he replied, 'Who are my mother and my brothers?' And looking at those who sat around him, he said, 'Here are my mother and my brothers! Whoever does the will of God is my brother and sister and mother'" (3:20–35).

Just before this climactic twelfth episode in the pattern, Mark has provided a narrative break, involving the investiture of his authority in the "twelve, whom he . . . sent out to proclaim the message, and to have authority to cast out demons" (3:13–19).[3]

19

We have heard of responses from those accepting the challenge to be disciples, from enthusiastic crowds, from the gratefully healed, and from hostile religious leaders. Mark's patterned episodes of authority-response conclude with the ominous response of Jesus's own family. Jesus's challenge to respond—repent and believe—involves complete commitment to the will of God: "Whoever does the will of God is my brother and sister and mother" (3:35).

The two main hearing cues, *authority* and *response*, emphasize the authoritative teaching and action of Jesus while preparing Mark's audiences, decades later and listening to this narrative, to assess their own responses. Where do they stand relative to the clear authority of Jesus, Messiah and Son of God?[4]

Within this pattern of twelve representative episodes, linked by the cues of authority and response, is Mark's message of repentance and salvation. Mark concludes with a devastating portrait of Jesus's own family's failure to respond properly to the offered good news.

Family, House, and Home: An Interwoven Pattern

Woven into Mark's tapestry of authority-response is a brief but complex pattern of family, house, home. Jesus has just added to the management and mission of the kingdom family by "appoint[ing] twelve, whom he also named apostles, to be with him, and to be sent out to proclaim the message, and to have authority to cast out demons. So he appointed the twelve," who are listed by name (3:14–19). The kingdom mission now includes apostles who are appointed with "authority," which has distinguished Jesus for the past few chapters. "Then he went home" (3:19).

Then he went home? Why include this unexplained detail about going home in the middle of a staccato-like string of episodes oriented around the authority of Jesus and typical responses from crowds, traditional Jewish leaders, and the disciples? Jesus appoints apostles to share in the kingdom task *and goes home.*

> Then he went home; and the crowd came together again, so that they could not even eat. When his family heard it, they went out to restrain him, for people were saying, "He has gone out of his mind." And the scribes who came down from Jerusalem said, "He has Beelzebul, and by the ruler of the demons he casts out demons." (3:19–22)

His family, concerned by reports that Jesus is out of his mind, wants to "restrain him." Perhaps they have also heard the rumors from the scribes that Jesus is in league with the devil.

The idea of family was implicit in Jesus's call of his original four followers, who left family and vocation to follow him. His new "family" has since expanded to twelve (thirteen with Jesus). And now Jesus's biological family wants to take him "home."

The story moves on to the mention of *house*: the house of Satan and the house of God, house against house—God, Jesus, and kingdom workers versus Satan and his minions (both earthly powers and those possessed by unclean spirits). Jesus is accused by earthly power, Jewish leaders, of dominating Satan and satanic power because he is Satan's own! But Jesus, the demon conqueror, responds by saying that Satan can't cast out Satan because a house divided against itself cannot stand (3:22–27).[5]

From kingdom family the narrative moves through references to the home and family of Jesus to the house of Satan and his demons, then circles back to the family of Jesus. The hearing cues, hovering around family and home/house, need to be connected:

- Jesus expanded his *kingdom of family workers.*
- *Then he went home.*
- *His family sought to restrain him.*
- Jesus raided *Satan's house.*
- "Then *his mother and his brothers came*; and standing outside, they sent to him and called him" (3:31).

With this last we have come full circle from the mysterious going home that began this little pattern—an unexplained event, unless we carefully attend to the pattern that follows.

Writ small, we hear biology: family of father, mother, sons, and daughters on the one hand, and workers in the kingdom on the other. Writ large, family and home are cosmic: the house of Satan and the kingdom reign of God. The "family" of God, we hear, takes utter precedence over normal family allegiance and honor. When his biological family—mother Mary, brothers and sisters—comes to his rescue, Jesus rejects their "help." Speaking to a crowd, Jesus asks, "Who are my mother and my brothers?" (3:33). Refusing an audience with his concerned family, Jesus looks "at those who [are sitting] around him" and says, "Here are my mother and my brothers! Whoever does the will of God is my brother and sister and mother"

(3:34–35). Jesus's family, God's kingdom, includes only those who do the will of God with an authority, conferred by Jesus, that challenges the traditional authority of family and tribe.

Sower, Seed, and Soils: A Parable about Response (Mark 4:1–34)

Mark breaks from the frenetic and intense pace of his opening salvo of authority-response for a parable reflecting on response.

The initial positive responses have given way to increasingly negative responses, especially on the part of religious leaders who sense their power being threatened. The religious leaders seek to catch Jesus in a religious violation, hanging out with sinners or healing on the Sabbath (and in a synagogue!). Jesus's final response to their incredulity is kindness to a person in desperate straits. Looking at these leaders in anger, and grieving about their hard-heartedness, Jesus restores a man's withered hand. They repeatedly reject Jesus's audacious, God-like authority. If they can destroy him, they will be free to continue to exert their own power, at the expense of the people they rule over. Mark completes this downward trajectory of responses with a presumably disconsolate Mary left outside without word from Jesus.

It is narrative time, judges Mark, to reflect on the meaning of this pattern of similar authority-response vignettes. So Jesus "began to teach beside the sea" about a farmer sowing seed on various kinds of soils (4:1–9)—one of only two substantial teachings of Jesus in Mark.[6] As a parable often is, this one proves mysterious at first. *What is he talking about?* the disciples wonder (4:10, 13).

Jesus explains. The parable isn't primarily about the sower (Jesus) or seeds (the word of God taught by Jesus); it's about soils—response. The seed represents the good news of God, and the sower is Jesus, who "sows the word," the gospel of God, the good news of the kingdom come. The focus is on the four types of soil, the range of responses to the words and deeds of Jesus. The seed sown on the first three types of soil—impenetrably hard ground, rocky soil, and thorny soil—produces no positive results. Only the seed that falls on the fourth soil takes root and produces ample grain. As we hear in the rest of Mark's narrative, no major character is good soil; none responds appropriately to the seed sown.

(1) The seed that falls on the hardened path is easy prey for Satan, who "immediately comes and takes away the word that is sown" (4:15). Here

the audience imagines the religious leaders, who are so hardened of heart they can't hear the word of God at all. Their "path" has been hardened by empty ritual, social position, and pride.

(2) When those represented by the rocky soil receive the word of God, they immediately and enthusiastically respond, but their moral and spiritual shallowness prevents God's word from taking root; their faith withers and dies in the face of "trouble or persecution" (4:17). This second type of soil represents the crowds, who are initially enamored—"astonished" and "amazed"—by Jesus's radical teachings and exciting powers. But their enthusiastic elation will devolve into a clamor for his crucifixion (15:13–15).

(3) The third soil foreshadows what will occupy the story's narrative spotlight, the disciples' increasingly dismal responses. This is the most promising of the ultimately losing soils: it represents those who "hear the word, but the cares of the world, and the lure of wealth, and the desire for other things come in and choke the word, and it yields nothing" (4:18). Cares of this world—social status, the desire to be great, and fear for life—overcome the kingdom demand to care for the needy. Such cares of this world will incite the increasingly tragic responses of Jesus's disciples, including faithlessness (9:19), betrayal (14:10), denial (14:30–31, 72), and desertion (14:37, 50).

(4) The fertile soil, the fourth, represents those who "hear the word and accept it and bear fruit, thirty and sixty and a hundredfold" (4:20). These embrace the good news of the kingdom proclaimed and demonstrated by Jesus, turning their lives around in repentance. As noted, no major character in Mark proves fertile ground for God's word.[7] But those listening to the story know about the fruits of good soil, including the later turnaround of Peter and the disciples.

Mark, recall, is writing a cautionary tale that is both warning and promise for would-be disciples of later generations, decades after the departure of Jesus. So when Jesus begins (4:3) and ends (4:23) his explanation of responses with "*Listen!*" Mark is directing his message to this audience: "*Listen!*" *Listening* means, the text adds, to "pay attention to what you hear" (4:24). The receptive soil represents hearing and doing, carefully attending to and then cultivating the good news within, along with kingdom action. And as the followers enter into God's flourishing kingdom on earth, "they bear fruit, thirty and sixty and a hundredfold" (4:8, 20).

Jesus's original challenge to his disciples becomes, in Mark's narrative, a resounding challenge to Mark's much-later audiences: Listen to the word of God's good news "sown" by Jesus and respond appropriately: repent

23

and obey. And remember always that "the one who endures to the end will be saved" (13:13).

Mark's first four chapters set the stage for a more leisurely and complex discussion of responses to the authority of Jesus and his good news of God's kingdom. The author completes this narrative preparation with a sower parable that both characterizes and explains the range of possible responses. Three of four soils prove resistant. What hope is there for the kingdom?

Within this opening section, Mark offers two bright spots, brief parables of assurance. "The kingdom of God is as if someone would scatter seed on the ground, and would sleep and rise night and day, and the seed would sprout and grow, he does not know how. The earth produces of itself, first the stalk, then the head, then the full grain in the head. But when the grain is ripe, at once he goes in with his sickle, because the harvest has come" (4:26–29). Even with infertile soil and so many thorns, God's kingdom will start small and grow slowly. But grow it will, surely; it will come to full bloom grandly: the kingdom "is like a mustard seed, which, when sown upon the ground, is the smallest of all the seeds on earth; yet when it is sown it grows up and becomes the greatest of all shrubs, and puts forth large branches, so that the birds of the air can make nests in its shade" (4:31–32).

We will hear in a following section that some listening to Jesus will experience the kingdom's humble beginnings (9:1).[8] Mark's audience, as gloomy as his story gets, should not be deterred by the kingdom's inauspicious beginnings and the disciples' failures. God's word, like the mustard seed, may appear puny, but it is powerful.

Conclusion: Responding to God's Good News of the Kingdom Come

Mark's repeated insistence on the radical response that the kingdom demands is highlighted in his conclusion of his dozen vignettes: "Who are my mother and my brothers?" (3:33). When Jesus asks, "Who is my family?" he is undermining some of our deepest commitments and values—cares of this world. Jesus's rebuffing of his mother and his siblings is a threat to normal human faithfulness and trust, which are built on, first and foremost, kin relations (family) and, secondly, extended kin relations (tribe). In God's kingdom, faith and trust are not based on biology and culture but on a radically reoriented commitment (repentance) to God and his

24

kingdom: *whoever does the will of God* is a member of Jesus's new spiritual family. By contrasting the faithfulness and trust required in God's family with the faithfulness and trust one normally finds in kin and tribe, Jesus is highlighting the very non-normal and demanding response that is required: turning from everyday familial and cultural commitments and norms to the way of God's kingdom.

Moreover, while kin and tribe are sources of good, they are also sources of favoritism, nepotism, out-group prejudice, and even violence—all of which are anathema to the kingdom of God. From the perspective of those who are in, the in-group is associated with good, family, friend, trust, while the out-group is associated with evil, competitor, enemy, and fear. The former sows seeds of trust, while the latter sows seeds of enmity and violence. By extending family to those who do the will of God, Jesus explodes the genetic and cultural boundaries of family, opening up his "family" to every human being. With every type and sort of person included in God's family, in-group and out-group boundaries are deconstructed, and with them the enmity and violence they carry in their wake.

The demanded response is severe—give up all normal familial and cultural commitments and values and *do the will of God*. By giving up all and following God's way, one becomes part of a radically inclusive kingdom of compassion and peace. Those who renounce family and friends will "receive a hundred times as much in this present age: homes, brothers, sisters, mothers, children and fields—along with persecutions—and in the age to come eternal life" (10:29 NIV).

Mark's audience has been challenged and forewarned concerning response: they should neither fear persecution nor yield to temptation, the ever-present "cares of the world" that make up everyday desire and fear. And they are offered hope: the kingdom, small as a mustard seed, will grow into the greatest of all shrubs, providing shade for all in need. By the end of this beginning section of Mark, the audience is well armed with warnings and promises about the good news of God's kingdom come near.

CHAPTER 3

"Do You Still Not Perceive or Understand? Are Your Hearts Hardened?" (Mark 4:35–8:21)

Good and Bad News

Mark's narrative focuses on how various people, from the crowds to the disciples, respond to Jesus's good news of God's kingdom come. The good news of God's compassionate, inclusive, and increasingly realized kingdom stands in stark opposition to Mark's bad news: from the crowd's call for crucifixion to the disciples' denial and desertion, all the major characters end up responding badly. This second section includes interwoven mini-patterns to drive the point home: boat rides and miraculous feedings that illustrate the disciples' increasingly poor responses, highlighted by contrast with the good responses of two women and the father of a very ill daughter.

Mark's narrative began, as we saw in the previous chapter, with brief examples of authority-response, ranging from astonishment to faithful commitment to murderous jealousy (1:21–4:34). In a concluding parable of soils, Jesus attributes the various responses to the conditions of people's hearts: soils ranging from hardened paths to fertile ground. The best of the insufficient soils/responses is the thorny soil, which represents an initial enthusiastic commitment that is easily distracted by "the cares of the world, and the lure of wealth, and the desire for other things" (4:19).

In a pattern of three boat scenes, Mark emphasizes disciple failure, which is further highlighted by contrast with a pattern of three good responses featuring two women and a sick girl's concerned father. Parallel feeding miracles further illustrate disciple failure. The three boat scenes contrasted with the three good responses in parallel with the feeding miracles work like a musical score with interwoven repeating themes.

Three Boat Rides (Mark 4:35–41; 6:45–53; 8:13–21)

The disciples are repeatedly overcome by normal "cares of the world," cares for their own safety and status, even fear over lack of food and security. Such anxieties can cause loss of faith, in spite of Jesus repeatedly demonstrating his power to provide, a power that Jesus has also shared with them (6:7–13). Jesus chides them for their "hardened hearts" (their thorny soil), which prevents their uncompromised belief in and embrace of "the will of God," which is to bring the kingdom of God to earth (1:14–15; 3:35).

First Boat Ride: Fear (Mark 4:35–41)

Immediately following the parable of the soils, with its attendant warnings and promises concerning responses to God's word, Jesus suggests to his disciples that they go by boat "across to the other side" into Gentile territory (4:35–36; 5:1). In treacherous seas, with their boat close to capsizing, the panicked disciples wake Jesus. They cry out in fear, "Teacher, do you not care that we are perishing?" (4:38). Jesus "rebuke[s] the wind, and [says] to the sea, 'Peace! Be still!'" (4:39).[1] With the waves calmed, Jesus asks, "Why are you afraid?" This simple rhetorical question, offered as a rebuke of his disciples, is quickly followed by an accusatory question: "Have you still no faith?" (4:40).

The disciples, "filled with great awe," ask, "Who then is this, that even the wind and the sea obey him?" (4:41). Although they have heard him teach with authority and seen his authority confirmed in miracles, they have little sense of who Jesus is and the scope of his power. Their awe, like the crowd's astonishment, is shallow: the seed of God's word can't flourish in such soil. While awe and astonishment are easily aroused, such visceral response does not constitute faith; they are just as easily vanquished—able to turn, in fact, to hostility. (The awe and astonishment of the crowds will soon give way to condemnation: "Crucify him!" they will cry out.) The disciples' apparent commitment to Jesus will give way to denial and desertion. In this second section, their fears of danger and deficiency lead to responses that elicit the double rebuke from Jesus: "Why are you afraid? Have you still no faith?"

Second Boat Ride: Hard Heart (Mark 6:45–53)

Following the miraculous feeding of more than five thousand persons, Jesus commands the disciples to "go on ahead to the other side [by boat], to Bethsaida." He remains, dismissing the crowds and going up a mountain to pray (6:44–46). "When evening came, the boat was out on the sea, and he was alone on the land. When he saw that they were straining at the oars against an adverse wind, he came towards them early in the morning, walking on the sea. He intended to pass them by" (6:47–48). Perhaps he intended encouragement, passing them while leading the way to the opposite shore.

Spying Jesus walking on the water—"a ghost"?—the disciples are terrified (6:49–50a). "Take heart, it is I," Jesus says; "do not be afraid" (6:50b). "Why are you afraid?" Jesus had asked during the first boat ride. Now, he gets into the boat, and the winds immediately cease. "And they were utterly astounded, for they did not understand about the loaves [Jesus had miraculously supplied loaves and fish for five thousand], but their hearts were hardened" (6:51–52). *But their hearts were hardened*—a condition of recalcitrant response echoing that of the pharaoh encountered by Moses (Exod. 7:3, 13) and of the Israelites themselves (Ps. 95:8).

"Astonishment" and "hardened hearts" are curiously coupled in Mark. While awe, astonishment, and amazement are typically positive terms, Mark's text shows them to be superficial, subject to disappointment and even a subsequent hardening of the heart. In Mark's narrative, easily impressed people are just as easily disappointed. Initial enthusiasm degenerates into indifference toward or even resistance to Jesus. People who respond enthusiastically to the good news of God with "amazement" have no root, so "immediately they fall away" (4:16–17). Throughout Mark's narrative we hear that the crowds, the disciples, and even Pontius Pilate are astonished.[2] Such surprise and awe can indicate the opposite of faith, as with the disciples in this scene: "They were utterly astounded, for they did not understand about the loaves; their hearts were hardened" (6:51). Awe and astonishment, like the *oohs* and *aahs* at the finale of a fireworks extravaganza, are involuntary gasps at displays of power; but like fireworks, they shine brightly and quickly fade away. Following Jesus, however, involves a considered choice from the depths of an open and willing heart. Faith in God's good news involves the daily and costly business of paying attention to others, following Jesus into God's kingdom come to earth (1:14–15).

Since instinctive responses of fear and awe are both normal and natural, the listening audience might well be drawn into the story as if they were in the boat with the disciples. Mark, then, implicitly asks audiences listening to this story: *How are you responding to the gospel of God's kingdom come?*

Third Boat Ride: Shut Eyes, Hard Hearts (Mark 8:13–21)

Jesus and his disciples once again are in a boat, and once again going "to the other side" of Lake Galilee, to a more Gentile-occupied territory (8:13, 22). Jesus warns his followers of the "yeast" of their religious leaders, the "Pharisees"—which resembles the self-seeking status of imperial leaders like Herod (8:15). Upon hearing the word *yeast*, the disciples immediately think loaves (food), which they had forgotten to bring on board. Jesus is talking about God's kingdom, but they can only think about lunch. Eager to explain the yeast metaphor in spiritual terms, Jesus is dismayed the disciples have descended to the level of appetites.

Their fear about no food overwhelms their sense of mission. How could they have so quickly forgotten his recent miracle of the multiplication of the loaves? "Do you still not perceive or understand?" he asks. "Are your hearts hardened? Do you have eyes, and fail to see? Do you have ears, and fail to hear? And do you not remember?" (8:17–18).

Hardened hearts, unseeing eyes, unhearing ears: the disciples appear closed off to understanding, to responding positively to God's will. So Jesus recounts the miracle of the loaves and asks rhetorically, "Do you not yet understand?" (8:21). The disciples' lack of understanding is more a matter of heart than intellect; their hardened hearts prevent their willingness to hear and reorient their lives toward God and his kingdom. The proper response of an open and willing heart to the good news was announced at the start: *repent (turn around), and believe in (trust) the good news of God's kingdom* (1:14–15).

What the eye sees and the ear hears, one typically believes. But just as a smoker can see and hear that smoking causes cancer, if she yet lacks the will to stop, her heart can resist what is otherwise crystal clear. Mark's narrative suggests that the proper orientation of one's heart is essential to understanding God's will. So Mark helps his audience get to the bottom of deficient response, its root cause.

Two Miraculous Feedings (Mark 6:35–45; 8:1–21)

A second mini-pattern weaves its way through the patterns of this second section, deepening the sense of the disciples' dismal responses to the authoritative teaching of Jesus and his show of kingdom power.

First Feeding and Failure (Mark 6:35–45)

Immediately after a flashback to John's beheading (6:14–29), "the apostles gathered around Jesus, and told him all that they had done and taught" as a result of their newly given kingdom power (6:7, 30). Given the bad news of John's death and the need for respite from exhausting kingdom work, Jesus invites the disciples to join him at a quiet place for a well-deserved rest (6:31). But given the crowd's eagerness for cures and comfort from Jesus, their respite cannot last long.

As Jesus and his disciples board their boat, they are recognized, and many curious people journey ahead to meet them on shore. Though weary, Jesus takes compassion on the people and starts to teach them the good news of God. Far removed from any food source, the time grows late and the people hungry. "Send them away," the disciples suggest, "so that they may go into the surrounding country and villages and buy something for themselves to eat." Jesus, however, asks for a response that takes responsibility. Although they have already been given kingdom power to solve problems like this (3:13–15; 6:7–13), they fail to take responsibility. They resist Jesus's request by asking, "Are we to go and buy two hundred denarii worth of bread, and give it to them to eat?" (6:37b). Jesus asks them instead to gather up all of the available food. From the five fishes and two loaves that they recovered, Jesus produces enough to feed five thousand with leftovers.

The disciples fail to "understand about the loaves," as we have seen, because their hearts are "hardened" (6:52). They have not trusted in the kingdom's good news and the kingdom powers conferred on them. "*You* feed them," Jesus asks—a simple and good request for those with kingdom powers. But they respond poorly: *You do it, Jesus.*

Second Feeding and Second Failure (Mark 8:1–21)

When Jesus cures a deaf man with a speech impediment, the crowds are astonished "beyond measure" (7:31–37). Curious, intrigued, and needy, the crowds follow after Jesus and, once again, end up far removed from any food source (8:1–3). In spite of Jesus's prior miraculous feeding, the disciples ask, "How can one feed these people with bread here in the desert?" (8:4). This time Jesus says nothing in response. Moved by compassion for the hungry, he multiplies seven loaves and a few fishes into a meal large enough for the four thousand people, again with leftovers (8:5–9).[3]

Once again, the disciples have forgotten both Jesus's kingdom power and their own. They, like the crowds, prefer seeing signs and wonders from Jesus. Mark includes here a brief interlude about the Pharisees seeking a sign, "to test him" (8:11). Jesus sighs deeply (8:12): perhaps the disciples, like the Pharisees, are testing him. They continue to follow, but at an increasing distance from the heart of their leader's kingdom mission and its power source. They want a show from Jesus, rather than showing up with their own invested power. Their failures of response are accentuated by Mark's grouping of the three boat scenes and repeated feeding scenes, interlocking patterns that illustrate on the one hand the kingdom power of Jesus and on the other hand the increasingly poor response of the disciples.

Two Little Daughters and a Bleeding Woman
(Mark 5:21–24, 35–43; 5:25–34; 7:24–30)

In the midst of these interwoven patterns of hard-hearted responses from both the traditional leaders and the new would-be leaders, there is a twist: two women and a concerned father combine to effectively highlight, by contrast, the disciples' dismal responses. In the three analogous sequences, these characters respond in faith by falling at Jesus's feet or bowing before Jesus.[4] The first two stories are so intertwined that one interrupts the other, which then comes to its resolve.[5]

(1a) A Father's "Little Daughter" (Mark 5:21–24)

The daughter of Jairus, "one of the leaders of the synagogue," is lying near death. Jairus comes to Jesus, *falls at his feet*, and begs him to cure his daughter (5:21–24).

We have already heard of the hostility to Jesus on the part of other religious leaders and of Jesus's justifiably angry response (3:1–6). But Jesus responds positively to this ranking synagogue official who, by falling at his feet, demonstrates his sincere belief in and submission to the authority of Jesus. "Come and lay your hands on her," the man pleads, "so that she may be made well, and live." So Jesus goes with him (5:23–24).

But then, an interruption.

(2) A Bleeding Woman (Mark 5:25–34)

A woman, "suffering from hemorrhages for twelve years," intrudes on the scene. In a society that viewed women as second class, bleeding as unclean, and suffering as punishment for sin, *woman, blood, suffering* combine here to create a ritually impure social outcast.

The woman apprehensively approaches Jesus from the rear, touches his cloak, and is cured. Sensing a release of healing power, Jesus stops, turns around, and asks who touched him. "The woman, knowing what had happened to her, came in fear and trembling, fell down before him, and told him the whole truth." Jesus responds to her with commendation. He says to her, "Daughter, your faith has made you well; go in peace, and be healed of your disease" (5:33–34).

The woman's *falling-down-before-him* faith, similar to the synagogue leader's falling down before the authority of Jesus, restores her to wholeness and peace. Of such are those rescued for kingdom well-being. In Mark, the kingdom of God is an inclusive community of restored outcasts.

(1b) The Father's "Little Daughter" (Mark 5:35–43)

Mark's narrative returns to Jairus's dying daughter. When people come from Jairus's house to inform him of his little girl's death, Jesus overhears and comforts the synagogue official: "Do not fear, only believe" (5:36).

The challenge *Do not fear, only believe* echoes, in reverse, the fear and lack of trust in the disciples.

Upon arrival at Jairus's grief-stricken house, Jesus enters the daughter's room with father, mother, and a few disciples. He gently takes the daughter's hand into his own and says to her, "Little girl, get up!" (5:41). She does so and walks about. Witnesses are "amazed" (5:42), an understandable but inadequate response. Astonishment, we hear repeatedly, is not faith. Unlike the bleeding woman and hopeful father who fall at the feet of Jesus in obedience to his words "fear not, only believe," the crowd displays its typically skin-deep astonishment.

Mark's story is fundamentally about response to the authoritative power of Jesus. To be amazed might appear as innocuous as it is natural. But to those who are simply amazed, Jesus is little more than a sideshow magician. While entertained, to the point of astonishment even, they lack a faith that believes-in and submits-to. Meeting the demand for magic (or deliverance from political enemies) has nothing to do with the gospel, the good news. Awe, astonishment, and amazement, which are responses to displays of power, can prevent a clear understanding of both who Jesus is and what he has come to do. Even the disciples (perhaps especially the disciples) increasingly fail to grasp the nature and mission of Jesus. So Jesus insists on secrecy: even those who have just witnessed the daughter's resurrection should tell no one (5:43).[6]

(3) A Mother's "Little Daughter" (Mark 7:24–30)

A little later in the narrative, a Gentile mother is rebuffed by Jesus. "Let the children [Israel] be fed first" is his standoffish answer to a request on behalf of her very ill daughter; "it is not fair to take the children's food and throw it to the dogs [Gentiles]" (7:27; at the time, associating with a Gentile was considered a defilement by Jews). Despite her humble and public admission of faith, Jesus refuses her request.[7]

But the woman will not be deterred. "Sir," she answers "even the dogs under the table eat the children's crumbs." Jesus changes tack. Has he learned something, on the spot? "For saying that," he tells the woman, "you may go—the demon has left your daughter" (7:28–29). Though a despised tribal outsider, and a woman to boot, the mother is honored by Jesus for her tenacious faith, which is sufficient for making her daughter whole. She returns home to find her child lying in her bed, healed. Her faith is clear from the start: "She came and bowed down at his feet" (7:25). All three illustrations of good response include falling down before the authority of Jesus. The woman's tenacious faith begins with her respect for the authoritative power of Jesus—she argues with Jesus on behalf of righteousness, of treating her and her daughter rightly, with equitable kingdom power. Such faith, inspired by the loving care of a mother on behalf of her ailing daughter, brings the daughter's liberation from death.

The parallel scenarios of life-bringing faith offer paradigms of faith in the authoritative power of Jesus. This mini-pattern serves as a foil to highlight the darkness of this section's major pattern: the boat and feeding scenes that illustrate the disciples' deficient responses to the authoritative power of Jesus and to his kingdom mission.

Conclusion: Submitting to and Accepting the Authoritative Power of Jesus

Both Mark's opening section and the section discussed in this chapter include two stories that set the narrative stage—confrontations between the authoritative power of Jesus and of Satan's demons. In both episodes, Jesus liberates men possessed by demons. The first occurs in a synagogue (of all places) and the second, "among the tombs" in Gentile territory.

In Mark 1, at the beginning of his mission, Jesus successfully commands an unclean spirit to leave the afflicted man's body, confirming his authority (1:21–28). In Mark 5, Jesus encounters a demon-possessed man so powerful he broke the shackles meant to restrain him. "No one could restrain him any more"; then, repeated, "No one had the strength to subdue him" (5:3–4). And he is unable to control himself, "always howling and bruising himself with stones" (5:4–5). Yet sensing Jesus's authority from far away, "he ran and bowed down before him; and he shouted at the top of his voice, 'What have you to do with me, Jesus, Son of the Most High God? I adjure you by God, do not torment me'" (5:6–7).

The meaning of this bowing is not entirely clear; it could be either the man's sincere faith in Jesus's authority or the demons' reluctant acknowledgment of Jesus's power. However, Mark's placement of this story at the beginning of a section in which three more people bow in faith gives us the simplest hearing cue we could hope for. We hear, in each bowing, the appropriate response to the authority of Jesus: believing-in and submitting-to.

Even demons and demon-possessed men recognize and heed what the disciples' fears and hard hearts preclude: appropriate response to the authority of Jesus. Jesus repeatedly chides the disciples for their poor responses, made all the more apparent by the stunningly positive responses of the demon-possessed men. Their poor responses are also highlighted by Mark's narrative twist of the unlikely *fall-at-his-feet faith* of a bleeding woman, a Jewish father and leader, and a Gentile mother.

The disciples' fears and hard hearts likewise preclude their understanding of and trust in God's compassionate kingdom. God's radically inclusive kingdom, Mark has shown us, includes Jews but Gentiles too, men but women too, societal members in good standing but outcasts too, adults but children too, religious leaders along with ex-demoniacs. The kingdom's compassionate power has cleaned and clothed the demon-possessed man, given life to a dying daughter, fed thousands, and healed a bleeding woman. Jesus has restored the physically, spiritually, and socially disenfranchised—candidates all to the *shalom* of the kingdom. The good news of the kingdom come is no longer merely news of what's to come. It is happening (1:14–15).

Ironically, the disciples, endowed with kingdom power, participated in some of these liberations and yet did not understand. Mark's exploration of response, with his brilliant exploration of the human heart, is aimed at cajoling and nudging and convincing his audience to respond to the authority of Jesus and the gospel of the kingdom in trust, not fear, and with repentance, not resistance.

CHAPTER 4

"Who Is the Greatest?" (Mark 8:22–10:52)

"Do You Still Not See?" The Anatomy of Failure

In spite of seeing and hearing Jesus, witnessing and even performing miracles, and experiencing the wonders of the kingdom, his disciples stubbornly resist appropriating the good news of God's remarkable kingdom. The last thing we've heard, concluding Mark's second section, came from the lips of an intensely irritated Jesus: "Do you still not perceive or understand? Are your hearts hardened? Do you have eyes, and fail to see? Do you have ears, and fail to hear? And do you not remember?" (8:17–18). Although they have seen, heard, and even participated with divine power in God's incipient but growing kingdom, they do not yet understand. They are blind. Jesus is trying hard to heal them, but they won't have it. In this crucial middle section, Mark explores what lies at the heart of this blindness—unwillingness to see.

Framing this middle section about disciple blindness are stories about blindness cured (8:22–26; 10:46–52). The hearing cue is clear: although not literally blind, the disciples cannot see. This blindness-healed framing[1] accentuates the metaphoric blindness (sight-but-can't-see) of the disciples; both blind men are healed (can see/understand), but the sighted disciples cannot see/understand.

The disciples' increasingly dismal responses to Jesus are likewise contrasted with Jesus's increasingly costly responses to the will of God. As Jesus humbly proceeds down the way of self-giving suffering, shame, and death, the disciples blindly assert their arrogant and shameful desires for status and glory, their desire to be great.

Woven in between these major movements are explanatory show-and-tell episodes in which we see played out failed response to the good news rooted, as noted, in the desire to be great.

Jesus's Way, the Disciples' Way: Three Intensifying Movements

Mark's central teaching is organized by a pattern of three parallel sequences (8:27–38; 9:30–37; 10:32–45). Each of these three sequences contains three movements:

1. Jesus suffering loss: he foretells his coming loss of honor and life and his rising from death.
2. Disciples seeking gain: they respond with talk about securing their own lives with positions of honor.
3. Repentance: Jesus explains to the recalcitrant disciples the need to reverse fields of attention and action from the evil of ordinary empires to the righteousness of God's kingdom.

Movement One (Mark 8:27–38)

After Peter identifies Jesus as Israel's promised Messiah, Jesus explains what being Messiah means.

Jesus Suffering Loss

We hear, for the first time, Jesus's foretelling of his suffering and death: "Then he began to teach them that the Son of Man must undergo great suffering, and be rejected by the elders, the chief priests, and the scribes, and be killed, and after three days rise again" (8:31–32a). But—and this will be repeated—death will not have the last word: Jesus will rise from death.

Disciples Seeking Gain

At this, Peter "took [Jesus] aside and began to rebuke him" (8:32b). While Peter does not want Jesus to suffer and die, he appears, in the context of this whole section, to be more concerned about his own prospects. Peter thinks he's found God's long-promised deliverer-king who will crush the Romans and ascend to Rome's emptied throne in power and honor. As the Messiah-King's devoted follower, Peter hopes to secure a powerful and glorious position in this new kingdom.

Repentance

Jesus rebukes Peter for setting his mind "not on divine things but on human things" (8:33)—satanic things, in fact. Here is an echo of the bad soil in the sower parable, a response that chokes out the seed of the word about God's kingdom by thorns like "the cares of the world, and the lure of wealth, and the desire for other things" (4:18–19). "Other things" include glory: of all such they need to repent, to reorient their lives and thinking. These normal "cares of the world," which Jesus will resist but the disciples will not, are diametrically opposed to kingdom attitudes. Jesus explains: "He called the crowd with his disciples, and said to them, 'If any want to become my followers, let them deny themselves and take up their cross and follow me. For those who want to save their life will lose it, and those who lose their life for my sake, and for the sake of the gospel, will save it'" (8:34–35). Instead of asserting themselves, seeking glory, and fearing death, the disciples, like Jesus, must deny themselves and take up the cross—the way of suffering, shame, and even death. In shunning shame, which Jesus says he must suffer, the disciples shun Jesus. By seeking power and glory, the disciples are, in effect, ashamed of Jesus. He goes on: "Those who are ashamed of me and of my words in this adulterous and sinful generation, of them the Son of Man will also be ashamed when he comes in the glory of his Father with the holy angels" (8:38). If the disciples are ashamed of him, he will be ashamed of them.

Movement Two (Mark 9:30–37)

The disciples' failures of belief and practice lead directly to a lengthy exploration, following a similar literary pattern, of what lies behind their blindness.

Jesus Suffering Loss

Again, Jesus tells his disciples of his impending betrayal, death, and resurrection (9:30–31).

Disciples Seeking Gain

Again, the disciples "did not understand" (9:32). So far are they from understanding Jesus's humble and self-giving way that they argue instead over "who [is] the greatest" (9:33–34). Thinking themselves first, they desire nothing but their own greatness.[2]

Repentance

The disciples' self-centered interests prevent them from hearing that "whoever wants to be first must be last of all and servant of all" (9:35). In God's kingdom, greatness is not achieved by elevating oneself above others (extorting or even forcing others to honor and serve one); it is achieved by humbly placing oneself below others, honoring and serving *them* (not *me* or *us*). To reinforce his point about true greatness, Jesus takes a child, the lowest in society, into his arms and says to the disciples, "Whoever welcomes one such child in my name welcomes me, and whoever welcomes me welcomes not me but the one who sent me" (9:37). If one wants to be greatest in his kingdom, one must lower oneself beneath and serve even a child.

Movement Three (Mark 10:32–45)

For a third time Jesus foretells his way of suffering, ridicule, and death, which will be followed by his rising from death. For a third time the disciples respond with the normal way of self-interest and status-seeking. And for a third time Jesus patiently teaches and demonstrates the self-sacrificial way of the kingdom and its cross, God's way of rescuing the lowly from oppression and misery.

Jesus Suffering Loss

Jesus again speaks of his forthcoming arrest, suffering, shaming, death, and resurrection. In a culture that so esteems honor (the glorification of self, family, and tribe), shame and ridicule should be avoided at all costs (death goes without saying). Again, the text makes clear the extent of the Son of Man's loss of honor—he will be mocked, spat on, and condemned unjustly to death; his flesh will be ripped from his naked body; and he will be hung on a criminal's cross. There is no glory or greatness here.

Disciples Seeking Gain

After Jesus dramatically and vividly tells of his impending horrific suffering, shame, and death, the disciples respond in effect, *Yes, yes, whatever. But what can you do for me?*

James and John callously ask their personal miracle worker to do whatever they ask. No doubt Jesus sighs as he plays along, "What is it you want me to do for you?" (10:36). They ask, in effect, for Jesus to make *them* great, to lift them above ordinary folk and seat them at the right and left hand of the Son of God: "Grant us to sit, one at your right hand and one at your left, in your glory" (10:37). In their desire to be great, they wish even to be on a par with God, ruling over the world with authority and power.

Repentance

If you want a place in God's kingdom, says Jesus, you must drink deeply the cup of suffering and death that I will experience. James and John respond affirmatively—"we are able"—but with an utter lack of comprehension. While Jesus presciently proclaims that they *will* drink his cup, he sees that they are still preoccupied with their own greatness (who, they still wonder, will sit at his right or left hand?). Mark clinches the disciples' preoccupation with greatness by immediately noting the bickering disciples, who are angry at the conniving James and John for beating them to the punch, asking Jesus to make them great. Jesus, however, refuses the disciples' arrogant aspirations to tyrannically lord their power over people. He offers, instead, the opposite way of "greatness" in God's kingdom: "Whoever wishes to become great among you must be your servant, and whoever wishes to be first among you must be slave of all" (10:43–44). Again, the disciples will come to humbly serve from below the little ones, bleeding women, and blind beggars. But for now, wishing to be great, they cannot see; they are, thus, unable to repent, turn around from normal aspirations to the way of God.

This way of God culminates, for Jesus, in his willingness to give up his very life for the sake of gathering others into the kingdom. And he expects the same from his disciples: "Whoever wishes to become great among you must be your servant" is followed by Jesus speaking of the extent to which he is willing to serve. Jesus grounds the disciples' self-sacrificial kingdom mission in his own: "For the Son of Man came not to be served but to serve, and to give his life a ransom for many" (10:45).

To *ransom*, in the context of the Hebrew Bible (Old Testament), is to serve others at extraordinary cost to oneself, a willingness to forfeit one's own comfort and desires for the purpose of delivering or rescuing another from various imprisonments and oppression. Jesus's radically other-regarding service liberates—ransoms—the oppressed and outcast from their demons or oppressors or illnesses, ushering them into God's compassionate and inclusive kingdom.

The disciples' kingdom mission—to rescue the least and neediest among them—likewise requires serving others at extraordinary cost to oneself. For their sake, one forfeits one's own glory to seek and find the in- glorious, the disfigured, the imprisoned, and the scapegoated and, kneeling beneath their feet, heal them. One finds the wicked, the demon-possessed, and those who have sinned against one; then one eagerly forgives them their sins, liberating them from sin's crushing power. Genuine liberation requires genuine compassion and concern; those who seek greatness nei- ther see nor care for those "beneath" them.

God's kingdom righteousness, characterized by humility, generosity, and compassion, runs clean contrary to most normal social values—glory, wealth, and power—and so is a threat to religious, social, and political lead- ers who both thrive on and control expressions of power. God's inclusive, peaceful, and growing kingdom is a threat to the hierarchical, prejudiced, and diminishing kingdoms of the world. So following Jesus is likely to in- cur the wrath of religious and political leaders; Jesus's is the costly way of suffering and death. And just as Jesus will give his life a ransom for many, the disciples will likewise make the ultimate sacrifice to ransom[3]—liber- ate—others for God's kingdom on earth.

Those who give their entire lives to rescue and then empower the dispossessed may also have to give up their lives to those whose power and prestige are threatened by God's alternative kingdom. It is a kingdom so near, emerging already, that loss of life itself will become a reality that some of them will experience (9:1).

Show-and-Tell, Woven between Movements

The Light of Transfiguration, the Shadow of Response (Mark 9:2–29)

After the first of the three repeated movements disclosing the willingness of Jesus to suffer shame and death juxtaposed with the disciples' zeal for their own glory, Jesus takes Peter, James, and John up a mountain where they have a foretaste of this kingdom. In the company of Elijah, Moses, and Jesus in "dazzling white," the awestruck but self-aggrandizing Peter suggests building dwellings to share exclusively in the reflected glory of these luminous presences (9:2–6). As Jesus shines in his glory, Peter reveals the shadow dogging him throughout the story: he wants to shine in glory with Jesus forever.

But from behind an overshadowing cloud, God booms, "This is my Son, the Beloved; listen to him!" (9:5–7). When Jesus asks the disciples not to say anything about what they had seen "until after the Son of Man [has] risen from the dead" (9:9), the uncomprehending disciples quibble over what rising from the dead could possibly mean (9:10). Their silly and irresolvable philosophical debate averts their attention from the rescue work they have been empowered to do—and so they immediately fail to free a child from satanic possession. The child's father comes to Jesus, upset. "I asked your disciples to cast it out, but they could not do so." A frustrated Jesus says to his ineffectual disciples, "You faithless generation, how much longer must I be among you? How much longer must I put up with you?" (9:18–19). Jesus heals the child and explains that the disciples' failure was due to lack of belief—"All things can be done for the one who believes" (9:23)—and lack of prayer (9:29).

The placement of this story after the story of the transfiguration—with the disciples' desire to bask forever in the reflected glory of the luminaries—suggests a common cause of both unbelief and lack of prayer: their desire to be great. This point is reinforced by a hearing cue—"child." Who is greatest? Jesus responds by taking "a little child and put[ting] it among them; and taking it in his arms, he [says] to them, 'Whoever welcomes one such child in my name welcomes me, and whoever welcomes me welcomes not me but the one who sent me'" (9:34–36).

Little Ones, Continued (Mark 9:38–10:16)

"If any of you put a stumbling block before one of these little ones who believe in me," Jesus goes on to say, "it would be better for you if a great millstone were hung around your neck and you were thrown into the sea" (9:42). Yet, after all this child talk, the disciples startlingly reprimand people for bringing little children to be blessed by Jesus. He responds, "'Let the little children come to me; do not stop them; for it is to such as these that the kingdom of God belongs. . . .' And he took them up in his arms, laid his hands on them, and blessed them" (10:13–16).

The Poor as Little Ones (Mark 10:17–31)

Mark moves on with Jesus inviting a man with money to join him in serving the poor, who are also portrayed in Mark's story as "little ones." Jesus tells the man, who has inquired about what to do to inherit eternal life, to sell everything and give the money to the poor; the man "went away grieving, for he had many possessions" (10:17–22).

When Jesus says that it is difficult for those who love wealth to enter God's kingdom, the disciples are perplexed. When Jesus tells them that "it is easier for a camel to go through the eye of a needle than for someone who is rich to enter the kingdom of God," they are stunned and ask, "Then who can be saved?" Jesus replies, "For mortals it is impossible, but not for God; for God all things are possible" (10:24–27). On one's own it is impossible to be rescued from one's normal needs and desires. But with God's assistance one can attain the radical reorientation of attitude and action required in God's kingdom (1:15; 6:12).

Mark concludes this central section with the refrain that runs throughout the entire section: "Many who are first will be last, and the last will be first" (10:31). Selfishly putting oneself first—minding the cares of this world, obsessing over one's own status and well-being—makes one last. But compassionately putting oneself last and serving others above oneself, in God's kingdom of similarly compassionate people, ensures that one will share in the joy of God's kingdom.

This section concludes as it began, with a story of a blind man cured, highlighting one more time the disciples' "blindness." As they are leaving Jericho, a blind beggar named Bartimaeus, sitting at the side of the dusty road, shouts, "Jesus, Son of David, have mercy on me!" When the crowd sternly demands that he be quiet, "he [cries] out even more loudly, 'Son of David, have mercy on me!'" Those seeking glory and honor, Jesus's self-important followers, couldn't be bothered to stop and help a "little one," a blind beggar. Helping dusty, no-account beggars is not, after all, the path to ordinary human glory. Jesus, on the other hand, who came to serve and to give his life, says, "Call him here." The blind man throws off his cloak, springs up, and makes his way to Jesus. Jesus asks him, "What do you want me to do for you?" The blind man says to him, "My teacher, let me see again." Jesus responds, "Go; your faith has made you well." "Immediately," we read, "he regained his sight and followed him on the way" (10:47–52).

Blind beggars—another of society's little ones—have had their concern for status and glory beaten out of them. Although they lack sight, they know how they are seen—as nothing or less than nothing. Their humility opens up room in their hearts for other-regarding faith and hope in mercy. The outcast has what the disciples lack—the *faith* that accepts suffering and shame for the sake of the lowliest rather than fear of not having and of not counting (10:52).

Jesus stops and makes the blind beggar whole. Given sight, the man is liberated from his exile on the dusty roadside (10:46) and restored to God's kingdom community. He stands, sees (understands), and then eagerly follows Jesus on his way of suffering, shame, and death (10:48–52).

Conclusion: Stupid or Hard-Hearted?

This entire middle section of Mark is framed by blind men seeing, which highlights by contrast the disciples' lack of seeing properly. Mark's hearing cues in this section begin, develop, and then circle back to this one central theme: *How can the disciples, who have eyes, not see (while the blind can see and follow)?* And Mark's answer—they are prevented from seeing and following by their desire to be great.

The disciples have revealed their aspirations for glory and their aversion to Jesus's self-sacrificial way on more than one occasion, by sternly telling parents not to bring little children to Jesus and wanting a blind beggar to shut up and leave Jesus alone (10:13, 48). The blind man, healed by Jesus, sees and follows; the disciples, while possessing Jesus's kingdom power, neither "see" nor follow. In the end, they will deny and desert Jesus. "The stupidity of Mark's disciples," John Drury argues, "is . . . instructive to his readers. We understand Jesus better than the people in the text usually do. Their incomprehension assists our comprehension. It signals the dead-end paths—namely, routes other than the road to the Cross, which the disciples, naturally, do not want to know about."[4] The stupidity of the disciples, we learn in this section, is not due to ignorance. The disciples have seen Jesus and his power, they have exercised that power, and they have felt the kingdom coming. Although seeing, they fail to understand. They cannot "see" because their hearts are captive to *cares of this world*—the third failed response in the sower-soil parable that concludes Mark's first section. Their desire for self-glorification and tyrannical power, hanging out with the glorified prophets or sitting at the right hand of God himself, prohibits the simple faith and hope required to see and follow the kingdom way of suffering and servant love.

CHAPTER 5

The Son of Man

Three Clusters: Distinct Definitions

In Mark, Jesus primarily refers to himself as "the Son of Man," in Jewish thought of the time a term suggesting divine judgment (as in Dan. 7:13). In Mark, the Son of Man does judge in glory, but he also suffers shame and death. Mark clusters three sequences that define Son of Man as: (1) wielding authoritative power; (2) suffering ignominious shame; and (3), judging in future glory.

Ironically, those closest to the authoritative power of the Son of Man end up the most confused about—or resistant to—who Jesus, Son of Man, truly is.

Authoritative Son of Man (Mark 2:10 and 2:28)

Mark goes on to explicate his understanding of Jesus as Son of Man in terms of Jesus's power to forgive sins and his Lordship of the Sabbath.

"Your Sins Are Forgiven"

Prevented by crowds from getting a paralytic to Jesus, four friends cut through a roof to lower the man into the presence of Jesus. To make a point about his authority, Jesus trades on the popular belief that such maladies are caused by one's own sin. Instead of healing the man's physical body, he replies, "Son, your sins are forgiven." His claim to forgive sins is taken as outrageous presumption of God's authority and power by some religious leaders who exclaim, "It is blasphemy! Who can forgive sins but God alone?" (2:6–7). Jesus confirms his authority by manifesting his power over paralysis: "'But so that you may know that the Son of Man has authority on earth to forgive sins'—he said to the paralytic—'I say to you, stand up, take your mat and go to your home'" (2:8–11). The Son of Man's authority to forgive sins is confirmed by his power over the alleged physical consequences of sin.

Lord of the Sabbath

A little while later, some religious leaders observe Jesus's disciples plucking heads of grain on the Sabbath and complain about their working on the sacred day of rest. Jesus replies, "The sabbath was made for humankind, and not humankind for the sabbath; so the Son of Man is lord even of the sabbath" (2:23–28). The Son of Man, as lord of the Sabbath, grants the hungry the right to pluck grain on this holy day just as God granted the hungry David and his companions permission to eat the bread of the Presence (see 1 Sam. 21:1–6). Likewise, the Son of Man has the authority and power to heal on the Sabbath (Mark 3:1–6).[1] The Son of Man assumes the divine authority to contravene the Sabbath rituals to protect, preserve, and enhance human life.

Shamed Son of Man (Mark 8:31, 38; 9:9, 12, 31; 10:33, 45)

Affirmations of the authority and power of the Son of Man must have seemed strangely compromised by Jesus's foretold ordeal. Jesus tells his disciples, in this second cluster of teachings on the topic, that in the days ahead the Son of Man will suffer greatly.

Mark places this cluster in his central section, with its focus on disciple failure. The reason is clear: the Son of Man willingly suffers on behalf of the kingdom, while the disciples refuse. The central section began with Jesus telling his disciples that the Son of Man will suffer, be rejected by religious leaders, and be killed (but rise from death) (8:31). He will, on his way to glory, be shamed (8:38).[2] His suffering and ignominy were prophesied in their scriptures: "it [is] written about the Son of Man, that he is to go through many sufferings and be treated with contempt" (9:12). He will be betrayed to the point of death (but rise again) (9:31). The religious leaders will hand him over to the Gentiles, who "will mock him, and spit upon him, and flog him, and kill him" (10:33–34). The Son of Man came

47

to serve, not to be served, willing to lose his life for the sake of bringing outsiders into the kingdom—"to give his life as a ransom for many" (10:45).

Jesus repeatedly urges his disciples to follow the Son of Man's way of shame and suffering, to sacrifice their very lives if need be. Although the disciples have seen Jesus manifest and confirm his authority and power and have likewise employed his authority and power successfully, they fail to follow the Son of Man on his path of shame, suffering, and death (6:52; 8:17).

Glorious Son of Man (Mark 13:26; 14:21, 41, 61–62)

Toward the end of Mark, in a third cluster of references, the suffering and death of the Son of Man is framed by the Son of Man's power and glory. Though he will die, "they will see 'the Son of Man coming in clouds' with great power and glory" (13:26).[3]

Although "the Son of Man is betrayed into the hands of sinners" (14:41), Jesus says, this is not the end of the story: "You will see the Son of Man seated at the right hand of the Power" (14:61–62). In the first and last references, the Son of Man is associated with ultimate glory—"coming in clouds with great power and glory." In between these twin affirmations of glory we hear, on the other hand, that the disciples, his closest friends, will betray him (14:21 and 14:41). Having betrayed and deserted Jesus, the disciples in Mark never get to hear about the risen Jesus, the Son of Man of glory.

Conclusion: The Son of Man and His Followers

Mark's audiences would know that the disciples had become true followers of Jesus and his way of serving others through self-giving suffering. Perhaps they had likewise heard of the disciples' desertion of Jesus, made all the more surprising by their beliefs in the risen, glorious Son of Man and the signs and wonders they have heard in God's kingdom. But Mark is keenly aware that his audiences' astonishment can be easily erased by the cares of this world. So his gospel is his cautionary tale about how a person can be this close to the Son of Man, just this side of glory, and yet fail to understand.

In Mark's Gospel, as the Son of Man's identity (authority-suffering-glory) is increasingly revealed, the glory-seeking disciples are increasingly befuddled and faithless. While they like Jesus's talk of power and glory, they think it includes them, now; they believe that Jesus has come to serve them, to make them great, rulers perhaps. And shame and suffering simply do not figure into their personal plans for self-glorification. They fail to understand that, just as the Son of Man came to serve, not to be served, Jesus called them to serve. As Jesus's identity as Son of Man is expanded, the disciples diminish as followers of Jesus. Mark artistically alternates between increasing our understanding of Jesus as Son of Man—his obedience through suffering and death, for example—and the disciples' increasing ignorance and disobedience. In the end, the self-seeking disciples deny Jesus completely in order to avoid suffering and death.

Mark's pattern of clustered explanations of "Son of Man" has been carefully calibrated to reinforce his understanding of Jesus. When these explanations are allied with Mark's overlapping patterns of repeated hearing cues, his audiences are warned in compelling fashion throughout the narrative: those who avoid the suffering and possible death in following the Son of Man likewise miss out on his glory.

CHAPTER 6

"The One Who Endures to the End Will Be Saved" (Mark 11:1–16:8a)

Mark's Unconcluding Conclusion

In Mark's final section, the suffering Son of Man loses whatever worldly honor had come his way, while losing his very life as well (chaps. 11–15). He rises from death, but with no one to inform the disciples, who have denied and deserted their Lord (16:1–8a).

As Jesus approaches death, we hear of the increasing treachery of his self-seeking disciples. Mark's narrative abruptly ends with the "messengers" of the resurrection frozen with fear, unable to bear the angel's command to inform the disciples (16:7–8). Mark's stark message—understand and follow God's way of suffering and death—is emphasized by this narrative exclamation point, a shocking ending that simply stops rather than concludes.

Immediately preceding this final section are the words of Jesus to a man cured of blindness: "'Go; your faith has made you well.' Immediately he regained his sight and followed him on the way" (10:52). Like the cured blind man but unlike the blind disciples, Mark's audiences need the eyes to see and follow the radical way of God's faithful and compassionate kingdom. We will see in Mark's concluding section the sorry responses of the religious leaders, the crowds, and the disciples themselves—the conclusion of the rhythmic beat throughout the story of authority-response, authority-response. Mark's listeners have been warned about their response, summarized by Jesus: "The one who endures to the end will be saved" (13:13)—and we are at the end of the story. And none have endured. For now, Mark knows, of course, what his audiences know, that the story kept going, with a turnaround by the disciples. Along with scary warning, then, Mark's audience is encouraged: *if even the disciples denied and deserted, there is hope for us!*

In this concluding fourth section, Mark rehearses the final responses of the story's major characters, along with Jesus's final speech to his disciples and a description of his death and its purpose.

Final Responses to the Authoritative Power of Jesus

Throughout, Mark has grouped his story's major characters as we see them in this last section: (1) the religious leaders, (2) the crowd, and (3) the disciples. What we have come to expect in the responses from each group to the authoritative teaching and power of Jesus regarding God's good news, the kingdom come, is fulfilled here at the end. There are no surprises for the alert audience.

Religious Leaders

As Jesus enters Jerusalem, he visits the temple. He looks around, retires for the evening, and returns the next morning, cursing a barren fig tree on the way (11:12–14). Later, the disciples see "the fig tree withered away to its roots" (11:20), echoing, again, the parable of the seeds and soils. Jesus's violent response to the misuse of God's "house"—"[driving] out those who [are] selling and those who [are] buying in the temple" (11:15)—is likewise a rebuke to the religious authorities who are party to the temple's economic defilement.[1] The religious leaders have taken God's house of prayer and "made it a den of robbers" (11:17).[2] Incensed at Jesus's challenge to their authority and threat to their economic well-being, the religious leaders keep "looking for a way to kill him" (11:18).

When the leaders ask Jesus, "By what authority are you doing these things? Who gave you this authority to do them?"[3] he deflects their question (11:27–33) and then tells a parable[4] in which these leaders appear as thinly disguised murderers against beneficent authority (12:1–11). When the religious leaders realize that the parable is directed "against them," they want to take him into custody but do not do so because they are afraid of the crowd.

Some Herodians and some Pharisees, seeking to trick Jesus, ask him if it's lawful to pay taxes to the emperor. In response, Jesus takes a Roman coin, points to the visage on it, and asks, "Whose head is this, and whose title?" When they correctly identify the emperor, he says, "Give to the emperor the things that are the emperor's,[5] and to God the things that are God's" (12:13–17). They are amazed at his reply. Then some Sadducees, who deny life after death, attempt to trick Jesus with a contrived theological conundrum. Jesus cuts through their arrogance and unbelief in the afterlife, asserting that the God who said to Moses, "I am the God of Abraham,

Isaac, and Jacob," is the God of the living, not the God of the dead. Finally, in response to the religious leaders' demand that he single out the greatest commandment of all, Jesus replies simply and profoundly: love God with all your heart and love your neighbor as yourself; this, not empty and showy ritual, is the stuff of God's kingdom (12:28–31).

Unable to get Jesus to incriminate himself, the religious leaders send an armed crowd to arrest Jesus. They take him to stand before a council of religious leaders who are unable to construct a viable case against him (14:55–56). Finally, when the high priest asks him, "Are you the Messiah, the Son of the Blessed One?" he replies, "I am" (14:61–62).[6]

They have heard enough. The religious leaders, again colluding with political power, "bound Jesus, led him away, and handed him over to Pilate" (15:1). Mark artfully highlights this collusion with the parallel questions linked by the hearing cue regarding identity:

- "The high priest asked him, 'Are you the Messiah, the Son of the Blessed One?' Jesus said, 'I am'" (14:61–62).
- "Pilate asked him, 'Are you the King of the Jews?' He answered him, 'You say so'" (15:2).

These questions, along with their answers, neatly conjoin and summarize Mark's thematic focus on response from the religious leaders to the authoritative power of Jesus as *the Messiah, the Son of the Blessed One, the Son of Man*, and *King of the Jews*.

The Jewish leaders want authority to procure their honor and wealth, but Jesus as Messiah is a decided threat. Rome's leaders want peace to maintain their dominion, but a Jewish "King Jesus," however paltry a figure, is a threat to the empire and its peace. The Jewish and Roman leaders, ironic bedfellows though they be, are complicit in the verdict: Jesus must die.

The Crowds

With news of his marvelous teachings and wondrous healings preceding him, Jesus is eagerly welcomed into Jerusalem by the crowd. He rides in on a colt, its back covered with their cloaks. Some in the crowd even drape their cloaks on the road, while others line the road with branches. Everyone is shouting: "Hosanna! Blessed is the one who comes in the name of the Lord! Blessed is the coming kingdom of our ancestor David! Hosanna in the highest heaven!" (11:8–10). Their highly favorable response to Jesus continues Mark's initial assessment of the crowd's response to Jesus: astonishment (1:22), amazement (1:27), and hope for healing and rescue (1:32–33).

But the people's elation, their being held spellbound by Jesus's teaching and healing, is a threat to the religious leaders, who keep "looking for a way to kill him; for they [are] afraid of him" because of the people's adulation (11:18; see 15:10).[7] The crowd listens to him "with delight" (12:37) as Jesus debates with the religious authorities, who forbear from overt action against Jesus because they are afraid of the crowd (12:12).

By now, Mark's audience connects astonishment and amazement with shallow and infertile soil, which receives the seed with exuberance but then fades, quickly (4:5–6, 16–17). The religious leaders have figured out a way to sway these malleable people in another direction. "A crowd with swords and clubs" (14:43) has been sent by the religious powers to arrest Jesus.[8] Shortly after his arrest, the people of Israel in Jerusalem get to choose whom they want released back into community: Jesus or the jailed ruffian, Barabbas.[9] With their astonishment fully extinguished, and with disappointment in this failed power broker, the people answer that they want Jesus killed and the criminal released in his place (15:11, 13–14). The crowd's initial euphoria, sown in shallow, rocky soil, has, in the end, become hysterically hateful.[10]

The Disciples

We have already heard Jesus's increasing exasperation with his disciples. As we near the end, Jesus appears downright desperate. "You will all become deserters," Jesus tells the twelve (14:27).

Between Jesus's dreadful prediction and Mark's abrupt ending (in which the prediction comes true, end of story), we hear in his final speech to his followers (13:3–37) the word *beware* four times, along with similar warning and encouragement: don't be alarmed (13:7); don't worry (13:11); endure (13:13); understand (13:14); pray that it may not be (13:18); don't believe false reports (13:21); be alert (13:23, 33); be on the watch (13:34); and keep awake (13:35, 37). In such exhortations to persist in faith we find not only Jesus's last thoughts for the disciples, but Mark's clear message for the audiences of his narrative.

Jesus had already warned his disciples to *"beware* of the yeast of the Pharisees and the yeast of Herod" (8:15). These leaders were motivated by their desires for wealth, power, and honor—the ordinary "cares of the world" (4:19). Jesus echoes his rejection of acceding to the temptations of wealth and respect in his first warning in the concluding section: *"Beware* of the scribes, who like to walk around in long robes, and to be greeted with respect in the marketplaces" (12:38).[11] Of course, we have already learned of the various manifestations of such self-seeking pride on the part of the disciples—of their desires to be the greatest, to be served by Jesus, to bask in the reflected glory of the prophets, and to sit at God's right hand. The desire to be great—like the ambition of the Pharisees and Herod—prevents their understanding the gospel.

And we know that the disciples' fears of losing social status and honor prevented them from following Jesus on the way of suffering and shame in service of the least among them—the physically afflicted, the social outcasts, the women, and the children. Since it is so easy to veer from the way of suffering, even if dimly seen glory awaits, Jesus warns, *"Beware* that no one leads you astray" (13:5).

Again, although Jesus is warning his disciples, Mark's likely audiences would feel implicated and challenged to examine their own possibly wavering responses. The warnings continue: *beware* of persecution (13:9); *beware* of the Son of Man's return in judgment (13:33). Jesus also warns of persecution from one's own family, perhaps implying that Jews will hurt and even kill fellow Jews. "Brother will betray brother to death, and a father his child, and children will rise against parents and have them put to death" (13:12).[12] And they can expect to "be hated," says Jesus, with all its attending ridicule and loss of honor, if not life itself (13:13). They, Mark's audiences, are invited to drink the cup of suffering that Jesus will offer his disciples (10:39; see 14:23, 36).[13]

Don't let go of the good news, Jesus says, because "the one who endures to the end will be saved" (13:13). The way of suffering is worth enduring because the Son of Man will return in power and glory to gather his faithful (13:26).

The Death of Jesus: Blood of the Covenant Poured Out for Many

At their last meal together, a Passover meal, Jesus asks his disciples to participate in his suffering on behalf of God's kingdom. This shared responsibility is symbolized by Jesus and his disciples eating from a common loaf and drinking from a common cup. "He took a loaf of bread, and after blessing it he broke it, gave it to them, and said, 'Take; this is my body.' Then he took a cup, and after giving thanks he gave it to them, and all of them drank from it. He said to them, 'This is my blood of the covenant, which is poured out for many'" (14:22–24). In Mark's Gospel, the pouring out of blood is for the ancient covenant and its fulfillment in the kingdom come, the reign of God on earth. That is, Jesus's blood seals the covenant between God and God's people.[14]

Jesus's death, in Mark, signifies the fulfillment of *the* covenant, which God made with Abraham and Moses: the reign of God's presence and blessing on earth. In Mark's Gospel this covenant is fulfilled in the earthly reign of God, which some will see before they die.[15] For the sake of God's kingdom Jesus has already relinquished honor and glory and status and wealth. Now he relinquishes his own life as a ransom, to free those in bondage to the satanic oppressions of possession and disease and isolation.

While only Jesus can reaffirm and extend the covenant, at the same time he is asking his disciples to participate in drinking from the common cup of wine, associated with suffering.[16] As Jesus has already suggested, followers must be willing to pick up their crosses and even give their lives for the sake of others; in this way they participate with Jesus in providing the ransom needed for many, ushering in God's kingdom. "Whoever wishes to become great among you must be your servant, and whoever wishes to be first among you must be slave of all. For the Son of Man came not to be served but to serve, and to give his life a ransom for many" (10:43–45).

A "distressed and agitated" Jesus, who is "deeply grieved, even to death," implores God to spare him from the death that awaits him. He then asks Peter, James, and John to "keep awake" (14:33–34). When he sees his disciples asleep, he says again, "Keep awake" (14:38). As he returns to his fretful and impassioned prayers, his disciples, in his time of greatest need, fall right back to sleep (14:41). Jesus is left to suffer alone while his disciples sleep. "Keep awake," Jesus has said, twice, in his final speech (13:35, 37). Although they have just shared the cup and bread with Jesus, the disciples' slumber betrays their unwillingness to drink from the cup of Jesus's suffering, to share in the work of ransoming others, the little ones, from their destitution.

Jesus predicts that his disciples will all desert him as they have deserted him in their slumbering. And while Peter ardently insists that he could never deny Jesus, Jesus says that Peter will deny him not once but three times (14:30) and, along with the rest of the disciples, will desert him entirely.[17]

Conclusion

In this final section, the crowd turns from adulation and adoration to derision and scorn; Judas betrays Jesus; the disciples sleep through his anguished prayers; Jesus is captured by a crowd carrying clubs, arrested, and, after a sham trial, sentenced to death. After Peter denies Jesus three times, Pilate appeases the crowd by handing Jesus over to be crucified. The soldiers mock him, spit on him, strip him, and crucify him. The crowd continues to disparage him. Jesus dies forsaken by his disciples and, in the anguished mind of Jesus, by God.

Though Jesus rises from the dead as promised, Mark's story ends with a retrospective focus on betrayal, denial, and desertion. When the three women at the empty tomb are told to share the news of the resurrection with the disciples, the terrified women say "nothing to anyone" (16:8a). End of story. The faithless disciples do not get to hear of the glorious resurrection—not in this story that Mark tells. (Again, Mark knows that the disciples do receive this news and are transformed. But this strange non-concluding conclusion serves Mark's purposes for *this* story: *Beware! Wake up!*)

Not everyone is faithless, however. A Roman centurion, of all people, stands at the foot of the cross and proclaims, "Truly this man was God's Son!" (15:39). This presumed enemy of the Jews joins the unlikely cast of minor characters, mostly sickly social outcasts, who respond positively to the Son of Man in Mark's Gospel. The children flock to Jesus, and blind beggar Bartimaeus believes and follows. Perhaps we can include the man with the unclean spirit, the leper, the paralytic, the man with the withered hand, some of the multitude who were miraculously fed, the demon-possessed, the near dead, the bleeding woman, the Syrophoenician woman, and the deaf man. Jesus came to serve the least in society, healing them and restoring them to health and life and flourishing within a compassionate and righteous human community.

But those who were closest to him, those who heard him teach with authority and serve with power, betrayed him. Those who shared his authority and power proved unwilling to share his suffering, to drink from his cup. Those he most deeply served refused, themselves, to become servants of others. And those who glimpsed his glory wanted to keep it to themselves, rather than suffer so that others could share in this glory. While we might expect poor responses to Jesus on the part of threatened leaders and shallowly committed crowds, surely the disciples who walked hand in hand with the Son of Man in authority and power would eagerly join the suffering Son of Man. But, wishing to be great, they refused Jesus's increasingly impassioned appeals to follow him on the way of suffering and shame. Those who refuse to drink the cup of suffering will not share in the cup of glory.

Mark's audiences, as suggested, know that the disciples have repented and are now sharing in the cup of suffering. Some have already been persecuted for the sake of the kingdom; most will die a martyr's death. They have drunk from the well of suffering and shared in Jesus's glory. So Mark's audiences would not have heard the gospel as a tragedy, and they will hear Mark's message—"wake up," "beware," "listen"—as a warning not only to the disciples but to themselves as well. It is a warning to hear and to heed and to repent and to follow.

Mark's literary artistry has created a powerful cautionary story, a compelling account of what it means to follow the Son of Man through suffering—and accompanied by glory, but on the Lord's terms, not theirs. They must serve, not be served; they must be willing to lose earthly honor and life itself, if required. And they are warned that they will be tempted by the normal cares of this world—for a life of comfort, say, or a portion of greatness, or status. On the contrary, they will be subject to shame and persecution. But Mark offers the ultimate comfort, which is also a challenge: "The one who endures to the end will be saved."

PART TWO

The Gospel of Matthew

CHAPTER 7

"Repent, for the Kingdom of Heaven Has Come Near" (Matthew 1:1–4:25)

The Fourth and Last Chapter in Israel's Story

Although Matthew is the beginning of what is called the New Testament, its author would be shocked to hear that he was offering up anything new. Matthew offers his narrative more as continuation and elaboration of God's ancient covenant with Israel than the start of some "new" covenant (testament). So when the intended audience heard that Jesus pours out his blood for *the* covenant (26:28), they would go back to where Matthew goes back (1:1), to the story of Israel starting with God's covenant promise to Abraham: that through Abraham's offspring all the peoples on earth would be blessed (Gen. 12:3).

This next (and final) chapter in Jewish history, as reckoned by Matthew, is the realization of God's kingdom on earth. Matthew begins this story by introducing this new beginning in the ages of Jewish epochs (1:1–18); by indicating God's control of both this history and this new epoch (1:19–4:16); and by insisting on the response of repentance required for experiencing this new age of God's kingdom on earth (4:17–25).

A New Beginning: The Fourth and Last Age of Israel's History (Matthew 1:1–18)

Matthew's opening genealogy affirms Scripture's message of Israel's God as in control, steadfast, and loyal in covenantal love. While modern readers might think this genealogy dull, the ancient audience would have found it an exciting overview of Israel's story along with its anticipation of a next chapter pointing to covenantal fulfillment.

So keen is Matthew to connect Jesus's teachings and mission to Israel's ancient covenant that he begins at the covenant's beginning, with Abraham: "An account of the genealogy of Jesus the Messiah, the son of David, the son of Abraham" (1:1). He divides the genealogy into three parts:

1. "From Abraham to David are fourteen generations."
2. "From David to the deportation to Babylon, fourteen generations."
3. "From the deportation to Babylon to the Messiah, fourteen generations" (1:17).

And he ends with Jesus: "Now the birth of Jesus the Messiah took place in this way" (1:18).

For each of the three main epochs Matthew spells out fourteen generations by name, tedious to the modern reader but indicating for the original listeners the sweep of the divinely overseen epochs of Israel's history. They heard that the God who worked through Abraham and the patriarchs, through David and the kings, and through the prophets in exile—in equal measurements of fourteen generations—is now working through Jesus the Messiah.

The pattern of repeated cues is a thing of mathematical precision, important for Matthew's theological perspective. Hearing cues knit together the generations but suggest also the deep meaning of the word *genealogy*, "beginning" and "birth."

- Phrases and numbers are repeated: *"from . . . to . . . are fourteen generations."* (*Fourteen generations* is repeated three times.)
- Words are repeated—most importantly *genesis*: "An account of the genealogy [*genesis*] of Jesus the Messiah, the son of David, the son of Abraham." Also: "Now the birth [*genesis*] of Jesus the Messiah took place in this way."

The birth of Jesus (*genesis*) is in the grand historical context of a genealogy (*genesis*), the latter *genesis* covering the entire story of Israel back to Abraham. And before: the hearing cue echoes and recalls the title of the Torah's first book, Genesis.

While such hearing patterns of even single words—*genesis, genesis, genesis*—contribute to the enjoyment of the story, they also embed meaning, the author's theological perspective. God is in control, from the very beginning of all things, and from the beginning of Israel's story and its continuing beginnings—fourteen generations times three—and from the new beginning represented by the birth of Jesus.

Fourteen,[1] of course, is *seven* doubled, the measure of time in days that God took to create in the first genesis (Gen. 1:1–2:4a). The mathematical orderliness and precise scope of the genealogy offer a theological perspective important to Matthew: God's faithfulness to Israel and control over its fortunes. The movement of genealogy (*genesis*) through Israel's three major epochs—from Abraham on, from King David on, and from the exile on—rises into a fourth age, a new beginning (*genesis*) with Jesus: a rebirth of the covenant for which Jesus pours out his blood (26:28). In this small initial pattern of mathematically measured epochs we hear the whole long and grand story, as Matthew sees it, of God's will for not only Israel but through Israel for all people from beginnings to end.

Matthew's story will proceed, like this small but theologically rich pattern, with overlapping patterns that give the story its shape and meaning.

Within these patterns a crucial message is often buried in a surprising twist. For example, the genealogy's mathematical precision and dominant patriarchy appear compromised by a twist. We hear mentions of women—not entirely respectable women at that. Abraham and David are, of course, men. And each key generation that Matthew mentions begins with "the father of." God seems to work exclusively with and through men, but five citations of women intrude:

1. Judah, the father of Perez and Zerah   *by Tamar* (1:3)
2. Salmon, the father of Boaz   *by Rahab* (1:5)
3. Boaz, the father of Obed   *by Ruth* (1:5)
4. David was the father of Solomon   *by the wife of Uriah* (1:5)
5. Jacob, the father of Joseph,   *husband of Mary* (1:16)

While the inclusion of women in a male-dominated genealogy is strange enough, a common thread (a hearing cue) of sexual and tribal "irregularities" compounds the peculiarity:

1. *Tamar* disguises herself as a prostitute, luring her stepfather Judah into a sexual relationship that produces offspring (Gen. 38:12–30).
2. *Rahab* "the prostitute," a non-Israelite, hides Joshua's spies and is spared when her city is destroyed (Josh. 2:1–21).
3. *Ruth*, another non-Israelite, seduces a rich landholder, initiating sexual contact that leads to the marriage that she and her mother-in-law Naomi have sought (Ruth 3:1–4:13).

4. *Bathsheba*, the wife of Uriah, a non-Israelite Hittite and one of David's key commanders, is seduced by the king, who kills her husband to cover up her pregnancy (2 Sam. 11:3–27).

5. *Mary*, who conceives out of wedlock, disturbs Joseph with her pregnancy; he plans to dismiss her quietly, "unwilling to expose her to public disgrace" (Matt. 1:19); Joseph "had no marital relations with her until she had borne a son; and he named him Jesus" (1:25).

In this twist to the genealogical pattern—its own mini-pattern focused on women—there is, as always, theological meaning: God uses and blesses both non-Jews and women (involved in irregular sexual relations!) to accomplish covenantal fulfillment. We hear in these repetitions God's valuation and affirmation of women as well as God's compassion for those known (and likely ostracized) for sexual irregularity.

Moreover, God's providence extends beyond Israel, thus breaking through tribal bonds that typically exclude and oppress outsiders. God's universal and inclusive concern for the marginalized within society and the oppressed outside of tribe emerges from twists in what would appear at first reading a straightforward, mathematically precise arrangement of three epochs of fourteen generations each. The fulfillment implicit in the *genesis* of Jesus points to the story's conclusion, with believers in Israel taking the good news of the kingdom to, and making disciples of, all nations (28:19–20).

Divine Direction: Stars Point, Dreams Direct, Scripture Is Being Fulfilled (Matthew 1:19–4:16)

Following the preface, Matthew strings together an elaboration on his opening message by way of the hearing cues *fourteen generations* and *genesis*, of God-in-control. Three interweaving mosaics (or "motifs," echoing themes) point to God's governance over human affairs. Matthew's composition here depends on the interplay of these motifs:

1. The fulfillment of Scripture
2. The appearances of stars above dictating movement below
3. Dreams providing precise road maps

These signals of divine control are highlighted below within an inter-weaving of the above three motifs. This way of structuring the narrative at this point indicates the orchestral way in which Matthew, like all ancient storytellers, proceeds. A motif is heard, then a second motif is heard, and then a third—all three occurring not randomly but carefully paced, playing off each other to produce the desired effect: *God is in control* (1:19–4:16).

- "Just when Joseph had resolved to [dismiss Mary], *an angel of the Lord appeared to him in a dream* and said, 'Joseph, son of David, do not be afraid to take Mary as your wife, for the child conceived in her is from the Holy Spirit. She will bear a son, and you are to name him Jesus, for he will save his people from their sins'" (1:20–21).
- "*All this took place to fulfill what had been spoken by the Lord through the prophet*: 'Look, the virgin shall conceive and bear a son, and they shall name him Emmanuel,' which means, 'God is with us'" (1:22–23).
- "After Jesus was born in Bethlehem of Judea, wise men from the East came to Jerusalem, asking, 'Where is the child who has been born king of the Jews? For *we observed his star at its rising*, and have come to pay him homage'" (2:1–2).
- "Calling together all the chief priests and scribes of the people, [the king] inquired of them where the Messiah was to be born. They told him, 'In Bethlehem of Judea; *for so it has been written by the prophet*: "... From you [Bethlehem] shall come a ruler who is to shepherd my people Israel"'" (2:4–6).
- "Then Herod secretly called for the wise men and learned from them *the exact time when the star had appeared*. Then he sent them to Bethlehem, saying, 'Go and search diligently for the child; and when you have found him, bring me word so that I may also go and pay him homage'" (2:7–8).
- "When they had heard the king, they set out; and *there, ahead of them, went the star that they had seen at its rising, until it stopped* over the place where the child was. When they saw that the star had stopped, they were overwhelmed with joy" (2:9–10).
- "*Having been warned in a dream* not to return to Herod, they left for their own country by another road" (2:12).
- "Now after they had left, *an angel of the Lord appeared to Joseph in a dream* and said, 'Get up, take the child and his mother, and flee to

Egypt, and remain there until I tell you; for Herod is about to search for the child, to destroy him'" (2:13).

- "Then Joseph got up, took the child and his mother by night, and went to Egypt, and remained there until the death of Herod. *This was to fulfill what had been spoken by the Lord through the prophet,* 'Out of Egypt I have called my son'" (2:14–15).
- "When Herod saw that he had been tricked by the wise men, he was infuriated, and he sent and killed all the children in and around Bethlehem who were two years old or under, according to the time that he had learned from the wise men. *Then was fulfilled what had been spoken through the prophet Jeremiah*: 'A voice was heard in Ramah, . . . Rachel weeping for her children'" (2:16–18).
- "When Herod died, *an angel of the Lord suddenly appeared in a dream* to Joseph in Egypt and said, 'Get up, take the child and his mother, and go to the land of Israel, for those who were seeking the child's life are dead'" (2:19–20).
- "Then Joseph got up, took the child and his mother, and went to the land of Israel. But when he heard that Archelaus was ruling over Judea in place of his father Herod, he was afraid to go there. And *after being warned in a dream,* he went away to the district of Galilee" (2:21–22).
- "[Joseph] made his home in a town called Nazareth, *so that what had been spoken through the prophets might be fulfilled,* 'He will be called a Nazorean'" (2:23).
- "In those days John the Baptist appeared in the wilderness of Judea, proclaiming, 'Repent, for the kingdom of heaven has come near.' *This is the one of whom the prophet Isaiah spoke* when he said, 'The voice of one crying out in the wilderness . . .'" (3:1).
- "When Jesus had been baptized, just as he came up from the water, suddenly the heavens were opened to him and he saw *the Spirit of God descending like a dove and alighting on him.* And a voice from heaven said, 'This is my Son, the Beloved, with whom I am well pleased'" (3:16–17).
- "Then *Jesus was led up by the Spirit* into the wilderness to be tempted by the devil" (4:1).
- "Then the devil left him, and suddenly *angels came and waited on him* (4:11).
- "Now when Jesus heard that John had been arrested, he withdrew to Galilee. He left Nazareth and made his home in Capernaum by the sea, in the territory of Zebulun and Naphtali, *so that what had been spoken*

through the prophet Isaiah might be fulfilled: 'Land of Zebulun, land of Naphtali . . . for those who sat in the region and shadow of death light has dawned'" (4:12–16).

This last indicator of fulfilled Scripture appropriately concludes the pattern of divine control, bringing the audience up to the present hour—a time of light coming to those sitting in darkness, a light dawning for those imprisoned within death's shadow (4:16).

The Kingdom's Requirement: Change Your Heart (Matthew 4:17–25)

At the conclusion of this orchestral arrangement of motifs indicating God's control, we hear of the need for human response. "From that time Jesus began to make his proclamation and to say, 'Change your hearts; for the Kingdom of the heavens has drawn near'" (4:17).[2]

This single word, *metanoia* (to repent, change your hearts, turn around),[3] is fundamental for entering God's kingdom drawing near. Matthew's implicit message at this point is this: while God has extraordinary control and concern, God won't or can't do everything; the heart's transformation, aided but not controlled by God, includes fundamentally the human response. God cannot force human response, but rather, as with Abraham, God is seeking human partners to bring God's blessing to the world.

As Jesus is walking by the Sea of Galilee, he sees two brothers fishing. *Turn around from your fishing*, Jesus says. "Follow me, and I will make you fish for people" (4:19). The fishermen follow as Jesus demonstrates the secret of fishing for people: "Jesus went throughout Galilee, teaching in their synagogues and proclaiming the good news of the kingdom and curing every disease and every sickness among the people. . . . They brought to him all the sick, those who were afflicted with various diseases and pains, demoniacs, epileptics, and paralytics, and he cured them. And great crowds followed him" (4:23–25). Great crowds of healed and whole people, the beginning of God's covenantal fulfillment, the kingdom of heaven come to earth through Israel: this is God's kingdom on earth envisioned by Isaiah, whose prophetic vision is inaugurated by Jesus.

Entry into God's kingdom is conditioned, as noted, on a turning around, repentance—*metanoeō* ("to make a change of principle and practice, to reform"). We hear of the importance of repentance from both Jesus and John the Baptist:

- "Change your heart," says John, "for the kingdom of heaven has come near" (3:2).
- "Change your heart," says Jesus, "for the kingdom of heaven has come near" (4:17).

The heart's transformation, in Matthew, is a complete change of life orientation, a *turning from* self-centeredness, self-righteousness, and the hypocritical appearance of law-keeping, and a *turning toward* the righteousness taught by Jesus, a purity of heart that shows mercy, fosters justice, and seeks peace.

Such a radical change of heart—of basic life orientation—results in a radical compassion that likewise fulfills the covenantal law. On the human side of things, then, this change of heart is how the reign of God on earth is inaugurated and entered. As Jesus says in his first long teaching in Matthew, "unless your righteousness exceeds that of the scribes and Pharisees, you will never enter the kingdom of heaven" (5:20).

God's kingdom is not off in the distant future or in another, postmortem realm of existence. The kingdom of which Matthew speaks is coming here, on earth, beginning now. In Matthew Jesus insists that some who are listening to him will, before they die, experience God's kingdom having come to earth (16:28). As Messiah, Israel's deliverer, Jesus will both proclaim and demonstrate to Israel this good news of God's incipient but inevitable kingdom, which those within Israel must then take to the world (28:19–20).

Conclusion

Matthew emphasizes providential control over Israel's past, present, and future in four patterns:

- repetition in the three sets of fourteen-generational epochs marking Israel's story
- repeated scriptures being fulfilled
- repeated appearances of stars above dictating movement below
- repeated dreams providing road maps, with precise timing

In his introduction, Matthew's overlapping patterns indicating divine control form the narrative cornerstone of his theological perspective: this sets the narrative stage for the fulfillment of the ancient covenant with Israel through the arrival of God's long-promised reign on earth, inaugurated by the Messiah.

Matthew's narrative, firmly rooted in God's covenantal love, tells of God's desire for a people whose change of heart returns them to covenantal faithfulness. What Israel's gracious and powerful God promised long ago is beginning and will be fulfilled.

According to Matthew, Jesus pours out his blood for renewal of this ancient covenant (26:28); he is the long-awaited Messiah who clarifies the covenantal law and who enables its being followed by being with his followers "always, to the end of the [kingdom] age" (28:20). Indeed, Jesus is "'Emmanuel,' which means, 'God is with us'" (1:23).

"Unless Your Righteousness Exceeds That of the Scribes and Pharisees" (Matthew 5–7; 23–25)

"Now Jesus Began to Teach"

Early in the so-called Sermon on the Mount (Matt. 5–7), Jesus boldly declares, "Unless your righteousness exceeds that of the scribes and Pharisees, you will never enter the kingdom of heaven" (5:20).

The respected and influential scribes and Pharisees held themselves to very high moral and spiritual standards—they prayed and tithed regularly, strictly adhered to the law and religious rituals, worshiped regularly in the temple, and were leaders in their religious communities. Yet, according to Matthew, one's righteousness must be better than theirs to gain salvation, entry into God's kingdom.

As we read on in Matthew, though, we learn that these leaders merely appear to be righteous but are not. They parade their virtue before others but inside are vicious; they practice the letter of the law but ignore its spirit (15:9). Simply put, they are hypocrites who look good on the outside but are morally and spiritually ugly within.

This focus of the first discourse, the "Sermon on the Mount," is paralleled—echoed—by the last of five discourses. The two are the longest by far of the five teachings that provide the shape of Matthew's main story, chapters 5–25.

Matthew presents these five teaching discourses as the clarion call of Jesus to a superior righteousness. Viewed as a whole, the five teachings and their connecting narrative explain both the beginning and ending of Matthew—the birth of the Messiah and the death and resurrection of the Messiah. Between beginning (chaps. 1–4) and end (chaps. 26–28) is the heart of Matthew (chaps. 5–25): entrance into God's righteous kingdom.

The Five Teachings about Righteousness
(Matthew 5–7; 10; 13:1–52; 18; 23–25)

Matthew orients the five discourses around the theme of righteousness that characterizes the kingdom of God.[1] The discourses are carefully arranged as parallels in reverse order (a *chiasm*, or ring composition)—with the last discourse echoing or paralleling the first, the second-to-last echoing the second—which leaves as a special focus the center discourse, the third.

The first and last of these discourses are the longest, intended for everyone—crowd, disciples, Jewish leaders—as is the very brief center discourse. The second and fourth are for the disciples only. This arrangement would have made it easier for the tuned ears of the intended audience to hear and remember in the many subsequent recitations:

1 Kingdom: law as covenant attitude and action   to all (Matt. 5–7)
  2 Kingdom: mission   to disciples (Matt. 10)
    3 Kingdom: snapshots and responses   to all (Matt. 13:1–52)
  2' Kingdom: mission   to disciples (Matt. 18)
1' Kingdom: law as covenant attitude and action   to all (Matt. 23–25)

The chiastic reversal of ring composition was a common technique of repetition in ancient preliterate cultures, found within but also outside the gospels in, for example, the book of Numbers[2] and Homer's *Iliad*.[3] Chiastic reversal is the most complex and perhaps most powerful of all ancient hearing cues.

The parallel first and last discourses, framing the parallel second and fourth discourses, present the Big Picture of righteousness (and its lack), including kingdom *blessing* and no-kingdom *woe*. The second and fourth parallel discourses, addressed to the disciples, concern the nature and challenges of the kingdom mission. The centerpiece discourse, the third, is a distillation of Matthew's primary message, offering narrative snapshots of the kingdom; it also includes teaching about what permits and what prevents a positive response to the gospel of the kingdom.

The First and Fifth Discourses (Matthew 5–7; 23–25)

In the music-like arrangement of the first and fifth discourses, we hear the multiple *woes* of the fifth echoing, in dark tones, the multiple *blessings*, in light tones. Matthew is taking us lyrically into the joyous world of the flourishing righteous kingdom in the first discourse and the vicious world of the self-satisfied hypocrite in the fifth. These two corresponding discourses are themselves marked by three parallel movements: (1) blessing (5:3–48) versus woe (23:2–12); (2) kingdom discipleship with threats from within (6:1–7:12) and from without[4] (24:1–25:30); and (3) mirroring pictures of the great judgment (7:21–24; 25:34–39).

Parallel Beginnings: Blessing (Matthew 5:3–48) versus Woe (Matthew 23:2–36)

Early in the first discourse we hear *blessing*, echoed in contrast by *woe* early in the fifth and last discourse.

Blessing and Law (Discourse One, Matthew 5:3–48)

"Unless your righteousness exceeds that of the scribes and Pharisees, you will never enter the kingdom of heaven" (5:20). Matthew 5 teaches that kingdom righteousness is most deeply a matter of attitude or heart:

> Blessed are the poor in spirit, for theirs is the kingdom of heaven.
> Blessed are those who mourn, for they will be comforted.
> Blessed are the meek, for they will inherit the earth.
> Blessed are those who hunger and thirst for righteousness, for they
>   will be filled.
> Blessed are the merciful, for they will receive mercy.
> Blessed are the pure in heart, for they will see God.
> Blessed are the peacemakers, for they will be called children of God.
>
> (5:3–9)

Those with rightly oriented hearts, those who yearn for righteousness, desire peace, love mercy, and hunger for justice, are likewise motivated and inspired to behaviors such as making peace and showing mercy—they don't just desire peace and mercy; they make peace and are merciful. In the kingdom, righteous attitudes produce just and merciful actions.

Jesus understands "righteousness" within the context of covenant and law. "Do not think that I have come to abolish the law or the prophets," Jesus insists; "I have come not to abolish but to fulfill" (5:17). And the law, according to Jesus, goes well beyond the letter, its literal meaning, to its spirit.

Consider the law regarding murder. Superior covenant righteousness requires dealing with the underlying and festering anger that can lead to murder:

- *Letter of the law*: "You have heard that it was said . . . , 'You shall not murder'; and 'whoever murders shall be liable to judgment.'"
- *Spirit of the law*: "But I say to you that if you are angry with a brother or sister, you will be liable to judgment; and if you insult a brother or sister, you will be liable to the council; and if you say, 'You fool,' you will be liable to the hell of fire" (5:21–22).

For kingdom righteousness, it is not enough simply not to kill; in the kingdom one must cultivate an inner disposition of kindness and compassion toward other people that would preclude the strife that makes murder possible in the first place.

Jesus's deep analysis of the law regarding murder begins a pattern of six examples that probe the spirit and purpose of the law. Each begins with *you have heard* or *it is written that* and concludes with *but I say*. The "but I say" not only does not negate the law; it makes it more challenging. The pattern of these repeated phrases helps to drive home what the kingdom law and the kingdom itself look like. For example,

- *Letter of the law*: "You have heard that it was said, 'You shall not commit adultery.'"
- *Spirit of the law*: "But I say to you that everyone who looks at a woman with lust has already committed adultery with her in his heart" (5:27–28).

Since adulterous acts result from lust, lust unchecked is unrighteous. Even more than a puritanical condemnation of lust-in-the-heart, Jesus is commending the sort of cultivated and loving commitment on which his eternal and peaceful kingdom is built.

- *Letter of the law*: "You have heard that it was said, 'An eye for an eye and a tooth for a tooth.'"
- *Spirit of the law*: "But I say to you, . . . if anyone strikes you on the right cheek, turn the other also; and if anyone wants to sue you and take your coat, give your cloak as well; and if anyone forces you to go one mile, go also the second mile. Give to everyone who begs from you" (5:38–42).

Acts of revenge and excessive demands for justice issue from a spirit of vengeance and self-concern, which likewise engender failures of compassion, generosity, and forgiveness such as turning the other cheek, offering one's coat (along with one's shirt), going the extra mile, or giving to the beggar. Jesus is not rejecting the legitimate demands of justice and the righting of wrongs; he is, more deeply, embracing the compassion, kindness, generosity, and forgiveness that cement the healthy bonds of the kingdom. When needs are empathetically anticipated and mercifully met, crime will drop dramatically and the need for retributive justice will decrease.

Jesus concludes with the most foundational attitude constituting superior covenant righteousness:

- *Letter of the law*: "You have heard that it was said, 'You shall love your neighbor and hate your enemy.'"
- *Spirit of the law*: "But I say to you, Love your enemies and pray for those who persecute you" (5:43–44).

While Jesus commends, like just about everyone, love of neighbor (those in one's tribe and family, those who can and do benefit oneself), he is not content to stop there. Tribal love leaves one stuck with only one's own: it results in tribalism and parochialism with its corresponding denigration of the "outsider," those outside of one's tribe or nation.

Radically, then, in a culture of intense family and tribal honor, Jesus commends love even of enemy. Since hatred of enemy is an obvious root of violence and even war, restricting love to neighbor would inadequately and insecurely motivate his ever-expanding peaceful kingdom. The blessed peacemakers are those who love enemies and pray for them.

Superior righteousness begins, first and foremost, with the energizing inner spirit of the law, the spirit of love—which of course is nothing without showing mercy. Toward the end of the first discourse (jumping ahead here), Jesus offers a simple and useful guide to superior righteousness: "In everything *do to others as you would have them do to you*; for this is the law and the prophets" (7:12). That is, if I am righteous, I take your good as my own. Thus motivated, the righteous heart then *does* that good for other people.

With all his talk of the spirit, one might think that Jesus has simply rejected the law and embraced love. But Jesus insists that he has come not to abolish but to fulfill the law and the prophets (5:17). For Jesus, righteousness is understood within the context of God's ancient covenant and covenantal law with Israel. Kingdom righteousness is covenant righteousness. However, he warns that merely keeping the letter of the law is a pretend righteousness, exemplified by the hypocritical religious leaders who skim over the surface of righteousness. Here is Matthew's full theological perspective: covenant righteousness begins with purity of heart and ends in superior behavior. With pure hearts and merciful actions we find the blessing of salvation, life in the kingdom of heaven come to earth (and without it only woe).[5] Jesus probes beneath the surface of the law to the depths of mercy in which the law finds expression.

Woe and Law (Discourse Five, Matthew 23:2–36)

The opening sections of the fifth discourse mirror the first, but in reverse: *woe* contrasts with *blessing*, each deepening the understanding of the other. In the fifth discourse's first section, Jesus condemns religious leaders to *woe* for practicing piety for show; they "tithe mint, dill, and cummin, and have neglected the weightier matters of the law: justice and mercy and faith" (23:23).

Early in the fifth discourse, we find a litany of *woes* that stand in stark contrast to the *blesseds* at the beginning of the first discourse. *Woe* suggests gloom, affliction, and impending doom or condemnation. "Woe to you" can be translated "Damned are you." *Blessed*, on the other hand, suggests a feeling of contentment and gratitude along with a palpable flourishing within the kingdom community. Hear Matthew's contrast:

- *"Woe to you*, scribes and Pharisees, hypocrites! For you lock people out of the kingdom of heaven. For you do not go in yourselves, and when others are going in, you stop them" (23:13–14).
  - *The blessed are inclusive in their mercy and peacemaking ways.*

- *"Woe to you*, scribes and Pharisees, hypocrites! For you cross sea and land to make a single convert, and you make the new convert twice as much a child of hell as yourselves" (23:15).
  - *The blessed reside in a kingdom of heaven, as children of God.*

- *"Woe to you*, blind guides, who say, 'Whoever swears by the sanctuary is bound by nothing, but whoever swears by the gold of the sanctuary is bound by the oath'" (23:16).
  - *The blessed are pure of heart and word.*

- *"Woe to you*, scribes and Pharisees, hypocrites! For you tithe mint, dill, and cummin, and have neglected the weightier matters of the law: justice and mercy and faith. It is these you ought to have practiced without neglecting the others" (23:23).
  - *The blessed are just, merciful, and faithful.*

- *"Woe to you*, scribes and Pharisees, hypocrites! For you clean the outside of the cup and of the plate, but inside they are full of greed and self-indulgence" (23:25).
  - *The blessed are people of integrity, with attitudes of mercy and merciful actions of a piece.*

- *"Woe to you*, scribes and Pharisees, hypocrites! For you are like whitewashed tombs, which on the outside look beautiful, but inside they are full of the bones of the dead and of all kinds of filth" (23:27).
  - *The blessed are pure of heart (so don't just appear righteous).*

- *"Woe to you*, scribes and Pharisees, hypocrites! For you build the tombs of the prophets and decorate the graves of the righteous . . . [but] I send you prophets, sages, and scribes, some of whom you will kill and crucify, and some you will flog in your synagogues" (23:29–34).
  - *Blessed are those who are persecuted for righteousness' sake, for theirs is the kingdom of heaven.*

In the opening sections of discourses one and five, then, Matthew contrasts the poor in spirit (those who bow before God in humble recognition of their spiritual impoverishment) with those who puff themselves up before God—presuming their spiritual and moral excellence. Matthew's "poor in spirit" are the polar opposite of the proud: they are meek, gentle, benevolent, and humane. "All who exalt themselves will be humbled, and all who humble themselves will be exalted" (23:12), which echoes the first discourse: "Blessed are the meek, for they will inherit the earth" (5:5). Unlike the imperious and self-serving hypocrites, the humble "meek" are gentle, kind, and forgiving; they will see God.

The pure in heart (5:8) stand in stark contrast to those who "clean the outside of the cup and of the plate, but inside . . . are full of greed and self-indulgence" (23:25). While the religious leaders display a clean face, their hearts are filthy; they are motivated by self-seeking pride and greed rather than by a pure and humble heart. The blessed have an integrity of pure hearts and righteous deeds, while the doomed parade their pious actions, disguising their inner impurity that generates wickedness. The pure in heart create communities of compassion, justice, and peace (communities of blessing), while these religious leaders create communities of greed, competition, and war (communities of woe). Such leaders create a kind of hell on earth, and they *pursue the righteous from town to town* to make them live in this hell (23:29–36); these make each of their converts "twice as much a child of hell" as they are (23:15).

In spite of pressure to accede to these powerful and influential forces, Jesus reminds his listeners that "those who are persecuted for righteousness' sake" are blessed, "for theirs is the kingdom of heaven" (5:10).

In the arrangement of *blessing* and *woe* as opposites within parallel discourses, both *blessing* and *woe* are not only clarified but, seen in the light of each other, are made all the more compelling in their theological meaning: the blessed inherit the earth and enter God's kingdom; the hypocrites are damned, lost to kingdom life.

Parallel Middle Sections: Kingdom Discipleship
(Matthew 6:1–7:12; 24:1–25:30)

In the parallel middle sections of the first and fifth discourses, Jesus narrows his focus to challenges that leaders of God's kingdom will face upon his departure. His message is also available to anyone within earshot. In the middle section of the first discourse, the emphasis for disciples is on the threat from within, the heart's meandering desires, whereas in the fifth discourse the threat is from without, opposition from opposing powers and overwhelming circumstances.

Threats from Within (Discourse One, Matthew 6:1–7:12)

"Beware of practicing your piety before others in order to be seen by them," Jesus warns his disciples (6:1). The kingdom's new leaders must avoid the failures of the traditional leaders of Israel, who so desperately seek honor, power, privilege, and wealth. It is precisely to those in leadership positions that status and wealth are both available and tempting. However, the new leaders, the disciples, must pay close attention to the heart, the seat of desire and longing.

While the corrupt religious leaders practice the law, they do so for selfish and social advantages. In various ways, Jesus concedes the reputational advantages of being thought holy, generous, and pious—as you gain respect and honor, your social stock rises and you gain increasing authority and power over those "beneath" you (6:1–5). But true righteousness begins in private, with prayer and fasting out of the public eye; you should give charitably with such a *not-for-public-notice* attitude that your left hand forgets what your right hand gave (6:3). Pray and fast, says Jesus, but in private, praying that God's kingdom in heaven, God's will of blessing for all, be accomplished on earth (6:7–18).

The social benefits of the pretenders who seek treasures—worldly honor, for example, and power—are perks subject to "moth and rust" and theft, whereas true righteousness yields treasures that are eternal, impervious to moth, rust, and theft (6:19–20). A series of admonitions follow with connected hearing cues about attending to and caring for the inner state of one's heart rather than attending to or worrying about external circumstances. What or who you serve (God or money), what you look at (longingly), how you spend your time, what or who you love, how you judge others, and what you fear—each reveals your inner light and your inner dark, your loves and hates, and your deepest desires and hopes.

- "The eye is the lamp of the body. . . . If your eye is unhealthy, your whole body will be full of darkness. If then the light in you is darkness, how great is the darkness!" (6:22–23).
- "No one can serve two masters; for a slave will either hate the one and love the other, or be devoted to the one and despise the other. You cannot serve God [loving God with all you heart] and wealth" (6:24).
- "Therefore I tell you, do not worry about your life, what you will eat or what you will drink, or about your body, what you will wear. . . . Strive first for the kingdom of God and his righteousness, and all these things will be given to you as well" (6:25, 32–33).
- "Do not judge, so that you may not be judged. . . . Why do you see the speck in your neighbor's eye but do not notice the log in your own eye? . . . You hypocrite, first take the log out of your own eye, and then you will see clearly to take the speck out of your neighbor's eye" (7:1–5).
- "Ask, and it will be given you. . . . If you then, who are evil, know how to give good gifts to your children, how much more will your Father in heaven give good things to those who ask him!" (7:7, 11).

If you love money, you will not share your possessions with those in need. If you look longingly at another person, you are on your way to committing adultery. If you worry about your daily life, you will lack the psychological resources to strive for righteousness. And if you judge, you will fail to notice your own moral failings (and take steps to eliminate them). The tight connection between motivation, attitudes, desire, and loves, on the one hand, and actions just or unjust, on the other, requires us to pay very careful attention to the former. So Jesus offers a simple summary of the law and prophets, with action and attitude intertwined: *"In everything do to others as you would have them do to you"* (7:12).

Threats from Without (Discourse Five, Matthew 24:1–25:30)

In the first discourse, Jesus warns his disciples to beware of threats from within—to beware of hypocrisy and fear and misplaced loves. The echoing alert, in this last discourse, concerns external threats. These threats from outside the kingdom community are in the near or distant future: they appear as apocalyptic in nature, referring in part to the end of the kingdom age with its day of judgment as precursor to the eschaton, a time of perfect peace. It's a bit daunting to pick through this entire picture of the near and distant future (24:1–25:46). We have chosen to follow the parallels between the last sections of discourses one and five, focusing here on the difficulties lying ahead "from without" (24:1–25:30) and ending with the great judgment (25:31–46).

When the disciples ask about "the end of the age" (24:1–3),[6] Jesus tells of great wars, famines, earthquakes, severe persecution, and even death. Resisting external threats takes courage and fidelity. "The one who endures to the end will be saved," Jesus says, both as warning and as promise (24:13).

Jesus's reply about "the end of the age" appears to include two time periods: (1) the time until the destruction of Jerusalem and the temple (70 CE) and (2) the time at the end of the kingdom age when the Son of Man returns in judgment. Given the threats they will endure in both time periods, Jesus extols endurance and faithfulness.

The destruction of Jerusalem and its temple, on the one hand, will be occasioned by a "desolating sacrilege standing in the holy place" (24:15). The end of time, on the other hand, will be occasioned by both human and cosmic chaos—the sun darkened, the moon failing in its light, and stars falling from heaven (24:29). The disciples are warned of the challenges to come:

- "The love of many will grow cold" and "many will fall away" (24:9–12).
- "Beware that no one leads you astray" (24:3–4).
- "The one who endures to the end will be saved" (24:13).
- "Take note, I have told you beforehand" (24:25).
- "Keep awake therefore . . ." (24:42; 25:13).

These evils and their suffering are the "birthpangs" of the kingdom of God, and when the good news has finally reached the four corners of the earth, "the end will come" (24:8–14). At that time, the end of the end time, "they will see 'the Son of Man coming on the clouds of heaven' with power and great glory" (24:30).[7]

Three parables strung together speak of being a "faithful and wise servant" of God. The faithful servant is like the slave in charge "whom his master will find at work when he arrives," as opposed to "that wicked slave [who] says to himself, 'My master is delayed,' and he begins to beat his fellow slaves, and eats and drinks with drunkards" (24:45–51); and like diligent bridesmaids with lamp oil in supply, waiting for their bridegroom, as opposed to the foolish, forgetting the oil (25:1–13); and like property managers who remain attentive while the landlord travels abroad (25:14–30). In this last parable, a landholder goes on a journey, entrusting his servants with possessions: five talents to one; two talents to another; one to a last. While the master journeys, the first two double their returns, while the last one, fearful of losing his one talent, buries it—and is severely punished, cast off the land into outer darkness (25:14–30).

Forewarned, then, the disciples are forearmed. In the absence of the physical Jesus, they should be like a faithful slave who is "put in charge of [the master's] household" (24:45), avoiding any dereliction of kingdom duty that might cause them to fall by the wayside. And, remember, Jesus says, "The one who endures to the end will be saved" (24:13).

Parallel Conclusions: The Great Day of Judgment (Matthew 7:21–27; 25:31–46)

The last sections of both discourses one and five focus on the day of judgment at the end of time. The preceding warnings about attack from within and from without come to a dramatic climax, by way of twin tales.

Discourse One, Matthew 7:21–27

At the conclusion of the first discourse we hear that "not everyone who says to me, 'Lord, Lord,' will enter the kingdom of heaven, but only the one who does the will of my Father in heaven" (7:21). Everyone will be judged in the end—those who say one thing but do another, and those who hear the word and do it. Jesus explains with a concluding tale: A wise man and a foolish man wanted to build themselves houses. The wise man built on rock, the foolish on sand. A storm wipes out the foolish man's house, "and great was its fall" (7:24–27). Jesus warns: those who hear his word but don't act on it are like the foolish man who built his house on the sand—great will be their fall.

Discourse Five, Matthew 25:31–46

In the echoing section of the last discourse we hear a similar tale about the day of judgment. At the gathering of nations, the Son of Man will separate the sheep from the goats. The righteous sheep did compassionate kingdom work: "I was hungry and you gave me food," the Son of Man tells them, "I was thirsty and you gave me something to drink, I was a stranger and you welcomed me, I was naked and you gave me clothing, I was sick and you took care of me, I was in prison and you visited me" (25:35–36). The goats, however, lacking the spirit of mercy and justice, ignored the hungry and the poor and the oppressed. And so "these will go away into eternal punishment, but the righteous into eternal life" (25:46).

Matthew's mirrored conclusions offer a compelling picture of what is at stake in choosing to enter into and steadfastly remain in the kingdom. These parallel tales of judgment implore the audience to consider the profound blessings of a superior righteousness versus the cruel consequences of hypocrisy, self-righteousness, rules-based religiosity, and pride.

Conclusion

We can summarize the concerns of the parallel discourses one and five by noting a short sequence in the first discourse that begins with a thought central to all of Matthew: "Unless your righteousness exceeds that of the scribes and Pharisees, you will never enter the kingdom of heaven" (5:20). This seemingly impossible challenge is echoed in the concluding verse to this sequence: "Be perfect, therefore, as your heavenly Father is perfect" (5:48). The first long discourse and its long echo join together to proclaim and explain—*this is what righteousness means.* Superior righteousness, covenant-kingdom righteousness, is grounded in a pure and merciful heart that moves one to act with compassion and justice. Superior righteousness is the perfect, God-like integration of love-motivated acts of justice and mercy.

Table 1. Hearing cues in discourses one and five

	DISCOURSE ONE (MATT. 5–7)	DISCOURSE FIVE (MATT. 23–25)
Beginning sections	"Blessed are you who . . ." (5:1–11)	"Woe to you who . . ." (23:13–36)
Middle sections	*Beware* of leadership hypocrisy! (6:1)	"*Beware* that no one leads you astray" (24:3–4)
	Beware, specifically: what not to do contrasted with what to do (6:2–7:12)	"The one who endures to the end will be saved" (24:13)
Concluding sections	Judgment:	Judgment:
	"Not everyone who says to me, 'Lord, Lord,' will enter the kingdom of heaven, but only the one who does the will of my Father in heaven" (7:21). Surprise awaits the smug who utter "Lord" phrases.	Separation of sheep and goats; consequences for true covenantal behavior, or not; for kingdom work, or its lack: judgment will prove surprising for the judged, both sheep and goats (25:31–46)

CHAPTER 9

"Proclaim the Good News, 'The Kingdom of Heaven Has Come Near'"

Parallel Discourses Two and Four, Central Discourse Three

Jesus has been traveling in "all the cities and villages, teaching in their synagogues, and proclaiming the good news of the kingdom, and curing every disease and every sickness" (9:35). Since the task of bringing God's kingdom to earth is immense, Jesus turns to his followers with a plea: "The harvest is plentiful, but the laborers are few; therefore ask the Lord of the harvest to send out laborers into his harvest" (9:37–38). The disciples themselves are the answer to this prayer. Jesus "summoned his twelve disciples and gave them authority over unclean spirits, to cast them out, and to cure every disease and every sickness" (10:1). Empowered and authorized by God, these new kingdom workers will, like Jesus, both teach and demonstrate the kingdom to the lost in Israel.

Dramatically alternating between righteousness and rule-keeping, blessing and woe, the little ones and those aspiring to be great, and peace and no peace, the symphonic structure of Matthew's grand narrative has five main movements, the discourses, with a four-chapter overture and a three-chapter finale. These five movements are united by a simple hearing cue, *kingdom*, repeatedly expressed or implied:

1 Kingdom explored: blessed are you!   to all (Matt. 5–7)
   2 Kingdom mission, kingdom opposition   to disciples (Matt. 10)
     3 Kingdom distilled   to all (Matt. 13:1–52)
   2' Kingdom mission, kingdom opposition   to disciples (Matt. 18)
1' Kingdom explored: woe to you!   to all (Matt. 23–25)

Movements one and five alternate, as we have seen, between blessing and woe, righteousness and hypocrisy, and the kingdom gained and lost.

In this chapter, we hear how the second and fourth movements sound forth the kingdom responsibility of the disciples as the new leaders of Israel in taking the gospel of the kingdom to Israel. And in the middle discourse of the entire ring, we hear a resounding declaration of *what the kingdom is like*.

The Second and Fourth Discourses: Getting the Disciples on Board (Matthew 10:1–42 and 18:1–35)

In both of these parallel discourses Jesus offers the particulars of the kingdom message, while warning about opposition to this message—from Israel's traditional leaders outside the kingdom community and from within this community itself. The reasons for opposing the message and messengers help to clarify the message itself. Because kingdom values threaten existing social structures, the disciples can expect opposition from those holding social power and position *outside* the kingdom. And, given the human condition, they can also expect increasing opposition from *inside* the kingdom as well, because of individual temptations to power and pride, and breakdowns in interpersonal relations.

The kingdom's message is directed as much to the kingdom workers as to those they seek to gain for the kingdom. And this message is clarified in and through the opposition they face.

Those whom the disciples are commanded to seek for the kingdom are fellow Jews. In the beginning of discourse two, Jesus restricts his disciples' mission to Israel: "Go nowhere among the Gentiles, and enter no town of the Samaritans, but go rather to the lost sheep of the house of Israel. As you go, proclaim the good news, 'The kingdom of heaven has come near.' Cure the sick, raise the dead, cleanse the lepers, cast out demons" (10:5–8). Their mission is clearly defined: teach and show God's kingdom to the lost sheep of Israel. In discourse four we hear again of the "lost sheep": "If a shepherd has a hundred sheep, and one of them has gone astray, does he not leave the ninety-nine on the mountains and go in search of the one that went astray? And if he finds it, truly I tell you, he rejoices over it more than over the ninety-nine that never went astray. So it is not the will of your Father in heaven that one of *these little ones* should be lost" (18:12–14). The disciples' mission in these parallel discourses, then, is to search for the lost sheep, the little ones, of the house of Israel.

The Kingdom Message of Discourses Two and Four

By the end of Matthew, the kingdom mission widens from those within Israel to all peoples of the earth (28:18–20). But first, as is made clear in discourses two and four, the kingdom good news is offered to those within Israel.

Message, Second Discourse (Matthew 10)

As in the beginning of discourse two, we repeatedly hear the essential kingdom message: "'The kingdom of heaven has come near.' Cure the sick, raise the dead, cleanse the lepers, cast out demons" (10:7–8). This message delivered by the disciples is a near replication of the fundamental message given by Jesus, who traveled about within Israel "teaching in their synagogues and proclaiming the good news of the kingdom and curing every disease and every sickness among the people . . . and they brought to him all the sick, those who were afflicted with various diseases and pains, demoniacs, epileptics, and paralytics, and he cured them" (4:23–24). At its heart, it is a message of kingdom peace (*shalom*): "As you enter the house, greet it," Jesus adds. "If the house is worthy, let your peace come upon it; but if it is not worthy, let your peace return to you" (10:12–13).

Jesus's awareness that some will reject their offer of peace hints at future opposition, accentuated by the hearing cue *sheep*. On the one hand, the disciples are told to seek lost sheep (10:6), but on the other hand, they themselves will be sent out as sheep "into the midst of wolves" (10:16). The traditional leaders within Israel, who are threatened by the new kingdom's radical values and attractive power, are the wolves.

Jesus concludes with encouragement to his disciples in their mission to Israel: "Whoever welcomes you welcomes me, and whoever welcomes me welcomes the one who sent me . . . and whoever gives even a cup of cold water to one of these little ones in the name of a disciple—truly I tell you, none of these will lose their reward" (10:40–42).

Echoed Message, Fourth Discourse (Matthew 18)

Jesus's teaching to the disciples in the fourth discourse echoes the parallel message of discourse two. A main echo is the focus on "little ones," "lost sheep." The discourse begins, however, with just the opposite, the disciples arrogantly thinking themselves superior to the little ones.

The disciples ask, "Who is the greatest in the kingdom of heaven?" (18:1). This very natural human tendency to be great is at decided odds with the kingdom of heaven. The kingdom of heaven come to earth is for the little ones, the poor, the lame, the outcast. We have already heard that kingdom righteousness requires that one be meek, mournful, poor in spirit—the very opposite attitudes of those who aspire to be great. It is both natural and wrong, from a kingdom perspective, to seek to be more significant or important or rich or handsome than one's neighbor or classmate or colleague. The kingdom is entered through humility, not pride. The proud feel entitled while looking down on those who are lesser, thinking them deserving of only scraps, shame, and dispossession. God's radically egalitarian and just kingdom is not for those who think themselves significant and deserving of greater notice than the other.

Jesus "answers" the disciples' question about greatness by placing a child (literally, *a little one*) within their midst and instructing them: "Unless you change and become like children, you will never enter the kingdom of heaven. Whoever becomes humble like this child is the greatest in the kingdom of heaven." To help in kingdom mission, one must, of course, have entered already, oneself. From the focus on the disciples as needing to become like children, Jesus concludes with their mission, to bring in the little ones: "Whoever welcomes one such child in my name welcomes me" (18:3–5).

The repeated hearing cue, *child*, focuses the message: one must become like a child in order to welcome the child.

- To enter the kingdom, you must become *like a child*.
- Whoever becomes humble *like a child* is the greatest in the kingdom.
- Whoever welcomes *one such child* in my name welcomes me.

Entrance to the kingdom requires *childlike* humility, and to be a co-laborer with Jesus is to *welcome the child*. In this one simple example, we find a key aspect of Matthew's theological perspective. Kingdom life involves a turnaround from *the proud demand for merit* (praise, power, riches) to *the humble hope for mercy* (forgiveness, healing, restoration). In Matthew the kingdom community is characterized by humility rather than the customary and cutthroat competition with others for significance. "Those who want to save their life will lose it," Jesus says, "and those who lose their life for my sake will find it" (16:25).

In its overall context, "little children" stands for all the dispossessed and disempowered "little ones" of the world. As humble people, then, the disciples will welcome the little ones into the kingdom just as they have been welcomed.

Discourse four continues with Jesus focusing on the little ones:

- "If any of you put a stumbling block before one of *these little ones* who believe in me, it would be better for you if a great millstone were fastened around your neck and you were drowned in the depth of the sea" (18:6).
- "Take care that you do not despise one of *these little ones*" (18:10).
- "It is not the will of your Father in heaven that one of *these little ones* should be lost" (18:14).

For both discourses, Jesus repeatedly instructs his disciples to care for, respect, honor, preserve, and act on behalf of "the little ones"—lepers and bleeding women, the emotionally tormented (the possessed), the frightened parents of gravely ill children, the lame, the blind, and the leper. Jesus's central message is that their rescue from physical, spiritual, and social suffering results in their restoration to full humanity within a thriving and inclusive community of compassion. This is their salvation: flourishing and peace within the kingdom of heaven come to earth.

Opposition to the Kingdom Message in Discourses Two and Four

Opposition to the message provides opportunity to clarify the message. In the second discourse, opposition comes from those within Israel who reject the kingdom message. Opposition in the fourth discourse appears as trouble within the kingdom.

The Opposition, Second Discourse (Matthew 10:1–42)

There are two sorts of opposition to the kingdom message from those in Israel refusing Jesus. First, and more benignly, some will indifferently dismiss the offer of kingdom peace; they will say "no thanks" and "please leave" and be done with it (10:12–15). Others, however, will be adamantly and actively hostile to the kingdom. So Jesus warns of hatred and persecution even from within one's own (biological) family: "I am sending you out like sheep into the midst of wolves. . . . Beware of them, for they will hand you over to councils and flog you in their synagogues. . . . Brother will betray brother to death, and a father his child, and children will rise against parents and have them put to death" (10:16–21). Given the temptation to acquiesce to such powerful threats, Jesus offers a challenge that serves also as a warning: "But the one who endures to the end will be saved" (10:22).

The idea of family members betraying each other, brother against brother, is repeated and expanded in the context of *peace*. This hearing cue can seem confusing because of its reversal from the earlier proclamation of peace as the heart of God's kingdom. Here Jesus says:

> I have not come to bring peace, but a sword.
>> For I have come to set a man against his father,
>> a daughter against her mother,
>> a daughter-in-law against her mother-in-law. (10:34–35)

In short, "one's foes will be members of one's own household" (10:36). Resistance to the turning of cultural values upside down often begins at home.

The hearing cue *peace* accentuates the prior demands of kingdom mission to preach and provide for peace:

- "As you enter the house, greet it. If the house is worthy, let your peace come upon it; but if it is not worthy, let your peace return to you" (10:12–13).
- "Do not think that I have come to bring peace to the earth; I have not come to bring peace, but a sword" (10:34).

Not peace, but a sword? Opposition to the kingdom message clarifies the message itself. Allegiance to self and kin constitutes a serious threat to kingdom peace, and so there must be the painful sword-like severing of the privileging and honoring of family if it comes at the expense of the privileging and honoring of God's family, Israel's little ones. "Whoever loves father or mother more than me is not worthy of me," Jesus adds, "and whoever loves son or daughter more than me is not worthy of me; and whoever does not take up the cross and follow me is not worthy of me. Those who find their life will lose it, and those who lose their life for my sake will find it" (10:37–39).

The audience has already heard what the fixation on *finding one's own life* looks like: a seeking after personal greatness and self-promotion. Such forms of pride are anathema to the flourishing life of God's radically inclusive and egalitarian kingdom. The kingdom, then, requires *losing one's life for Jesus's sake*—a commitment that, rather than seeking one's own advancement or the honoring of one's family at the expense of others, embraces the relentless pursuit of mercy and justice for the world's undesirables, its little ones.

Kin affection, then, threatens communal welfare. First, favoring kin has detrimental effects on the distribution of communal resources. Second, kinship creates such powerful in-group allegiances that it fosters a spirit of *them-versus-us*: *we* are family and friends; *they* are the enemy. Family allegiance resists the solidarity within the kingdom's ever-expanding community. Jesus's radically inclusive kingdom re-creates familial compassion but without privileging one's own biological kin at the expense of others.

Opposition to the kingdom in the second discourse comes primarily from outside the kingdom, from those within Israel, including one's own family, whose resistance to God's kingdom ranges from indifferent refusal to active hostility. This section concludes, however, on a hopeful note with the hearing cue *the little ones*, returning the audience once again to God's mercy: "Whoever gives even a cup of cold water to one of these little ones" will not "lose their reward" of life in God's kingdom come (10:42).

The Opposition, Fourth Discourse (Matthew 18:1–35)

In the fourth discourse the opposition comes not from outside the kingdom family, but from within the kingdom itself. Again, the kingdom message comes into clearer focus as opposition to that message intensifies.

Each individual, Jesus warns, will be confronted by self-centered appetites and habits that thwart life in and service to the kingdom. With hyperbole, Jesus points to the seriousness of this kingdom threat: "If your hand or your foot causes you to stumble, cut it off and throw it away" (18:8). That is, pay radical attention to and beware of what your hands grasp for, and avoid the corridors of power and greed that your feet long to tread. The message is clear: kingdom commitment demands constant reevaluation of your deepest priorities, loves, and desires.

Anticipating contentiousness within God's kingdom, Jesus offers instruction for restoring peace: graciously *confront* and then mercifully *forgive* the offending parties (18:15–20). Since contention is inevitable, confrontation and forgiveness are essential for maintaining unity. Jesus so prizes communal unity that he offers an astonishing claim, that "if two of you agree on earth about anything you ask, it will be done for you by my Father in heaven. For where two or three are gathered in my name, I am there among them" (18:19–20). *The kingdom is here*, with Jesus *among us*, in communities of astounding unity.

Though confrontation is difficult and forgiveness is demanding, Jesus requires both for the ongoing health of the kingdom. Peter, in his characteristically volatile and voluble way (14:28; 16:22), challenges Jesus's demands, asking how many times he must forgive those who sin against him: "As many as seven times?" Jesus replies, "Not seven times but, I tell you, seventy-seven times" (18:21–22). If the offending party should concede their error, be ready to forgive—unceasingly. Since believers are so likely to hurt other believers (and be hurt by them), Jesus requires a generosity of heart toward those who offend, who "sin" against you.

Jesus offers a tale to make the point. A king forgives the debt of a slave, who in turn mercilessly demands payment from another slave. The king angrily confronts the ungenerous slave and hands him over to be tortured. "So my heavenly Father will also do to every one of you," Jesus warns in the conclusion to this fourth discourse, "if you do not forgive your brother or sister from your heart" (18:23–35).

The kingdom mission requires rescuing the little ones from desperation and oppression and restoring them to communal flourishing. Mission workers must remain vigilant in the face of opposition from those in power outside the kingdom community, but also from those within the community, including themselves, who lust for glory and who fail to confront and forgive. Opposition to the kingdom helps define and refine its message of repentance: to enter the kingdom and enjoy its blessings, one must turn from self-aggrandizing and tribal ways toward the radically other-regarding and inclusive kingdom ways of compassion and forgiveness.

The Third and Central Discourse:
The Kingdom Crystalized (Matthew 13:1–52)

At the center of the ringed (parallel) discourses we find a teaching about the kingdom's essence. In pithy summaries both of the kingdom and of responses to the good news of its arrival we find a focused picture of what the kingdom is like. What are the proper and inappropriate responses to the kingdom? In reply, Jesus tells parables, perfect for distillation and crystallization of his gospel, God's heavenly kingdom come to earth.

Parable of the Soils (Matthew 13:1–23)

A farmer scatters seeds. Some land on the well-worn path and are snatched away immediately by birds. Other seeds land on rocky ground and spring up quickly, but with no depth of soil the seedlings are scorched to death. Still other seeds land in thorns and are choked. Some, however, land on fertile soil and flourish.

Is it just bad luck for the seeds landing on unfavorable soil? The answer is not immediately clear, which leads the disciples to ask Jesus why he teaches in parables, why he says things no one can understand. Jesus says that the disciples have been given the secrets to the kingdom but they have not been revealed to others; the latter can see but not perceive, hear but not understand (13:11–13). Jesus attributes personal responsibility to those who can neither perceive nor understand the secrets to the kingdom: in fulfillment of Scripture, says Jesus, "this people's heart has grown dull, and their ears are hard of hearing, and they have shut their eyes" (13:15).[1] The "bad" soil is the result of bad choices.

The problem of those not understanding the parables, then, is their own, explained in terms of the soils as follows:

- The hard-worn path represents lack of understanding.
- The rocky ground stands for those receiving the word about the kingdom with joy but falling away at the first sign of trouble.
- The thorny soil is the "lure of wealth" and ordinary "cares of the world" that choke off any initial interest in the kingdom (13:18–22).

The good soil, however, is the result of good choices: "this is the one who hears the word and understands it, who indeed bears fruit" (13:23). The parable's point is that many people within Israel "have shut their eyes" to the kingdom of heaven.

Parable of the Seeds: Wheat and Weeds (Matthew 13:24–30, 36–43); Parable of the Kingdom's Small, Slow Start (Matthew 13:31–35)

A farmer sows wheat, but his enemy sneaks in and sows weeds. The seeds grow together, side by side. Field hands come to the landholder and ask, "Do you want us to go and gather [the weeds]?" He replies, "No; for in gathering the weeds you would uproot the wheat along with them. Let both of them grow together until the harvest; and at harvest time I will tell the reapers, Collect the weeds first and bind them in bundles to be burned, but gather the wheat into my barn" (13:28–30).

Let both of them grow together, the evil with the good? Doesn't the kingdom mission require assessing and rooting out evil? Before addressing such questions, Matthew inserts two tiny parables recommending patience and realistic expectations. "The kingdom of heaven is like a mustard seed . . . the smallest of all the seeds," but finally, when it "becomes a tree . . . , the birds of the air come and make nests in its branches" (13:31–32). And another: "The kingdom of heaven is like yeast that a woman took and mixed in with three measures of flour until all of it was leavened" (13:33). Pay attention, and be patient and persistent: the kingdom is coming and will flourish.

The disciples ask Jesus to explain "the parable of the weeds" (13:36). Jesus explains that the one sowing the weed seed is the devil, and the one sowing the good seed is the Son of Man, and that only at the end of the age will God judge and burn the weeds (13:37–43). Followers must nurture everyone as best they can and leave the fate of the weeds up to God (13:24–30). Don't focus on evil and try to eliminate it: give your energy to the fostering of good. In the end, doers of evil will be judged and thrown into a furnace of fire, but "the righteous will shine like the sun in the kingdom of their Father" (13:43).[2] This day of judgment will come at the end of kingdom growth—at "the end of the age" (13:39–40, 49). Resist the impulse to get rid of evil, which will prevent proper nourishing of kingdom goodness. Let God take care of the rest.

Pearl of Great Price; Good Fish; Judgment Day (Matthew 13:44–50)

The center discourse concludes, like the first and last discourses, on a note of choice and consequence. The kingdom is immensely valuable, worth everything—"like treasure hidden in a field, which someone found and hid; then in his joy he goes and sells all that he has and buys that field" (13:44), or "like a merchant in search of fine pearls" who, "finding one pearl of great value," sells all to buy that one pearl (13:45–46). One must choose the kingdom.

This choice for or against the kingdom has consquences. At the end of the kingdom age, there will be judgment, "like a net that was thrown into the sea and caught fish of every kind; when it was full, they drew it ashore, sat down, and put the good into baskets but threw out the bad. So it will be at the end of the age. The angels will come out and separate the evil from the righteous and throw them into the furnace of fire, where there will be weeping and gnashing of teeth" (13:48–50). At the heart of Matthew's theological perspective we have heard that "unless your righteousness exceeds that of the scribes and Pharisees, you will never enter the kingdom of heaven" (5:20). To enter is joy and peace; not to enter is to suffer the anguish of loss.

Conclusion

"When Jesus had finished these parables, he left that place. He came to his hometown and began to teach the people in their synagogue, so that they were astounded and said, 'Where did this man get this wisdom and these deeds of power?'" (13:53–54). In the five discourses, we have heard Jesus's remarkable wisdom regarding the kingdom of heaven. Matthew's careful orchestration of these teaching discourses converges on this one theme: the wisdom of superior righteousness, of kingdom compassion and inclusiveness.

CHAPTER 10

Deeds of Power: From Telling to Showing

Telling and Showing

"Where did this man get this wisdom and these deeds of power?" asks the astonished crowd (13:53–54). In Matthew's tell-and-show it's hard to know what impresses the crowd more, the wisdom or the action, the *telling* or the *showing*. We've heard the kingdom *tellings* in the discourses on the kingdom's teachings on superior righteousness. We've also heard of the dire consequences of the religious leaders' hypocrisy both for themselves and for their followers. Matthew is also keen to authorize and illustrate Jesus's tellings of God's kingdom realized through dramatic *showings*, compelling anecdotes, and additional explanation. The reason for the people's astonishment at the teaching of Jesus was that "he taught them as one having authority, and not as their scribes" (7:29), an authority backed by deeds of power. Combined, wisdom and power indicate both that the kingdom has come and the kind of kingdom that has come.

The Kingdom Shown: First Discourse to the Second Discourse (Matthew 8–9)

We have heard about the kinds of people, those of superior righteousness, in God's kingdom—people who are merciful, meek, and pure in heart; people who seek peace and hunger for righteousness and justice. Such people, Jesus taught over and over, are *blessed* by virtue of sharing in the kingdom's communal peace, justice, and mercy. How are these tellings of the kingdom reinforced by Jesus's showings of power?

In Matthew, Jesus's deeds of power are on behalf of the little ones, the diseased and oppressed. For example, after the first discourse, a leper comes to Jesus, kneels before him, and says, "Lord, if you choose, you can make me clean" (7:28–8:2). The leper's desperate plight provides Jesus the opportunity to show what he has been teaching about the kingdom. "He stretched out his hand and touched him, saying, 'I do choose. Be made clean!' Immediately his leprosy was cleansed" (8:3). In the leper's cleansing, we see the kind of healing mercy that permits, for the first time, his flourishing within a community of inclusion and justice.

Matthew carefully and successively arranges the deeds of power:

- Jesus heals a leper (7:28–8:2).
  - Lepers were untouchables who lived in solitary desperation.

- Jesus heals the paralyzed servant of a Roman military official (8:5–13).
  - Roman military officers were the enemy and the oppressor of Jews.

- Jesus relieves the fever of Peter's mother-in-law (8:17).
  - Women were second-class citizens.

- Jesus frees the demon-possessed (8:28–34).
  - The demon-possessed were ritually scorned social outcasts.

We also hear of the extent of Jesus's power. The calming of the storm (8:23–27) shows Jesus's power over nature, and the release of the demon-possessed men shows his power over God's greatest adversary, Satan. Through these deeds, Jesus demonstrates his power to secure the personally and communally fulfilling life he has been teaching, a blessed life shared by the righteous in God's inclusive kingdom—inclusive of all the outcasts and little ones of Israel (Jesus will extend inclusion to all nations in his last words to the disciples).

In so doing, Jesus likewise shows a complete transformation of values from normal living, the self-seeking tribe-honoring habits of ordinary life, to kingdom flourishing. In such showings of the kingdom, Jesus illustrates the possibilities of full humanity for the dispossessed and disheartened within God's community of compassion. In God's kingdom, the leper, the demon-possessed, and the enemy are healed body and soul by being shown boundless mercy, fearless peace, and divine justice. No longer leper or enemy, they are children of God (5:45). As repentant members of this compassionate community, they will become, themselves, merciful and healing peacemakers. They will welcome into their new way of life the oppressed and the outcast, and even their enemy. In these brief stories of the kingdom in action, Jesus shows what he tells, a kingdom of wholeness, peace, connection, courage, sharing, health, and mutual flourishing.

The kingdom way of living threatens normal cultural values in a variety of ways, as seen in the freeing of two demoniacs from their tormentors (8:28–34). Jesus sends the released demons into some pigs, who "rushed down the steep bank into the sea and perished in the water" (8:32). The swineherds, concerned more by their loss of livelihood than by the plight of the demon-dominated men, run into the town to tell their version of the story. The whole town charges out and pleads with Jesus to leave (8:32–34). The entire town, in effect, says *no* to kingdom values that would cripple business interests.

God's radically inclusive and mutually fulfilling kingdom, however, keeps on coming. Matthew's rapid succession indicates artistic purpose — hear Jesus teach and see his teachings fulfilled:

- Desperate friends of a paralyzed man carry him on a pallet to Jesus. When Jesus sees their faith, he says to the paralytic, "Take heart, son; your sins are forgiven," and cures his paralysis; the man picks up his pallet and walks home (9:2–8).
- A distraught father, "a leader of the synagogue," kneels before Jesus, begging him to lay his hands on his dead daughter. Jesus enters the girl's room and raises her up from death to new life (9:18–19, 23–26).
- A fearful woman whose bleeding has been out of control for twelve years sneaks up on Jesus from behind, thinking, "If I only touch his cloak, I will be made well." Sensing the flow of energy at the touching of his garment, Jesus turns around and blesses her. She is cured (9:20–22).
- Two blind men cry out, "Have mercy on us, Son of David!" They follow Jesus, who goes into a house; turning to them, Jesus asks if they believe he is able. "Yes, Lord," they answer. They are given their sight (9:27–31).
- A man who can't speak, his tongue held by a demon, is cured, the demon cast out (9:32–34).

Before moving into discourse two, Matthew offers a summary of what we have seen connecting discourses one and two — Jesus's *showing* of the kingdom: "Jesus went about all the cities and villages, teaching in their synagogues, and proclaiming the good news of the kingdom, and curing every disease and every sickness. When he saw the crowds, he had compassion for them, because they were harassed and helpless, like sheep without a shepherd" (9:35–36). This *show* part of Matthew's grand structure of tell-and-show displays Jesus's radically inclusive mercy in giving people sight and light—and life within a compassionate community. Matthew then returns to the *tell* part of his symphonic structuring. The kingdom mission requires further explanation.

The Kingdom Shown: Second Discourse to the Third Discourse (Matthew 11–12)

"Now when Jesus had finished instructing his twelve disciples [second discourse], he went on from there to teach and proclaim his message in their cities" (11:1). We will find, again, a showing that elaborates on what Jesus has been telling his audience about kingdom righteousness and kingdom entrance.

Imprisoned, John hears what the Messiah is doing and sends word to Jesus by way of his disciples. "Are you the one who is to come, or are we to wait for another?" (11:3). Jesus answers with a reminder of his powerful deeds. "Go and tell John what you hear and see: the blind receive their sight, the lame walk, the lepers are cleansed, the deaf hear, the dead are raised, and the poor have good news brought to them" (11:4–5). The kingdom taught and shown is the kingdom come.

After praising John, Jesus denounces those unwilling to repent by turning their lives around from self-centered habits to the other-serving way of God (11:7–20). From the negative response to himself and John, Jesus moves on to three towns in Israel that are even worse than the infamously wicked Tyre, Sidon, and Sodom—which, bad as they were, would have repented had they seen Jesus and his compassionate deeds of power (11:21–24). And for those repenting, Jesus offers (with John's demise firmly in mind) profound encouragement: "Come to me, all you that are weary and are carrying heavy burdens, and I will give you rest. Take my yoke upon you, and learn from me; for I am gentle and humble in heart, and you will find rest for your souls. For my yoke is easy, and my burden is light" (11:28–30).

But how can Jesus's yoke be easy and his burden light when we've just heard that following Jesus requires taking up one's cross and losing one's life? And we've heard repeatedly that without a righteousness that exceeds the scribes and Pharisees, one cannot enter the kingdom. What, then, makes Jesus's yoke easy? The yoke and burden borne by followers of Jesus is light not because following Jesus is not demanding, costing everything really, or that genuine righteousness is not demanding. Jesus's yoke is light because Jesus helps lift it: "I will give you rest" (11:28–29). The focus in this passage is not on the yoke, which is heavy indeed, but on Jesus, with whom the believer is yoked, who helps us lift.

Later we will hear Jesus criticizing religious leaders who "tie up heavy burdens, hard to bear, and lay them on the shoulders of others; but they themselves are unwilling to lift a finger to move them" (23:4). Those religious leaders almost certainly bogged people down with excessive religious strictures (15:9; 12:1–13). More important, though, was the religious leaders' "unwillingness to lift a finger" to help their followers keep the law. Burdens prove heavy when the soul is bogged down by religious strictures, like Sabbath rules prohibiting the gleaning of grain or healing—which Jesus and his disciples break (12:1–13). Attacked, Jesus responds by noting that God desires "mercy and not sacrifice" (12:7).

In the following two stories, we see Jesus mercifully lifting his fingers to feed the hungry and to heal a man's withered hand—but in violation of the religious leaders' excessive and often harmful Sabbath restrictions. The leaders are incensed at Jesus's impropriety in disregarding their understanding of the law. And they are threatened by his attractive compassion, which they take as a threat to their power. Thus viciously motivated, they seek his destruction (12:14). So Jesus moves on, warmly reassuring the crowds and healing those in need (12:15). He gently and humbly asserts his profound calling (11:29); he will not "break a bruised reed or quench a smoldering wick until he brings justice to victory" (12:20). And the kingdom's justice and peace will spread beyond Israel: "in his name the Gentiles will hope" (12:21).

Matthew's spare plotline is marked by the rising hostility of the religious elite. Demonstration of flourishing kingdom life is narratively offset with demonstration of malicious opposition to God's kingdom: the accusers of Jesus resort to alleging his allegiance with the devil, of working on behalf of Satan, Beelzebul (12:24). Jesus has just rescued one of the little ones, a person possessed by a demon who has made him blind and mute (12:22), and he now responds to the Pharisees by pointing to his kingdom power: "If it is by the Spirit of God that I cast out demons, then the kingdom of God has come to you" (12:28). The kingdom is not just near; it is here.

The religious leaders continue to resist, taking a different tack. They insist that Jesus prove himself. Immediately after Jesus has made a blind man see, they demand to see a sign from Jesus (12:38). Jesus will comply but not now and not in any expected or even expectable way. "An evil and adulterous generation asks for a sign," Jesus answers, "but no sign will be given to it except the sign of the prophet Jonah" (12:39; repeated word for word in 16:4). "For just as Jonah was three days and three nights in the belly of the sea monster," Jesus goes on, "so for three days and three nights the Son of Man will be in the heart of the earth" (12:40). Jesus will give them just one more sign, a sign to beat all signs—his resurrection.

But, Jesus argues, the problem isn't with the signs; it's with them: "The people of Nineveh will rise up at the judgment with this generation and condemn it, because they repented at the proclamation of Jonah, and see, something greater than Jonah is here!" (12:41). These leaders repeatedly refuse to reorient themselves from their self-aggrandizing ways to the kingdom ways (that is, to repent). They are incapable of seeing because they are unwilling to hear. They are blind to the signs and deaf to the wisdom of Jesus. "The queen of the South will rise up at the judgment with this generation and condemn it," Jesus continues, "because she came from the ends of the earth to listen to the wisdom of Solomon, and see, something greater than Solomon is here!" (12:42). Though Jesus is much greater than Solomon in both power and wisdom, they neither see nor hear.

God's wisdom, entrusted to Jesus and authenticated by the sign of Jonah, inaugurates an entirely new age, a new order of reality—the kingdom of heaven come to earth. But, in spite of the sign of Jonah and the wisdom greater than Solomon's, some will not see or listen. Clamoring for power and prestige, they see Jesus as a nuisance at best and a threat at worst. They denigrate his works of compassion (insisting on themselves as sole arbiters of God's law) and vilify his healings (suggesting that Satan is Jesus's source of power). The leaders have failed to accede to the wisdom and power of Jesus and to respond by repenting. So the wicked but repentant Ninevites and the queen of the South who sought out Solomon's wisdom will rise up to judge and condemn them.

Immediately following we hear what might seem a random insertion of what-came-next: "Look, your mother and your brothers are standing outside, wanting to speak to you," a messenger tells Jesus. Hearers of Matthew's narrative could fill in the blanks with echoings recalled; what appear to the modern reader as narrative gaps suggested implicit and powerful transitions and forward progress to the alert listener. Here the gap is filled in by the implicit comparison of the family of Jesus, including his mother

Mary, to the nonlistening, unrepentant leadership: each group did not come to listen but to talk.

Although Jesus does not go out to speak to his family, he asks, with brutal pointedness, "Who is my mother, and who are my brothers?" Jesus answers his own question. "Pointing to his disciples, he said, 'Here are my mother and my brothers! For whoever does the will of my Father in heaven is my brother and sister and mother'" (12:46–50). The kingdom overturns one's primary orientation to family and the privileging of tribe. Jesus's biological family is not with him; they are outside the house in which he is speaking. And he will leave the house for his kingdom family: "That same day Jesus went out of the house and sat beside the sea" to teach everyone about the kingdom. For all who will listen to this centerpiece discourse about response to the kingdom, he shares his distilled wisdom, in parables. This is his true family.

The Kingdom Shown: Third Discourse to the Fourth Discourse (Matthew 13:54–17:27)

What has been taught about the kingdom and response to it in discourse three is followed immediately by anecdotes *showing* various responses to the *telling*, to what Jesus has been explaining about the kingdom.

For example, Jesus has just taught about the response of unbelief to his teaching, quoting from the prophet Isaiah that "this people's heart has grown dull, and their ears are hard of hearing" (13:15). Following this response is a demonstration: Jesus's hometown neighbors take offense at him (13:54), and so "he [does] not do many deeds of power there, because of their unbelief" (13:58). But Jesus, despite such negative responses, continues with his kingdom work, demonstrating his teaching. Seeing a great crowd, "he had compassion for them and cured their sick" (14:14). The main point of all that Jesus teaches concerns the revolutionary nature of the kingdom, this radical paying attention to the needs of the little ones.

In successive scenes, Jesus continues to pay attention to the little ones, demonstrating the kingdom-in-action: feeding the hungry (14:13–21), healing the sick (14:34–36), and freeing those imprisoned by Satan (15:21–39).

We hear of Herod's fear of the crowd if he were to pursue his plan to kill John (14:3–5). And, despite witnessing these astounding displays of wisdom-endorsing power, the disciples, when push comes to shove, are, like Herod, gripped with fear. While struggling in their boat in rough seas and high winds, they see Jesus walking on the water and are terrified, fearing a rapidly approaching ghost. But Jesus says to them, "Take heart, it is I; do not be afraid" (14:24–27). Peter, eager to meet Jesus, impetuously attempts to walk on the water. But when Peter notices the high winds, he "[becomes] frightened" and starts to sink. Jesus catches Peter and rebukes him, "You of little faith, why did you doubt?" But when Jesus gets into the boat, the winds cease and the disciples proclaim, "Truly you are the Son of God" (14:28–33).

The hostile response of the religious leaders escalates as the scribes and Pharisees attack Jesus for threatening their self-proclaimed authority to expound the law. For example, they ask, "Why do your disciples break the tradition of the elders? For they do not wash their hands before they eat" (15:1–2). Their hypocritical and spiritually impoverished response is exposed by Jesus, who quotes Isaiah: "This people honors me with their lips, but their hearts are far from me; in vain do they worship me, teaching human precepts as doctrines" (15:7–9). They burden others with their empty rules, while ignoring weightier matters of the heart.

Like Jesus's neighbors (13:57), these leaders take offense at Jesus's teachings and actions. According to Jesus, however, what is truly offensive is what comes out of the mouth, because what comes out of the mouth proceeds from the heart. And "out of the heart come evil intentions, murder, adultery, fornication, theft, false witness, slander. These are what defile a person, but to eat with unwashed hands does not defile" (15:19–20). The religious leaders focus on trivial external rule-keeping, all the while ignoring their glory- and power-seeking hearts. Again, the religious leaders cannot see the wisdom of Jesus and so are blind guides, leading their blind followers into a pit (15:14). Unrepentant hearts prevent seeing and hearing the wisdom of Jesus.

The disciples are warned to guard against the hypocritical leaders' shiny appearance but dark heart. "Beware of the yeast of the Pharisees and Sadducees," Jesus says to them (16:6). This bad "yeast"—their self-righteous and hypocritical teachings—gets inside and taints the entire loaf (16:12).

Given the traditional teachings of the respected leaders and the radical new teaching of Jesus, who should one believe? When Jesus asks his disciples who people think "the Son of Man" is, he is in effect asking who is the authoritative person with privileged access to God (Dan. 7). Peter responds, "You are the Messiah, the Son of the living God" (16:16). Jesus affirms both Peter and his response: "I tell you, you are Peter [*petros*, stone], and on this rock [*petra*][1] I will build my church [*ekklēsia*, assembled people], and the gates of Hades will not prevail against it. I will give you *the keys of the kingdom of heaven*" (16:18–19).[2]

Following Peter's remarkable response and Jesus's equally remarkable assignation of kingdom mission and power to his disciples, Jesus speaks soberly of the powers conspiring in his forthcoming suffering and death (16:21–23). He then, all the more remarkably, invites the disciples to share in his suffering and death: "If any want to become my followers, let them deny themselves and take up their cross and follow me" (16:24), which echoes, of course, Jesus's prediction of his own suffering and death (16:21). Choosing to follow Jesus, the narrative makes clear, is choosing suffering and maybe even death. But death will not have the last word. Jesus, we hear, will die but rise again on the third day, and God will repay those who suffer for his sake.

There are only two possible responses, according to Matthew, with just two corresponding consequences: follow Jesus's path of both suffering and joy and inherit eternal life in God's kingdom, or refuse to follow and inherit God's wrath—"for the Son of Man is to come with his angels in the glory of his Father, and then he will repay everyone for what has been done." Then Jesus says to his disciples assuringly, "Truly I tell you, there are some standing here who will not taste death before they see the Son of Man coming in his kingdom" (16:27–28).

The disciples are then granted a glimpse of God's completed kingdom (and offered opportunity to respond). On a high mountain, in the company of Moses and Elijah, Jesus is gloriously transformed, his face shining "like the sun" and his clothes a "dazzling white" (17:1–8). The disciples' immediate response is to short-circuit their earthly mission and luxuriate in the divine presence forever. God, however, interrupts. "This is my Son, the Beloved; with him I am well pleased," God says to Peter, James, and John. "Listen to him!" (17:6).

Face to face with the glory of God, as in the boat on the stormy sea, the disciples are overwhelmed with fear; they fall face down on the ground. Again, Jesus touches them and says, "Get up and do not be afraid" (17:7). They cannot share in the glory, they will be learning, until they suffer along with Jesus. The kingdom cannot come, will not come, without first the suffering and death of Jesus and second their own cross-bearing kingdom work.

On their way down the mountain, Jesus commands the three disciples to "tell no one about the vision until after the Son of Man has been raised from the dead" (17:9). Although they have seen the glory of God and gained power "over unclean spirits, to cast them out, and to cure every disease and every sickness" (10:1), they still have not yet understood Jesus and his kingdom. We are reminded of their misunderstandings, their infidelity, in a final story. "I brought [my epileptic son] to your disciples," complains a father to Jesus, "but they could not cure him." Jesus turns to his disciples and rails against them, "You faithless and perverse generation, how much longer must I put up with you?" (17:16–17). When they ask Jesus directly why they failed, he says to them, "Because of your little faith. For truly I tell you, if you have faith the size of a mustard seed, you will say to this mountain, 'Move from here to there,' and it will move; and nothing will be impossible for you" (17:20).

So Jesus reminds them, once again, what he is facing (which, again, they will face) on behalf of the kingdom: "The Son of Man is going to be betrayed into human hands, and they will kill him, and on the third day he will be raised." But they still do not understand the kingdom way. So we read, "And they were greatly distressed" (17:23).

The sequences between discourses three and four have focused on showing the challenges of response, which were reviewed in the conclusion to discourse three. The response is demonstrated following discourse three with Jesus's neighbors taking offense at Jesus as a no-good local boy (13:54–57), moving on immediately to the more deadly concern of King Herod, who has John the baptizer beheaded (14:1–12). The hometown folks respond with dismissive unbelief, Herod with fear. We hear repeated echoes of fear and unbelief on the part of both the disciples (fearing ghosts, waves, and God) and the religious leaders (fearing loss of self, power, and prestige). The religious leaders' failure to understand, attributed to their wicked hearts, when later allied with political power ensures the suffering and death of Jesus.

As we move into discourse four we find a shift in focus on the weakness of the disciples, dubbed by Jesus as a "faithless and perverse generation" (17:17). When they learn that Jesus will be betrayed and killed, they are "greatly distressed" (17:23). So they need more focused teaching, which they get in discourse four.

The Kingdom Shown: Fourth Discourse to the Fifth Discourse (Matthew 19:1–23:1)

The disciples have received their second debriefing of their kingdom mission and its opposition in discourse four. Between discourses four and five, the last two, we hear of the great and gracious deeds of kingdom action on behalf of the little ones: "When Jesus had finished saying these things, he left Galilee and went to the region of Judea beyond the Jordan [where] large crowds followed him; and he cured them there" (19:1–2). What follows are example after example of such inclusive mercy (which Jesus has been telling his disciples is the business of the kingdom come).

Jesus teaches about inclusive mercy, deepening our understanding of "the little one," in a series of brief episodes. "Some Pharisees came to him, and to test him they asked, 'Is it lawful for a man to divorce his wife for any cause?'" (19:3). Divorce in this culture was permissible for males of power and means. (Women, unlike men, were not permitted under any circumstances to divorce men.) Jesus, instead, affirms a deeper union governing marriage (19:4–6), making an exception only for infidelity (19:9). The self-appointed rule-keepers retort, "Why then did Moses command us to give a certificate of dismissal and to divorce her?" Jesus replies, "It was because you were so hard-hearted that Moses allowed you to divorce your wives, but from the beginning it was not so" (19:7–8). Simply by securing a certificate, a husband could divorce his wife, thus consigning her, in that day and age, to a life of poverty and estrangement. Divorced women, who were by and large dependent on husbands for their livelihood, were instantly third-class citizens (as women they were already second-class citizens). By virtue of losing their breadwinner, they would be impoverished; by virtue of being divorced, they would be ostracized. Lose-lose for women. Moses's decree, Jesus explains, was little more than a concession to the hard and indifferent hearts of husbands incapable of treating their beloveds with compassion. In such a profound affirmation of marriage, Jesus is ensuring that women are granted socio-personal wholeness in the kingdom. As such, they can't be cast aside, doomed to poverty and oppression.

Matthew's narrative on mercy toward little ones shifts from women to children. When little children are brought to Jesus, the disciples, who consider this an impropriety, rebuke the people who brought them (19:13). Jesus, however, rebukes his disciples for failing to understand: "Let the little children come to me, and do not stop them; for it is to such as these that the kingdom of heaven belongs" (19:14).

All of the little ones, the children and women, the diseased and possessed, reveal the kingdom concern of Jesus but also the crippling lack of mercy on the part of privileged and powerful men. The importance of the powerless to the kingdom is repeated over and over, from "Blessed are the meek" (5:5) to "Whoever welcomes one such child in my name welcomes me" (18:3–5) to "Let the little children come to me . . . for it is to such as these that the kingdom of heaven belongs" (19:14). Jesus's kingdom is not especially for men, for important people, for politicians, for the wealthy, or for the powerful. If anything, his kingdom is especially for the little ones—the oppressed, the outcast, and the diseased. Although God's kingdom is for everyone, whoever enters must do so as a child.

Matthew's kingdom theme of mercy continues. When a young man asks Jesus what he should do to gain eternal life, Jesus replies, "Keep the commandments." When the man asks, "Which ones?" Jesus recites those commandments that concern our treatment of other human beings: don't murder, commit adultery, steal, bear false witness, and so on. Jesus goes on, "You shall love your neighbor as yourself." The man claims that he has done all of this, to which Jesus responds, "'If you wish to be perfect, go, sell your possessions, and give the money to the poor, and you will have treasure in heaven; then come, follow me." Then we read, "When the young man heard this word, he went away grieving, for he had many possessions" (19:16–22). Although the man claimed to love his neighbor as himself, he couldn't bring himself to part with a single possession to share with the poor (the little ones). As a rich man, he didn't need to murder, steal, or bear false witness. All fine and good. But he lacked mercy. This man was unwilling to give up his greatest love—money—to rescue the little ones and ensure their flourishing within God's kingdom. Jesus says to his disciples, "It is easier for a camel to go through the eye of a needle than for someone who is rich to enter the kingdom of God" (19:24). The man's treasure, we hear, is money, not God.

His disciples, shocked at such give-up-everything-and-follow-me righteousness, ask, "Then who can be saved?" Jesus looks them in the eye and says, "For mortals it is impossible, but for God all things are possible" (19:25–26)—especially with the advent of Emmanuel, the God who is with you (1:23). I will make your yoke easy and your load light, he says; I will lift a finger to help you carry this enormous load. "And remember," Jesus will say—the last words of the story—"I am with you always" (28:20).

But Peter objects, "We have left everything and followed you. What then will we have?" (19:27). Jesus gives the disciples hope of future reward: they will sit beside him in glory, will receive a hundredfold of all they have renounced, and will inherit eternal life. But—Jesus returns again to the kingdom's complete transformation of value—the first will be last, and the last will be first.

The desire to be first is not found just in the wealthy or the powerful. The obsession with greatness, to be first, comes in a wide variety of guises, even in a parent's aspirations for their children. So we hear the mother of James and John ask Jesus to grant special glory and honor to her sons: "Declare that these two sons of mine will sit, one at your right hand and one at your left, in your kingdom." Jesus answers, "You do not know what you are asking. Are you able to drink the cup that I am about to drink?" When they say, "We are able," he responds, "You will indeed drink my cup, but to sit at my right hand and at my left, this is not mine to grant" (20:20–23).

Once again we hear an echo: "Who is the greatest in the kingdom of heaven?" Our very natural but lamentable desire to be great is the most serious roadblock on the way of and to the kingdom. Jesus's cure for selfishness and self-aggrandizement is *repentance*—a complete change of heart, which requires a turning away from nearly all cultural norms: "Whoever wishes to be great among you must be your servant, and whoever wishes to be first among you must be your slave; just as the Son of Man came not to be served but to serve, and to give his life a ransom for many" (20:26–28).[3] Repentance requires, on the one hand, giving up all our normal (selfish) aspirations to honor and glory and wealth and, on the other hand, reorienting our desires toward mercy and justice.

Jesus tells, then Jesus shows. Two blind men, sitting at the side of the road, cry out for mercy: "Have mercy on us, Lord, Son of David!" (20:30–31). Jesus is leaving Jericho, on his way to the big city, preoccupied with the ordeal that awaits him. Jesus, however, allows an interruption of "important business" by outcasts in need. The attentive listener will hear and connect *blind men* with *little ones*, gaining a new understanding of "lord," "the least," and "the lost." Jesus shows what being Lord and Master in the kingdom looks like. He stops and, moved with compassion, kneels down and touches their eyes. Regaining their sight, they are restored to light and life. This Master is their servant. Jesus makes himself, according to society's values, last and the blind men first.

Finally entering Jerusalem, Jesus assumes the social position of a lowly peasant riding a donkey.[4] He is greeted with cheers from the crowd, who mistake him for a political messiah (21:1–10). But their adulation will turn to profound disappointment and a murderous roar: "Let him be crucified!" (27:22). Theirs is a mistaken notion of political reign, which the crowd

comes to realize after Jesus's arrest and trial. The people want tribal greatness and power, or at least relief from the oppression of another tribal
power, specifically that of Rome. Jesus offers, instead, a new sort of community of God's people caring for *the least of these*, including even the
enemy. Thus, when Jesus enters it, the city is in turmoil. "Who is this?"
they ask (21:10).

The cleansing of the temple, which occurs next, is typically portrayed
as Jesus's zealous rejection of commerce at a high place of worship. But,
more importantly, co-opting the temple for commercial purposes crowds
out space for the little ones—about whom we hear: "The blind and the
lame came to him in the temple, and he cured them" (21:14). That is, the
kingdom's Lord heals, in "God's house," the previously excluded or overlooked little ones. As he heals, we hear of "children crying out in the temple, 'Hosanna to the Son of David'"—which made the religious leaders
angry (21:15). The last shall be first in God's kingdom, and the first—the
leaders—will be last.

Conclusion

We have heard, in the discourses, of opposition to the kingdom. In response to the verbal assaults of the traditional leaders, Jesus offers parables
on authority and power, and their proper (and improper) use (21:18–44).
The leaders are predictably unhappy: "When the chief priests and the
Pharisees heard his parables, they realized that he was speaking about
them. They wanted to arrest him, but they feared the crowds, because they
regarded him as a prophet" (21:45–46). As more incriminating parables
follow, the Pharisees plot "to entrap him in what he said" (22:15). So they
ask Jesus once again, "Which commandment in the law is the greatest?"
(22:36). One wonders at this point if even the disciples, who have shown
a decided lack of understanding and faith, know.

Matthew concludes the narrative material connecting discourses four
and five with a focus on kingdom opposition from religious leaders, and
on the little ones despised by them but honored by Jesus. Discourse five
follows up with a focus on these leaders and their inevitable destruction,
a long teaching sequence followed by the story of their help in getting
Jesus killed—a short-lived victory, as we hear in the concluding section of
Matthew. God is in control and the kingdom is coming: the last will be first.

"This Is My Blood of the Covenant, Which Is Poured Out for Many" (Matthew 26–28)

Death Conquered and Divine Control: Revisiting Matthew's Introduction

Tell-then-show: after the five "telling" (teaching) discourses, we are given the greatest "showing" of all: the power of God in raising Jesus from death. The risen Messiah must leave, but not without a promise of being forever present (28:20) that echoes the name given Jesus in the beginning, "Emmanuel," *God-with-us* (1:23). In Matthew's conclusion we revisit, as well, his emphasis on divine control through repeated scriptural fulfillments and repeated titles for the Messiah.

Matthew gets right to the point at the beginning of his final section: "When Jesus had finished saying all these things, he said to his disciples, 'You know that after two days the Passover is coming, and the Son of Man will be handed over to be crucified'" (26:1–2). This is the sixth time we have heard Jesus tell his disciples about the coming death of "the Son of Man."[1] The religious leaders, the target of Jesus's previous long teaching, "conspired to arrest Jesus by stealth and kill him" (26:3).

This final discourse concludes (as does the first) with the great judgment: those who have chosen the kingdom will enter into the heavenly kingdom's "eternal life," while those who have refused "will go away into eternal punishment" (25:46). This apocalyptic conclusion to the final epoch of Israel's story (1:1–18) reminds the reader of the eschatological vision running throughout the Hebrew Scriptures, beginning with the promise to Abraham, that through his blessed nation blessing would spread to the world (Gen. 12:1–3)—a promise whose final stages were envisioned by Isaiah, on whom Matthew relies. The day of judgment will usher in the final phase of the kingdom of God—fulfilled entirely. "Go therefore and make disciples of all nations," Jesus concludes in his last words to the disciples, "teaching them to obey everything that I have commanded you. And remember, I am with you always, to the end of the age" (28:19–20).

Up to the Arrest: Episode Explaining Episode (26:1–56)

Matthew's conclusion moves briskly, chronologically, and with explanatory logic—with subsequent episodes expanding on the meaning of the prior episode.

A Little One's Love Upsets the Disciples (26:6–13)

The story of the Lord of the kingdom being killed by religious and political leaders begins with a story about a "little one" crashing the dinner party of the kingdom's future leaders, the disciples.

A woman, uninvited, shows up among the men and goes to Jesus, bathing his head in "a very costly ointment" (26:6–7). The woman's lavish love is juxtaposed with the men's cautious circumspection. The disciples are angry at the woman and for a noble reason: the ointment could have been sold and the profits given to the poor (26:8–9).

In a rebuke of the disciples, Jesus commends the woman: she is, he says, preparing him for burial. With echoes of the rich young ruler (19:16–30), we hear of a person—a woman, a little one—willing to give everything to honor Jesus. He concludes, "Wherever this good news [of the kingdom] is proclaimed in the whole world, what she has done will be told in remembrance of her" (26:13). Unrecognized by the disciples themselves, the kingdom of God is happening in front of these easily offended males.[2]

Love Money versus Blood Money (26:14–16)

We soon hear of a disciple, Judas, seeking blood money. He is granted thirty pieces of silver by the rulers of Israel for the betrayal of his Lord, and "from that moment he [begins] to look for an opportunity to betray him" (26:14–16). We hear echoes of Jesus's temptations, especially Satan's offer of the kingdoms of the world with its perks of wealth and power. Unlike Judas, Jesus resists Satan's temptation to worldly power, remaining steadfast in his pursuit of God's kingdom even though it will cost him his life.

Surrounding the death of Jesus, then, we hear of money lavishly spent on his honor and money treacherously gained on his betrayal. The compassionate woman, spending and loving extravagantly, will be honored throughout the world. The self-serving man, selling his soul for a few pieces of silver, will be dishonored throughout the world. The little one worships God with all of her heart, soul, and mind. The one who would be great accedes to his dark and dismal heart.

Kingdom gained, kingdom lost.

Blood: What Does This Death Accomplish? (26:17–30)

Jesus begins a typically celebratory Passover meal by gravely announcing his betrayal. His announcement, however, is accompanied by his seventh repetition of divine control over what lies ahead. Jesus already knows about it, and Scripture has foretold it (26:17–21). "The Son of Man goes as it is written of him," he tells his disciples, "but woe to that one by whom the Son of Man is betrayed!" (26:24).

During the meal, "Jesus took a loaf of bread, and after blessing it he broke it, gave it to the disciples, and said, 'Take, eat; this is my body.' Then he took a cup, and after giving thanks he gave it to them, saying, 'Drink from it, all of you; for this is my blood of the covenant, which is poured out for many for the forgiveness of sins'" (26:26–28). Just as those who honored the covenant in the days of Moses, the kings, and the prophets would have their sins forgiven—so too Jesus is affirming God's covenant mercy toward those who acknowledge their sins while striving for the kingdom's superior righteousness. The poured-out blood of Jesus for this covenant and its righteousness, extends forgiveness to those faithful to the covenant.

This day of Passover refers to two primary acts from the story of Israel involving the sacrifice of blood: the blood of oxen administered by Moses in sealing the covenant and the blood of a paschal lamb in the deliverance of Israel from the bondage in Egypt.

Moses poured out the blood of oxen to seal the covenant, a partnership agreement represented by half of the blood being sprinkled on the altar of God and half on the people (Exod. 24:6). Then, as John I. Durham, notes, "Moses read the newly written Book of the Covenant to the people, and they responded with the set phrase of commitment, to which is added here the additional assurance that they will *pay attention and take seriously the words of Yahweh*, all of which they have previously promised to do."[3] Jesus, Lord of the kingdom, likewise expects a response of commitment—the disciples must "pay attention and take seriously the words of Yahweh" (as taught by Jesus in his five discourses).

The poured-out blood at this Passover ceremony also refers to the scene of deliverance from Egypt where blood was sprinkled on door lintels so that God would "pass over" that house, sparing the angel's slaying of its eldest son. Passover is Israel's annual "remembrance" (Exod. 12:14) of this "passover of the LORD" (Exod. 12:11). What Jesus provides in his resealing of the covenant is a deliverance, not from the enemy, but from the bondage of sin and its dire consequences. Jesus provides an escape, a "ransom," a freeing from the way of living leading to death, a deliverance from sin that enables one to follow God's way of life (Matt. 20:28). As the angel had told Joseph, Mary's son "will save his people from their sins" (1:21), through—as the story ahead explains—covenantal faithfulness and righteousness empowered by Emmanuel, God-with-us (1:23). "Remember," Jesus says in his last words, "I am with you always, to the end of the age" (28:20). His divine presence provides daily release from the power of sin and forgiveness for our lapses.

Before this Passover ceremony we hear that Jesus will be betrayed by a disciple; just after the meal Jesus foretells the denial and desertion of all of his disciples (26:31–35). Judas will not be forgiven, because he has forsaken the covenant entirely; his sin leads to death. The other disciples will be forgiven because they remain committed to the covenant despite their flaws—demonstrated by their presence with the Lord after his resurrection. Judas, understanding the horror of his betrayal, kills himself; the remaining disciples return to the Lord, their sins of denial and desertion forgiven.

Jesus has urged this covenant participation. *Take these pieces of bread, my broken-apart body, and eat! Participate in the brokenness to come. Drink the wine, my poured-out blood, and participate with me as partners in God's covenant with his people* (26:26–29). "One cannot gain salvation—life in the kingdom—without keeping the covenant, within which dynamic forgiveness of sins is included."[4] Keeping the covenant means full participation in that covenant, with Jesus: "Whoever does not take up the cross and follow me is not worthy of me" (10:38). And later: "If any want to become my followers, let them deny themselves and take up their cross and follow me" (16:24).

The disciples' participation in the brokenness and suffering of Jesus, picking up their own crosses, will likewise liberate people from Satan's power to possess, to inflict debilitating disease, and to impoverish: the disciples will continue to usher in the kingdom. They will, with pain and suffering, do the kingdom's work by encouraging people to resist their unjust attitudes and actions toward outsiders—women or children or non-Jews.[5] In their striving for glory, however, the disciples are as yet unable to drink the cup of suffering Jesus has offered them (20:22–23). But they do drink from the cup of wine, signifying a willingness that will come to fruition after the resurrection.

After singing a hymn together, they depart with Jesus for the Mount of Olives (26:30).

Asleep in a Garden: Prelude to Betrayal, Denial, and Desertion (26:31–56)

Jesus goes with his disciples to a garden to pray. He takes Peter, James, and John aside, sharing with them his grief and agitation. He asks them to stay awake with him (26:37–38). They don't.

Jesus asks his Father, if possible, to "let this cup pass" from him (26:39). Three times Jesus returns to find his disciples asleep (26:40–46). Three times sleeping, and for Peter, three times denying: such repetition of hearing cues underscores the kingdom challenges awaiting these disciples upon the departure of Jesus. They can't resist the urge to sleep; how will they resist the more palpable temptations to desert Jesus?[6] Despite their unfaithfulness to him at this point, Jesus will remain faithful to the covenant and its kingdom, and he will be always present, "to the end of the age" (28:20).

Judas arrives on the scene with a large crowd, sent by the religious leaders, armed with swords and clubs. Denial and desertion are capped off by outright betrayal. After the betrayal by Judas, the scene ends with all followers implicated: "Then all the disciples deserted him and fled" (26:56b).

Who *Is* this Man Facing Death? A Cluster of Titles

Within Matthew's conclusion, the final three chapters, we find repeated references to authoritative titles for Jesus used previously in the story, though in this climactic section those asserting the titles mostly fail to understand them. Instead, they conspire in rejecting the Teacher and his teachings and the Messiah and his kingdom. They derisively mock Jesus in his various roles and then kill him. Yet running through this pattern of titles we hear the same theological perspective that marks the patterns of hearing cues in the four introductory chapters: God's implacable and compassionate control in bringing the kingdom of heaven to earth through the Messiah, the anointed deliverer of Israel.

The manner of deliverance through covenantal faithfulness into the kingdom provided by God is accomplished through Jesus in his roles as Teacher, Messiah, Son of Man, Son of God, and King of the Jews.

Teacher

It is impossible to separate the teaching from the teacher. Jesus teaches the kingdom of heaven—which he, as Messiah, both inaugurates and empowers—based on his deep understanding of covenantal faithfulness. Even his betrayer recognizes Jesus as teacher, though in the end he rejects his teachings.

- At the scene of Jesus's arrest, Judas "came up to Jesus and said, 'Greetings, Rabbi [Teacher]!' and kissed him" (26:49).
- Just before, at the Passover meal, Judas had asked about the betrayer, "Surely not I, Rabbi?" (26:25).
- Jesus calls himself "the Teacher" (26:18).[7]
- When they come to arrest him, Jesus says, "Day after day I sat in the temple teaching, and you did not arrest me'" (26:55).

Messiah

While many expected the Messiah to be a powerful political liberator,[8] Jesus's self-understanding was entirely different: deliverance his way would come through suffering and death. Moreover, rather than ruling in power over people, he served from below, attracting people into the kingdom through compassion and justice.

Jesus shared the burdens of the lonely and the little ones, comforting the afflicted. Earlier on Jesus had "sternly ordered the disciples not to tell anyone that he was the Messiah" until they understood that *this* Messiah would deliver not by mighty armies but by suffering, death, and resurrection (16:20–21).

- "The high priest said to [Jesus], 'I put you under oath before the living God, tell us if you are the Messiah, the Son of God'" (26:63).
- "Prophesy to us, you Messiah! Who is it that struck you?" (26:68).
- "Pilate said to them, 'Whom do you want me to release for you, Jesus Barabbas or Jesus who is called the Messiah?'" (27:17).
- "Pilate said to them, 'Then what should I do with Jesus who is called the Messiah?' All of them said, 'Let him be crucified!'" (27:22)

Son of Man

In Matthew Jesus refers to himself as the Son of Man thirty times, a title derived from the apocalyptic writing of Daniel. Daniel envisions "one like a human being . . . [who] came to the Ancient One and was presented before him" (7:13). The text of Daniel goes on to note an end point to an eschatological age with this *one like a human being*—the *son of man*—in charge:

> To him was given dominion
>   and glory and kingship,
> that all peoples, nations, and languages
>   should serve him.
> His dominion is an everlasting dominion
>   that shall not pass away,
> and his kingship is one
>   that shall never be destroyed. (7:14)

So when Matthew refers to Jesus as the Son of Man, he means that Daniel's vision has come true in Jesus, Israel's Messiah and Lord of God's kingdom of heaven come to earth—an eschatological age that will conclude in an apocalyptic last day of judgment (Matt. 26:64). In Jesus, the authoritative king, knowing that nations of the future will eagerly serve him, is humbly willing to endure suffering, betrayal, and death to ensure and enhance God's kingdom on earth (26:2, 24, 45).

- "You know that after two days the Passover is coming, and the Son of Man will be handed over to be crucified" (26:2).
- "The Son of Man goes as it is written of him, but woe to that one by whom the Son of Man is betrayed! It would have been better for that one not to have been born" (26:24).

- "Then he came to the disciples and said to them, 'Are you still sleeping and taking your rest? See, the hour is at hand, and the Son of Man is betrayed into the hands of sinners'" (26:45).
- "Jesus said to [the high priest], 'You have said so. But I tell you, From now on you will see the Son of Man seated at the right hand of Power and coming on the clouds of heaven'" (26:64)

Son of God

Son of God is a term of royalty designating a dynastic heir to the throne of King David (in Ps. 2, for example, the "anointed" one is the son of God in charge of nations); in Matthew, Son of God also means a beloved servant of God (3:17; 12:18; 17:5).

"The paradoxical nature of the central figure of Matthew's narrative," Donald Hagner notes, is that on the one hand he is "declared the unique Son, the powerful anointed one (in the analogy of triumphant king)," while on the other hand he is "the humble Servant who obediently accomplishes the will of God, eventually through suffering and death."[9] Using "Messiah" and "Son of God" as synonyms (26:23) suggests that the Messiah is, as God twice asserts, "my Son, the Beloved" (3:17; 17:5). Of course, God's estimation of his Son throughout the narrative contrasts sharply with the derision of the high priest and the unruly crowds.

- "The high priest said to him, 'I put you under oath before the living God, tell us if you are the Messiah, the Son of God'" (26:63).
- "You who would destroy the temple and build it in three days," shout the crowd below the cross, "save yourself! If you are the Son of God, come down from the cross" (27:40).

King of the Jews

Beginning with the three wise men from the East, Jesus is implicitly and explicitly called the king of the Jews, the dynastic "Son of David" (1:1; 9:27; 12:23; 15:22; 20:30, 31; 21:9, 15; 22:42) and "Son of God," Israel's deliverer, the Messiah. In this final section, however, the title is used derisively. "Are you the King of the Jews?" (27:11) asks Pilate, with an implicit *yes* from

Jesus,[10] but the Roman ruler refuses to "pay him homage" as did the wise men (2:2). Hearing the clustered string of references together emphasizes for the modern reader what would have sounded a staccato beat of significance for the ancient listener:

- "Now Jesus stood before the governor; and the governor asked him, 'Are you *the King of the Jews?*' Jesus said, 'You say so'" (27:11).
- "After twisting some thorns into a crown, they put it on his head. They put a reed in his right hand and knelt before him and mocked him, saying, 'Hail, *King of the Jews!*'" (27:29).
- Over his head they put the charge against him, which read, "This is Jesus, *the King of the Jews*" (27:37).
- "He saved others; he cannot save himself. He is *the King of Israel*; let him come down from the cross now, and we will believe in him" (27:42).

While Jesus could save himself, King Jesus saves others, serving them as ransom throughout his brief career and finally forfeiting his own life on behalf of the kingdom (1:21). Jesus's kingship is like the work of a shepherd who looks after and protects his sheep: "From [Bethlehem] shall come a ruler who is to shepherd my people Israel" (2:5–6).[11]

For his claim to be King of the Jews, the religious authorities find Jesus guilty of blasphemy and hand him over to Pilate for sedition. The manipulative Jewish leaders want Pilate to feel threatened by Jesus, but Pilate recognizes their ploy. He suggests letting the crowd decide between the release of a notorious criminal or the innocent Jesus (27:15–18). He thinks, wrongly, that the crowd will choose Jesus. But the crowd, having been deceived by their leaders, prefer the release of the criminal Barabbas over the teacher Jesus (27:20–21). Stunned, Pilate asks, "Then what should I do with Jesus who is called the Messiah?" They respond, "Crucify him!" Pilate, overwhelmed at the severity of the punishment, asks "Why, what evil has he done?" whereupon "they [shout] all the more, 'Let him be crucified!'" Pilate accedes to their vicious wishes, washing his hands of the whole mess (27:22–24).

The Dying King

The denial and desertion of Jesus by his disciples is accentuated by Peter's three-time denial of ever having known Jesus (26:69–75). King Jesus has, so it seems, lost the first members of his kingdom.

Earthly rulers compound the loss. The Jewish religious leaders have instigated the people's refusal of Jesus, and the Roman leader, Pilate, in collusion with the Jewish leaders, finds Jesus innocent but out of cowardice accedes to public pressure and hands Jesus over for crucifixion. Roman soldiers mockingly clothe Jesus in purple and spit on him (27:26–30). Finally, Jesus is hung on the cross for an excruciatingly painful dying.

The King appears defeated and his kingdom lost. The disciples have deserted him, and Peter has denied him. Judas has betrayed him and then killed himself. The mayhem is captured and clarified by Matthew in a small pattern of hearing cues:

1 "Two *bandits were crucified with him*, one on his right and one on his left" (27:38).
   2 "Those who passed by derided him, shaking their heads and saying, 'You who would destroy the temple and build it in three days, save yourself! If you are *the Son of God, come down from the cross*'" (27:39–40).
   2' "He is the King of Israel," say the leaders; "let him *come down from the cross* now, and we will believe in him. He trusts in God; let God deliver him now, if he wants to; for he said, 'I am *God's Son*'" (27:42–43).
1' "The *bandits who were crucified with him* also taunted him in the same way" (27:44).

Between the frame of thieves—the king dying with bandits (1 and 1')—we hear the taunts of the commoners and the elite beneath the cross (2 and 2'). In this juxtaposition, we hear that the people and their leaders are like the thieves, who "taunted him in the same way."

These three elements of society—ordinary persons, the power elite, and criminals—are equally enmeshed in the unrighteous kingdom of this world. Rome and Israel are in collusion.

But the triumphal authority of the "King of the Jews" is dramatically manifested in events surrounding Jesus's death, in just four verses (27:50–53)—a mini-pattern of resonating hearing cues:

- The temple curtain separating the people from the holiest of holy (from God) is "torn in two."
- The earth shakes.
- Rocks split.
- Tombs open.
- Bodies of dead saints rise and walk around Jerusalem.

Jesus's heavenly authority is backed up by supernatural signs. In these echoing hearing cues (cosmic and temporal upheaval and tearing apart), the original listening audience would have heard the musical poetry of this powerful affirmation of the King and his teaching, and the extraordinary context and consequence of his actual dying. His resurrection is the final substantiation of his authority.

It Had to Be, and Will Be: Scriptural Fulfillment

The substantiation of Jesus's mission as Israel's Messiah begins and ends with references to God's control over what seems hopeless below. As evidence of the divine master plan, Matthew clusters fulfillments of Scripture in both the introductory four chapters and concluding three chapters:

Introduction: The Birth (chaps. 1–4)
- "to fulfill what had been spoken by the Lord through the prophet" (1:22)
- (again) "to fulfill what had been spoken by the Lord through the prophet" (2:15)
- "fulfilled what had been spoken through the prophet Jeremiah" (2:17)
- "so that what had been spoken through the prophets might be fulfilled" (2:23)
- "so that what had been spoken through the prophet Isaiah might be fulfilled" (4:14)
- "for so it has been written by the prophet" (2:5)

Conclusion: The Death (chaps. 26–28)
- "as it is written of him" (26:24)
- "for it is written" (26:31)
- "How then would the scriptures be fulfilled, which say it must happen in this way?" (26:54)
- "so that the scriptures of the prophets may be fulfilled" (26:56)
- "Then was fulfilled what had been spoken through the prophet Jeremiah" (27:9)

This repetition of scriptural continuities, particularly in these introductory and closing chapters, suggests God's control over the birth and death of

Jesus, the Messiah and Son of God.[12] The Scriptures, as well as Jesus, know what will happen. Like God, and guided by God's word, Jesus has seen into the future both of his death and resurrection and of his coming kingdom.

In the final words of the risen Jesus, the disciples are instructed to fulfill what God has planned since his covenant with Abraham—to bless all the nations through Abraham. He reminds them that "all authority in heaven and on earth has been given to me," which is to be theirs: "Go therefore and make disciples of all nations, baptizing them in the name of the Father and of the Son and of the Holy Spirit, and teaching them to obey everything that I have commanded you" (28:18–20a). The disciples are both charged and empowered, and then sent off with the promise: "Remember, I am with you always, to the end of the age" (28:20b). The kingdom is coming, it is here and now, and it will, without fail, be fully realized.

Conclusion: Blessings to All

God's great plan is coming true: through Abraham's descendants God will bless all peoples (Gen. 12:3; Matt. 28:19). Matthew assures his listeners that God's grand eschatological plan, in place from the start, is nearing fulfillment in the kingdom of heaven on earth.

Just as Matthew connects Jesus's mission with God's promise to Abraham, he connects Jesus's suffering and death with Isaiah's picture of the end times in which the kingdom is ushered in through suffering and death (Matt. 8:17; Isa. 53). Though the kingdom of God has come in nascent form, the Lord of the kingdom must first suffer and die before it can spread to all nations through his faithful disciples. According to Matthew, God took the humble and costly way of kingdom building—populating it with the little ones and requiring the suffering and death of its Lord.

Covenant righteousness marks the citizenry of this kingdom, which honors partnership with God and the blood of Jesus poured out for this covenant.

The kingdom's demanding righteousness is matched by God's merciful forgiveness. Matthew begins with the announcement that Jesus will save his people from their sins (1:21). Before his death, Jesus forgave sins (9:5–6). Finally, Jesus pours out his blood to renew this covenant and its promise of forgiveness for those seeking to honor the kingdom way taught by Jesus (26:28).

In the kingdom, God's merciful forgiveness is matched by the people's covenantal faithfulness, which requires daily tending to the transformation of heart from selfishness toward kingdom righteousness (3:2, 8; 4:17; 11:20; 12:41; 27:3).

The kingdom's superior righteousness is empowered, as we have seen, by the presence of Jesus, God-with-us, with which Matthew bookends his narrative:

- From Isaiah we heard, "'Look, the virgin shall conceive and bear a son, and they shall name him Emmanuel,' which means, 'God is with us'" (Matt. 1:23).
- Jesus says in his crucial postscript, "And remember, I am with you always, to the end of the age" (28:20).

Heard whole, Matthew's carefully crafted story makes a compelling case for the teaching of Jesus regarding the kingdom and the basis of the clarified law on which it rests: here is the hope of Israel and, through redeemed Israel, hope for all peoples of the world.

Matthew begins with the proclamation that in Jesus God is with us, and ends with Jesus promising to be *God-with-us* until "the end of the age." Until the end, the kingdom's completion on earth and the day of judgment, the kingdom will grow within a context of opposition, as Jesus warns the disciples. They will all suffer, and some will die. Like Jesus, the disciples are empowered and encouraged to follow the humble and costly way of kingdom building. But fear not, Jesus says, *I am with you—always.*

PART THREE

Luke-Acts, I:
The Gospel of Luke

CHAPTER 12

"So That You May Know the Exact Truth" (Luke 1:1–79)

Luke's Orderly Account

Luke-Acts, which accounts for nearly one-quarter of the New Testament, is the only comprehensive story within the Bible of the events surrounding and resulting from the life of Jesus; the author's purpose, we hear, is to recount these events in an orderly narrative (Luke 1:1). And yet Luke-Acts is one of the gospels that has been, in N. T. Wright's judgment, forgotten—or, at the least, confused.[1] By capturing the artistic crafting of Luke's unified and coherent whole, we rescue the meaning lost to many modern readers. As we carefully attend to the message found in the medium of these orally influenced texts, Luke's surprising theological perspective will emerge. From his prefatory words, we understand the author to have taken special pains to get it right. Together with our readers, we aim to do so as well.

Luke's Preface: Striving for "the Exact Truth" (Luke 1:1–4)

Luke begins his two-volume story by telling Theophilus, "lover of God,"[2] that he's written his "orderly account" of Jesus so that the listener can "know the exact truth." This four-verse preface is packed with meaning:

> Inasmuch as many have undertaken to compile an account of the things ["events," NRSV] accomplished among us, just as they were handed down to us by those who from the beginning were eyewitnesses and servants of the word, it seemed fitting for me as well, having investigated everything carefully from the beginning, to write it out for you in consecutive order, most excellent Theophilus; so that you may know the exact truth about the things you have been taught. (1:1–4 NASB)

We gather from what is and is not said here that "in Luke's mind all is not well with the *many*'s accounts"—that the audience needs to have "a firmer grasp of the true significance of the tradition" they have received from other sources.[3] Luke intends for his audience to recognize *his* story as the complete and definitive version of the Jesus story. One decided advantage of Luke's account over the other accounts is his continuation and completion of the story of Israel, the kingdom, and the Holy Spirit in Acts. Luke-Acts, then, offers the most comprehensive gospel in the New Testament.

Although not explicitly stated, at the time there were likely many disorderly, incomplete, and mistaken accounts of Jesus. And if we assume, as is likely, that Luke had examined Mark and at least portions of Matthew,[4] we can determine at least three events, among the several that Luke found missing, without which, in Luke's mind, the competing accounts failed to grasp the full significance of Jesus:

1. The salvation of Israel, as prophesied in Scripture and rehearsed in the first nine clustered poems of Luke (1:13–6:49), is fulfilled in Acts.
2. Through those "who belonged to the Way" (Acts 9:2)—redeemed Israel, "servant Israel" (Luke 1:54)—the kingdom of God spreads like wildfire.
3. Jesus sends the Holy Spirit to empower the striving necessary to attain salvation, that is, entrance into the kingdom (Luke 13:24–30; Acts 2:17–18, 33).

These three events in Acts, in addition to accounts of Jesus's birth, teaching, miracles, death, and resurrection in Luke, complete Luke's "orderly account" offered to Theophilus.[5]

Luke begins with astounding promises by God's messenger Gabriel to a priest, Zechariah, and to a young woman, Mary. The respective messages are heard as poetry, the arrangement of language best suited to convey matters of greatest import in the fewest possible words.[6] Gabriel's poem-messages are the first two of nine early poems clustered together by Luke that focus on Israel and its restoration as God's people. Luke's introduction concludes with a third and fourth poem, by Mary and Zechariah respectively: these remind the audience of God's merciful covenant with Israel, a covenant repeatedly abandoned by Israel but not by God. The two main characters of the opening dramatic scenario poetically illuminate the joyous expectation of what lies ahead for Israel—which Luke shows coming true in Acts.

Luke's Introductory Action: Parallel Stories and Poems (Luke 1:4–79)

We have just heard Luke's intention to offer an orderly narrative of "the exact truth" about the events surrounding Jesus. The action, which begins with the Messiah's birth, is no straightforward account, but rather a repeated story of an angel who comes with improbable news of conception, and the birth of those who will figure prominently in the deliverance of Israel. In the crucial aspect of this doubled story—the poor response by a priest to God's message in contrast with the splendid response of a young virgin—the moral emerges: blessed are those who hear the word of God and respond well. This message is central to all of Luke-Acts, defining the requirements for salvation, entrance to God's kingdom.

Parallel Stories: Improbable Conceptions, Contrasting Responses

The very old priest, Zechariah, is told that his barren and old wife, Elizabeth, will bear him a son. The young virgin, Mary, is promised a child, Jesus.

Similar reassurance and promises are given to Zechariah and Mary by the angel Gabriel, with precise words and order repeated:

- "Do not be afraid, Zechariah" (1:13).
- "Do not be afraid, Mary" (1:30).

Then, similar commands from God's messenger to name each child:

- "You will name him John" (to Zechariah, 1:13);
- "You will name him Jesus" (to Mary, 1:31).

Each will play similarly crucial roles in the deliverance of Israel and the establishment of God's kingdom:

- John, says the angel to Zechariah, "will turn many of the people of Israel to the Lord their God" (1:16).
- Jesus, says the angel to Mary, will be given "the throne of his ancestor David. He will reign over the house of Jacob forever, and of his kingdom there will be no end" (1:32–33).

But the word of God is received in opposite ways:

- "Zechariah said to the angel,
  - 'How will I know that this is so?
    - For I am an old man, and my wife is getting on in years'"
      (1:18).

- "Mary said to the angel,
  - 'How can this be,
    - since I am a virgin?'" (1:34).

While Zechariah's "How will I know?" expresses a skeptical resistance, Mary's "How can this be?" expresses joyous wonder.

In case we missed the profound difference in responses to the two "how" questions, note the respective consequences: while Zechariah is chastised, Mary is praised.

- Having asked *how will I know?* Zechariah is struck mute. "Because you did not believe my words," says Gabriel to the priest, "which will be fulfilled in their time, you will become mute, unable to speak, until the day these things occur" (1:20).
- After asking *how can this be?* Mary is given an answer, a promise: "The power of the Most High will overshadow you," says the angel (1:35). In contrast to the priest's silence, Mary bursts into speech, delivering a magnificent poem of praise (1:46–55).

The priest's question manifests his disbelief and doubt, while Mary's manifests a trusting curiosity. "Here am I," she tells the angel Gabriel, "the servant of the Lord; let it be with me according to your word" (1:38).

Such variation at the end of the pattern with precise echoing reveals profound meaning. "The authors of the biblical narratives," notes Robert Alter, "astutely discovered how the slightest strategic variations in the pattern of repetitions could serve the purpose of commentary, analysis, foreshadowing, thematic assertion, with a wonderful combination of subtle understatement and dramatic force."[7] Mary's and Zechariah's similar but different questions illustrate a "strategic variation." The purpose of "commentary" and "foreshadowing" in the case of Luke's beginning suggests the narrative's fundamental assumption on which its moral vision rests: *Those who hear and obey the word of God as taught by Jesus will enter into the kingdom's eternal life.*[8] Luke's thematic premise, that salvation requires hearing the word of God taught by Jesus and living in faithfulness to that word, appears in different narrative guises—in differing words, images, and anecdotes echoed over and over throughout Luke-Acts. Attentively hearing the word of God taught by Jesus accompanied by striving to obey brings entrance into God's kingdom come to earth.

Poems 1 and 2: Parallel Poems from Gabriel Regarding Israel's Deliverance

The angel Gabriel has spoken to the priest Zechariah of the miraculous birth of a son, John, who will call God's people to return to their covenant relationship with God:

> Do not be afraid, Zechariah,
> for your prayer has been heard.
> Your wife Elizabeth will bear you a son,
> and you will name him John.
> You will have joy and gladness
> and many will rejoice at his birth. . . .
> He will turn many of the people of Israel to the Lord their God.
> With the spirit and power of Elijah he will go before him
> to turn the hearts of parents to their children,
> and the disobedient to the wisdom of the righteous,
> to make ready a people prepared for the Lord. (1:13–17)[9]

The role of the priest's prophetic son, we hear, is to turn recalcitrant Israel back to their covenantally faithful God:

- *turn many in Israel back* to the Lord their God (1:16)
- *turn the hearts of parents back* to their children (1:17)
- *[turn] the disobedient back* to the wisdom of righteousness (1:17)

This simple hearing cue *turning back* highlights Luke's repeated message of repentance (*metanoeō*, "turn around") that will rescue Israel from its disobedience and return the people, in faithfulness, to their covenantal God.

In a similar poem, the same angel tells Mary of an improbable conception and of Israel's imminent restoration (again, we take the prose of the NRSV and transpose it into the poetry it is):

Do not be afraid, Mary,
for you have found favor with God.
And now, you will conceive in your womb and bear a son;
you will name him Jesus.
He will be great
and will be called the Son of the Most High.
And the Lord God will give to him the throne of his ancestor David.
He will reign over the house of Jacob forever;
of his kingdom there will be no end. (1:30–33)

The salvation of Israel, with Jesus on the throne of King David, will bring a kingdom with "no end." Unlike previous dynasties and kings, which began with promise and ended in disaster, King Jesus will rule his righteous kingdom forever.

Table 2. A visual of the hearing cues of the twin messages from God

GABRIEL TO PRIEST	GABRIEL TO MAIDEN
"Do not be afraid, Zechariah,	"Do not be afraid, Mary,
for your prayer has been heard [by God].	for you have found favor with God. . . .
Your wife Elizabeth will bear you a son, and you will name him John. . . .	You will . . . bear a son, and you will name him Jesus.
He will be great in the sight of the Lord. . . .	He will be great . . . the Son of the Most High. . . .
He will turn many of the people of Israel to the Lord their God. . . . With the spirit and power of Elijah he will go before him . . . to make ready a people prepared for the Lord." (1:13–17)	The Lord God will give to him the throne of his ancestor David. . . . He will reign over the house of Jacob forever, and of his kingdom there will be no end." (1:30–33)

Poems 3 and 4: Parallel Poems of Praise for Israel's Deliverance: Mary, then Zechariah

Mary (Luke 1:46–55)

As noted, Mary's good hearing of the word from God, by way of Gabriel, leads to magnificent speaking, a splendid poem that has come to be known as the Magnificat. It begins with praise:

> My soul magnifies the Lord,
> and my spirit rejoices in God my Savior. (1:47)

And it concludes with her motivation for praise:

> [God] has helped his servant Israel
> in remembrance of his mercy,
> according to the promise he made to our ancestors,
> to Abraham and to his descendants forever. (1:54–55)

Mary begins by expressing deep personal gratitude to God *her* Savior and concludes with a declaration of God's saving help for "servant Israel." God has looked with favor on her, and in the end we hear that God looks with favor on "servant Israel."

The status of Israel as God's servant is echoed in Mary herself: as God's lowly "servant" (1:46–48), Mary is among the first members of "servant Israel." From her we learn of the servant's need for humility and the dramatic reversal of lowly and proud in the kingdom: "[God] has looked with favor on the lowliness of his servant" (1:48) is followed up with "[God] has brought down the powerful from their thrones, and lifted up the lowly" (1:52). According to this poem, God's kingdom does not operate in accord with typical, earthly ways of accruing and assigning sociopolitical value, such as power, prestige, wealth, social status, looks, health, gender, race, or religion. Echoing Hannah, the mother of Samuel,[10] Mary proclaims that God will scatter the proud, bring down rulers, and send away the rich. God brings mercy, however, to those who fear him, lifting up the humble and feeding the hungry (1:51–53). Israel's rescue, as Acts will demonstrate, will inaugurate kingdom values, which God initiated with Abraham—a life of blessing (Gen. 12:3; Acts 3:25) at odds with the death-dealing ways of earthly kingdoms with their honoring of the self-centered powermongers and the self-aggrandizing ways of ordinary individuals.

Zechariah (Luke 1:68–79)

His punishment of silence over, Zechariah offers a poem that matches Mary's for magnificence, paralleling Mary's assurance of God's mercy toward Israel. "Blessed be the Lord God of Israel," he begins,

> for he has looked favorably on his people and redeemed them.
> He has raised up a mighty savior for us
> in the house of his servant David. (1:68–69)

God has redeemed Israel, starting now and lasting forever. God "has remembered his holy covenant," sings Zechariah,

> the oath that he swore to our ancestor Abraham,
> to grant us that we, being rescued from the hands of our enemies,
> might serve him without fear, in holiness and righteousness
> before him all our days. (1:72–75)

Mary sang of "servant Israel," here shown as God's fulfillment of the covenant with Abraham to make of Israel a great nation to be servant to all peoples of the world, bringing salvation's blessing from God (Gen. 12:1–3; see Peter's address in Acts 3:25).

The priest's reference to a savior in the house of David echoes Gabriel's statement to Mary about Jesus: "He will reign over the house of Jacob forever."

Hearing the two echoing poems in tandem, we hear that Israel is a "redeemed" people through its "mighty savior," Jesus, and as such will serve God in the world.

Zechariah's poem closes as it opens, with a focus on Israel:

> The dawn from on high will break upon us [Israel],
> to give light to those who sit in darkness and in the shadow of death,
> to guide our feet into the way of peace. (1:78–79)

God's grand purpose for all is summarized in the last lines of Zechariah's poem: God's guidance "into the way of peace."

Conclusion

The events that Luke is anxious for Theophilus to understand conclude with the joyous arrival of God's promised kingdom on earth, starting with the salvation of Israel. Luke may have been concerned that these two climactic events, Israel's redemption and the kingdom's beginning, were being downplayed or confused in other accounts. In Luke's narrative, "servant Israel" is shown mercy (1:54) *and* Israel's glory is realized in its beginning to become a light to the nations.[11] God's kingdom, which Jesus said would come in a slow, small way (Luke 13:19, 21), arrives and spreads in Acts through servant Israel.

In Acts, Peter connects the kingdom to the covenant between God and Abraham: "You are the descendants of the prophets and of the covenant that God gave to your ancestors." Moreover, in the spreading kingdom, Peter sees the fulfillment of God's promise to Abraham, that "in your descendants all the families of the earth shall be blessed" (3:25). Luke's artfully structured preface, offering promise and hope to the entire world, would have appealed to the sensibilities of traditional Jew and curious Gentile alike.[12]

CHAPTER 13

"God Has Looked Favorably on His People and Redeemed Them" (Luke 1:13–6:49)

From Peace to Love: Five More Poems

Starting with the shocking news of miraculous conceptions, delivered as poems by God's messenger Gabriel, Luke clusters nine poems in close succession. We have seen four of them in Luke's introduction already (1:5–79). They constitute a pattern of gathered hearing cues regarding Israel and blessing and covenant that would ring in the ears of Luke's audience.

In oral cultures, stories and poetry were performed aloud partly for the sheer pleasure of the language. When we read the gospel writers' written form, the pleasure of the poetry in particular is part of the profit: when we hear the stories repeatedly, we discover meaning, which in sacred narrative is the author's theological vision. In Luke we hear a lyrical affirmation of liberation, of salvation. All the more important, then, to try hearing as the original audience heard—the pattern of all poems in tandem, theme bouncing off theme with reinforcement and elaboration.

Unfortunately, many translations obscure Luke's poems with prose renderings that flatten their delicately balanced and intricately organized lines, obscuring his vision, making it harder to hear. Heard together, as if mini-movements of a symphony, Luke's nine poems sing in harmony of Israel's restoration and its impact on the kingdom age, "the year of the Lord's favor" (4:19). Israel will both enjoy and share God's kingdom blessings.

One of the major fulfilled events referred to by Luke in his letter to Theophilus is the restoration of Israel as "servant Israel"—its covenantal role in bringing light and blessing to all nations (Acts 3:25). We have seen the two poems by the messenger Gabriel and the two poems by Mary and Zechariah: all four hover around the idea of Israel's restoration as "servant Israel." The fourth poem, Zechariah's, closes as it opens, with a focus on Israel:

The dawn from on high will break upon us [Israel],
to give light to those who sit in darkness and in the shadow of death,
to guide our feet into the way of peace. (1:78–79)

We move on to the remaining five poems with their narrowing focus on Jesus as God's "holy servant" to Israel (Acts 4:27, 30).

Poem 5: God's Glory in Heaven Is Earth's Peace (Luke 2:14)

God's grand purpose is summarized in the last lines of Zechariah's poem: guidance "into the way of peace." Angels sing of this kingdom goal in the very next poem, to the shepherds. Peace lies at the heart of the kingdom way.

It is night. The Jewish shepherds keep themselves awake in their fields outside town, guarding their sheep. The heavens open with flashing light and celestial song.

Glory to God in the highest heaven,
and on earth peace among those whom he favors! (2:14)

In addition to the shock of hearing an angelic choir bursting forth from the skies above, these dispossessed shepherds hear that they, of all people, are favored and will experience God's grace and peace. Luke's listeners will later hear that such communal compassion and *shalom* (peace, wholeness, fulfillment, and harmony) are the heart and soul of Israel's radically inclusive salvation in the coming kingdom of God. If we reorganize it a bit and listen as it is read more slowly—

- in the highest heaven,
  - glory to God;

- on earth,
  - peace among those whom he favors!

—its meaning emerges: *God's glory* above echoes *peace* below, on earth. That is, God is glorified by the realization of peace on earth.

The context for this shortest of the early nine poems is the birth of Jesus. Joseph and Mary have traveled to David's city, Bethlehem, where

Jesus is born (2:1–7). Jesus is laid in a barn's feeding trough, a manger, since there is no room at the inn (2:7). The lowly birth to the lowly couple is news to the lowly shepherds. Those who first harken to the herald are the lowly within Israel, spoken of by Mary in her poem of praise: the lowly will be lifted up.

An angel has told the shepherds that "the Messiah, the Lord" has been born in David's city (the focus on Israel and its redemption weaves its way through each poem in its immediate literary context). This single angel is joined by "a multitude of the heavenly host" who sing their brief version of the gospel, the good news of God's kingdom come. Communal *shalom* is the goal of the divine will and human participants—the covenantal fulfillment that comes true in Acts.

The lowly handmaiden and the rustics from the field hear of Israel's salvation, brought through their Messiah, their Lord—born in David's city and occupying his throne forever, as promised in the Hebrew Scriptures. The brilliant little poem sung by the angels offers a cosmic perspective involving the lowliest of human creatures—among those whom God favors.

Poem 6: "A Light for Revelation to the Gentiles" (Luke 2:29–32)

When Jesus is taken to the temple for ritual purification,[1] an old man, the "righteous and devout" Simeon, takes baby Jesus in his arms and praises God. He has been "looking forward to the consolation of Israel" (2:25), and now he is holding the fulfillment of God's great promise in his arms.

> For my eyes have seen your salvation,
>> which you have prepared in the presence of all peoples,
> a light for revelation to the Gentiles
>> and for glory to your people Israel. (2:29–32)

What Simeon hopes for as "the consolation of Israel" (2:25) he goes on to express here, in poetry, as a salvation prepared "in the presence of all peoples"—"a light for revelation to the Gentiles" that would come through God's "people Israel" and redound to their glory. For this they were chosen as God's covenantal partner in service: to bring God's light to all non-Jews of the world (Gen. 12:3; Acts 3:25).

After Simeon blesses the family, he turns to Mary with a prophecy: "This child is destined for the falling and the rising of many in Israel" (Luke 2:34). In Acts we will hear that the "rising" are the redeemed, those turning to Jesus as their Messiah by the thousands (Acts 2:41) upon thousands (4:4) upon thousands (21:20). But those within Israel who reject God's salvation, those "falling . . . in Israel," will be "utterly rooted out of the people" (3:23).

But this rosy picture of the rising within Israel conceals pain: Simeon follows up with a strange and ominous warning to Mary, that "a sword will pierce your own soul" (Luke 2:35). In Luke we will find at least two occasions—before the crucifixion—when Mary's soul is pierced by her own son, as Simeon forecasts.

Simeon, along with Mary, is an early representative of servant Israel. The covenant fulfillment for which he has longed is here, in his arms. "Master," he prays, "now you are dismissing your servant in peace" (2:29). His eyes have seen Israel's salvation, which will spread as "revelation to the Gentiles." Simeon's expectation of Israel's salvation, the expectation of Luke's audience, is realized in Acts.

Poem 7: "All Flesh Shall See the Salvation of God" (Luke 3:4-6)

We hear that Jesus is growing up and becoming strong, "filled with wisdom" and with "the favor of God . . . upon him" (2:40). Once more, just a few verses away: "And Jesus increased in wisdom and in years, and in divine and human favor" (2:52). The meaning in such echoing between 2:40 and 2:52? Jesus, we hear, *grew* in wisdom and *increased* in the favor of God. Jesus was not the ready-made Teacher of God's way, the law clarified; he learned, listened, and grew, pleasing God more and more. Jesus the Teacher, for Luke, serves as a model for his pupils of both the Way and the striving required to follow the Way.

And we hear of the grown-up John rehearsing the word of God for his fellow Israelites, "proclaiming a baptism of repentance for the forgiveness of sins" (3:3). John's mission as "the voice of one crying out in the wilderness" echoes words from the prophet Isaiah:

Prepare the way of the Lord,
    make his paths straight.
Every valley shall be filled,

> and every mountain and hill shall be made low,
> and the crooked shall be made straight,
> and the rough ways made smooth;
> and all flesh shall see the salvation of God. (3:2–6; see Isa. 40:4)

The poem concludes with a proclamation of the ancient covenant made with Abraham, referred to in Mary's poem above: God is acting "according to the promise he made to our ancestors, / to Abraham and to his descendants forever," that Israel's blessing will bring blessing to the entire world (1:54–55; see Acts 3:25). John is paving the way for Jesus, filling valleys, straightening paths, and making the rough ways smooth—so that, in the end, "all flesh shall see the salvation of God."

John then calls Israel to "bear fruits worthy of repentance," required for a kingdom way of life, which is utterly opposed to the ways of ordinary living (3:7–14).

Poem 8: "The Year of the Lord's Favor" (Luke 4:18–19)

"When all the people were baptized, and when Jesus also had been baptized and was praying, the heaven was opened, and the Holy Spirit descended upon him in bodily form like a dove. And a voice came from heaven, 'You are my Son, the Beloved; with you I am well pleased'" (3:21–22).

Luke, preparing his audience for the first poem by Jesus, refers to Isaiah to define what it means to be Israel's Messiah. A genealogy traces his lineage back to the "son of Adam, son of God" (3:23–38). From Adam, son of God, we move immediately forward to Jesus, whom God has just called "my Son, the Beloved." Jesus is being tested by God's great opponent, the devil. But Jesus is "full of the Holy Spirit"—a key theme in Acts; Jesus defeats the devil, refusing the perks of earthly power in favor of honoring God and the priorities of God's coming kingdom (4:1–13).

Jesus returns home. He is in the synagogue, as is his practice. He stands up to read from Scripture; his chosen passage is about himself, the Anointed One, the Messiah:

> The Spirit of the Lord is upon me,
> because he has anointed me to bring good news to the poor.
> He has sent me to proclaim release to the captives

and recovery of sight to the blind,
    to let the oppressed go free,
to proclaim the year of the Lord's favor.

(4:18–19; from Isa. 61:1; 58:6)

Here we find the start of an answer to the question from the angels' song about those whom God favors (2:14). God has anointed Jesus to proclaim and bring the good news, and a sign of God's favor, to the poor, the captive, the blind, and the oppressed. This "year of the Lord's favor," the age of God's kingdom, is inaugurated with both the proclamation and the demonstration of the good news that provides release from all oppressions.

Jesus takes his seat in the synagogue and speaks about Israel's stubborn refusal to accept the prophet's words; he implicitly places himself alongside Isaiah, whom he has just quoted in predicting his own vocation as Messiah (4:20–27). His fellow Jews, "filled with rage," take him to the edge of a cliff to hurl him to his death. "But he passed through the midst of them and went on his way" (4:28–30).

Jesus then *demonstrates* the good news of release from oppression (4:18) by releasing a demon-possessed man from his imprisonment (4:31–37). A woman "suffering from a high fever" is freed from her illness (4:38–39). "All those who had any who were sick with various kinds of diseases brought them to him; and he laid his hands on each of them and cured them" (4:40). Since inaugurating the kingdom on earth for a redeemed Israel is the immediate goal of Jesus, he continues "proclaiming the message in the synagogues of Judea" (4:44).

For this kingdom to come, Jesus needs help; he challenges Peter, James, and John to leave their catching of fish to help him bring people into the kingdom. They follow (5:1–11). A leper is cured, and "now more than ever the word about Jesus spread abroad; many crowds would gather to hear him and to be cured of their diseases" (5:12–15). A paralytic is cured, and his sins forgiven—to the consternation of the leaders: "Who can forgive sins but God alone?" they ask. The people glorify God (5:17–26).

Another kingdom helper, the tax collector Levi, is added. He immediately gives "a great banquet"—again, to the consternation of the leaders: "Why do you eat and drink with tax collectors and sinners?" they ask. Because, answers Jesus, "I have come to call not the righteous but sinners to repentance" (5:27–32). The leaders persist. Why don't your disciples fast

139

and pray (5:33–39)? Why do they pluck grain to eat on the Sabbath? "The Son of Man is lord of the sabbath," Jesus concludes, implying authority over the Sabbath (6:1–5). To the consternation of the leaders, he heals on the Sabbath (6:6–11). The work of releasing those in need, for the kingdom, is a seven-day-a-week challenge.

Poem 9: "Do to Others As You Would Have Them Do to You" (Luke 6:20–49)

After a night in prayer on a mountain, Jesus completes his choosing of twelve disciples to assist him, both in the present and after his departure (6:12–16): these will be the leaders of redeemed Israel. They descend the mountain. Jesus is standing "on a level place, with a great crowd of his disciples and a great multitude of people from all Judea, Jerusalem, and the coast of Tyre and Sidon." They have come to hear his kingdom proclamation and to be released from oppressions. "All in the crowd were trying to touch him, for power came out from him and healed all of them" (6:17–19).

"He looked up at his disciples and said . . ." We come to the last, longest, and climactic ninth poem,[2] a crystal-clear clarification of the law: striving to obey this law is essential for kingdom entrance (13:24–30). Again: the prose of most translations, here the NRSV, dulls the power of the poetry, which includes three linked sequences: (1) *the blessed and the damned* (6:20–26); (2) *love your enemies* (6:27–38); and (3) *hear the word and do it* (6:39–49).

Section 1: *The Blessed and the Damned (Luke 6:20–26)*

"He looked up at his disciples and said, 'Blessed are you who are poor / for yours is the kingdom of God'" (6:20).

We find, again, the kingdom's great reversal of values that was foreshadowed in Mary's poem with the poor and lowly lifted up, the proud and wealthy brought down. In his prior poem, Jesus had said that he was sent in order to bring the gospel to the poor (4:18–19). This first section of the ninth poem expands on the meaning of *poor*: the hungry (6:21a); the mournful (6:21b); those hated and reviled "on account of the Son of Man," who will receive their reward "in heaven," that is, in the sight of

God (6:22–23). For those, however, who cling to their cultural norms of pride and wealth, who refuse to embrace poverty and the impoverished, he proclaims damnation:

> Woe to you who are full now,
>> for you will be hungry.
> Woe to you who are laughing now,
>> for you will mourn and weep. (6:24–25)

Section 2: Love Your Enemies (Luke 6:27–38)

The second section, the heart of the poem, expresses the way of God, which is the way of love, even of enemies. It has three stanzas marked by parallel starting lines, highlighted below.

> *Love your enemies,*
>> do good to those who hate you
>> bless those who curse you,
>> pray for those who abuse you. . . .
>> Do to others
>> as you would have them
>> do to you. (6:27–31)

> *If you love those who love you,*
>> what credit is that to you?
>> For even sinners love those who love them.
>> If you do good to those who do good to you,
>> what credit is that to you?
>> For even sinners do the same.
>> If you lend to those from whom you hope to receive,
>> what credit is that to you?
>> Even sinners lend to sinners, to receive as much again. (6:32–34)

> *Love your enemies,*
>> do good, and lend, expecting nothing in return.
>> Your reward will be great;
>> you will be children of the Most High;

> he is kind to the ungrateful and the wicked.
> Be merciful, just as your Father is merciful.
> Do not judge, and you will not be judged. . . .
> for the measure you give
> will be the measure you get back. (6:35–38)

The middle stanza of this little love poem offers the normal cultural way of loving those who love you, norms even sinners can live up to: love of friends and family. The parallel first and third stanzas, echoing each other, express the radical way of God's kingdom: "Love your enemies."

In the culture of Jesus's place and time, as in most cultures, we find exclusively familial and tribal "love,"[3] caring for those who are blood related to you or those who can benefit you (that is, kin and community). We are biologically hardwired to love our family members, especially our children. If we see our own child in need—falling into a fire or in front of a car—we instantly leap into action, even at the cost of life or limb. Extending that sort of self-sacrificial concern beyond kin is difficult, especially difficult if one's family and community define, as they often do, the outsider as "enemy." In Jesus's kingdom, love has no limits. It extends beyond genetic and communal boundaries or categories to embrace "enemy."

Even sinners "love" those who love them, though such "love"—doing good for those who are good to you—is little more than economic exchange (6:33).[4] Kingdom love, "love your enemies," turns these essentially selfish "quid pro quo" cultural norms upside down. More importantly, opening one's heart to "the enemy" breaks the sorts of cultural boundaries that would preclude the expansion of God's kingdom of compassion "to all flesh."

Jesus concludes with simple advice for the kingdom: "Do to others as you would have them do to you" (6:31). Kingdom love involves both the attitude and action of helpfulness, seeking to understand and support another's best interests—even those of the outcast, prisoner, or enemy.

When Israel (temporarily) rejects his love-based making of peace, Jesus weeps (19:41–42).[5]

Section 3: Hear the Word and Do It (Luke 6:39–49)

Jesus begins this section with a prohibition on judging others:

> Do not judge,
> and you will not be judged;
> do not condemn,
> and you will not be condemned.
> Forgive,
> and you will be forgiven;
> give,
> and it will be given to you. (6:37–38)

"Why do you see the speck in your neighbor's eye / but do not notice the log in your own eye?" Jesus asks (6:41).

Connecting this prohibition against judging to the previous section, we see its embrace of the love of enemy, threatened by our instinctive judging and putting down of others. Look inward, honestly; when looking out, act lovingly—as you would want others to do for you.

Jesus returns to the major assumption underlying all of Luke-Acts, the requirement for entering the kingdom's salvation: hearing the word of God and doing it. (We heard it first, implicitly, in the juxtaposition of responses to the word brought by the messenger Gabriel to Zechariah and Mary.)

> Why do you call me "Lord, Lord"
> and do not do what I tell you?
> I will show you what someone is like
> who comes to me, hears my words, and acts on them.
> That one is like a man building a house
> who dug deeply and laid the foundation on rock;
> when a flood arose, the river burst against that house
> but could not shake it, because it had been well built.
> But the one who hears and does not act is like
> a man who built a house on the ground, without a foundation.
> When the river burst against it, immediately it fell,
> and great was the ruin of that house. (6:46–49)

The blessings and woes that began with Mary and Zechariah (Mary blessed; Zechariah temporarily experiencing woe) are echoed here: blessing to those who hear and heed the word of God; woe to those who don't.

This last of nine poems, tied together within six chapters and featuring the theme of Israel's salvation, spells out the radical turnaround from Israel's business as usual, loving their own, all the while ignoring the poor and despising their enemies. Their salvation will be their entrance into a kingdom of outcasts and enemies, anyone who seeks release from oppressions and illnesses and seeks peace.

Conclusion

Each of the nine poems focuses on Israel's salvific role as "servant Israel." An angel announces the miraculous births of two persons, John and Jesus, who will prove pivotal in the turnaround of Israel to God.

Mary the mother of Jesus praises God for being faithful "to the promise he made to our ancestors, to Abraham and his descendants forever," with Zechariah the father of John following up with praise for "the Lord God of Israel" who "has raised up a mighty savior for us in the house of his servant David."

At the birth of Jesus, angels sing a poem of praise to God for peace on earth for those who favor God; Simeon, following, praises the merciful God for preparing salvation "in the presence of all peoples, a light for revelation to the Gentiles" bringing "glory to [God's] people, Israel."

The adult John quotes a poem that is a call for preparation of "the way of the Lord" so that "all flesh [through Israel] shall see the salvation of God."

This cluster of introductory poems concludes with two others, both by Jesus. The first, as crucial as it is brief, is borrowed from Isaiah and is about the anointing of Israel's deliverer, who provides release for *all* who are oppressed—in a word, ushering in the kingdom age, "the year of the Lord's favor." The last of the nine poems, about the covenantal law as a principle of love—even of enemy (within and beyond the house of Jacob)—concludes on a note of judgment, based on one's hearing of God's word and doing it. We are taken back, by way of the hearing cue, to the contrasting responses of Mary and Zechariah: she responded well to the word of God and was honored by the angel. This last and longest of the nine early poems, by Jesus, provides a preview of a ten-chapter teaching pattern (9:51–19:44), which clarifies the law in compelling fashion. This, for Luke, is "the way of God" as taught by Jesus (20:21).

CHAPTER 14

"Release to the Captives": The Gospel of Jesus Demonstrated, with Its Cost (Luke 4:33–9:50)

Interweaving Motifs

Reading from Isaiah, Jesus has identified himself as the one anointed (Messiah, Son of God) to liberate those shackled by poverty, blindness, imprisonment, and oppression in order "to proclaim [and demonstrate] the year of the Lord's favor," the age of God's kingdom come to earth (4:18–19). Within six chapters of the first section of Luke (4:33–9:43), Luke arranges a pattern of thirteen miracles, instances of the repeated release of captives.

But there is a motif of cost as well, repeated indications of the heavy price paid by the leaders of the early kingdom movement. Jesus, of course, will give his life. And a dark shadow hangs over John's parents, Zechariah and Elizabeth, as they await word on their son's fate in prison, and then receive the news of their son's being murdered; a similar shadow awaits Mary. Her soul is to be pierced twice even before she witnesses her son's cruel death.

We hear about cost willingly borne but also cost decidedly avoided by the otherwise well-intended disciples. And John has had haunting doubts in prison about whether Jesus is really the one promised. Like most of the great biblical narratives—recall the story told in Genesis from Abraham through Joseph—the grim and gritty reality of shadows and cost are interwoven into the Luke-Acts account of Jesus and his followers and the kingdom come.

Luke underscores this dark undertow by contrasting it with the kingdom's joyous birthing. Luke's arrangement of his first major section (1:1–9:50) is a complex interweaving of orchestral motifs, some wonderfully upbeat (the nine poems and subsequent thirteen miracles of release provided by Jesus) punctuated by dark undertones—minor-key motifs of pain and suffering and death.

"If any want to become my followers," says Jesus toward the end of this section, "let them deny themselves and take up their cross daily and follow

145

me" (9:23). We will explore first the repeated and remarkable instances of kingdom release, followed by the inevitable cost along with some avoidable disciple failure.

Release from Oppression: Thirteen Miraculous Demonstrations (Luke 4:33–9:43)

After the joyous and expectant words of Jesus's anointing (4:18–19), we hear thirteen examples of miraculous release performed by Jesus. By arranging them mostly in tight succession, Luke is able to establish a narrative rhythm of tell-and-show, of *kingdom proclaimed* (in the poems) and *kingdom demonstrated* (in the miracles).

1. Man released from possession by unclean spirit (4:33–37)
2. Woman released from fever (4:38–39)
3. Leper released from disease (5:12–16)
4. Paralytic released from lameness (5:17–26)
5. Man's arm released from its withered state (6:6–11)
6. Roman centurion's slave released from illness (7:2–10)
7. Widow's only son released from death (7:12–15)
8. Wind and raging seas calmed (8:22–25)
9. Wild man released from demons (8:26–39)
10. Woman released from hemorrhaging (8:43–48)
11. Daughter released from disease (8:41–42, 49–56)
12. Crowd released from hunger (9:12–17)
13. Son released from demons (9:38–43)

The good news of God's kingdom—with the jubilant release of so many captives—is evident from the start of this new era, "the year of the Lord's favor."

Luke frames these thirteen miracle stories with accounts of release from satanic power: a man released from demonic possession (miracle one, 4:33–37) and a son released from demons (miracle thirteen, 9:38–43). A third instance occurs in the middle with a wild man released from a host of demons (miracle nine, 8:26–39). Satan is, in Luke, God's chief adversary. This demonic force is front and center in the case of demon possession, and, according to Luke, Satan is behind all oppressions and captivities, from political powers to the ravages of disease.

Satan is also implicated in cosmic and natural dis-ordering. Jesus's implicit power over Satan in the calming of treacherous seas is followed immediately by the third explicit instance of conquering Satan (miracles eight and nine). The kingdom struggle is cosmic: through Jesus, God is battling Satan himself—the dragon in the sea.[1] The wildness of seas and the chaos of Satan are neatly juxtaposed by Luke, whose sense of orderliness works in small matters like this pairing and within the greater architecture, the clustering of thirteen instances of the coming righting-of-wrong in God's healing kingdom. Moreover, since Luke sees demonic influence behind all oppression, each demonstration of kingdom release—from illness, hemorrhaging, paralysis—is release from the devil and his demons. *Satan binds,* Luke tells us; *Jesus releases.*

Release from impairment defeats the binding of Satan. A leper is healed (miracle three), a paralytic walks (miracle four), and a man's withered limb is restored (miracle five). These three successive acts of goodness are contested by those who are dark in heart and deed. Once released, the afflicted are restored to health and life and flourishing in community.

When a leper—in an age when lepers were considered ritually unclean, untouchables—asks for healing, Jesus stretches out his hand, touches him, and the leprosy leaves him (a parallel to demons who *leave* their possessed; miracle three, 5:12–16). By touching "the unclean," Jesus violates a social convention, which would strike the Jewish leaders as shameless. In the immediately following miracle, before healing the paralytic, Jesus forgives the man his sins, again riling the religious leaders, who exclaim, "Who is this who is speaking blasphemies? Who can forgive sins but God alone?" (miracle four, 5:17–26).

"After this he went out and saw a tax collector named Levi, sitting at the tax booth; and he said to him, 'Follow me.' And he got up, left everything, and followed him" (5:27). When the despised tax collector throws a lavish banquet for Jesus and friends, "The Pharisees and their scribes [complain] to his disciples, saying, 'Why do you eat and drink with tax collectors[2] and sinners?'" (5:29–32). The leaders then complain to Jesus about his disciples eating and drinking rather than fasting, like John's (5:33–38). Further, "some of the Pharisees [say], 'Why are you doing what is not lawful [picking grain to eat] on the sabbath?'" (6:1–5). To cap off his offense against the authorities, Jesus heals again on the Sabbath, restoring a man with a withered hand to wholeness (miracle five, 6:6–11). The religious leaders are incensed by the "rabbi" who touches the unclean, forgives sins, dines with sinners, and heals on the Sabbath.

By juxtaposing release from Satan's oppression with human opposition, Luke presents a compelling vision of human resistance that parallels the opposition of Satan, ruler of all demons and demonic activity (11:15). The religious leaders are in cahoots with Satan, exacerbating the oppressions. Leprosy is disease, a dis-ordering of Satan, and the religious leaders make the suffere's problems even worse by shunning the leper, consigning the diseased to a life of desperate isolation.

Luke pauses to summarize humanity's desperate need: large crowds come "to hear [Jesus] and to be healed of their diseases; and those who were troubled with unclean spirits were cured. And all in the crowd were trying to touch him, for power came out from him and healed all of them" (6:18–19). The crowds include everyone: Jew and Gentile, male and female, son and daughter, slave and free, leader and ordinary person. All are freed from their oppression—released from their captivity—to a life that is whole, within a community of compassion, peace, and justice in God's kingdom come to earth.

We have come to Jesus's long poem on a plain, with its radical demand of love for enemy (6:20–49). Jesus's love-telling in the last and great poem is reinforced by Jesus's love-showing. Immediately following the poem we hear an example of loving one's enemy: Jesus heals the son of a Roman official, an enemy of Jews (miracle six, 7:2–10). In his healing of the son of an enemy, Jesus is doing what he has been teaching—opposing the strife and striving that Satan encourages, like hatred of one's enemy. Then Jesus sees a weeping widow whose only son, on whom she relies for sustenance and succor, has just died. "He had compassion for her and said to her, 'Do not weep.' Then he came forward and touched the bier, and the bearers stood still. And he said, 'Young man, I say to you, rise!'" He rises, "and Jesus [gives] him to his mother" (miracle seven, 7:11–17). These companion miracles, the enemy's son healed and the widow's son revived and returned to his mother, show the wide range of love for the oppressed: from enemies to forlorn widows, from the great and powerful to the "little ones" (17:2).

Luke's orderly arrangement expands his picture of the kingdom, providing light to various dark imprisonments. Following the son raised from the darkness of death comes a sequence on John the Baptist in the darkness of a literal prison. Confused, John sends some of his disciples to ask Jesus if he is the Messiah that God promised to Israel. Jesus responds, "Go and tell John what you have seen and heard," which in effect is a picture of the kingdom in action: "the blind receive their sight, the lame walk, the lepers are cleansed, the deaf hear, the dead are raised, the poor have good news brought to them" (7:22). Between John's question and Jesus's answer, Luke inserts a brief note: "Jesus had just then cured many people of diseases, plagues, and evil spirits, and had given sight to many who were blind" (7:21). *Go and tell John that God's kingdom has come.*

*   *   *

At this point in Luke's narrative, there is a break in miracle activity and a triple focus on women. A sequence of three anecdotes centered on women suggests, perhaps, a subtle form of miracle: the elevation of the status of women to full humanity.

After the sequence on John the Baptist, Luke continues with portraits of response to Jesus's teaching and miraculous deeds. In the first, a woman, an outsider and sinner, crashes an all-male dinner party and demonstrates love for Jesus in a startling and humble way: "She stood behind him at his feet, weeping, and began to bathe his feet with her tears and to dry them with her hair. Then she continued kissing his feet and anointing them with the ointment" (7:38). Kingdom people, we learn, are outcasts, outsiders, and sinners. Kingdom compassion, we hear, weeps, kneels, and bathes grimy feet. "She has shown great love," says Jesus (7:47). Of such sinners and self-sacrificial love is the kingdom of God.[3] Jesus forgives the woman her sins with these words: "Your faith has saved you; go in peace" (7:50). Peace (*shalom*) in Luke-Acts is communal; it is the wholeness and flourishing one finds only through deeply other-regarding relationships, among people mutually committed to one another. This outcast woman is no longer isolated; she is *saved* by entering into God's compassionate and inclusive kingdom. *Go in peace.*

Luke moves from this lowly yet loving woman to his second portrait of response, lesser-known but no less crucial female followers of Jesus. For the hectic and demanding work of the kingdom, Jesus is assisted by "the twelve" but also by, we are told, "some women who had been cured of evil spirits and infirmities: Mary . . . and Joanna . . . and Susanna, and many others who provided for them out of their resources" (8:1–3).

Luke's third portrait of response is less positive. "Your mother and your brothers," someone tells Jesus, "are standing outside, wanting to see you." He responds, "My mother and my brothers are those who hear the word of God and do it" (8:20–21). Because Jesus doesn't take the time to go speak with his mother or his brothers, they are clearly rebuffed. Recall Simeon's promise to Mary that baby Jesus would one day become "a sword [that] will pierce your own soul" (2:35).

Between the two pictures of positive responses and the negative portrait of the mother and siblings of Jesus, Luke places a parable explaining the variety of response to Jesus's words and miraculous deeds. Jesus speaks of those who spurn the good news of this kingdom, as well as those "who, when they hear the word, hold it fast in an honest and good heart, and bear fruit with patient endurance" (8:4–15). Seed is sown on four differing soils, only one of which is receptive, able to "bear fruit." The parable's point about listening carefully and following faithfully, bearing fruit, is reinforced by Jesus's shocking rejection of his own mother and brothers—especially jarring in juxtaposition with Jesus's joy-filled embrace of the lavish love shown him by the party-crashing woman. Parable and narrative combine to warn: only those who listen to the word of God and do it are members of God's kingdom (Jesus's new family).

*   *   *

Luke moves on with a final litany of stories of miracles: a wild sea is calmed, releasing the disciples from fear (miracle eight, 8:22–25); a demon-possessed man, released from the chaos of uncontrolled forces, crazed nakedness, and shackles, is seen "sitting at the feet of Jesus, clothed and in his right mind" (miracle nine, 8:26–39); a woman is released from her twelve-year hemorrhaging and, without saying it, its associated shame and stigma (miracle ten [interrupting miracle eleven], 8:43–48); a synagogue leader's only daughter is healed (miracle eleven, 8:41–42, 49–56); a crowd's hunger is miraculously assuaged (miracle twelve, 9:12–17), and finally, a son is released from demons (miracle thirteen, 9:38–43).

All who are lost—men and women, adult and child, healthy and diseased—are welcomed into Jesus's new family, God's kingdom, in which they find wholeness, acceptance, and peace (15:4). Perhaps some, like the hungry thousands who were fed miraculously, only nibble at the kingdom's largesse, subsequently refusing the arduous path leading into the kingdom (13:24); but all have tasted of the kingdom's goodness, a quality of life offered by no ordinary earthly kingdoms.

Kingdom Cost

We have seen John in prison, and we later hear that King Herod has had him beheaded, costing John his life and his once joyous parents a son. The explicit early parallels of hearing cues between John and Jesus intensify at the point of John's beheading; the shadow of death now hangs over the story of Jesus: he will die and Mary will lose a son.

Twice we find a focus on the pain of Mary, echoing Simeon's vision of soul-piercing in her future (2:35). And at the climax of this first long section, Luke arranges five successive failures on the part of the disciples, evasions in attitude and action, of kingdom responsibility. The disciples have been given full power to heal in their kingdom mission, but fail.

Mary's Soul-Piercings

Holding baby Jesus, "the peace of Israel," Simeon turns to the child's mother and tells her that a sword will pierce her soul (2:25–35). She has to witness her son's gruesome death at a young age. But twice before this death Mary's pain is detailed both explicitly and implicitly.

"Child, Why Have You Treated Us Like This?" (Luke 2:41–52)

Joseph, Mary, and their twelve-year-old son travel to Jerusalem for the annual festival of the Passover. At festival's end the parents return home, only to discover after a day's journey that their child is missing: "The boy Jesus [had] stayed behind in Jerusalem" (2:43). After searching unsuccessfully through their entourage, they return to Jerusalem and search the city to no avail. At the end of day three, they find him sitting in the temple among the teachers. The distraught and agitated Mary, as might be expected, is none too happy with her wayward son.

When she tells Jesus, "Look, your father and I have been searching for you in great anxiety," he responds, "Why were you searching for me?" He adds, "Did you not know [you should have!] that I must be in my Father's house?" (2:48–49). In effect, the young Jesus is telling his biological mother and father that his real parent is his Father in heaven! To parents anxiously searching for their lost son, the boy's responses would not have been consoling. They don't know what to make of it: "they did not understand what he said to them" (2:50).

My Mother and My Brothers? (Luke 8:19–21)

Jesus has just told a tale about a farmer whose seed does well in only one out of four soils. The most promising yet disappointing soil is one with thorns that choke out fruitfulness with "the cares and riches and pleasures of life" (8:14). *Pay attention, listen,* we hear (8:18). Jesus's point about listening carefully and following faithfully is reinforced by his shocking rejection of his family members. When the adult and very busy Jesus is told that his mother and brothers have come but can't press through the crowd, he stays put and sends a message: "My mother and my brothers are those who hear the word of God and do it" (8:21).

These two related family events share obvious hearing cues having to do with relinquishment. In the latter, Jesus declares that his true father and mother and brothers are those who hear and do the word of God: further light is cast, here, on the earlier words to his distraught parents, "Why were you searching for me? Did you not know that I must be in my Father's house?" For Jesus, as for all who would enter the kingdom, the business (the will) of God must loom over ordinary business, including that of one's nuclear family, regardless of their anguish.

In the upcoming teaching sequence (9:51–19:44), we hear echoes of "family." In one such parallel, Jesus teaches about the inevitable divisions within families as a consequence of the kingdom come to earth (12:49–13:9), and then, in an echoing sequence, Jesus insists that the true disciple must actively relinquish ties to family for the sake of the kingdom (14:25–35). Only those who hear and do the word of God are members of Jesus's new family, God's kingdom. Family provides, or at least represents, a refuge from the chaotic storms that rage outside. Stereotypically, mothers care and fathers protect and provide. When the world overwhelms, family provides peace. So when Jesus rejects his biological family in favor of kingdom family, he releases our deepest fears: that in our cold and uncaring world, there is neither family nor home.

After we hear "My mother and my brothers are those who hear the word of God and do it," Luke tells the following story. Jesus and his followers are at sea, fearful of "the wind and raging waves." Where is the solace of home, the comfort of kin? The little scene provides an answer: Jesus releases them from their terror by releasing the sea from its chaos, from the "dragon of the sea." With amazement, the new brothers of Jesus wonder, "Who then is this, that he commands even the winds and the water, and they obey him?" (8:22–25). You may leave family and friends, we hear, but your new family, with the Master's power over chaos, is your new place of peace.

Disciple Failure to Bear the Cost: Five Successive Instances

Women, outcasts, sinners, and even enemies are released from the demons and death that oppress them. And we learn that God's radically inclusive kingdom includes the poor, the oppressed, second-class citizens, and the demon-possessed. We also learn that its members show a new kind of lavish and self-sacrificial love that makes ordinary familial love pale in comparison. However, in contrast to the light and life and love of the kingdom, Luke offers a dark prelude that bears down unrelentingly on the disappointing disciples.

Luke begins his report regarding the disciples on a high note: Jesus calls and empowers the disciples to work with him for the kingdom of God (9:1–2)—which they do, with great success (9:6, 10; 10:17). But the narrative veers sharply downward with a clustered series of disciple failures. They are far from ready to take this power to a higher level of kingdom effort.

First Failure of the Disciples (Luke 9:12–17)

The disciples report to Jesus "all they had done" on their mission trips (9:10), exercising the healing powers Jesus has given them (9:1–6). But shortly after, witnessing a large crowd in a desert place gathered to hear Jesus and experience his power, they ask Jesus to send the people away to get themselves something to eat. But he says to the disciples, "You give them something to eat" (9:13). They don't (though Jesus evidently thinks the power he invested in them is sufficient to the task). They fail to respond adequately to Jesus's challenge that they feed the hungry crowd (9:13). Jesus takes over and gives the crowd something to eat (miracle twelve, 9:12–17).

Second Failure of the Disciples (Luke 9:28–36)

Peter, James, and John are taken up a mountain by Jesus, who, in the company of Moses and Elijah, suddenly becomes "dazzling white." The three are talking about the coming departure of Jesus. A weary Peter, James, and John see "his glory" but apparently don't hear their conversation (9:28–32). Peter, "not knowing what he [is saying]," expresses his desire to make permanent dwellings at this site of glory (9:33). Peter's failure to understand Jesus's messianic mission is clear. He thinks glory is *now*, exclusively for him and his buddies in realms of resplendence with Jesus, Moses, and Elijah. Although the three disciples missed the conversation among the three luminaries, they cannot miss the voice of God speaking to them. It is just one word, repeated often in Luke-Acts: *Listen!* "This is my Son, my Chosen; listen to him!" (9:35). There will be much to hear, recounted by Luke in his central section of kingdom teaching by Jesus.

Third Failure of the Disciples (Luke 9:37–43a)

A man begs Jesus to release his demon-possessed son after the disciples have failed to do so. Jesus turns angrily on his disciples: "You faithless and perverse generation," he exclaims, "how much longer must I be with you and bear with you?" (9:37–41). Jesus performs a healing that could have been done by the disciples had they not considered the demon-possessed child beneath them. Just as Jesus gave the raised-from-death son back to his widow mother, so here, Jesus rescues a son from being "dashed . . . to the ground in convulsions." He "rebuked the unclean spirit, healed the boy, and gave him back to his father" (9:42). *Giving back* is a small but powerful hearing cue. Giving back, restoration, release from captivities: of such is the kingdom of God.

But the motif of disciple failure looms larger and more ominously. Their failure to heal the child manifests their insidious desire to be great, distracting them from concern for the little boy and his plight. Although given the kingdom power to give this broken boy back to his father, whole, they failed.

Fourth Failure of the Disciples (Luke 9:43b–48)

Listen, we have heard over and over again. Immediately following their failure with the possessed son, Jesus says to his disciples, "Let these words sink into your ears" (9:44). Jesus is preparing his followers for their momentous journey to Jerusalem by repeating, over and over, *listen.* Here the words are somber, even threatening, to the disciples: "The Son of Man is going to be betrayed into human hands." The disciples "did not understand; . . . they could not perceive it" (9:44–45). We immediately find out the root of the disciples' failure to understand. The blockage is not in the ear or in the head but in the heart: "An argument arose among them as to which one of them was the greatest" (9:46). Once again, their desire to be great prevents their understanding of the Messiah.

Since teaching hasn't worked, Jesus resorts to example. He sets a little child by his side, showing his disciples true greatness: "Whoever welcomes this child in my name welcomes me, and whoever welcomes me welcomes the one who sent me; for the least among all of you is the greatest" (9:47–48), immediately echoing the disciples' lack of concern for the possessed son. The disciples' desire to be great has prevented them from taking the path of self-denying service to "the least among you." Their desire to stand with transfigured Glory has precluded their kneeling down to heal a child in need. If they want to be great in God's kingdom, they must relinquish their desire to be great and, rather, be willing to serve the lowest among them.

Fifth Failure of the Disciples (Luke 9:49–50)

Immediately, and again ironically, a response comes that is the opposite of what Jesus is teaching: "John answered, 'Master, we saw someone casting out demons in your name, and we tried to stop him, because he does not follow with us'" (9:48–49). Given its location within Luke's pattern of disciple failure, the audience is prepared to supply the connection between what Jesus has said and John's apparently unrelated response. What is the connection between the kingdom successes of others and the disciples' desire to be great? John is saying, in effect, *We are the great ones. Not them. They are not us. We hang out with you, Jesus, and with the transfigured Moses and Elijah. God speaks to us. Not them. We are the greatest.* But Jesus rebukes their petty zero-sum game of greatness, saying, "Whoever is not against you is for you" (9:50).

Conclusion

The unmistakable pattern of disciple failure in chapter 9 constitutes a prelude to Luke's long teaching section (9:51–19:44). Since Jesus will soon be departing, the disciples need to be taught if they are to carry on kingdom work. The future leaders of the kingdom need to learn what commitment to the kingdom of God involves. They need help from their "Teacher."

Jesus has been Teacher all along, of course, both showing and telling the good news of God's incipient kingdom. And just as Abraham left his home and own to bring God's blessing to the world (Gen. 12:1–3), Jesus breaks out of his brutal hometown and away from his uncomprehending family to inaugurate God's kingdom. The blessing of the kingdom is already clear: women, outcasts, sinners, and even enemies are released from the demons that oppress them. And so we learn that God's inclusive kingdom includes the poor, the oppressed, second-class citizens, and the demon-possessed. We also learn that its members show a radically new kind of lavish and self-sacrificial love that makes mere biological, familial love pale in comparison.

CHAPTER 15

"Things That Make for Peace," Part One: The Goal (Luke 9:51–12:12; 17:1–19:44)

Going in Circles

This teaching section of Luke, sometimes called "Journey to Jerusalem" (9:51–19:44), begins determinedly: "When the days drew near for him to be taken up, he set his face to go to Jerusalem" (9:51). But for all the seriousness of this journey, it can't be mapped—it has few geographical markers and very little sense of going anywhere, though Jesus and his followers do end up in Jerusalem. It is, however, a metaphoric journey of themes that go in circles, in what scholars call a "ring composition" or "chiasm."[1] For example, a teaching about peace and messengers (9:51–10:24) opens the journey and is repeated, ten chapters later at journey's end, with messengers and peace (18:31–19:44). And so on: theme two is repeated as the second to last theme, an echo. The ring progresses in this fashion, narrowing down to the bull's eye or center point, the heart of the thematic message. In Luke's case, the heart of Jesus's teaching is the need to strive to enter into God's kingdom—the continual appropriation of the good news heard and obeyed. This is the journey's destination. While Jerusalem is the literal destination, God's kingdom is the thematic destination, both merging at the center point of this ring composition.

This journey through the law, as clarified by Jesus, is vital given the failures of the disciples we've just heard about. Jesus, the Teacher, will be taken up to his Father, leaving the disciples with the responsibility of proclaiming and demonstrating the gospel of the kingdom come.[2] And so Jesus teaches: *Hear the word of God—"the things that make for peace"* (19:42)—*and do it*. These "things" appear in an artistic arrangement, as seen in the chart below. The first five themes and their echoes—the outermost rings (highlighted below)—will be the subject of this chapter; in the following chapter we take up the middle themes (six through eleven).

1 Kingdom goal: communal peace (9:51–10:24)
  2 "What must I do to inherit eternal life?" (10:25–42)
    3 Prayer: How do I pray and for what? (11:1–13)
      4 How can I be sure about all this? (11:14–32)
        5 What's inside: faithlessness and hypocrisy (11:33–12:12)
          6 Don't worry about money and security (12:13–34)
            7 Perks and privilege (12:35–48)
              8 Family (12:49–13:9)
                9 Sabbath and the religious tradition (13:10–17)
                  10 Kingdoms human and divine (13:18–21)
                  11 Kingdom entrance (13:22–30)
                  10' Kingdoms human and divine (13:31–35)
                9' Sabbath and the religious tradition (14:1–24)
              8' Family (14:25–35)
            7' Perks and privilege (15:1–32)
          6' Don't worry about money and security (16:1–31)
        5' What's inside: faith and integrity (17:1–19)
      4' How can I be sure about all this? (17:20–37)
    3' Prayer: How do I pray and for what? (18:1–14)
  2' "What must I do to inherit eternal life?" (18:15–30)
1' Kingdom goal: communal peace (18:31–19:44)

Some of these themes and their echoes are easily discerned—for example, the second theme: a laywer and a ruler both ask, "What must I do to inherit eternal life?" (10:25; 18:18). The crisp thematic sequences on prayer (the third theme) are easily spotted as well (11:1–13; 18:1–14).

Other circling themes, we will see, require closer attention to both explicit and implicit (indirect) hearing cues. But all of the cues point to an underlying concern, that what Jesus teaches must be truly heard and rigorously obeyed: *blessed is the one,* says Jesus, *who "hears my words, and acts on them"* (6:47).

At the end of this long teaching, in the echoing portion of the outermost ring (theme 1', 18:31–19:44), we find Jesus weeping. What moves him so is the sight of Jerusalem and the recognition that so far the bulk of Israel has refused the word of God he has been teaching. Israel has not "recognized . . . the things that make for peace!" (19:42). This peace is the communal experience of justice, mercy, and harmony in God's kingdom come to earth. Luke borrows his conception of peace (*shalom*) from the Hebrew Scriptures: "The effect of righteousness will be peace," wrote Isaiah, and "the result of righteousness [is] quietness and trust forever" (Isa. 32:17). In Luke and Acts peace as communal flourishing, *shalom*, is both demonstrated and explained, detail by detail. The outer rings explain the positive "things" that make for *shalom*, while the inner rings teach what must be relinquished for *shalom* to work.

First Theme: The Beginning and End of the Journey

Messengers of the good news of the kingdom appear in both the first and last parallel teachings. Since the continuance of the kingdom requires proclaimers of the gospel, they must be well taught. In each sequence, first and last, communal peace, *shalom*, is the gospel's goal.

Theme 1: Kingdom Goal: Communal Peace (Luke 9:51–10:24)

Setting his face for Jerusalem in order to depart, to be "taken up" (9:51–52), Jesus sends messengers ahead of him. They return, having been rebuffed by a Samaritan village. The disciples want to call down hellfire on the village that has refused to welcome Jesus and grant them all safe passage.[3] But Jesus rebukes them (9:52–55). Only later will it become clear that the mission of followers is never judgment and always blessing, the offer of peace.

The message is summarized in one word: "peace." Aware of the need for more mission workers, Jesus appoints seventy more disciple messengers and sends them out with the instruction, "Whatever house you enter, first say, 'Peace to this house!' And if anyone is there who shares in peace, your peace will rest on that person; but if not, it will return to you" (10:5–6). The disciples are instructed to bring the message of peace not only in word but also in deed, welcoming everyone, breaking bread with everyone, and healing the sick (10:8–9).[4] If a town should reject their offer of peace, the disciples are instructed to leave with their offer of peace intact, rather than be filled with resentment; God, not the disciples, is the judge of those refusing peace (10:12–16).

The seventy return with astonishing stories of success, excitedly telling Jesus that even Satan's demons submitted to them. Jesus rejoices with them but warns, "Do not rejoice at this, that the spirits submit to you, but rejoice that your names are written in heaven" (10:17–20). *Do not rejoice over earthly power; rejoice that you are known by God; the former is fleeting, the latter is eternal.*

Theme 1': Kingdom Goal: Communal Peace (Luke 18:31–19:44)

The last leg of the journey mirrors its beginning, in part, by once again emphasizing Jesus's proclamation of peace. Although it concludes with Jesus weeping over the failure of Israel to recognize "the things that make for peace," it begins more optimistically:

> The whole multitude of the disciples began to praise God joyfully with a loud voice for all the deeds of power that they had seen, saying,
>> "Blessed is the king
>>> who comes in the name of the Lord!
>> Peace in heaven,
>>> glory in the highest heaven!" (19:37–38)

The peace envisioned by God in heaven, the angels sing, is also peace on earth (2:14).

But here at the end of this particular journey, Jesus is filled with sorrow over Israel's heedlessness to "the things that make for peace" (19:42). Israel has neither heard nor heeded these things.

At journey's end we also discover Jesus's own disciples' resistance to the things that make for peace. Just outside the big city, a blind beggar cries out for Jesus and is rebuffed by the crowd but recognized and honored by Jesus, who releases the man from his blindness (18:35–43). Jesus creates a scandal when he accepts an invitation to dine at the home of a Jewish tax collector for Rome (19:5). Everyone who sees this interaction, presumably including the disciples, begins to "grumble," saying, "He has gone to be the guest of one who is a sinner" (19:1–10). In the case of each outcast, beggar, and tax collector, Jesus himself shows compassionate mercy, revealing once again, in show-and-tell, what he has been teaching about the kingdom's offer of blessing and peace.

Just before this sequence of two outcasts, Jesus tried to explain to the disciples about his coming dishonor and shame upon arrival in Jerusalem, that he will be "insulted and spat upon" and killed (though raised up again). "But they understood nothing about all these things; in fact, what he said was hidden from them, and they did not grasp what was said" (18:31–34). Jesus is asking his followers to share in his suffering, to be willing to embrace dishonor and ridicule for caring about a beggar and a tax collector. But they understand nothing. Their trouble, as the text continually implies, is not with their head but with their heart.

The disempowered outcasts, unlike the empowered but ignorant disciples, lack all social capital according to their culture's value system. But human value, Jesus has already explained, lies not in earthly power (having "a name" on earth) but in being loved by God (having one's name written in the book of life). The blind man, crying out for mercy from the son of David, has been judged by the crowd and disciples as unworthy of Jesus. But Jesus seeks him out and releases him from his prison of blindness: seeing, the man follows Jesus, "glorifying God" (18:35–43). Zacchaeus, the Jew collecting taxes for Rome and hated by fellow Jews, is also judged severely but ends up giving away half his possessions and entertaining Jesus at his home—to the horror of those following Jesus.

With both show and tell, Jesus has taught the way of peace (*shalom*), a radically inclusive, deeply merciful, and unfailingly just community, one radically opposed to the exclusive, status-hungry, power-wielding, us-versus-them disharmony of the surrounding culture. Luke's audience sees in Jesus what his disciples do not: the things that make for peace.

Second Theme: "What Must I Do to Inherit Eternal Life?"

On two occasions, eight chapters apart, Jesus is asked a crucial question that is close to the heart of Luke's theological vision: "What must I do to inherit eternal life?" The wording is precisely the same. The questioners are both persons of high rank. One genuinely asks the question, while the other uses the question to gain advantage over Jesus.

Theme 2: A Lawyer Asks the Question (Luke 10:25–42)

"What must I do to inherit eternal life?" asks a religious lawyer, standing up "to test Jesus" (10:25). This lawyer, who knows the law exhaustively, wants to know if the Teacher holds to Torah fundamentals—asking in a way to stump the Teacher, showing himself brilliantly clever in the questioning. The testing is ambiguous. Perhaps he really wants an answer?

Jesus asks the lawyer, "What is written in the law?" and the lawyer responds, "You shall love the Lord your God with all your heart, and with all your soul, and with all your strength, and with all your mind; and your neighbor as yourself." Jesus tells him, "You have given the right answer. Do this and you will live" (10:26–28).

The lawyer's self-righteousness and concern with his own status now become apparent. "Wanting to justify himself," the lawyer asks, "Who *is* my neighbor?" (*just in case I should run across someone who qualifies for my love*).

Jesus answers with a parable, the so-called parable of the good Samaritan. Someone is stripped naked by bandits and left half dead on the side of the road. Two religious leaders pass by. They see the suffering person but ignore him, moving quickly to the other side. (Wounded and bleeding, the man is in a state of religious impurity—and so the religious sorts might have rationalized that he was untouchable.) A Samaritan, despised by Jews, slows down, sees the suffering man, takes pity, and stops to help. He treats the man with painstaking care at no small financial cost, taking him to a lodging and promising payment for any expenses (10:30–36).

"Which of these three," asks Jesus, "do you think was a neighbor to the man who fell into the hands of the robbers?" (10:36).

There's something strange here. The neighbor, we've assumed, is the one lying needy in the ditch. Jesus confounds the matter when he asks who was the neighbor to the man in need? The lawyer's question has been brilliantly subverted. His smug "Who is my neighbor?" has become a challenge to himself! Jesus shifts perspective from self to other, and from noun to verb. Jesus is saying that the question of neighbor is not about *who-out-there* is my neighbor, but *am-I-being* a neighbor. In the former case, the lawyer is asking a question about the limits of his obligations. But, Jesus says, love, which has no limits, requires *being* a neighbor—tending to anyone in need. The lawyer is forced to answer this new question, "What does it mean to be neighborly?" The neighbor, he says, is "the one who showed him mercy." Lesson on neighbor complete. "Do likewise," concludes Jesus (10:37).

The lawyer's original question does not go unanswered. As Jesus tells the story, the audience hears that the vaunted religious leaders were strangers, while the lowly Samaritan was a neighbor, one who showed mercy. As half Jew and half Gentile, Samaritans were looked down on by "pure" Jews. The full-blooded Jews of Jesus's time had no contact with Samaritan half-breeds. Jesus, then, is indirectly saying that acting neighborly in God's kingdom includes attention to social outcasts. The neighborly Samaritan, acting within the framework of loving God, inherits eternal life by virtue of acting justly and mercifully, not by virtue of ethnic purity or social power.

There's more in what follows, although no explanatory transition helps us. We need to lean in for the implicit hearing cues.

Jesus goes to the home of sisters Martha and Mary to teach the word of God. This would have been doubly offensive in the day—a single adult male would never visit the home of women, and women would never be taught Torah. Sister Mary sits at the feet of Teacher Jesus and listens, which bothers older sister Martha. When Martha chastises Mary for not pitching in, Jesus responds, "Martha, Martha, you are worried and distracted by many things; there is need of only one thing," which Mary has chosen—listening to God's word (10:41–42). Martha is distracted by and anxious about her performance as hostess; the lawyer is distracted by and anxious about his performance as law expert. Taken in tandem, as Luke has arranged these stories, we hear Jesus's clear teaching about the kingdom. Martha and the lawyer is distracted from following Jesus by selfish anxiety about their proper place in society. Mary and the Samaritan, on the other hand, jointly constitute the model disciple in the kingdom of God: Mary listens to the word of God, and the Samaritan does it.

Theme 2′: A Rich Ruler Asks the Question (Luke 18:15–30)

A ruler asks the same question as the lawyer: "What must I do to inherit eternal life?" (18:18). Unlike the lawyer's attempt at self-aggrandizement, however, the ruler appears sincere in his desire to know. Jesus answers almost as the lawyer did: don't murder, steal, lie, etc. (18:20). But Jesus omits any mention of the essence of the law, loving God. Why? The good listener stays tuned.

When the ruler claims he has always kept the law, Jesus replies, "There is still one thing lacking. Sell all that you own and distribute the money to the poor, and you will have treasure in heaven" (18:22). The ruler becomes sad, for he is "very rich" (18:23). By this response, the rich man reveals, for the tuned listener, his failure to love *God* with all of his heart, mind, and soul: his heart is fixed on wealth, not on God.

In an aside to his disciples, Jesus comments that the ruler's chance of inheriting eternal life, like any wealthy person's, is less than that of a camel's going through the eye of a needle (18:25). "Then who can be saved?" ask his incredulous disciples (18:26). The disciples are worried. Since we all so deeply desire wealth, honor, fame, and power, who is capable of loving, above all else, God and neighbor? Jesus offers hope: "What is impossible for mortals is possible for God" (18:27). The answer will not come until Acts, when Jesus sends to individuals striving to enter the kingdom the enabling Holy Spirit (Acts 2:33). With God within, what is impossible for mortals becomes possible.

Third Theme: Prayer—How Do I Pray and for What?

Two brief treatises on prayer appear within the ordered reversal of thematic sequences. The first time, Jesus goes off to pray, communing with his Father, which of course involves listening—like Mary at the feet of Jesus.

Each sequence builds on the bedrock of persistence: *stay at it* (11:8); and *pray always and do not lose heart* (18:1). In each theme statement, how to pray is answered in part with the single idea: *persistence*.

Theme 3: "Lord, Teach Us to Pray" (Luke 11:1–13)

When his disciples ask Jesus to teach them to pray, Jesus offers a model prayer, concluding with the encouragement to ask for God's empowering Holy Spirit.[5]

Jesus's model prayer (11:2–4) includes praise (*holy is your name*) and submission (*your kingdom come*). His prayer requires an awareness of dependence on and trust in God (*give us each day our daily bread*), and a sense of our moral and spiritual frailty allied with largesse toward others (*forgive us our sins, for we ourselves forgive everyone indebted to us*). His teaching on prayer concludes on a note of hope: "How much more will the heavenly Father give the Holy Spirit to those who ask him?" (11:13). This is the best gift the heavenly Father can give: the Spirit, who empowers the otherwise impossible kingdom entrance.

Theme 3': "[The] Need to Pray Always and Not to Lose Heart" (Luke 18:1–14)

In the echoing sequence, the disciples are again instructed to pray persistently, but this time for two things that God deeply cares about: justice and mercy. Jesus explains with back-to-back stories.

In the first, a woman repeatedly begs a wicked judge, who loves neither God nor neighbor, for justice. Her request is finally granted, "so that she may not wear [the judge] out by continually coming" (18:2–8). Taking this story solely as a testament to the woman's persistent faith, as it often is, misses Jesus's full explication of the story's meaning: "And will not God grant justice to his chosen ones who cry to him day and night? Will he delay long in helping them? I tell you, he will quickly grant justice to them" (18:7–8).

In the second story, about asking the Father for mercy, a Pharisee and a tax collector go to the temple to pray. The "pious" Pharisee thanks God—in his prayer—that he is "not like other people—thieves, rogues, adulterers, or even like this tax collector." He reminds God of how good he is, referring to his exemplary habits of prayer and tithing. The tax collector, in contrast, humbly bows before God and asks, "God be merciful to me, a sinner!" (18:13).[6] Where the former approaches God in smug self-righteousness (God is lucky to have him!), the tax collector approaches God in humble recognition of his moral failings and need for forgiveness. "I tell you," Jesus concludes, "this man [the tax collector] went down to his home justified rather than the other; for all who exalt themselves will be humbled, but all who humble themselves will be exalted" (18:14; "justified" in the Greek and in this context means "vouched to be good and true"). Those who strive for notice, for status, for power ranking will be brought low; those recognizing their need will be honored by God.

Justice and mercy, two of the things that make for peace, characterize the kingdom we pray to come. For the kingdom to come, though, Jesus's frail and fallible followers will need, and so must ask for, the gift of the empowering Spirit.

Fourth Theme: How Can I Be Sure about All of This?

Since the teachings of Jesus are lofty and demanding, people want proof that Jesus really is the Messiah. Luke, recall, begins his gospel with the priest Zechariah asking how he can be sure of God's message (1:18). Although God rebukes Zechariah—and will rebuke "this evil generation" for its demand for a sign—Luke is not insensitive to the very human need for assurance. Jesus offers hope, and Luke wants his Zechariah-like audiences, however skeptical and uncertain, to be assured that faith in God's word is not misplaced.

Theme 4: "Blessed Are Those Who Hear and Obey" (Luke 11:14–32)

When Jesus casts out a demon, some are amazed, yet some accuse him of being in cahoots with the demon master, Beelzebul. Others, "to test him," ask for "a sign from heaven" to prove that he is the Messiah. His initial and famous response, "a house divided against itself cannot stand," is aimed at effectively undermining the claim that he's a demon working against demons (11:14–19). But focusing on this issue is, in the first place, to miss the deeper reply: his liberating power over demons is a sign, one they refuse to recognize, that the kingdom of God has come (11:20). Jesus has given them a sign of his kingdom power to bring peace on earth, namely, his power over demons and the dis-ease they cause. Like many exorcisms in Luke, *shalom* is the peace of re-ordered life, whole, at ease—a life restored to community. And yet, like a petulant child, they demand more.

Others turn to their own status as the only sort of "sign" they care about, Jesus or no Jesus, kingdom or no kingdom. Take the case of a woman who looks for something "out there" to vindicate her existence, to make it all worthwhile. "A woman in the crowd raised her voice and said to him, 'Blessed is the womb that bore you and the breasts that nursed you!' But he said, 'Blessed rather are those who hear the word of God and obey it!'" (11:27–28). Resisting the incessant demand for a show requires a purity of heart that hears and obeys God's word.

The desperate hankering for signs to make one sure of a secure place in the world indicates both an impurity of heart and a desire for false security. Jesus concedes to their demand, thinking perhaps, *If you want a sign, I'll give you a sign—the resurrection:* this "evil generation" will see no more signs until "the sign of Jonah" (11:29–30). Recall that Jonah, after lying in the belly of the whale for three days, returned to Nineveh to preach their repentance. Because they have ignored Jesus, who is after all greater than Jonah, this evil generation will be judged by the repentant Ninevites. Consider "the queen of the South" who "came from the ends of the earth to listen to Solomon's wisdom, and see, something greater than Solomon [myself] is here!" (11:31). Ignoring Jesus in their hankering after a sign—rather than the word of God he teaches—will bring judgment (11:32). Blessed, after all, are those who hear and obey. For now, this "evil generation" will see no more signs until "the sign of Jonah" (11:29–30).

Theme 4': "The Kingdom Is Not Coming with Things That Can Be Observed" (Luke 17:20–37)

The crowd and its leaders have seen signs of God's peaceable kingdom, signs of justice, peace, and mercy: lepers cleansed, demons cast out, tax collectors embraced, and sinners forgiven. But they have seen no earthly king marching with armies in defiant opposition to Rome. God's kingdom and its way of securing peace through compassion and justice are very different from all cultural norms within earthly empires. Jesus has planted seeds of mercy and justice but not amassed armies and weapons and territory. People have been added to God's kingdom through compassion, not through conquest. Jesus tells those expecting an earthly king coming to power in thunder and lightning, "The kingdom of God is not coming with things that can be observed" (17:20).

Sign seekers will not be able to point to a decisive display of earthly power and say, "Look, here it is!" or "There it is!" (17:21). Indeed, they have already missed God's signs in the small acts of compassion that mark the kingdom—a leper released from disease and isolation, the demoniac freed from loneliness due to uncontrollable forces, the bleeding woman delivered from her life of humiliation and rejection. Looking for military might and Roman submission, they can't see that God's kingdom is already, as Jesus says, "among you" (17:21). The cleansing and liberation of ten helpless and hopeless lepers is all the sign they need to see that God's kingdom is here (17:11–19).

Echoing Luke's allusion to the prophet Jonah in the first instance of this thematic focus on ostentatious signs versus kingdom humility is the ark-building Noah. At a word from God, Noah built the ark, with no evidence of rain. Because Noah's neighbors were so immersed in their own selfish interests—"eating and drinking, and marrying and being given in marriage"— they complacently ignored God right up "until the day Noah entered the ark, and the flood came and destroyed all of them" (17:27). Their flood-worthy sin was like the evil of Sodom, whose great sin—according to Jesus—was not rape or homosexuality, but in "eating and drinking, buying and selling, planting and building" (17:28). Perhaps Jesus is drawing on Ezekiel 16:49: "This was the guilt of your sister Sodom: she and her daughters had pride, excess of food, and prosperous ease, but did not aid the poor and needy." The point, explains Jesus, is that "those who try to make their life secure" with objects, with possessions—signs of their own self-procured status and comfort but immune from the needs of the outcast—are lost (17:33). We hear an echo of the religious leader thanking God that he's better than others, of people "wanting to justify themselves" by pointing to signs of their piety.

Jesus is, in effect, reversing society's status quo: in God's kingdom, one's value is not based on one's own efforts or one's societal value system; one is not valued by the size of one's crop or one's house or one's wealth, or the beauty of one's wife or the number and success of one's children. One is not "justified" by one's attempts to make one's own life, one's own self, secure. Only those who take God's word seriously will secure their life: "Those who try to make their life secure will lose it, but those who lose their life will keep it" (17:33).

Fifth Theme: What's Inside a Person—Hypocrisy versus Faith

In these echoing sequences, we hear dire warnings about one's interior: woe to leaders within the traditional religious establishment who parade their goodness while hiding rot in their hearts (first sequence); and warnings of woe to the new leadership of a delivered Israel who would fail to cultivate true faith and integrity within (echoing sequence). Since religious leaders, indeed all people in power, are prone to hypocrisy, Israel's new leaders must constantly cultivate the genuine faith that unfolds compellingly in the echoing sequence.

Theme 5: "You Tithe . . . and Neglect Justice and the Love of God" (Luke 11:33–12:12)

Luke begins his discussion of hypocrisy with a powerful call to look inward: "Consider whether the light in you is not darkness" (11:35). If you are indeed righteous, the light will shine from inside out.

Luke returns to his metaphor of light at the end of this section, where he warns: "Beware of the yeast of the Pharisees, that is, their hypocrisy," because hidden wickedness will inevitably become known; "whatever you have said in the dark will be heard in the light, and what you have whispered behind closed doors will be proclaimed from the housetops" (12:1–2). Between this frame of darkness revealed in light, Luke sandwiches his denunciation of religious hypocrisy in its various forms.

The traditional religious leaders chastise Jesus for not ritually cleansing himself before dining with them; he faults them for cleaning the outside of their "cup" while inside they "are full of greed and wickedness" (11:39). While they appear pious and act religious, it's all appearance and show—they have ignored the wickedness within their hearts.

But Jesus is just warming up, and he begins reciting a litany of the traditional religious leaders' woe-deserving hypocritical acts:

- "You tithe mint and rue and herbs of all kinds, and neglect justice and the love of God" (11:42).
- "You love to have the seat of honor in the synagogues and to be greeted with respect in the marketplaces" (11:43).
- "You load people with burdens hard to bear, and you yourselves do not lift a finger to ease them" (11:46).
- "You have taken away the key of knowledge; you did not enter yourselves, and you hindered those who were entering" (11:52).

While these leaders believe themselves morally exemplary, worthy of great honor and respect, Jesus rejects them for neglecting the things that make for peace: justice and mercy (11:42–43).

Theme 5′: Do Not Expect Thanks; Always Give Thanks (Luke 17:1–19)

In the repeated sequence, Jesus speaks directly to his disciples about the inevitable temptations of hypocrisy: "Be on your guard," he warns (17:1–3). Jesus is so concerned with the corrosive effects of hypocrisy that he warns, in the strongest possible terms, against causing the little ones[7] to stumble.[8] Instead of lording power over the little ones in the guise of piety, Jesus commends a deep and genuine faith, one that integrates one's faithful heart with righteous and compassionate actions.

Luke arranges a series of vignettes that build on each other to a climax expressing the deepest moral truth: rather than expecting anything in return for doing the right thing, including being thanked, be always grateful, giving thanks.

1. *Forgive, over and over.* Jesus demands forgiveness for anyone who repents; and, he goes on, if they should sin against you seven times and repent seven times, you must forgive them seven more times (17:3–4).

2. *Have faith.* When the apostles ask Jesus to increase their faith, Jesus rebukes them, saying that if they had faith the size of the miniscule mustard seed, they could command a mulberry plant to uproot itself and jump into the sea; since they can't, they lack even that small amount of faith (17:5–6).

3. *Act without regard for reward.* Do the works of love that faith demands without thought of reward—as slaves do what their master expects of them without regard for praise or reward (17:7–10).

4. *Always give thanks.* Rather than expecting recognition and thanks, be always ready to give thanks (17:11–19).

In the concluding story of the ten healed lepers, only one explicitly expresses gratitude, gives thanks, to Jesus: "He prostrated himself at Jesus's feet and thanked him" (17:16a). Here is the height and depth and breadth of true faith: a humble heart that always expresses gratitude. By returning to praise and thank Jesus, this one out of ten shows that he's been healed—both inside and out. While he has been physically transformed, more importantly he has been spiritually transformed.

"And he was a Samaritan" (17:16b). As if being weighed down with debilitating pain were not enough, lepers were shunned, alienated, and ostracized—forced to live in lonely and devastating poverty outside of a human community. Unlike the religious leaders who were beautiful on the outside, lepers were clearly ugly on the outside; unlike the religious leaders, they were deeply aware of their need for physical healing and meaningful human relationships. But dehumanizing lepers simply contributed to the religious leaders' sham sense of superiority. And this man is a half-breed (Samaritan) to boot, worthy of derision, not inclusion, in the Jewish community. The humble gratitude of the leper, which Jesus calls his healing faith, unmasks the faithless and self-sufficient religious leaders' hypocrisy. Jesus says to the leper but not to the religious leaders, which Luke makes abundantly clear in his patterned excursus on faith, "Your faith has made you well" (17:19).

Conclusion

Jesus has instructed his disciples, at the beginning and the end, to do the things that make for peace. The next four themes spell out some of those:

- loving God with all your heart and your neighbor as yourself
- praying fervently
- doing what one hears Jesus teaching
- having faith (versus being a hypocrite)

If one digs deeper into the text, as Luke invites his hearers to do, one finds the deep connections between kingdom love, prayer, actions, and faith on the one hand and kingdom peace and communal flourishing on the other.

Faith, to take them in reverse order, prevents selfishness from masquerading as religion, pride from manifesting itself as piety. In everything, the hypocrites seek self-advantage, lording their power over those beneath them, all the while neglecting justice, mercy, and peace. Faith, in contrast, grounds the grateful and healthy humility that can forgive and forgive and forgive and act for others without concern for self or reward.

If one hears and then does what Jesus teaches—the things that make for peace—one is well on the way to the other-regarding, other-doing compassion the kingdom demands. However, if one wishes to be self-secure, through possessions or status or power, one is diametrically opposed to communal flourishing. "The kingdom of God is not coming with things that can be observed" (17:20). It comes from a radical, other-regarding love from within. One either submits to self or to God.

Prayer, then, is the sign of submission to God required for the attainment of the things God cares about: justice and mercy. Indeed, the ultimate prayer is for divine assistance, for the empowering Spirit, to do the things that make for peace.

Undergirding it all, of course, is love: loving God with all one's heart, soul, mind, and strength, and loving neighbor as one loves oneself. One must not love false gods—those anathema to communal flourishing, like money—in the place of God. And one must be so detached from wealth that one is willing to share it all with those in need. The faithless hypocrite, the rejector of Jesus, the neglecter of prayer, and the lover of self and wealth share one thing in common—their exclusive and competitive regard for self thwarts the compassion and justice required for communal flourishing (peace). Such flourishing requires the other-regarding, radically inclusive, other-delighting attitudes and commitments that produce acts of justice and mercy. The kingdom of God, Luke is saying, is within.

CHAPTER 16

"Things That Make for Peace," Part Two: The Journey (Luke 12:13–16:31)

Striving to Enter the Kingdom's Salvation

After successfully inaugurating the kingdom by liberating outcasts oppressed by demons and disease, Jesus has recruited more followers for the work of the kingdom. But they need to learn about both faith and covenantal fidelity.[1] We have just heard the first five themes of this teaching: peace, loving God and neighbor, prayer for the Spirit and for justice and mercy, true security, and finally, true faith. Luke structures this middle portion of the journey, its inner rings, in a deepening realization of the challenges that plague one's journey on the way of God (20:21).

As Luke deepens our understanding of the kingdom and its required relinquishments, he deftly guides us to the literary center point of the journey. In this chapter we highlight the inner rings of the journey as they head to the center point, the thematic destination: kingdom entrance.

1 Kingdom goal: communal peace (9:51–10:24)
  2 "What must I do to inherit eternal life?" (10:25–42)
    3 Prayer: How do I pray and for what? (11:1–13)
      4 How can I be sure about all this? (11:14–32)
        5 What's inside: faithlessness and hypocrisy (11:33–12:12)
        6 Don't worry about money and security (12:13–34)
          7 Perks and privilege (12:35–48)
            8 Family (12:49–13:9)
              9 Sabbath and the religious tradition (13:10–17)
                10 Kingdoms human and divine (13:18–21)
                  11 Kingdom entrance (13:22–30)
                10′ Kingdoms human and divine (13:31–35)
              9′ Sabbath and the religious tradition (14:1–24)
            8′ Family (14:25–35)

7' **Perks and privilege (15:1–32)**
6' **Don't worry about money and security (16:1–31)**
5' What's inside: faith and integrity (17:1–19)
4' How can I be sure about all this? (17:20–37)
3' Prayer: How do I pray and for what? (18:1–14)
2' "What must I do to inherit eternal life?" (18:15–30)
1' Kingdom goal: communal peace (18:31–19:44)

Increasingly Jesus addresses, alternately, the new religious leaders in God's kingdom (his disciples) and the old religious leaders of a misappropriated Israel (the scribes and the Pharisees). As we learn about their radically different visions of God's relationship to his people, as mediated by the law, we also learn about their membership and their leadership. Given the failures of the traditional leaders in this regard, Jesus's hope lies in the new leaders, the disciples. The successive topics (6-7-8-9 / 9'-8'-7'-6') concern relinquishing conventionally crucial "things" that work against the "things" making for peace.

Sixth Theme: Don't Worry about Money and Security

Anxiety, we learn, is a multiheaded monster that, to enter the kingdom, must be tamed. People are normally anxious about money and security, status, family honor, and even their religious tradition. Genuine faith, according to Jesus, is the shield against these externally located anxieties.[2] While anti-kingdom forces rage and wreak havoc, your soul is in God's hands (12:4–7).

Theme 6: "Sell Your Possessions, and Give Alms" (Luke 12:13–34)

Concern for money and security snowballs into the vice of greed—those who value their life in direct proportion to the amount of their possessions.

A successful farmer, Jesus describes, devotes himself entirely to building bigger and bigger storehouses for his abundant and increasing "grain and goods" so that *he* can guarantee *himself* many years to "relax, eat, drink, and be merry." God, however, visits the deluded hoarder and says, "You fool! This very night your life is being demanded of you." Jesus concludes, "So it is with those who store up treasures for themselves but are not rich toward God" (12:20–21). The reliance on wealth to relieve one's fear of the future is a substitute and silly deity, while being rich toward God, trusting him and him alone, frees one from worry. Jesus goes on to explain, "Do not worry about your life, what you will eat, or about your body, what you will wear." Life, after all, "is more than food, and the body more than clothing" (12:22–23).

Jesus calls attention to ravens, which, although they "neither sow nor reap," are fed by God; and, he adds, humans are vastly more valuable to God than are birds. So Jesus instructs the rich to sell everything, give their profits away, and put their trust (treasure) in God (12:24–34).

Theme 6': "Make Friends for Yourselves by Means of Dishonest Wealth" (Luke 16:1–31)

In this mirrored sequence, Jesus qualifies his previous response to the issue of money and security. If money gets in the way of your entering the kingdom, give it all away, we have just heard him say. Now he qualifies the categorical demand to live in poverty.

Jesus tells a story about a "shrewd" manager, which is not intended to downplay the manager's moral and social defects—he's dishonest, self-serving, lazy, shifty. As a result of his incompetence and profligacy, he has lost much of his rich master's estate. When called to account by his boss, the manager seeks to curry favor with his master's debtors so that when he's unemployed, they will welcome him into their homes; so he slashes each of their debts (16:1–7). Surprisingly, the master commends the steward's shrewdness for his use of money to gain friends. What is the point of this odd story?

While Jesus is not commending the use of, say, drug money to fund famine relief (he opposes the dishonest use of money in chaps. 10–12), he uses this startling story to make a point about the purpose of money. Money, we should hear, is not for the selfish accumulation of wealth, something to be considered as one's own. Wealth, he is saying, should be used "to make friends for yourselves" in the realm of the kingdom—"eternal homes" (16:9). Jesus, then, is demanding a renunciation of the spirit of owning property and money for simply one's own use. Use your possessions, rather, to build a compassionate and mutually committed community, including friends welcoming your communal presence in the realm of the kingdom.

Luke concludes this mirrored sequence on possessions with another, more conventional story emphasizing the proper use of money (16:19–31). Day after day a wealthy man ignores the entreaties of Lazarus, a destitute beggar at his door. When they die, the rich man is sent to Hades while Lazarus is sent to heaven. The agonized rich man beseeches Father Abraham to send Lazarus with some water to quench his thirst. Abraham replies that since he received many good things during his lifetime but ignored the poor and dispossessed, there is simply no possibility of relief (salvation).

By ignoring his earthly obligation to relieve the suffering of the lost, the rich man himself becomes lost, outside the precincts of salvation. Within the precincts of salvation are the "eternal homes," the goal of the story of the shrewd manager. Be shrewd in handling your possessions and money—with a constant eye to the needs of others in God's kingdom.

The mirrored sequences on money and possessions are mutually reinforcing and expansive: making God your heart's singular desire means serving God's interests, not your own. Possessions and wealth are to be held lightly and easily shared; they are not one's to own but gifts to be used for the needs of others. For those who trust exclusively in themselves, who build increasingly larger storehouses for their bounty, Jesus demands that they give it all away, for "where your treasure is, there your heart will be also" (12:34). Clinging to money indicates a problem of misplaced trust. For those who fail to share their God-given bounty with those in need, Jesus warns that they will soon cross an unbridgeable chasm, placing themselves outside the domain of salvation. Clinging to money also indicates a problem of compassion and justice. In both sequences Jesus asks us to relinquish, for the sake of the kingdom, what we normally and urgently grasp—the means to our self-focused, self-designed, and self-ensured cozy and comfy future.

Seventh Theme: Perks and Privilege

"To whom much has been entrusted, even more will be demanded," Jesus says. And, to an elder malcontent son, a father says tenderly, "This brother of yours was dead and has come to life; he was lost and has been found." Therefore rejoice.

Theme 7: "To Whom Much Has Been Entrusted, Even More Will Be Demanded" (Luke 12:35–48)

In this first sequence Jesus warns Israel's new religious leaders, the disciples, against abusing their positions to garner the ordinary perks of power over others. Jesus warns his disciples to think of themselves as servants rather than masters, as leaders are typically tempted to do; as servants they should attend to the rescue and protection of the "little ones"—the poor, the oppressed, the imprisoned, the possessed, the widow, the sick, and the orphaned. In God's kingdom, leaders diligently and vigilantly serve the little ones as service to the Son of Man (12:35–40).

When Peter asks if this servant's message is for the disciples only or for everyone, Jesus clarifies that it is for the disciples, who are like "the faithful and prudent manager whom his master will put in charge of his slaves" (12:42). The manager's faithfulness to the absent master entails material care for the needs of the slaves; the unfaithful manager, however, abuses the master's slaves and uses his work for his own benefit. In short, the disciples have been equipped and taught to diligently and materially care for members of God's kingdom, not to mistreat them or benefit from them. Jesus concludes, "From everyone to whom much has been given, much will be required; and from the one to whom much has been entrusted, even more will be demanded" (12:48). Relinquish the normal perks of power in ruling over others (by taking from them); rather, selflessly serve those God has put under your care.

Theme 7': "This Fellow Welcomes Sinners and Eats with Them" (Luke 15:1–32)

Jesus wants the traditional leaders, the Pharisees especially, to cooperate with him in the kingdom enterprise. He appeals to them sincerely, putting the case for serving rather than lording it over in the most cogent terms.

As social outcasts clamor to hear Jesus, "the Pharisees and the scribes [are] grumbling and saying, 'This fellow [Jesus] welcomes sinners and eats with them'" (15:1–2). What Jesus says here is essentially an elaboration of what, in the first theme sequence, he has told the new leaders, his disciples: their sense of prestige and privilege prevents them from appreciating and appropriating God's grace on behalf of the little ones.

Jesus offers three interconnected tales focused on the theme of rejoic-ing over the return of the lost sinner:

1. Just as a truly good shepherd leaves his ninety-nine secure sheep to seek and find his one lost sheep, rejoicing when it is found (15:3–7), so too "there will be more joy in heaven over one sinner who repents than over ninety-nine righteous persons who need no repentance" (15:7).
2. When a woman finds the lost one of her ten coins through painstak-ing measures—lighting the lamp, sweeping the entire house, and then searching carefully—she rejoices; so too "there is joy in the presence of the angels of God over one sinner who repents" (15:8–10).
3. Finally, a loving father of two sons rejoices when his one "lost" son returns home (15:25–32).

Jesus's concern for the sinner-outsider flies in the face of the religious lead-ers' presumption of righteousness. They are like the obedient elder son in the third tale who refuses to rejoice over the return of his lost brother. He thinks that by virtue of his obedience, he deserves to be celebrated. He complains to his dad, "Listen! For all these years I have been working like a slave for you, and I have never disobeyed your command; yet you have never given me even a young goat so that I might celebrate with my friends. But when this son of yours came back, who has devoured your property with prostitutes, you killed the fatted calf for him!" (15:29–30). Nary a goat for the obedient son! The son's sense of worthiness prevents him from graciously welcoming his brother back, as his father has. His presumption precludes graciousness or generosity on his part. His father replies, "Son, you are always with me, and all that is mine is yours. But we had to celebrate and rejoice, because this brother of yours was dead and has come to life; he was lost and has been found" (15:31–32).

In these mirrored sequences, Jesus challenges the old and new leaders about the nature of the kingdom—one made up of slaves and sinners. As servants, the disciples owe gratitude to their master, the Son of Man; they are undeserving of special privilege or honor. As managers, they humbly serve by obeying the Master's desire to care for the little ones, with all the zeal of the shepherd and the woman searching for the one thing lost, and with the generous joy of a heartbroken father upon his wastrel son's return home.

The grumbling and complaining religious leaders, like the elder son, are so convinced of their own righteousness that they are unable to delight in the salvation of the sinner in God's kingdom; their presumption prevents the graciousness and generosity required of leaders in God's new kingdom. *To whom much has been given, much is expected.* The heavenly Father grieves over the shriveled hearts of those religious leaders who, given so much, care only for their own power and its perks. The presumptions of power and reward and righteousness must be relinquished for the sake of God's kingdom.

Eighth Theme: Family

Here we find one of Jesus's most challenging but important teachings: the communal well-being of God's kingdom must be pursued at all costs, even at the cost of family. If one's biological family compromises or opposes kingdom peace, it must be relinquished.

Theme 8: "From Now on Five in One Household Will Be Divided" (Luke 12:49–13:9)

About ties to family Jesus says that he came to bring fire and division: "Do you think that I have come to bring peace to the earth? No, I tell you, but rather division!" (12:51).[3]

Jesus's teachings seem to conflict with Luke's proclamations on communal peace. Pitting followers against families seems a clear and certain obstacle to peace. Jesus says, however, and in the strongest terms, that any ties that compromise kingdom commitment are ties that threaten peace. Jesus has already shown how favoritism based on wealth and privilege threatens communal peace. Hoarded wealth benefits a small percentage of power holders at the expense of the vast majority "beneath" them. The socially and politically privileged, puffed up with pride, gain social status at the cost of those "beneath" them. Now Jesus is denouncing favoritism based on blood relations. Granting special favors to family members typically means ignoring the needs of those outside one's family. In God's kingdom, as Acts will make clear, everyone is equal with regard to living well, with benefits of possessions and wealth distributed not according to kin-relation but instead "as any had need" (Acts 2:45; 4:32).

Theme 8': "Whoever Does Not Hate Father and Mother Cannot Be My Disciple" (Luke 14:25–35)

This parallel statement is even more dramatic in rejecting the sort of familial favoritism that gets in the way of kingdom commitment: "Whoever comes to me and does not hate father and mother, wife and children, brothers and sisters, yes, and even life itself, cannot be my disciple" (14:26). Followers of Jesus "hate"[4] their biological family members, relinquishing the honoring of biological family above God's family. Honoring God's family—which requires unyielding commitment to the kingdom—trumps loyalty to one's nuclear family. The honoring of family, tribe, and clan—which invariably endanger peace—must be subsumed to the honoring of God. This is an unthinkable reversal from what is considered normal and even honorable, especially in the culture of the day. Such a turnaround from loyalty first and always to family highlights the most demanding of relinquishments required for commitment to God's kingdom family.

Even the preservation of one's life itself, if it supersedes commitment to the other members of God's kingdom, must be relinquished.

Kingdom commitment collides with familial relations, constituting for some in Luke's audience an insurmountable obstacle to following Jesus. The demands of God's family will almost certainly result in acrimony with one's biological family. But the favoritism of family is a serious obstacle to the radical equality and universal empathy and compassion required for kingdom peace. Family, then, must be relinquished for kingdom peace.

Ninth Theme: Sabbath and the Religious Tradition

These paired themes lie near the center of the ringed theme composition, nearly at the destination point of God's kingdom (13:24–30). In each sequence, Jesus heals on the Sabbath, drawing criticism for breaking the religious rule—*keep the Sabbath!* Jesus criticizes the religious leaders who fail to understand the law's deeper love of the outcast and enemy. Their religion has become an obstacle to the realization of God's kingdom.

Theme 9: "You Hypocrites!" (Luke 13:10–17)

Jesus is teaching in the synagogue on the Sabbath and sees a woman who has been crippled for eighteen years. He says to her, "Woman, you are set free from your ailment," and she stands and rejoices (13:10–13). When a leader of the synagogue reprimands Jesus for working on the Sabbath, he calls the leaders "hypocrites" for untying their livestock and leading them to water on the Sabbath but then complaining when a person is freed from debilitating pain on the Sabbath. "And ought not this woman, a daughter of Abraham whom Satan bound for eighteen long years, be set free from this bondage on the sabbath day?" (13:16). The leaders were shamed as the crowd rejoiced.

Theme 9′: "Is It Lawful to Cure People on the Sabbath, or Not?" (Luke 14:1–24)

In this mirrored sequence, Jesus is on his way to a Sabbath meal with a Pharisee. In front of him is a man with edema.[5] This time he asks the religious elite to consider: "Is it lawful to cure people on the sabbath, or not?" (14:3). When they respond with silence, Jesus cures the man. Then he asks them if, on the Sabbath, they would pull out their child or ox who has fallen into a well. Again, they are silent (14:4–6).

In both sequences, Jesus challenges the religious leaders' lamentable misunderstanding of Israel's law—religion as the relishing of rules over helping people. Jesus is not asking for an abandonment of the law, but for a deeper understanding of the compassion that informs and motivates it. Jesus will heal, Sabbath or not—regardless of "the rule." Their religion is judged by the law of compassion that governs God's covenant people. Jesus is clearly demanding his followers relinquish any self-righteous and self-serving understanding of the law as shallow and self-serving rule keeping.

Tenth Theme: Kingdoms Human and Divine

As we approach the center point of Jesus's teachings, as organized by Luke, we hear a shocking contrast between God's kingdom of peace and the "holy" city of Jerusalem, "the city that kills the prophets and stones those who are sent to it!" (13:34).

Theme 10: "To What Should I Compare the Kingdom of God?"
(Luke 13:18–21)

We have already learned of God's kingdom and justice. We know that it is marked by radical compassion and inclusion, and populated with restored sinners and outcasts. And despite appearances, it is alive and growing. God's kingdom is starting small and slowly—without splash or conspicuous triumph. But its outcome is as sure as a tiny mustard seed growing into a tree large enough to accommodate countless birds. Or consider that a pinch of yeast is enough to raise dough sufficient to feed 150 people (13:18–21).

What is the relationship of God's kingdom to the religious leaders' understanding of Israel, the temple, God, and the law?

Theme 10′: "Jerusalem, Jerusalem, the City That Kills the Prophets"
(Luke 13:31–35)

The "holy" city Jerusalem, once the center of Israel's cultic practice with the temple of God shining in glory, is now the dark and doomed city that kills prophets and stones those sent to it (13:34). They also will soon kill the Son of Man, whom Simeon declared a light for "glory to your people Israel." The sun is setting on Jerusalem and its mistaken and legalistic understanding of the law, with its temple desacralized into a center of false prophets and self-seeking power, and with its leaders little more than hypocrites who cling to power and status at the expense of the "little ones." This, in spite of God's good will: "How often have I desired to gather your children together as a hen gathers her brood under her wings, and you were not willing!" And so God judges Jerusalem: "See, your house is left to you" (13:34–35). It is a house that will be destroyed, as Jesus has foretold.[6]

For now, Jesus is doomed: "I must be on my way," he says, "because it is impossible for a prophet to be killed outside of Jerusalem" (13:33). But his crucifixion is the death knell for Jerusalem and all that it represents. The glory that was once located in the temple in the holy city, Jerusalem, will dramatically shift to Jesus and his kingdom. As Acts will illustrate, the risen Jesus will be the new locus of Israel's worship, as God's kingdom is realized through servant Israel.

The contrast in these parallel sequences is between God's thriving new kingdom and Jerusalem's gaudy but dying kingdom. And though it may not be obvious now, the kingdom of God has come and will grow into a home large enough for all of God's children.

Eleventh Theme: The Journey's Destination—"Strive to Enter through the [Kingdom's] Narrow Door" (Luke 13:22–30)

Luke has presented a carefully ordered account of God's new, thriving and growing kingdom in contrast to the religious leaders' dying and soon dead religion. In addition to increasing his audience's understanding of the kingdom, he is also motivating seekers to see that *all of God's action is now here, in the kingdom.* Then Jesus offers the very sober entrance requirements to God's kingdom: "Strive to enter through the [kingdom's] narrow door; for many, I tell you, will try to enter and will not be able" (13:24).

The entire teaching journey, ten chapters' worth, comes down to this: kingdom entrance, through which we realize God's blessed salvation, depends on strenuously striving toward the goodness of this kingdom. Such striving, we have already heard, involves striving for communal well-being within God's kingdom, continually choosing and showing compassion and justice to the little ones. Israel's traditional leaders, however, strive for status and power while ignoring the poor, the outcast, and the sinner. Servant Israel must strive for compassion and peace and justice, all the while relinquishing status and power and wealth.

Strive for God's kingdom, we hear, *or else.* On the day of judgment, those who have refused the kingdom's invitation will learn that they cannot enter into the joy of God's eternal presence: "There will be weeping and gnashing of teeth when you see Abraham and Isaac and Jacob and all the prophets in the kingdom of God, and you yourselves thrown out" (13:28). Some of those who are rejected, such as the religious leaders, will be shocked, thinking themselves eminently deserving of entry (13:26). People from all over the world—from east and west, from north and south—will enter into the heavenly kingdom (13:29). *But not them.* Thinking themselves first, they will be shocked and dismayed to learn which people are invited to God's banquet: "Indeed, some are last who will be first, and some are first who will be last" (13:30). Presumption of one's own status, power, and merit leads to being last, excluded from the joy of God's kingdom. Strive, therefore, to enter God's kingdom of compassion and peace—and join in the eternal banquet!

Conclusion: "The Things That Make for Peace"

With purpose and determination Jesus has set his face toward Jerusalem, the center of Jewish religious and political life. As he nears, Jesus greets the cheering crowds with an outburst of tears, lamenting, "If you, even you, had only recognized on this day the things that make for peace!" (19:41–42). The religious leaders' failures to recognize "the time of your visitation from God" and to respond to his invitation to the kingdom spell Jerusalem's doom—their enemies will crush them (19:43–44). God's peaceable kingdom, on the other hand, though starting small and growing slowly, will grow surely and widely and into eternity.

God's kingdom come to earth, as represented in the first set of echoing themes, is marked by communal wholeness, fulfillment, and harmony—in a word, peace.

Kingdom principles include peace, love, prayer, hearing and doing the word, and sharing one's possessions with those in need. And kingdom members—the poor, the outcast, the blind and lame, the sinner—are mutually devoted to one another's well-being. They serve one another as slaves serve their masters. They relinquish the favoritism of families for the radical egalitarianism of the kingdom. Their relationships are marked by the deep compassion and justice at the heart of the law, not by the pride and legalism of the letter of the law. As a result, entering and living in the kingdom is no easy task. In order to enter the kingdom of God and experience eternal life, one must repent. Kingdom life is a continual repenting, a daily turning around from normal cultural ways to God's way.[7]

The audience, attentive to Luke's hearing cues, learns in this teaching about the salvation of God and the challenges of securing kingdom peace. The making of peace, we hear at the center point of Luke's chiastic structure, is a monumentally difficult task. So those entering the kingdom of *shalom* must continually strive to do so. God's way requires understanding and striving to follow the teaching of God's word as Jesus lays it out on this journey to Jerusalem. The striving for righteousness Jesus is calling for is a disciplined hearing and difficult doing of the word of God, a continual turning around from the intuitive and comfortable ways of one's culture to the demanding way of God (20:21).

Teaching finished, Jesus sets his face toward Jerusalem.

Appendix: A Review of the Repeated Themes in a Question-and-Answer Format

First Question, Repeated

What is the central kingdom goal?
Answer: Communal peace (9:51–10:24; 18:31–19:44).

Second Question, Repeated

"What must I do to inherit eternal life?"
Answer: Hear the word and do it (10:25–42; 18:15–30).

Third Question, Repeated

How do I pray, and for what?
Answer: Ask God, unceasingly, for the things that last: the Holy Spirit, who enables salvation (11:1–13); *and justice and mercy* (18:1–14).

Fourth Question, Repeated

How can I be sure about you and this kingdom?
Answer: Let go of doubts based on securing your own interests (11:14–32; 17:20–37).

Fifth Question, Repeated

What is faith?
Answer: Fake faith is having others noticing your piety (11:33–12:12); *true faith is faithfulness in doing what is right for its own sake, not for notice* (17:1–19).

Sixth Question, Repeated

But what about money and possessions, security for me and my family?
Answer: Do not worry so much. Dispossess yourself of the spirit of possessing for the sake of your new family of God (12:13–34; 16:1–31).

Seventh Question, Repeated

But what about the perks and privilege I deserve?

Answer: "From everyone to whom much has been given, much will be required; and from the one to whom much has been entrusted, even more will be demanded" (12:35–48; 15:1–32).

Eighth Question, Repeated

But what about my family, my kids, my spouse?
Answer: Accept the family of God to threaten birth-family stability (12:49–13:9); in fact, make it happen (14:25–35).

Ninth Question, Repeated

But what about my religious tradition, what my family holds to?
Answer: Move beyond, into the inclusive true religion of the radically inclusive kingdom of God (13:10–17; 14:1–24).

Tenth Question, Repeated

God's kingdom versus earthly empires?
Answer: The kingdom of God will look small and slow at the start, lacking in power (13:18–21); earthly empires, like that of Jerusalem, are formidable, acting with seductive power (13:31–35).

Central Question, Heart of the Journey

Who then can be saved? And how?
Answer: Only those who strive to enter the kingdom; all others are lost to its salvation (13:22–30).

CHAPTER 17

Authority: Who Will Lead Israel? (Luke 19:45–24:53)

The Final Events of Volume One

Jesus has just finished clarifying the law, ten paired themes or principles to guide everyday living in God's peaceful kingdom (9:51–19:44). It has been a literal journey to Jerusalem and a metaphorical journey into the kingdom. When at his literal journey's end he spies Jerusalem, Jesus pauses and weeps: "If you, even you, had only recognized on this day the things that make for peace!" (19:41–42).

Next we find Jesus cleansing the temple (19:46), which has become a "den of thieves," one more sign that God is not in the temple (or in the religion it has come to represent) but in the new and emerging kingdom. The religious leaders, realizing the threat of the growing kingdom to their prestige and power, plot to kill Jesus. But they are thwarted by the en-thralled worshipers surrounding Jesus (19:47–48).

In dialogue with Israel's traditional leaders, Jesus establishes his own authority to rule Israel. And with his friends, his disciples, Jesus explains the near and distant future as preparation for their assuming leadership of the kingdom (22:29): the near future of his coming death, resurrection, and departure; the not-too-distant future of Jerusalem's desolation and the destruction of its temple; finally, the distant future—after the kingdom has spread to all the peoples of the world—of the return of Jesus as Judge at the end of ordinary time.[1]

This final section of Luke is divided in two. The first, inside the temple, is organized around the verbal sparring between Jesus and the traditional leaders regarding authority (19:45–21:38). In the second, outside the tem-ple, the conflict over authority is extended, leading to the killing of Jesus. Luke concludes with a grand reversal—the ultimate vindication of Jesus as the authoritative leader of Israel, its Messiah: God raises Jesus from death.

Inside the Temple (Luke 19:45–21:38)

This first long sequence in the temple parades all the lead characters and their response to Jesus: the religious authorities, the disciples, the crowd—concluding with a widow who is praised. The temple scene begins and ends with parallel words, "Every day he was teaching in the temple" (19:45–47; 21:37), and with parallel references to the hostile leaders foiled by the people's high regard for Jesus (19:45–48; 21:37–22:2).

Traditional Leaders: "By What Authority Are You Doing These Things?" (Luke 19:45–21:4)

A long dialogue begins in the temple between Jesus and the religious leaders. The stakes are high. Who has the authoritative view of the Hebrew Scriptures, and what is that view? Who has legitimate rule over Israel—the traditional rulers or Jesus? And who will rule over Israel after the departure of Jesus?

The religious leaders have asserted various forms of coercive or domineering power over people to force acceptance of their authority and their understanding of the law. Jesus, on the other hand, uses the attractive and invitational power of compassion, enticing people with the good news of God's kingdom, without fear or coercion. The traditional leaders, who rely on instilling fear, ironically fear the people's devotion to Jesus and Jesus's threat to their status as leaders. So they seek to kill Jesus while maneuvering around the people—until the time is right to strike.

We hear the verbal battle between Messiah Jesus and the traditional leaders with *authority*, in various guises, as a hearing cue.

Authority, Part 1 (Luke 19:45–20:8)

When Jesus clears the temple of robbers and thieves,[2] the religious leaders protest, asking him, "By what authority are you doing these things?" Jesus responds to their question with a question of his own about the status of John. When they can't think of a good reply, partially because of the people's respect for John,[3] they say they don't know if John was authorized by heaven or humans. Jesus, in turn, refuses to reveal his source of authority.

Authority, Part 2 (Luke 20:9–26)

Jesus then tells a tale about the abuse of authority, aimed at the religious rulers supposedly serving God: A vineyard master has tenants who are abusing their master's trust. After unsuccessful attempts to get word from messengers about his vineyard, the owner sends his "beloved son," thinking that surely there will be respect for the authority vested in the person of his son. But the son is killed by the greedy tenants, who are then destroyed, in turn, by the owner.

Entrusted with the owner's holdings, the tenants in the story squander the owner's trust for their own profit and comfort and kill his son.[4] "Heaven forbid!" the leaders exclaim (20:16). But when they realize that the parable is aimed at them, they want "to lay hands on him at that very hour," but their fear of the people keeps them from doing so (20:19).

Following this, they keep watching him and send spies who pretend to be honest (20:20). They ask if it's permissible for them to pay taxes to the emperor. Jesus tells them to "give to the emperor the things that are the emperor's, and to God the things that are God's" (20:25). This enigmatic response reduces the spies to silence.

Authority, Part 3 (Luke 20:27–47)

Some Sadducees, who don't believe in the general resurrection, try to trap Jesus in a question about the legalities of marriage in heaven (20:27–33). Jesus uses the occasion to support the idea of the resurrection from their own Scripture and to argue that there is no marriage in the afterlife (20:34–38). The Pharisees, who believe in the resurrection, applaud: "Teacher, you have spoken well" (20:39). Luke concludes by pointing out that "they no longer dared to ask him another question" (20:40).[5]

Jesus concludes this authority contest by pointing out that the leaders' self-proclaimed greatness vanishes under scrutiny. "Beware of the scribes," he warns, "who like to walk around in long robes, and love to be greeted with respect in the marketplaces, and to have the best seats in the synagogues and places of honor at banquets." In addition, their presumed authority isn't merely groundless; it's harmful: "They devour widows' houses and for the sake of appearance say long prayers" (20:45–47). The scribes' hypocrisy is made all the more apparent when Jesus points to rich people who give "out of their abundance," while an impoverished widow, who is just entering the temple, "put in all she had to live on" (21:1–4).

Follow the widow; beware of the scribes' hypocrisy.

Israel's New Leaders: "Be on Guard" and "Be Alert" (Luke 21:5–21:38)

As the traditional leaders fade from the temple scene, the new leaders come to the fore: Jesus needs to teach them about their role, and about the future. In the coming days, the dissembling and self-serving traditional leaders will violently oppose God's kingdom. But that is just a foretaste of challenges the disciples must face. Foreign powers will ravage Jerusalem and destroy its temple. Two periods of devastation lie ahead, says Jesus, local and worldwide.

The Future, First Phase: Jerusalem's Destruction (Luke 21:5–24)

Jesus warns of the perilous times facing the disciples. The first phase of challenge and calamity surrounds the desolation of Jerusalem and the destruction of its temple: "the days will come when not one stone will be left upon another; all will be thrown down" (21:6). But even before the temple falls (in 70 CE), says Jesus to his followers, Jewish leaders "will arrest you and persecute you; they will hand you over to synagogues and prisons, and you will be brought before kings and governors because of my name" (21:12). Although betrayed even by family, and imprisoned and possibly killed, by being placed on trial, the disciples will be given an opportunity to testify to the coming kingdom; although hated, they will not perish (21:12–18). And, to make clear that God is on their and the kingdom's side and not on the side of Jerusalem and the temple, and the degenerate and dying religion they represent, its citizens "will fall by the edge of the sword and be taken away as captives among all nations."

The Future, Second Phase: The Times of the Gentiles and Continuing Distress (Luke 21:25–36)

At the end of the previous section we hear that "Jerusalem will be trampled on by the Gentiles, until the times of the Gentiles are fulfilled" (21:22–24).

The Gentiles, then, are the instrument of God's judgment on Israel's traditional leaders and their followers. *Their* time—the times of the Gentiles—is part of God's grand plan for the world (Gen 12:3; Acts 3:25). *The times of the Gentiles*, promised in the early poems of Luke and by Paul at the end of Acts, are also the time for Gentiles to embrace Jesus and his gospel of the kingdom.

During the times of the Gentiles, followers of Jesus must beware. "Be on guard" and "be alert," we hear (21:34, 36): from the time of Jerusalem's destruction to the end of time, the havoc that preceded the fall of Jerusalem will continue. But fear not, they are comforted; "by your endurance you will gain your souls" (21:19). Upon the fulfillment of the times of the Gentiles, then, a third phase of horror will ensue, a period of earthly and cosmic chaos.

These will be difficult times. "There will be signs in the sun, the moon, and the stars, and on the earth distress among nations confused by the roaring of the sea and the waves. People will faint from fear and foreboding of what is coming upon the world, for the powers of the heavens will be shaken" (21:25–26). With such cosmic mayhem, people will faint dead away with fear, but through the advent of these horrific events "they will see 'the Son of Man coming in a cloud' with power and great glory" (21:27). Jesus will return, in clouds of glory, to judge the old world and to rule over his new world (10:14, 11:31–32; Acts 2:20).

When the destruction of Jerusalem is complete, the times of the kingdom's openness to the Gentiles will continue until the Son of Man comes in power to judge the world (21:27). The age of kingdom growth among both Jews and Gentiles concludes, its fulfillment ushered in by signs, distress, and confusion (21:25–27). When you witness this mayhem, says Jesus, know that the time of fulfillment of the "kingdom of God is near" (21:31).

Jesus adds a final and mysterious word: "Truly I tell you, this generation will not pass away until all things have taken place" (21:32).[6]

Outside the Temple: The Story's Conclusion (Luke 22–24)

"Now the festival of Unleavened Bread, which is called the Passover, was near. The chief priests and the scribes were looking for a way to put Jesus to death, for they were afraid of the people. Then Satan entered into Judas called Iscariot, who was one of the twelve" (22:1–3). The dramatic scene moves from Jerusalem's temple to the city itself.

Luke is putting his audience on high alert: Jesus is in Jerusalem as the Passover celebration of God's deliverance of Israel from the Egyptians is near; the murderous intentions of the religious authorities stay ramped up. Satan has reentered the story at just this critical moment, the "opportune time" mentioned by the author earlier, at the conclusion of the three wilderness temptations (4:13). Satan will have a last go at tempting Jesus away from his steadfast commitment to the way of God and God's kingdom.

Jesus has won the battle of authority with the religious leaders, as he had against the devil (4:1–13).

Accentuating the shift from Jerusalem to God's kingdom and from the temple to the Gentiles and the world, Jesus and his followers are outside the temple, first in a private home for his final meal, and then in a private garden on the Mount of Olives for prayer. The end of Jesus's earthly time fast approaches. If he's killed, what becomes of the gospel's hard-won authority? What becomes of God's kingdom?

In an extraordinary climax to the story of Jesus's time on earth Jesus passes on to his disciples the authority vested in him by the Father. Jesus then confers on his followers the responsibility for the kingdom—just as the Father had conferred on Jesus his kingdom (22:29).

A Room: Sealing of the New Covenant by Blood (Luke 22:7–38)

Preparations have been made for the annual Passover meal together. "I have eagerly desired to eat this Passover with you before I suffer," says Jesus; "for I tell you, I will not eat it until it is fulfilled in the kingdom of God" (22:15–16). He passes around a cup of wine, asking them to divide it among themselves—because "from now on I will not drink of the fruit of the vine until the kingdom of God comes" (22:17–18). And then he takes a loaf of bread and after giving thanks he breaks it and hands it to them, saying, "This is my body" (22:19a). Then he invites them to drink the wine, his blood.[7]

At this meal we find the fullest reflection by Jesus (and Luke) on the meaning of Jesus's death on the cross. Meanings that would later attach themselves to what the gospels are saying about the death of Jesus—about why he died and what was accomplished—would come from many sources and later traditions other than this account in Luke-Acts. If we pay attention to Luke's hearing cues—eat and drink—it is more a message of hope for the future than a clinging to the past or a fear of the present. Jesus has the disciples participating in this common and shared meal ritual to remind them of a future shared meal: "You are those who have stood by me in my trials; and I confer on you, just as my Father has conferred on me, a kingdom, *so that you may eat and drink at my table in my kingdom,* and you will sit on thrones judging the twelve tribes of Israel" (22:28–29). *My table, my kingdom—with you!* But there is a challenge, as always in Luke, in these very words of hope. Sharing in the eternal banquet is "for those who have stood by me in trials." Those who are faithful to Jesus, during these very difficult times, are promised a seat at the kingdom banquet above.

Moreover, there are hints that the disciples may be asked to do more than stand beside Jesus in his trials: just as Jesus will have to bear the cross in utter denial of himself, his followers must "deny themselves," as Jesus says, "and take up their cross daily" (9:23). Share in his suffering and you will share in his glory.

Following their shared meal, Jesus brings up the shock of betrayal: "The one who betrays me is with me, and his hand is on the table. For the Son of Man is going as it has been determined, but woe to that one by whom he is betrayed!" Each looks to the other with the question about "which one of them it could be who would do this" (22:20–23). Yet each will, in his own way, betray Jesus. We learn of what motivates their darkness and hides their true nature from their selves: "A dispute also arose among them as to which one of them was to be regarded as the greatest" (22:24). At this hour of shared bread and promised blood poured out for the covenant, we hear of one more grab on the part of the disciples for status and power. Jesus counters their selfish understanding of and grasp for greatness: "The greatest among you must become like the youngest, and the leader like one who serves" (22:26). The disciples have reasserted the self-aggrandizing and self-promoting way of the scribes and Pharisees, forgetting already the way of self-giving, the kingdom way of Jesus, modeled in their final meal together: "I am among you as one who serves" (22:27).

A Garden: "If You Are Willing, Remove This Cup from Me" (Luke 22:39–46)

The disciples' failure to understand how to serve is put to immediate test: in response to Jesus's request to "pray that you may not come into the time of trial," they fall fast asleep. Their failure is all the more ironic when placed beside Jesus, who prays for his cup of suffering to pass. In these carefully intertwined experiences of the darkness ahead, we hear an important refrain:

- "Pray that you may not come into the time of trial" (22:40).
  - "Father, if you are willing, remove this cup from me" (22:42).

- "Pray that you may not come into the time of trial" (22:46).

With his own prayer, Jesus is asking, like the disciples, that *he* may not come into *his* time of trial. But since the Father is unwilling to remove the cup from Jesus, Jesus willingly accepts his cup. The disciples, we should hear, must, like Jesus, willingly accept theirs.[8]

Arrest and Death: Authority versus Authority (Luke 22:47–23:55)

Emerging from the garden, Jesus sees Judas among an assembly of religious leaders. Jesus asks Judas a prescient question that exposes both Judas's hypocrisy and Jesus's authority: "Judas, is it with a kiss that you are betraying the Son of Man?" (22:48).[9] With the Satan-driven Judas on their side, the religious leaders are portrayed as embracing Satan's power of darkness. Again we are reminded that, early in the story, the devil "departed from [Jesus] until an opportune time" (4:13). Here, at the opportune time, Satan leads the assault on Jesus and God's kingdom. Judas fails in his hour of trial, as will all the disciples.

When Jesus is interrogated by the chief priests and scribes, he is asked if he is the Messiah (22:67). His self-identification as "Son of Man," who "will be seated at the right hand of the power of God" (22:69), is an unambiguous yes. When asked if he is "the Son of God," Jesus's reply, "You say that I am," is likewise an unambiguous yes. Indeed, since "Messiah" and "Son of God" both meant "the Davidic ruler of an age of peace," Jesus's affirmation of being Israel's Messiah is his yes to being the Son of God (22:70). Incensed at his presumption, the religious leaders take Jesus to Pilate, Roman procurator of Judea, claiming that Jesus sought to usurp Rome's authority and subvert the Jewish nation (23:2–3). "He stirs up the people by teaching throughout all Judea, from Galilee[10] where he began even to this place," the leaders explain (23:5). Pilate, finding no basis for "an accusation against this man," sends him over to Rome's representative in Galilee, Herod,[11] who quickly returns him to Pilate (23:6–11).[12]

Pilate, finding Jesus innocent, refuses the religious leaders' demand to have him killed. "I will therefore have him flogged and release him," Pilate determines (23:16). But "then they all [leaders and people] shouted out together, 'Away with this fellow! Release Barabbas for us!' (Barabbas had been put in prison for insurrection and murder.) Pilate, wanting to release Jesus, addressed them again; but they kept shouting, 'Crucify, crucify him!'" (23:18–21). After resisting their demands another time, Pilate finally concedes (23:22–25). Jesus is handed over for crucifixion. The vicious powers of Israel have successfully maneuvered the reluctant power of Rome into killing Jesus.

While Jesus hangs on the cross, the surrounding characters mock him with sarcastic calls to save himself. Some religious leaders challenge him similarly: if he is the Messiah of God, surely he can save himself (23:25). Roman soldiers chime in: "If you are the King of the Jews, save yourself!" (23:36–37). And finally, from a cross next to Jesus's, a criminal says, "Are you not the Messiah? Save yourself and us!" (23:39). But saving himself would involve the same sort of self-seeking and self-aggrandizing power exercised by the religious leaders and offered to him by Satan in the wilderness. Jesus willingly accepts the will of his Father—his suffering and death—for the good of the kingdom family.

Not everyone relishes Jesus's death. Some women follow Jesus to the site of his execution, "beating their breasts and wailing for him" (23:27). Later "the crowds who had gathered there for this [crucifixion] spectacle" return home, "beating their breasts" (23:48). While one of the two criminals hanging on crosses mocks Jesus, the other asks, "Do you not fear God?" (23:40). Unlike us, the latter says, Jesus is innocent: "We are getting what we deserve for our deeds, but this man has done nothing wrong" (23:40–41). When this contrite and god-fearing criminal asks for mercy—he asks to be remembered when Jesus comes into his kingdom—Jesus replies, "Today you will be with me in Paradise" (23:43).

As the dying Jesus hangs on the cross, darkness falls over the land, and the temple veil is torn in two. Then Jesus, dying, cries out in a loud voice, "Father, into your hands I commend my spirit" (23:44–46a). "Having said this," Luke tells us, "he breathed his last" (23:46b).

A Roman centurion praises God, proclaiming, "Certainly this man was innocent" (23:47).[13] The Roman is joined in his approbation by "a good and righteous man named Joseph, who, though a member of the council [of Jewish leaders], had not agreed to their [the Jewish leaders'] plan and action. He came from the Jewish town of Arimathea, and he was waiting expectantly for the kingdom of God" (23:50–51). He asks a Roman official for the body of Jesus, which he wraps in linen and lays in a tomb (23:52–53).[14]

Authority Determined: God Raises Jesus from Death (Luke 24:1–43)

On the third day after Jesus's death, some women, taking spices to the tomb, find it empty and hear from two men in dazzling clothes that Jesus has risen as foretold. When the three women plus others tell the men of Jesus's resurrection, the disciples think it just "an idle tale, and they [do] not believe them" (24:8–11). Peter, however, runs to the tomb, sees "the linen cloths by themselves," and then goes home, "amazed at what had happened" (24:1–12).

"On that same day" two men tell a stranger about their dashed hopes. This stranger—Jesus, as yet unrecognized—patiently explains, through Scripture, that God had promised to raise the suffering Messiah from death (24:25–27; for Luke, this is the definitive scriptural prophecy regarding Israel's coming Messiah: his being raised from death by God). When Jesus eats with them, they finally recognize him—as they later recount to the disciples—"in the breaking of the bread" together (24:35).

When the disciples later see Jesus, however, they are terrified, thinking him a ghost. He asks them to touch and see; then he eats some pieces of fish: Jesus is definitely not a ghost (24:36–43).

Last Words (Luke 24:44–53)

Jesus needs to convey an important message to his followers before his departure from earth, reminding them of what he had told them about their immediate future: "I confer on you, just as my Father has conferred on me, a kingdom" (22:29). Now he gets more specific about their kingdom mission.

After proving that he is no ghost, Jesus offers these final words: "Thus it is written, that the Messiah is to suffer and to rise from the dead on the third day, and that repentance and forgiveness of sins is to be proclaimed in his name to all nations, beginning from Jerusalem. You are witnesses of these things. And see, I am sending upon you what my Father promised; so stay here in the city until you have been clothed with power from on high" (24:46–49). Jesus is reasserting his authority in terms of both teacher and teachings, but he is also asserting the authority of his disciples to take the good news of the kingdom to all peoples, empowered by God's Holy Spirit. They become "servant Israel" (1:54) to the world, the core leaders of the kingdom that appears in its nascent form in Acts. Jesus, God's "holy servant" (Acts 4:27, 30), is redeeming the faithful within Israel (Simeon's reference to the "rising"; Luke 2:34), transforming them into "servant Israel" to the world (Luke 1:54).

As the leaders of servant Israel, the disciples must include in their preaching and teaching these three points:

- Resurrection: as Scripture had foretold, Jesus overcame his suffering and death by rising from death;
- Repentance: change of heart, and its attending forgiveness of sins;
- Holy Spirit: the need for empowerment of God for kingdom entrance and witness.

As servant Israel to the world, the disciples have finally learned of their mission and message.

Conclusion

"Then he led them out as far as Bethany, and, lifting up his hands, he blessed them. While he was blessing them, he withdrew from them and was carried up into heaven. And they worshiped him, and returned to Jerusalem with great joy; and they were continually in the temple blessing God" (24:50–53). The disciples return to the temple, blessing God. What now? Luke's story is half finished. We are now prepared to hear Luke's story of the kingdom coming in the second part of Luke-Acts. Only in Acts will we see the promises of God's kingdom spreading to all peoples on earth fulfilled. But Acts is comprehensible only if its audiences first understand Luke's presentation of Jesus and his proclamation of the good news about the kingdom coming, about the things that make for peace.

PART FOUR

Luke-Acts, II:
The Acts of the Apostles

CHAPTER 18

"The Rising of Many in Israel" (Acts 1:1–3:26)

The Redemption of Israel

Luke tells his audience, in the very beginning of his two-volume narrative, that his purpose is to provide an orderly narrative of "the events that have been fulfilled among us" (Luke 1:1). One of these major events is the promised deliverance of Israel through its Messiah, Jesus, which is chronicled in Acts.

In Acts we find, for example, the fulfillment of Simeon's vision of "the rising of many in Israel" (Luke 2:34), of Mary's vision of God helping "his servant Israel" (Luke 1:38), and of Zechariah's claim that God is "rais[ing] up a mighty savior for [Israel]" (Luke 1:68–69). As Israel's Messiah, Jesus redeems Israel by distilling the law, sealing the covenant with his blood, and sending the Holy Spirit to empower those who seek to follow God's word.

The action in Acts is primarily the extraordinary spread of God's word (6:7) and the explosion of numbers of those within Israel embracing Jesus as their Messiah and turning to his teaching of "the way of God" (Luke 20:21; 9:51–19:44). This is the "rising of many in Israel" predicted by Simeon (Luke 2:34)—by the thousands upon thousands upon thousands (Acts 2:41; 4:4; 21:20).

As the Jesus movement takes off, his followers become known not by a name (in Acts they are called *Christians* twice but only derisively)[1] but by their way of life: they are those who belong to "the Way" (Acts 9:2), the way of God taught by Jesus. They have turned from their normal, selfish ways toward the "way of salvation" (16:17), "the way of peace" (Luke 1:79)—the communal flourishing and mutual sharing of God's kingdom come to earth (reported in Acts 2:41–47; 4:32–37).

His followers preach that Jesus's way is authorized by the resurrection, *God's raising Jesus from death*. Even more, the resurrected and ascended Jesus graciously sends the Holy Spirit to believers (Acts 2:33) to empower them for the very first time to follow this way of God that he taught. This is a key event "fulfilled among us," God's raising Israel's deliverer from death.

Jesus departs, the Spirit comes, and the redeemed of the Lord from within Israel fan out—from Jerusalem up through Asia Minor into Macedonia and Greece. While throughout Acts Israelites continue to repent in great numbers, the "falling" within Israel (predicted by Simeon in Luke 2:34) remain stubborn in their rejection of Jesus; with jealousy and zeal they attack his authoritative teaching as preached by the apostles. The falling within Israel are no longer part of true Israel; they are, Peter says, "rooted out of the people" (Acts 3:23). Luke sets the stage for the dramatic rise of God's kingdom in his brief preface.

Luke's Preface (Acts 1:1–11)

Luke begins with a reminder that in his first volume he "wrote about all that Jesus did and taught from the beginning until the day when he was taken up to heaven" (1:1–2). In the forty days between his resurrection and ascension, Luke writes, Jesus spent his time "speaking about the kingdom of God" (1:3)—the focal point of the first volume (Luke 4:43).

Jesus then informs his disciples of their coming empowerment through baptism "with the Holy Spirit" (Acts 1:5–8), which is necessary both for salvation and for their kingdom mission. For all believers, baptism enables faithfulness to the kingdom way. The kingdom mission will extend throughout Jerusalem, Judea, and Samaria to "the ends of the earth" (1:8). Luke concludes his prefatory note by reporting, as in Luke, on Jesus's being "lifted up" and into heaven (1:9–11; see Luke 24:51).

Peter's First Three Speeches (Acts 1:15–26; 2:14–39; 3:12–26)

Before the kingdom can become reality, two things are needed: the empowerment of the Holy Spirit and a twelfth apostle to complete the leadership of redeemed Israel (with Judas gone, there are only eleven).

As instructed by Jesus (Luke 24:49), some within Israel who have already turned to Jesus as their Messiah, about 120, have gathered to await the Holy Spirit's arrival (Acts 1:12–14). They are the nucleus of "servant Israel" to the world (Luke 1:54)—just as Jesus has been God's "holy servant" to Israel (Acts 4:27, 30).

In rapid succession we hear three speeches by Peter to Israel, each based on the word of God as taught by Jesus: first, to the one hundred-plus who have already risen within Israel; then to fellow Israelites and God-fearers[2] gathered for Pentecost from around the known world; and third, to the Israelites astonished at Peter's power in curing a lame man.

Peter's First Speech: To the New Leaders of Israel (Acts 1:15–26)

"In those days Peter stood up among the believers" (1:15). Peter's first speech focuses on the scriptures prophesying Judas's betrayal and demise (1:16–20).

Resurrection

Peter asserts the need for a replacement for Judas and sets some job requirements: Judas's replacement must be "one of the men who have accompanied us during all the time that the Lord Jesus went in and out among us," and most critically he "must [be] a witness with us to his resurrection" (1:21–22). Here is one of many reminders that the linchpin of salvation is God's raising Jesus from death, which both affirms his status as Messiah and authorizes his teaching of the way of God.

Peter sets up the choice by lot, with prayer, leading to the selection of Matthias. The disciples' authority as the new leaders of Israel—representing all twelve tribes—was commissioned by Jesus (Luke 22:30). These leaders will be most dramatically on view in a pivotal council meeting about "admitting" Gentiles into the kingdom (Acts 15).

Holy Spirit

Following the appointment of Matthias, Israel's leaders and dozens of other Jewish believers await the fulfillment of Jesus's promise of "power from on high" (Luke 24:49), the "promise of the Father," mentioned in Luke's preface to Acts: "John baptized with water, but you will be baptized with the Holy Spirit" (1:4–5).

On the day of Pentecost, the empowering Spirit of God descends as "divided tongues, as of fire, . . . a tongue rest[ing] on each of them" (2:3). This brilliant streaking light is accompanied by "the rush of a violent wind," the life breath of God—like the descent of the Spirit on Jesus in the form of a dove.[3]

Peter's Second Speech: To All of Israel (Acts 2:14–39)

The annual feast of Pentecost has drawn "devout Jews from every nation under heaven" (2:5)—all of Israel! Listening to the Spirit-filled disciples speak, these listeners from many nations are able to hear the disciples' words in their own languages, and each is therefore astonished that they can understand "them speaking about God's deeds of power" (2:11–12). Others, unimpressed by what they hear as a cacophony of noise, sneer and say, "They are filled with new wine" (2:13).

Peter begins and ends this speech speaking of the Holy Spirit. These people, he assures the mockers, are not drunk; they are filled with God's Spirit, as prophesied. Hearing cues that are shared in most of the subsequent speeches are: *resurrection*, the authoritative seal on Jesus as Teacher and Messiah; the need for the reorienting *repentance* that makes the kingdom possible; and the *Holy Spirit*, who empowers the turning around required for the salvation of kingdom entrance.

Resurrection/Authority

After citing Scripture about the coming of the Holy Spirit, the major portion of Peter's speech focuses on God's raising Jesus from death (2:22–35). Though you had Jesus "crucified and killed," Peter declares, "God raised him up" (2:23–24), as prophesied by David, who "spoke of the resurrection of the Messiah" (2:31).[4] By paying attention to what is repeated, as always with an orally derived text, we hear the importance of the resurrection to Acts.

Throughout Acts, God's raising up of Jesus from suffering and death is central to God's plan of salvation as the Scriptures foretold and as Jesus taught (Luke 24:45–46).[5] "Therefore," says Peter, "let the entire house of Israel know with certainty that God has made him both Lord and Messiah, this Jesus whom you crucified" (Acts 2:36). The resurrection certifies that Jesus authoritatively represents the true understanding of God's word.[6]

Repentance

After hearing of the resurrection, "They were cut to the heart and said to Peter and to the other apostles, 'Brothers, what should we do?'" (2:37)

The alert audience, having listened attentively to volume one, anticipates the answer: "Repent,"[7] he says. And "be baptized every one of you in the name of Jesus Christ so that your sins may be forgiven" (2:38a).

To be baptized *in the name of Jesus* requires repentance, a renunciation of one's former allegiances to self and family. One rises from the water of baptism facing in an entirely new direction, toward God's way of serving the needs of others under the lordship of Jesus. In Acts, "signs and wonders are performed through the name of [God's] holy servant Jesus" (4:30).

Holy Spirit

Commitment to the lordship of Jesus as Messiah brings with it the power to transform one's life and live within the kingdom: "You will receive the gift of the Holy Spirit," Peter concludes (2:38b), citing a key aspect of God's grace in Luke-Acts.[8]

The prophet Joel had said that God's Spirit would at some momentous point in history be poured out "upon all flesh" (Acts 2:16–21). That time, Peter asserts, is now. In the first manifestation of communal power, God's Spirit allows the various tongues to be unscrambled in the hearing process—a reversing of the tongue-scrambling curse on the builders of the tower of Babel (Gen. 11:9).

As Acts unfolds, we will find Peter and Paul crediting the Spirit with empowerment to work miracles, to speak boldly in the face of persecution, and, most importantly, to repent—by reorienting one's life from "wicked ways" (3:26) to God's "Way" (9:2, 18:25, 19:9, 24:14, 22). "Everyone who calls on the name of the Lord shall be saved," Peter concludes, quoting the prophet Joel (2:21).

"So those who welcomed his message were baptized, and that day about three thousand persons were added" (2:41).

The Kingdom Shown

Salvation, according to Peter, means being rescued from "this corrupt generation" (2:40) and acquiring the benefits of being part of a life-giving, life-enhancing community of like-minded believers.

The thousands of Jews who call on the name of the Lord (2:41) are empowered to enter into the kingdom: "All who believed were together and had all things in common; they would sell their possessions and goods and distribute the proceeds to all, as any had need" (2:44–45). Salvation, as Peter understands it, includes both freedom from sin and wholeness of life within a community of believers deeply committed to one another's well-being—a commitment marked most conspicuously and practically, as taught by Jesus, by relinquishing ownership of possessions and money for distribution according to need.

Peter's Third Speech: Again to the People of Israel (Acts 3:12–26)

Peter both speaks about and demonstrates the good news of the kingdom that we heard throughout Luke in the teaching and healing mission of Jesus (Luke 4:43). Likewise, following his major speech to all Israel, Peter illustrates the kingdom power vested in him and the other apostles by Jesus (Luke 9:1–2), as well as what kingdom workers do.

On their way to the temple, Peter and John encounter a lame man begging them for alms. "Peter looked intently at him, as did John, and said, 'Look at us'" (3:4). Had the beggar been reluctant to look up? Peter then says, "'I have no silver or gold, but what I have I give you; in the name of Jesus Christ of Nazareth, stand up and walk.' And he took him by the right hand and raised him up; and immediately his feet and ankles were made strong. Jumping up, he stood and began to walk, and he entered the temple with them, walking and leaping and praising God" (3:6–8). From weak to strong, from immobility to walking, from sorrow to praise: of such is the kingdom of God as shown in both Luke and Acts.

Peter's kindness releases the man from a debilitating ailment, for sure. But even more, the man is released from the oppressive poverty that such ailments carried in their wake, from the humiliation of begging for pennies—he could hardly look Peter and John in the eye—and from his culturally relegated status as outcast. Now walking and leaping and praising God, he enters the new kingdom in which people love radically and unconditionally and share mutually their hearts and lives. The incident prompts awe at Peter's powers, which he opposes in very strong words: *This is the work of the Holy Spirit!*

The Holy Spirit

Although the people are amazed by his healing of the lame man, Peter deflects their praise from himself. "Why do you stare at us, as though by our own power or piety we had made him walk?" he asks (3:12). He points away from himself to God, whose power has been manifested through the Holy Spirit: "By faith in his name [Jesus], his name itself has made this man strong, whom you see and know; and the faith that is through Jesus has given him this perfect health in the presence of all of you" (3:16). Power in the name *Jesus* is not a magician's trick; it comes through the Spirit sent by God almighty (2:33).

Resurrection/Authority

God's raising up of Jesus from suffering and death is the divine seal of authority on the lordship of Jesus. Jesus, first and foremost, *serves God*: "The God of Abraham," Peter goes on, "the God of Isaac, and the God of Jacob, the God of our ancestors has glorified *his servant Jesus*" (3:13). But, he continues, "you killed the Author of life, whom God raised from the dead" (3:15). Peter offers a scriptural affirmation of Jesus's authority: "Moses said, 'The Lord your God will raise up for you from your own people a prophet like me. You must listen to whatever he tells you. . . . Everyone who does not listen to that prophet will be utterly rooted out of the people'" (3:22–23).[9] Jesus, says Peter, is that prophet, God's uniquely authorized teacher. *Listen!*, then, Peter tells us, to what Jesus taught, the word of God that we now repeat to you.

Repentance

"And now, friends, I know that you acted in ignorance, as did also your rulers. . . . Repent therefore, and turn to God so that your sins may be wiped out" (3:17–19). Accepting the gospel brought by Jesus ("the good news of the kingdom of God") is an embrace of the Messiah that begins with repentance, as Peter concludes: "When God raised up his servant [Jesus], he sent him first to you, to bless you by turning each of you from your wicked ways" (3:26). Repentance is not mere renunciation: this *turning from wicked ways* is also a *turning toward kingdom ways*, the way of God. And forgiveness is granted for those who repent: "Repent therefore, and turn to God so that your sins may be wiped out."

Those who repent—"servant Israel" (Luke 1:54)—are to be a blessing for all the families of the earth: "You are the descendants of the prophets and of the covenant that God gave to your ancestors," Peter declares to his fellow Israelites, "saying to Abraham, 'And in your descendants all the families of the earth shall be blessed'" (Acts 3:25). Peter calls the coming reign of God, brought about by the repentance of Israel, a "universal restoration" (3:19–21)—a covenant whose blessing now includes the fulfilled promise to Abraham, that all peoples will experience God's blessing.[10]

Conclusion

"When God raised up his servant, he sent him first to you, to bless you by turning each of you from your wicked ways," Peter concludes (3:26). Immediately following we hear: "While Peter and John were speaking to the people, the priests, the captain of the temple, and the Sadducees came to them, much annoyed because they were teaching the people and proclaiming that in Jesus there is the resurrection of the dead. So they arrested them and put them in custody" (4:1–3). The narrative movement from these who are rising in Israel to the falling is abrupt, helping to emphasize the polarity of Israel's response to Jesus, spoken of by Simeon (Luke 2:34). These traditional religious powers are among the falling in Israel. But Luke makes sure that his audience hears the positive, that the rising far outnumber the falling: "Many of those who heard the word believed; and they numbered about five thousand" (Acts 4:4; this in addition to the prior three thousand in 2:41).

The thousands upon thousands rising within Israel belong to "the Way" (9:2)—not to an institution, but to a way of living foretold and taught by Jesus as God's *kingdom way*.[11] The relationship between Israel's redemption and the kingdom's coming is clarified by noting the cues revolving around "Way." Those within Israel being redeemed now belong to "the Way." In practical terms, they meet together for worship and prayer, in gatherings or assemblies, whenever and wherever followers of the Way gather together. Such gatherings are the kingdom in miniature, manifest in the sharing of meals, worship, and all possessions. This is the "way of salvation" (Acts 16:17) central to the early nine poems in Luke.[12]

"My eyes have seen your salvation," Simeon says, holding the infant Jesus in his arms, a redemption "which you [God] have prepared in the presence of all peoples, a light for revelation to the Gentiles and for glory to your people Israel" (Luke 2:25, 30–32). Peter sees this glory of Israel in the fulfillment of the covenantal promise in which Israel becomes "servant Israel" (Luke 1:54) to all the non-Jews of the world, the Gentiles (Acts 3:25). The restoration of Israel as "servant Israel" to the nations is essential to the kingdom's growth in Acts. With the addition of Matthias there are now twelve disciples again, the full complement of judges and guides of Israel and the emergent kingdom of God.

By the time Peter has finished his two major speeches to Israel (2:14–39; 3:12–26), thousands upon thousands have been added to the number of those rising within Israel (2:41; 4:4). Israel is being redeemed, and the kingdom, beginning with a restored Israel, is growing dramatically. The promised and once future kingdom, envisioned in Luke and preached by Peter, is now.

CHAPTER 19

"The Falling of Many in Israel" (Acts 4:1–7:60)

Unbelievers Rooted Out of Israel

In the first volume of Luke-Acts, Zechariah exclaims, "Blessed be the Lord God of Israel, for he has looked favorably on his people and redeemed them" (Luke 1:68). In Acts, the redeemed are measured in the thousands upon thousands upon thousands (2:41; 4:4; 21:20). But Peter, in his third speech to fellow Jews, quotes Moses, who said that anyone within Israel "who does not listen to that prophet [to come] will be utterly rooted out of the people" (3:23). Peter believes that "the prophet" is Jesus, who Simeon predicted would be the cause of "the falling and rising of many in Israel" (Luke 2:34). Those *falling* will be, Peters warns, rooted out.

Rooted out, maybe, but not without a fight: "They [the Jewish leaders] will arrest you and persecute you," Jesus had warned; "they will hand you over to synagogues and prisons, and you will be brought before kings and governors because of my name" (Luke 21:12). Jesus and his apostles have parallel experiences of hostility from traditional Jewish leaders. The spread of God's word as taught and demonstrated by Jesus and his apostles and the rapid growth of a revitalized Israel as the nascent kingdom of God on earth result in arrests and interrogations, jailing and persecution, and even death.

Luke clusters four speeches by believers to, or about, the oppressive leaders within Israel. Each is responding to specific hostilities.

First Speech	Peter (his fourth)	4:8–12
Second Speech	All twelve	4:24–30
Third Speech	All twelve	5:29–32
Fourth Speech	Stephen	7:1–53

In all four addresses, God's raising Jesus from death is cited to establish the authority of Jesus—and his followers—in their interpretation of God's word and the gospel of God's coming kingdom. In both Luke and Acts, it's the resurrection, not the death, that is featured—God's authorization of Jesus as Israel's Messiah and authority is based on God's raising Jesus from his unjust death. Jesus is Israel's new teacher, replacing Moses while also providing an exodus, not from the land of a foreign power to a promised land, but from the power of sin to God's kingdom on earth.

First Speech: Peter, to Israel's Traditional Leadership (Acts 4:8–12)

"Much annoyed because they were teaching the people and proclaiming that in Jesus there is the resurrection of the dead," the religious leaders "arrested [Peter and John] and put them in custody" (4:2–3). It couldn't have helped matters that this "teaching" of the people had led to thousands forsaking Israel's traditional leaders to embrace Jesus and his followers. "By what power or by what name did you do this?" ask Annas and the high priestly family the next day (4:5–7).

Resurrection/Authority

In response to the question of their authority, Peter replies, "Rulers of the people and elders, . . . let it be known to all of you, and to all the people of Israel, that this [previously lame] man is standing before you in good health by the name of Jesus Christ of Nazareth, whom you crucified, whom God raised from the dead" (4:8–10).

Quoting the psalmist, Peter goes on to affirm Jesus's foundational role in the restoration of Israel: "This Jesus is 'the stone that was rejected by you, the builders; it has become the cornerstone'" (4:11; see Ps. 118:22). The cornerstone is a resurrected, living stone. I stand before you, Peter is saying, by the power and authority of Jesus Christ, *whom God raised from the dead.*

Repentance

"There is salvation in no one else," Peter goes on, "for there is no other name under heaven given among mortals by which we must be saved"

(4:12). Although Peter does not mention it explicitly, the audience would associate salvation with repentance, a complete turning away from normal cultural and religious ways, and toward the only name under heaven by which one can be saved, participating in the communal joy of God's kingdom come. The religious leaders have heard and seen the power that authorizes Jesus as God's messenger and the sole source of salvation, but they have not listened and repented.

The Holy Spirit

"When they bring you before the synagogues, the rulers, and the authorities," Jesus said to Peter and the twelve, "do not worry about how you are to defend yourselves or what you are to say; for the Holy Spirit will teach you at that very hour what you ought to say" (Luke 12:11–12).

Luke cites what Peter does not mention, that the Holy Spirit is empowering Peter to face the religious establishment: "Then Peter, filled with the Holy Spirit, said to them . . ." (Acts 4:8). Luke expands the theological point of resurrection power and authority to include the Holy Spirit, who gives the disciples the *power* to overcome their very legitimate fears and *authorizes* them and their message by showing their connection to Jesus. And so we read, "Now when [the Jewish authorities] saw the boldness of Peter and John and realized that they were uneducated and ordinary men, they were amazed and recognized them as companions of Jesus" (4:13). They ordered Peter and John "not to speak or teach at all in the name of Jesus" (4:18). The two leave, but not without a parting word: "Whether it is right in God's sight to listen to you rather than to God, you must judge; for we cannot keep from speaking about what we have seen and heard" (4:19–20). God's authority is vested in Jesus, exercised now by the disciples themselves.

Second Speech: The Twelve, Praying about Evil Leadership (Acts 4:24–30)

The new leaders of servant Israel are overjoyed when Peter and John are released from jail. Their natural response is to join their voices as one in praise and petition to God.

The Holy Spirit

"Sovereign Lord," the new leaders begin in unison,

> "who made the heaven and the earth, the sea, and everything in them,
> it is you who said by the Holy Spirit through our ancestor David, your
> servant:
>> 'Why did the Gentiles rage,
>>> and the peoples imagine vain things?
>> The kings of the earth took their stand,
>>> and the rulers have gathered together
>>> against the Lord and against his Messiah.'" (4:24–26)

The recently poured-out Holy Spirit has been active throughout Israel's history, which has come to a focal point: "For in this city, in fact, both Herod and Pontius Pilate, with the Gentiles and the peoples of Israel, gathered together against your holy servant Jesus, whom you anointed" (4:27). The new leaders both invoke and hope for the empowering Spirit who granted his divine power to God's servants at key points in history.

They will surely need that power to speak with boldness in the face of persecution and even death. "Grant to your servants to speak your word with all boldness," the twelve conclude, "while you stretch out your hand to heal, and signs and wonders are performed through the name of your holy servant Jesus" (4:29–30). In the minutiae of kingdom work—a lame man healed, an outcast invited in—God's power over all things and people is made manifest. The twelve—a mere twelve—will speak God's word with boldness; their hands, the healing hand of God, will perform "signs and wonders . . . through the name of your holy servant Jesus." So the word of God spreads and great numbers are added to the kingdom (6:7; 4:17; 10:37; 13:49).

After their prayer, the Holy Spirit is felt: "When they had prayed, the place in which they were gathered together was shaken; and they were all filled with the Holy Spirit and spoke the word of God with boldness" (4:31). Even the room in which they pray cannot keep itself still. Such hearing cues as *Holy Spirit* would take on the power of a repeated refrain in a choral symphony, the reader's voice hushed for emphasis: *the place in which they were gathered together was shaken.*

Immediately following this powerful prayer spoken in one voice to a miniature of the kingdom, we hear of a wide-lens picture of the kingdom.

Luke offers another detailed view of the kingdom, nearly identical to his earlier one (2:43–47): "Now the whole group of those who believed were of one heart and soul, and no one claimed private ownership of any possessions, but everything they owned was held in common. With great power the apostles gave their testimony to the resurrection of the Lord Jesus, and great grace was upon them all. There was not a needy person among them, for as many as owned lands or houses sold them and brought the proceeds of what was sold" (4:32–34). Luke has structured the teaching of Jesus, for example, to emphasize in parallel sequences the relinquishment of—the liberation from—the tyranny of possessions and money as part of the striving required for entering the kingdom (Luke 12:13–34; 16:1–31). What in volume one may have made little sense in the abstract gets played out in Acts in astonishingly concrete terms. In this modest assembly in the kingdom, Luke offers a paradigm of the kingdom come.

In the two-volume Gospel according to Luke, the "good news" of God's kingdom growing on earth involves a radical orientation of the will from self toward God and God's people. In God's kingdom, everyone serves and is served, with possessions shared in common and distributed according to need—so that everyone enjoys *shalom*, a communal enjoyment of justice and mercy in which all needs are anticipated and met. Everyone pools all their resources, including material goods, and the collected resources are distributed "to each as any [has] need" (4:35). The core of kingdom good news that Jesus taught is lived out by the believers in Acts.

Luke offers his first glimpse of kingdom living with the information that "about three thousand persons were added" to those comprising redeemed Israel, servant Israel (2:41), and that "day by day the Lord added to their number those who were being saved" (2:47). And just before the healing of the lame man and subsequent prayer of the twelve, we are told that "many of those who heard the word believed; and they numbered about five thousand" (4:4).

The thousands of believers within Israel live the kingdom way—a total commitment to a radically reoriented, mutually compassionating life. When Ananias and Sapphira, who belong to this Way, lie about holding back some of the proceeds from selling their house, they are struck dead (5:1–10). From Ananias and Sapphira we learn that kingdom salvation is lost by "put[ting] the Spirit of the Lord to the test" (5:9). After this incident the assembled believers are seized by a "great fear" (5:11): following the Way requires an utter purity of heart. The kingdom, as presented in Acts, is joyous but serious business.

The word continues spreading, along with its power manifested and authority demonstrated in continued healings and liberations ("signs and wonders" repeatedly: 2:22, 43; 4:30; 5:12; 6:8; 14:3; 15:12). As news of the word and its authorizing power spreads, "more than ever believers [are] added to the Lord, great numbers of both men and women" (5:14).

Third Speech: The Twelve Speak to Israel's Evil Leaders (Acts 5:29–32)

While kingdom work proceeds apace, the attention generated by the apostles' signs and wonders creates predictable resentment. "Filled with jealousy," the high priest and Sadducees arrest the twelve, putting them in prison. An angel opens the prison doors at night, and the apostles escape, returning to the temple to teach (5:17–26). Once again, they are apprehended and brought before the religious council, where the high priest addresses them, saying, "We gave you strict orders not to teach in this name, yet here you have filled Jerusalem with your teaching" (5:27–28).

Resurrection/Authority

Peter responds, along with the other apostles: "We must obey God rather than any human authority" (5:29).

As we heard in their earlier speech to these false human authorities, Peter and John had similarly argued, "Whether it is right in God's sight to listen to you rather than to God, you must judge; for we cannot keep from speaking about what we have seen and heard" (4:19–20). We submit, they are saying in both speeches, to God's authority alone, which is found in Jesus Christ as attested to by God's raising him from death. "The God of our ancestors," the twelve continue, "raised up Jesus, whom you had killed" (5:30); not only raised from death but raised to glory, God "exalt[ing] him at his right hand as Leader and Savior" (5:31a).

Repentance

Jesus was raised and exalted by God so "that he [God] might give repentance to Israel and forgiveness of sins" (5:31b). Sitting at the hand of

Power, Jesus has been able to send the promised Holy Spirit (2:33) as grace extended by God for empowering the difficult and humanly impossible turning-around required by repentance (Luke 18:22–26). With daily repentance God forgives—forgiveness given because God is merciful.

The Holy Spirit

Through the empowering gift of the Holy Spirit, God *gives* repentance to Israel—covenant faithfulness is now possible through the enabling Spirit. "And we are witnesses to these things," the twelve continue to the established powers, "and so is the Holy Spirit whom God has given to those who obey him" (5:32). Believers seeking to obey are enabled to do so.

But, as we saw in Luke, the traditional leaders are jealous of this "upstart" power to the point of murder: "When they heard this, they were enraged and wanted to kill them" (5:33). What is "this" that so enrages the leaders of the Sanhedrin? Although not stated, it is implied that righteousness is possible only through the gift sent by Jesus, God's empowering Spirit (2:33). Not having availed themselves of the Spirit, the leaders realize that *their* righteousness is thereby declared inadequate, and demonstrably so. Their rage at being declared disobedient to God turns murderous. After Gamaliel urges caution, the twelve are let off with a flogging (5:33–39). And yet "every day in the temple and at home they did not cease to teach and proclaim Jesus as the Messiah" (5:42).

As redeemed Israel continues its remarkable growth as servant Israel (disciples "increasing in number" [6:1a]), Israel's new leaders face increasingly challenging issues—from within. "Widows were being neglected," for example; and so "the twelve called together the whole community of the disciples and said, 'It is not right that we should neglect the word of God in order to wait on tables'" (6:1b–2). While kingdom reality elicits fierce opposition from external power structures, the communal expansion of God's kingdom also has its own growing pains.

So the entire community chooses Stephen and six others (6:5–6). "The word of God continued to spread," we hear next, and "the number of the disciples increased greatly in Jerusalem, and a great many of the priests became obedient to the faith" (6:7). Then, back to Stephen: "Full of grace and power, [he] did great wonders and signs among the people" (6:8). Opponents "could not withstand the wisdom and the Spirit with which he spoke" (6:10). We come to a speech to his fellow Jews that will cost Stephen his life.

Fourth Speech: Stephen, to Israel's Evil Leaders (Acts 7:1–53)

Under false charges, Stephen is brought before the religious council. Facing death, he is radiant: "All who sat in the council looked intently at him, and they saw that his face was like the face of an angel" (6:15).

Stephen is charged with blasphemy against Moses and against God, and for speaking against the temple and against Mosaic law: "For we have heard him say that this Jesus of Nazareth will destroy this place and will change the customs that Moses handed on to us" (6:14). The high priest asks, "Are these things so?" (7:1).

The speeches and the speech-oriented action of Acts build to the extraordinary speech of Stephen, a speech powerful enough to get him killed.

"Brothers and fathers, listen to me," Stephen begins (7:2). His eyes blazing, Stephen offers an overview of God's presence with the patriarchs as backdrop to the pouring out of the Spirit, focusing on the charges against him involving Moses, affirming the greatness of this patriarch and his "living oracles" offered to Israel. He situates Moses within a context of other patriarchs who, like Moses, journeyed from their homeland, experiencing the presence of God always with them—anticipating every believer's empowerment by the continuing presence of God, the Holy Spirit.

Abraham

"The God of glory appeared to our ancestor Abraham when he was in Mesopotamia, before he lived in Haran, and said to him, 'Leave your country and your relatives and go to the land that I will show you'" (7:2-3).

While the audience would have known that Abraham left the land of his people for a place to be revealed by God, Stephen emphasizes God's continual presence alongside Abraham during the journey. God, likewise, was present with Israel when they were "resident aliens in a country belonging to others" (7:6). "And so Abraham became the father of . . . the twelve patriarchs" (7:8).

Joseph

"The patriarchs, jealous of Joseph, sold him into Egypt; but God was with him" (7:9). Stripped of his family and religious/tribal connections, Joseph ended up in prison, *but*—and here is the main thread of Stephen's speech—*God was with him.*[1]

The implication of the traditional leaders is hard to miss: like Joseph, the apostles, held "in high esteem" by the people, had been thrown in prison by the traditional leaders, "being filled with jealousy" (5:12–18). God's presence with Joseph empowered his rise to leadership. In his rise, like Jesus, Joseph won favor and showed wisdom (7:10; Luke 2:52: "Jesus increased in wisdom . . . and in divine and human favor"). God was with Joseph. Just as God was with Joseph—through the Holy Spirit—God was with Jesus when the same Holy Spirit descended on him like a dove. (Many of the hearing cues in Acts, as in Stephen's speech, are intertextual, alluding to the Hebrew Scriptures and the parallel experience of patriarchs with those of Jesus and his followers.)

The significant difference between then and now, Acts demonstrates, is that the Holy Spirit empowers all believers, not just leaders like Abraham, Joseph, and Moses. As Joel prophesied—and Peter has affirmed—God will "pour out [his] Spirit" on each and every individual believer (Acts 2:16–18). As such, the covenant for which Jesus pours out his blood, at least in part, is "new."

Moses

Stephen concludes with Moses, the penultimate word-bearer of Israel and precursor to Jesus.[2]

Like Abraham and Joseph, Moses journeyed—always accompanied by the presence of God. Moses, Stephen notes, fled from his birthplace in Egypt to Midian, where he settled as an alien. Moses returned to Egypt to lead Israel out into the desert for forty years.[3] God was present with Moses, an alien in Midian and a wanderer in the wilderness. He experienced God's presence in a burning bush, on "holy ground" (7:30).[4]

Moses was sent back to Egypt to lead the people out of slavery, and he performed "wonders and signs in Egypt, at the Red Sea, and in the wilderness for forty years"—yet "our ancestors were unwilling to obey him; instead, they pushed him aside, and in their hearts they turned back to Egypt" (7:36, 39). But God gave them "the tent of testimony," and Solomon built the temple, a house for God. "Yet the Most High does not dwell in houses made with human hands" (7:44–48). The Creator of heaven and earth is too great to be housed in a tent, or a temple, or a city. Stephen is clearly denouncing the traditional leaders and their infidelity to the covenant and their temple and their city—houses made with human hands. They have repeatedly resisted the Holy Spirit and killed the Messiah. He ends his speech sharply: "You stiff-necked people. . . . You are the ones that received the law as ordained by angels, and yet you have not kept it" (7:51, 53).

With Stephen's finger firmly pointed at them, "they became enraged and ground their teeth at Stephen. But filled with the Holy Spirit, he gazed into heaven and saw the glory of God and Jesus standing at the right hand of God" (7:54–55). Stephen had begun by asking these fellow Jews to listen, but now "they covered their ears" (7:57).

As they stone him to death, Stephen, like Jesus, asks God not to hold the sins of his killers against them (7:58–60).

"And Saul approved of their killing [Stephen]" (8:1a). Stephen would not be alone in suffering for following Jesus. "That day," the text continues, "a severe persecution began against the assembly of believers in Jerusalem, and all except the apostles were scattered throughout the countryside of Judea and Samaria" (8:1b). Saul, who would later be known as the apostle Paul, author of nearly half of the New Testament, is at this point in his life "ravaging different gatherings of believers[5] by entering house after house," dragging them off to prison (8:3). His turning away from such darkness toward the light and joy of God's rule is such a wondrous repentance that Luke repeats the experience three times.

Conclusion

The persecution following Stephen's stoning would have a remarkable effect on spreading the gospel: "Now those who were scattered because of the persecution that took place over Stephen," we hear later, "traveled as far as Phoenicia, Cyprus, and Antioch, and they spoke the word to no one except Jews," focusing on the continued success of bringing Israelites to an embrace of their Messiah (11:19). And God was with them, as with Abraham, Joseph, and Moses.

While the rising within Israel increases, those falling become increasingly envious, embittered, and murderous. In their struggles with the religious establishment, the believers demonstrate part of what Jesus meant in saying that it takes striving to enter God's kingdom (Luke 13:24), a willingness to bear one's cross on behalf of this kingdom (Luke 9:23).

The twelve have spoken, in one voice, to their opposition and then to God about the power of God and God's Messiah to Israel. Stephen concludes these successive speeches with opposition to the religious establishment on their own terms, the Mosaic law and patriarchs; he exposes their inauthentic allegiance to the covenant of their ancestors. God was present then, Stephen says, just as God is present now through the Holy Spirit; and just as Israel resisted God back then, so too the leaders are resisting God's Spirit now.

Luke's clustering of these four speeches, in the face of adversity, manifests Jesus's hopes for a clear witness to the gospel of God's kingdom (Luke 24:44–49). When met with sword and stones by the unfaithful and vicious leaders, the twelve, empowered by God's Spirit, respond in speech and with grace.

Gentiles Welcomed: "Anyone Who Fears Him and Does What Is Right" (Acts 8:1–15:21)

Allowing Gentiles into the Kingdom

We have heard Peter speak of unbelieving Jews being "rooted out of the people" of Israel, lost to the kingdom (3:23). Now we hear of those outside of Israel being allowed in—but not without a lot of fuss and consternation.

Following the death of Stephen, Peter repents of his rejection of Gentiles and Paul repents of his persecution of followers of the Messiah. In effect, Paul repents of his entire life. Their turnarounds are drastic, with astounding consequences for the growth of God's kingdom. We focus here on the four clustered speeches to or about the godly Gentiles who are turning to Israel's Messiah—three by Peter and one by Israel's new leader of the apostles, James.

Paul appears in this narrative flow dominated by Peter and his outreach to Gentiles, emphasizing the unity of their missions to both Jews and Gentiles. Peter had alluded to Israel's role as "servant" to Gentiles in his reaffirmation of the covenant with Abraham—that through Abraham's seed God would bless *all* peoples on earth (Acts 3:25; Gen. 12:1–3). Jewish believers become, as Paul will put it, a "light both to our people and to the Gentiles" (26:23).

The action of this sequence in chapters 8–15 is oriented, as always in Acts, around speeches—four major speeches addressed to Gentiles, or to Jewish believers about Gentiles being "allowed in" as full members of God's kingdom on earth.

Between Stephen's Speech and Peter's Speech to Gentiles

Ironically, the killing of Stephen and subsequent persecution of followers of the Way propel the kingdom outward from Jerusalem and Samaria "to the ends of the earth," as promised by Jesus (Acts 1:8). Those believers "rising" in Israel "were scattered, [going] from place to place proclaiming the word" (8:4). Philip "went down to the city of Samaria and proclaimed the Messiah to them" (8:5).

A Non-Jew Baptized

Told by an angel to go south toward Gaza, Philip meets up with a court official of the Ethiopian queen (8:26–38). This official, a "God-fearer," has come to Jerusalem to worship and is returning home, reading the prophet Isaiah. When he asks Philip what it means, Philip "proclaim[s] to him the good news about Jesus." The official, a non-Jew, embraces Jesus and is baptized. The expansion of God's people to those beyond Israel has begun.

Paul's Repentance: An About-Face in Support of Jesus as Messiah (Acts 9:1–30)

Just after Stephen's death, Luke mentions a certain "Saul" who "approved of their killing him [Stephen]" (8:1). Philip's mission has taken him beyond Jerusalem. "Meanwhile Saul, still breathing threats and murder against the disciples of the Lord, went to the high priest and asked him for letters to the synagogues at Damascus, so that if he found any who belonged to the Way, men or women, he might bring them bound to Jerusalem" (9:1–2). Granted permission, Saul travels to Damascus where he encounters Jesus en route. Saul's extraordinary turnaround (recounted three times) will lead to the further spread of God's word beyond Jerusalem and to the ends of the earth. "Meanwhile," we hear again, "the assemblies of believers throughout Judea, Galilee, and Samaria had peace and [were] built up. Living in the fear of the Lord and in the comfort of the Holy Spirit, [they] increased in numbers" (9:31).

Peter's Repentance: About-Face Regarding the Gentiles

Peter's initial repentance, turning his life around from fisherman to follower of Jesus, requires constant reassessment and renewal. As with all of Jesus's followers, he must continually strive to turn from normal cultural ways to God's way. While Peter cites Genesis regarding God's covenantal promise to bless all peoples through Israel (Gen. 12:3; Acts 3:25), he himself, ironically, requires a confrontation with God to repent of his attitudes and actions regarding non-Jews.

We read, "In Caesarea there was a man named Cornelius, a centurion of the Italian Cohort. . . . He was a devout man who feared God with all his household; he gave alms generously to the people and prayed constantly to God" (10:1–2). In a vision, an angel tells Cornelius to seek out Peter—and he sends men immediately (10:3–8). At noon the next day, with Cornelius's men on the way, Peter, while praying, has a vision of food considered unclean by Jews—and is told to eat it. "By no means, Lord," says Peter, the good Jew. The voice repeats itself three times with the words "What God has made clean, you must not call profane" (10:15–16). And just as Peter three times denied knowing Jesus, in this vision he says three times, "By no means, Lord." But Peter will soon eat Gentile food with a Gentile family—an extraordinary breakthrough for servant Israel.

The men arrive and take Peter, with "some of the believers from Joppa," back to Cornelius (10:23). Upon arrival, Peter awkwardly acknowledges to Cornelius the impropriety of accepting the invitation, because "it is unlawful for a Jew to associate with or to visit a Gentile" (10:28a). But, he hurries on, "God has shown me that I should not call anyone profane or unclean. So when I was sent for, I came without objection" (10:28b–29). Then Cornelius, a Gentile working for despised Rome, asks Peter, a Jew and follower of Jesus, to tell "all that the Lord has commanded [him] to say" (10:33).

Four Speeches Concerning the Gentiles

Both Peter and Cornelius have visions of what might otherwise might be shocking or abhorrent. Peter has learned something startling about the God whose kingdom he serves.

First Speech: Peter Speaks to Cornelius and His Family (Acts 10:34–43)

Peter's first speech, to Cornelius and his family, expands on Jesus's authoritative vision of the kingdom: empowered by the Holy Spirit, the kingdom's radically reoriented believers will live and breathe God's message of peace to all peoples.

An Impartial God

Peter begins his speech to Cornelius and his family by announcing a new perspective: "God shows no partiality." Moreover, he has been made aware that "in every nation anyone who fears him and does what is right is acceptable to him" (10:34–35). Peter goes on to articulate a main thematic focus of Luke-Acts: "You know," he says to his Gentile audience, "the message he sent to the people of Israel, preaching peace by Jesus Christ—he is Lord of all" (10:36). We hear echoes of earlier cues: Zechariah's note of the light for those in darkness, guiding their feet "into *the way of peace*" (Luke 1:79; see also Luke 2:14; 10:5–6; 19:42). In God's kingdom, Gentile and Jew alike live together in strife-free, mutually satisfying harmony. This is the message, Peter says: peace among all peoples through Jesus.

Resurrection/Authority

Peter goes on: "They put him to death by hanging him on a tree; but God raised him on the third day" (10:39–40).

God's raising of Jesus from death is God's seal of approval on the new leader of Israel and the one who is judge of all, both Jew and Gentile. "He commanded us," Peter points out, "to preach to the people and to testify that he is the one ordained by God as judge of the living and the dead" (10:42). The resurrection of Jesus vouchsafes his sole authority to teach the word of God and to be the judge of all people. Paul, in his sole speech to the Gentiles, will make this same point.[1]

Repentance, Forgiveness

"All the prophets testify about him," Peter continues, "that everyone who believes in him receives forgiveness of sins through his name" (10:43).

Believing in Jesus, we have seen, requires a turnaround *from* following ways of individual and tribal interests and *to* the way of God taught by Jesus. Such a reorientation of one's entire life is required, Jesus has said, to enter the kingdom's salvation and gain forgiveness of sins (Luke 13:24–30).

The Holy Spirit

As the speech ends, something remarkable happens: "While Peter was still speaking, the Holy Spirit fell upon all who heard the word. The circumcised believers who had come with Peter were astounded that the gift of the Holy Spirit had been poured out even on the Gentiles" (10:44–45).

Jesus, John had promised, "will baptize you with the Holy Spirit and fire" (Luke 3:16). But, given their reaction, it is clear that the circumcised believers, the Jews, thought God's greatest gift, the Holy Spirit, was reserved for them. God shows them, and Luke shows his audience, God's impartial love by dramatically opening up the kingdom at this very moment to Gentiles. The kingdom of God is both renewed—as Peter and his cohort are made to realize God's impartial love—and expanded as it is graciously opened up to non-Jews such as Cornelius and his family.

The concluding sentence sums up kingdom life: "Then they invited him to stay for several days" (10:48)—Jew and Gentile eating together, sleeping under the same roof, gathering for fellowship around the Lord and his teachings, and sharing with those in need.

Second Speech: Peter to Servant Israel, Urging Repentance Regarding Gentiles (Acts 11:1–17)

When "the apostles and the believers" hear that "the Gentiles [have] also accepted the word of God," they are concerned. "The circumcised believers" criticize Peter, saying, "Why did you go to uncircumcised men and eat with them?" (11:1–3).

Peter's speech continues to orient the action of Acts while also offering the meaning of the action: God's grace is expansive and inclusive. Peter begins "to explain it to them, step by step" (11:4). His story begins with a recounting of his vision, a sheet coming down from heaven with "unclean" animals accompanied by a voice saying, *kill, eat.* "But I replied," Peter tells his fellow believers, "'By no means, Lord; for nothing profane or unclean has ever entered my mouth'" (11:5–8). He recounts the story of Cornelius and his family to the other leaders of Israel. Peter's personal story speaks honestly of his transformation from unwillingness and resistance and reluctance to, through the power of the Holy Spirit, acceptance and sharing of God's grace. We will observe a key point in Peter's speech to his fellow leaders: *make no distinction between them and us.*

The Holy Spirit

Peter's reluctant transformation from Gentile-excluder to Gentile-includer is attributed to the empowering Spirit: "The Spirit told me to go with [Cornelius's messengers] and not to make a distinction between them and us" (11:12), which goes against the human grain. The Spirit that transformed Peter was also the Spirit at work in these Gentiles. "As I began to speak" to these God-fearing Gentiles, Peter reports, "the Holy Spirit fell upon them just as it had upon us at the beginning. And I remembered the word of the Lord, how he had said, 'John baptized with water, but you will be baptized with the Holy Spirit.'" Peter could scarcely resist God's logic: "If then God gave them the same gift that he gave us when we believed in the Lord Jesus Christ, who was I that I could hinder God?" (11:15–17).

Repentance

Although the new leaders of Israel initially are "silenced" by Peter's words, they quickly marvel at the extent of God's grace: "They praised God, saying, 'Then God has given even to the Gentiles the repentance that leads to life'" (11:18). Many of Peter's fellow Jews have been persuaded, turning around from deeply held biases to the new way of inclusivity, of allegiance to an impartial God.

While manifestations of the kingdom's impartial and inclusive compassion are accompanied throughout Acts by praise and joy, "the Gentile problem" persists. While Peter realizes that believing non-Jews are included among the people of God, other Jewish believers are not so sure. In his last of seven speeches, Peter will address a problem that could thwart the emerging kingdom: the circumcision of Gentile male believers—the most significant religious and clan marker within Israel.

We hear of "those who were scattered because of the persecution that took place over Stephen"; they traveled "as far as Phoenicia, Cyprus, and Antioch, and they spoke the word to no one except Jews" (11:19). Some of them "spoke to the Hellenists [Greek Gentiles[2]] also, proclaiming the Lord Jesus" (11:20). Gentiles are again hearing the word of God and entering into the kingdom.

Paul, who has joined those whom he had persecuted, is now being persecuted himself by the traditional Jewish religious establishment. After his first speech, he is stoned by them, dragged out of the city, and left for dead (14:19). But he recovers and moves on to other cities, ending up in Antioch. ("It is through many persecutions that we must enter the kingdom of God," Paul reminds the many disciples in Iconium and Antioch [14:22].) After more traveling, Paul and Barnabas return to Antioch where they first encounter the controversy about the status of uncircumcised Gentile believers. "Certain individuals came down from Judea and were teaching the brothers, 'Unless you are circumcised according to the custom of Moses, you cannot be saved'" (15:1). Because of the dissension between these Jewish believers and Paul, Paul and Barnabas and some others are appointed to go to Jerusalem to discuss the matter with the new leaders of Israel; they are heartily welcomed (15:2–5).

Some believers belonging to the sect of the Pharisees stand up and say, "It is necessary for them to be circumcised and ordered to keep the law of Moses" (15:5). These Israelites, Pharisees who, like Paul, have turned to Jesus as their Messiah, speak with conviction. After lengthy debate, Peter stands up and speaks to them (15:7a).

Third Speech: Peter Speaks Again about Becoming Servant Israel to Gentiles (Acts 15:7–11)

"My brothers," Peter begins, addressing his Jewish family, "you know that in the early days God made a choice among you, that I should be the one through whom the Gentiles would hear the message of the good news and become believers" (15:7b).

Hearing cues often come in discordant echoes. We have already heard of God's appointment of *Paul* as "an instrument whom I have chosen to bring my name before Gentiles and kings and before the people of Israel" (9:15). But here Peter claims that God has chosen *him* to proclaim the good news to the Gentiles. Paul's story, recall, is inserted within this predominantly Peter-centered narrative in order to highlight the two-as-one, twin missioners in the greater story of servant Israel's role in the world (as a "light both to our people and to the Gentiles" [26:23]). Peter and Paul, here, are identified as one, acting in accord with God's goal to bring blessing to all peoples through servant Israel (Gen. 12:3; Acts 3:25).

The Holy Spirit

The proof that Gentile believers are fully included in the kingdom, Peter asserts, is God's "giving them the Holy Spirit, just as he did to us" (15:8). The *giving of the Holy Spirit*, echoing the just-prior "gift of the Holy Spirit," affirms God's largesse to Gentile believers (10:45). Hearing cue within hearing cues: the best gift one can request of God, Jesus said in his first theme statement about prayer, is the Holy Spirit (Luke 11:13), given now to Jew and Gentile alike.

Make No Distinction

We have already heard of the kingdom breakthrough regarding Gentiles, that all followers are one family. "The Spirit told me to go with them," Peter has told his brothers about visiting Cornelius and his family, "and *not to make a distinction between them and us*" (11:12).

   Again we hear the same words: "In cleansing their hearts by faith," Peter says about the Gentile followers, "[God] *has made no distinction between them and us*" (15:9). Just as we have been given God's Holy Spirit, Peter says, so have they (15:8). Just as our hearts have been turned around by the power of the Spirit, so too theirs. The communal life of God's kingdom come is a family like no other earthly family, tribe, or empire: with one heart and mind, the good of God's kingdom family is impartially implemented.

No Additional Yoke

Let us not test God, Peter concludes, by imposing "a yoke that neither our ancestors nor we have been able to bear" (15:10).

   Peter and Jews like him "could not be expected to know or practice all the details of legal tradition," the minutiae of rules added to the essential law for identification as a Jew in good standing.[3] Such codes would prove onerous in the light of God's growing rule on earth. God has given Gentiles the Holy Spirit and cleansed their hearts, not by their practice of purity code rituals, the detailed commandments and prohibitions so difficult to fulfill, but by their embrace of Jesus as Lord and Teacher of the distilled law (15:8–9).

There can be now "no distinction between them and us" in terms of religious purity and acceptability before God (15:9). "Woe also to you [religious] lawyers," Jesus said on this same point, "for you load people with burdens hard to bear, and you yourselves do not lift a finger to ease them" (11:46).

The Grace of Our Lord Jesus

We are one communion of people on a level playing field before God, Peter suggests, with "no distinction between them and us," since "we believe that we will be saved through the grace of the Lord Jesus, just as they will" (15:11).

Such "grace of the Lord Jesus," according to Peter and the other believers in Acts, is twofold: (1) Jesus as God's Teacher of the law and the coming of the kingdom; and (2) Jesus as the one to send God's gift of the Holy Spirit to empower those striving after faithfulness in God's kingdom (Acts 2:33; Luke 13:24; 18:26–27). Gentiles, Peter argues, have the same access to God's grace and kingdom *shalom* that Israel has. *We will (all) be saved through the grace of the Lord Jesus.* At these concluding words, "the whole assembly [keep] silence" as Paul and Barnabas describe the "wonders God had done through them among the Gentiles" (15:12).

Fourth Speech: James—"We Should Not Trouble Those Gentiles Who Are Turning to God" (Acts 15:13–21)

Peter's speech has been a plea to his fellow Jewish believers, including Pharisees, on behalf of Gentiles turning to God. All eyes turn to James, the decision-maker of Israel's new leadership (12:19). He offers the final decision on the debate concerning whether or not non-Jews can be full and equal members of the restored people of God.

James is keen to show that Peter and Paul's theological insights are nothing new. Indeed, they are rooted in the deepest understanding of God's purposes as revealed in Holy Scripture. "My brothers, listen to me. Simeon has related how God first looked favorably on the Gentiles, to take from among them a people for his name. This agrees with the words of the prophets."[4] He then quotes from Amos:

"After this I will return
and I will rebuild the dwelling of David, which has fallen;
    from its ruins I will rebuild it,
    and I will set it up,
so that all other peoples may seek the Lord—
    even all the Gentiles over whom my name has been called."
        (15:16–17; quoting Amos 9:11–12)

James's citing of "the prophets" provides an authoritative theological context for understanding the role of restored Israel as "servant Israel" to the peoples of the world.

God will rebuild and restore "David's fallen tent" so that *all* of humanity may seek the Lord—*even Gentiles*. This, we can be assured, is the word of God, "who has been making these things known from long ago" (15:16–18). God not only *says* these things but is *doing* them as well. Peter and Paul don't offer a new theology of inclusion; they are in line with God's gracious plan from the very beginning. Israel may be God's chosen, but they were chosen for a reason—to share God's grace with the world (Gen. 12:3; Acts 3:25).

James goes on to reject any conditions for entry into the kingdom: "Therefore I have reached the decision that we should not trouble those Gentiles who are turning to God [with circumcision, for example], but we should write to them to abstain only from things polluted by idols and from fornication and from whatever has been strangled and from blood" (15:19–20). James's ruling is in the spirit of Peter's rejection of a deadly reliance on the law imposed as "a yoke that neither our ancestors nor we have been able to bear" (15:10). We heard it in Luke: "Woe also to you [religious] lawyers! For you load people with burdens hard to bear, and you yourselves do not lift a finger to ease them" (11:46). Acts represents the resolution to problems of law viewed as restrictive codes—shown to be a burden on the people in Luke. Here indeed is "the year of the Lord's favor" Jesus came to inaugurate (Luke 4:18–19), a turning upside down of the entire world order.

Conclusion: The World Turned Upside Down

In their momentous decision to include Gentiles in the kingdom without circumcision, the new leaders have truly and deeply repented of their initial tribalism and legalism. The transformations from tribe to all humanity and from law-as-rules to law-as-liberation are of monumental importance in Acts. In fully grasping God's message of inclusive and expansive grace spoken to prophets like Amos, followers like Peter, Stephen, Cornelius, James, and Paul are guilty as charged of "turning the world upside down" (Acts 17:6).

Israel's open arms make possible the kingdom's worldwide realization. Acts opens with Jesus teaching forty days about the kingdom (1:3) and closes with Paul teaching about the Lord Jesus Christ and the kingdom for two years (28:31). Jesus's and Paul's teachings about the kingdom constitute the frame for the entire second volume.

This kingdom does not remain the small Jewish sect of its infancy; its boundaries grow to include all peoples. What Peter proclaimed about the covenant with Abraham is coming true: Israel is fulfilling the divine dream, God's will that all peoples share in the blessing of God's salvation, through Israel (Gen. 12:1–3; Acts 3:25). Peter's speeches chronicle his journey toward understanding the inclusive and impartial will of God. He returns to his fellow Jewish leaders to persuade them to journey with him to the Gentiles. His spiritual journey is a microcosm of Israel's journey as "servant Israel" (Luke 1:54).

Mission accomplished at the gathering of servant Israel's leadership regarding the Gentiles, Peter no longer plays an active role in the narrative. The story shifts to Paul, but with clear echoes back to Peter. Carefully patterned hearing cues indicate parallels between Peter and Paul in both action and word. Luke's purpose emerges as a focus on redeemed Israel, those many "rising" to woo fellow Jews and Gentiles. It is important for Luke that we catch the cues that link Peter and Paul as spiritual twins in their mission to Israel and, through servant Israel, to the world. What Jesus spoke of in Luke becomes reality in Acts: followers with his kingdom power ransom the lost, assisting their entrance into the kingdom.

CHAPTER 21

To Fellow Jews and to Greek Gentiles:
The Gospel according to Paul (Acts 13:15–41; 17:22–31)

Paul, Back to Peter, Then Paul Exclusively

Just before Peter's encounter with the Gentile Cornelius and his family, leading to their welcome into the kingdom family of God (chap. 10), we hear the first of three accounts of Paul's repentance (9:1–30), his turn to God's way from persecuting Jesus followers with a hoped-for rise in status among his religious peers.

After the council in Jerusalem and the decision by James that believing Gentiles should be allowed into God's kingdom without having to keep restrictive Jewish codes like circumcision, Paul offers his first of seven major speeches. It is one of only two speeches directed exclusively to fellow Jews.

Encountering Paul (then "Saul") in the middle of a lengthy narrative segment devoted to Peter (chaps. 10–15) might seem strange unless we consider two narrative factors. First, the immediate context of the spreading persecution following Stephen's murder highlights Saul as the great persecutor: "And there was Saul, approving of his destruction. And on that day a great persecution broke out against the assembly in Jerusalem. . . . Saul wreaked havoc upon the assembly, entering house after house, hauling off both men and women and delivering them to prison" (8:1–3). The spreading opposition and persecution surprisingly parallels the rapid spread of God's word and the emerging kingdom, "the number of disciples increas[ing] greatly," including some traditional leaders: "many of the priests became obedient to the faith" (6:7).

A second literary reason for interjecting Paul within the narrative focus on Peter is to emphasize the intertwined theologies of Peter and Paul. Just as Peter does and says nothing theologically contrary to Paul, so too Paul concurs with the theological perspective of Peter. Luke's orderly design underscores the unity of vision that inspires both Peter and Paul.[1]

This chapter focuses on Paul's first two speeches: the first of two speeches to an exclusively Jewish audience (13:15–41), and his only speech to an exclusively Gentile audience (17:22–31).

Peter and Paul, Twins

In word and action, Peter and Paul are presented by Luke as spiritual twins. Identical twins, nearly: each is chosen, for example, as *the* messenger to the Gentiles. And Peter and Paul share parallel action and speeches.

Twin Missioners to the Gentiles

It is almost as if Luke has made a literary mistake.

First there is Paul, the one chosen to serve the Gentiles. Concerning Paul, God says to Ananias, "Go, for he is an instrument whom I have chosen to bring my name before Gentiles and kings and before the people of Israel" (9:15). Later, Paul tells his fellow Jews the same about the Lord's commission: "The Lord has commanded us, saying, 'I have set you to be a light for the Gentiles, so that you may bring salvation to the ends of the earth'" (13:46–47).

Then there is Peter, the one chosen to serve the Gentiles. "After there had been much debate [among leaders of servant Israel], Peter stood up and said to them, 'My brothers, you know that in the early days God made a choice among you, that I should be the one through whom the Gentiles would hear the message of the good news and become believers'" (15:7).

But Luke is too skilled a literary craftsman to have made a mistake here. The two gospel bearers equally absorb the will of God throughout all the Scriptures—that Israel becomes a holy people to bring God's blessing to all peoples of the world (Gen 12:1–3; Acts 3:25). Beyond the overlap of major themes in their respective speeches we hear the echoing cues associating both Peter and Paul with Jesus.

Twins in Word and Deed

After the council decides to include believing Gentiles as full members of God's people (chap. 15), the narrative focuses on Paul. But Paul makes no advance on the meaning of the gospel proclaimed by Peter, who makes no advance on the gospel proclaimed by Jesus. In word and deed, Peter and Paul are similar.

The effect of such overlapping is to stress the commonality of mission and message: "the rising" of many within Israel will serve all peoples of the world, while "the falling" will be, in the words of Peter, "utterly rooted out of the people" of God (3:23). Other hearing cues link Peter and Paul as spiritual twins:

- Both Peter and Paul raise the dead (Peter, 9:36–41; Paul, 20:9–12).
- Both confront a magician (Peter, 8:14–24; Paul, 13:6–12).
- Both heal a lame man (Peter, 3:2–10; Paul, 14:8–10).
- Both fend off praise after healings (Peter, 3:11–12; Paul, 14:8–18).
- Both first and foremost address their fellow Israelites (Peter, 1:15–25; 2:14–39; Paul, 13:16–41).
- Both lead many fellow Israelites to their Messiah (Peter and Cornelius; Paul throughout his mission).

Luke's listeners might well have picked up what the modern reader easily misses of the echoing between Jesus and one or both of the two apostles to the Gentiles:

- Jesus raises the dead, heals the lame, and proclaims the kingdom (the good news).
- People are called to respond to the message of the good news by repenting.
- Paul, like Jesus, takes a momentous journey to Jerusalem to face arrest and death.
- Jesus and the new leaders of Israel confront the violence of the established religious authorities.
- Jesus and Paul suffer unjust deaths when Jewish leaders collude with Rome.

And there is more. When Jesus suffers an unjust death at the hands of Jewish leaders in collusion with Roman rulers, he asks his Father to forgive them since they do not know what they are doing (Luke 23:34);[2] when Stephen is dying after being stoned by Jewish leaders, he asks God not to hold their sin against them (Acts 7:60). Jesus comes to be God's "holy servant" to Israel (Acts 4:27, 30), while "the many rising in Israel" become "servant Israel" to the Gentiles (Acts 3:25).

Perhaps surprisingly, then, only one of Paul's seven speeches is to Gentiles. But in his seventh and final speech, which concludes Acts, Paul declares to his Jewish brothers and sisters that servant Israel will now focus on Gentiles (28:25–28). Let us consider, in order, Paul's speeches.

Paul's First Two Major Speeches, to Jews and to Gentiles (Acts 13:15–41; 17:22–31)

These two speeches cover the witness of Paul first to his Jewish family and then to non-Jews.

Emphasizing Paul's and Peter's intertwined missions, Paul's first speech occurs in the middle of Peter's mission to Cornelius and the Gentiles. Following the account of his momentous turnaround from opposing the way of God to joining it—Luke's prize example of repentance—Saul ("also known as Paul" [13:9]) and his companion Barnabas travel to Antioch, Syria, a seaport town in the northeast corner of the Mediterranean Sea.

"On the sabbath day [Paul and his companions] went into the synagogue and sat down" (13:13–14). "'Brothers,'" they are asked by the synagogue leaders, "'if you have any word of exhortation for the people, give it.' So Paul stood up and with a gesture began to speak" (13:15–16).

Paul's Major Speech, to Fellow Jews (Acts 13:15–41)

"You Israelites, and others who fear God,[3] listen," commands Paul (13:16). *Listen* and *hear* are key repeated words, going back to early Luke. At the most radical point of his countercultural message and mission, Jesus says, "I say to you that listen, Love your enemies, do good to those who hate you" (Luke 6:27). *Listen* is a command that signals the need for full attention. "Let anyone with ears to hear listen!" says Jesus about a key teaching (Luke 8:8); and again, "Pay attention to how you listen" (Luke 8:18). And God, quoted only once, says only one key word in describing the response to Jesus: "This is my Son, my Chosen," God says. "Listen to him!" (Luke 9:35). "My mother and my brothers," says Jesus, "are those who hear the word of God and do it" (Luke 8:21). Paul's challenge to listen carries the same message: *Hear the word of God and do it.*

Repentance

"Before his [Jesus's] coming," Paul declares, "John had already proclaimed a baptism of repentance to all the people of Israel" (13:24). Luke's audience would know this central term, *repentance*, as continual life-changing turns from sinful ways of normal life to God's kingdom way. Paul has offered a six-verse history of Israel (13:17–22) that stresses God's gifts of deliverance out of Egypt and in subsequent years through the means of judges, prophets, and King David, from whose line Israel's ultimate deliverer comes: the "Savior, Jesus, as he promised" (13:22–23). Jesus saves by teaching the way of God (Luke 20:21) and sending the Holy Spirit—fundamentals echoed over and over again. Jesus brings salvation, pointing to the way of repentance and liberation from sin's power.

Resurrection and Authority

On what basis does Luke think Jesus is the final word on the meaning of God's word? Throughout Acts, the answer is the resurrection. "We bring you the good news," Paul claims, "that what God promised to our ancestors he has fulfilled for us, their children, by raising Jesus" (13:32–33; the salvific work of Jesus, for Paul—and for Luke throughout his two volumes—is in the resurrection, not the cross). Here, with the help of Luke's careful selection and arrangement of hearing cues, Paul makes sure his point is heard:

- "They asked Pilate to have him killed. . . . They took him down from the tree and laid him in a tomb. *But God raised him from the dead*" (13:28–30).
- "We bring you the good news that what God promised to our ancestors he has fulfilled for us, their children, *by raising Jesus*" (13:32–33).
- "As to *his raising him from the dead*, no more to return to corruption . . ." (13:34).
- "Therefore [God] has also said . . . , 'You will not let your Holy One experience corruption [of death]'" (13:35).

- "David, after he had served the purpose of God in his own generation, died, was laid beside his ancestors, and experienced corruption; but *he whom God raised up experienced no corruption*" (13:36–37).

Paul's repeated reliance on God's raising Jesus from death underscores its centrality in God's plan of salvation for Israel, confirming both the power of God and the Son's appointment as Messiah and Teacher.

God used his power to make Israel prosper as slaves in Egypt. God used his power to liberate Israel from slavery. God used his power to conquer seven nations so that Israel might have land. God used his power to appoint judges and kings to rule on his behalf. But Israel repeatedly turned away from God. Paul's repeated insistence that God's power is fulfilled in raising Israel's Savior from death emphatically confirms Jesus's authoritative teaching of God's word and his power over sin: "Let it be known to you therefore, my brothers, that through this man forgiveness of sins is proclaimed to you; by this Jesus everyone who believes is set free from all those sins from which you could not be freed by the law of Moses" (13:38–39).

Repentance and Forgiveness

Before the coming of Jesus, John the Baptist had already proclaimed what Jesus would likewise proclaim—the forgiveness of sins conditioned on repentance (Luke 3:3, 8; 5:32; 13:3, 5; 15:7). But unlike John the Baptist, Jesus also offers the power to *set free* those who repent. These who follow Jesus, the Teacher replacing Moses (Luke 20:21, 28), are "set free from all those sins from which you could not be freed by the law of Moses" (13:39). Jesus liberates his followers from the power of sin through the Holy Spirit that empowers those repenting to follow Jesus and his kingdom teachings. Faithfulness to the covenantal relationship is finally possible through God's enabling Spirit.

Such liberation—being "set free" (*dikaioō*) from the power of sin—is through "the grace of God." Paul's speech is a continual reminder of God's gracious and faithful power on behalf of Israel over various apparently insurmountable obstacles. God repeatedly fulfilled his promises to "our ancestors"; what God promised "our ancestors," Paul says, is now fulfilled in its entirety through God's raising Jesus from the dead. "As to his raising him from the dead, no more to return to corruption, he [God] has spoken in this way: 'I will give you the holy promises made to David'" (13:34). Paul reduces these "promises" to one momentous and fulfilled event: "Of this man's [David's] posterity God has brought to Israel a Savior, Jesus, as he promised" (13:23). This is the good news, "that what God promised to our ancestors he has fulfilled for us, their children, by raising Jesus; as also it is written in the second psalm" (13:32–33).

God liberated Israel from its oppressors, Paul points out, leading them out of Egypt; God overthrew seven nations so that Israel could inherit its promised land. God gave it judges and kings and, finally, God sent them a Savior. But how, with Israel's long history of failure, does Paul envision Jesus saving them?

The question is crucial, taking the audience back to Luke's first volume. Zechariah, for example, praised God for "look[ing] favorably on his people and redeem[ing] them"—by "rais[ing] up a mighty savior for us in the house of his servant David" (Luke 1:68–69). And the angels sang to the shepherds, "To you is born this day in the city of David a Savior, who is the Messiah, the Lord" (2:11). How did Zechariah and the angels, and Paul himself, understand "Savior"? The answer has been playing itself out from the beginning of Luke (1:68; 24:21): *Jesus clarifies God's word and then sends the Holy Spirit to empower following it.*

To the disappointment of many, the Savior is not a powerful, nationalistic king who would restore Israel to glory in the promised land. Jesus is Savior, says all of Luke-Acts, by delivering believers from the power of sin through repentance. Empowered by God's Spirit, believers can enter into the kingdom of God with all of its blessings. As Savior, Jesus delivers—but not from sociopolitical oppression to the Romans into a restored national and tribal power under the reign of a mighty king. Much to the disappointment and later murderous rage of hopeful Jews, Jesus offers no continuation of a nationalistic dynasty of David; rather, he sets believers free from sin and death and alienation into the righteous and life-giving and inclusive kingdom of God, under the reign of Jesus as Lord.

Paul closes negatively, anticipating a response from those "falling" within Israel. "Look, you scoffers!" Paul warns, quoting Scripture (Habakkuk). "Be amazed and perish, for in your days I am doing a work, a work that you will never believe, even if someone tells you" (13:41). The work to which he refers is the kingdom age when Israel becomes, in fulfillment of the holy covenant made with Abraham (Gen. 12:1–3; Acts 3:25), servant Israel to the world—just as Jesus was God's "holy servant" to Israel (Acts 4:27, 30). This "mighty work" is one of the major "events being fulfilled among us" to which Luke refers in the beginning of his orderly account (Luke 1:1–4).

Many listening to Paul, of course, respond positively to the Messiah and his "work" of the kingdom's inauguration: "When the meeting of the synagogue broke up, many Jews and devout converts to Judaism followed Paul and Barnabas, who spoke to them and urged them to continue in the grace of God" (13:43).

Between Paul's First and Second Speech

After Paul's speech to his fellow Jews, he encourages them to continue "in the grace of God" (13:43). Word about Paul and his gospel spreads. "The next sabbath almost the whole city gathered to hear the word of the Lord" (13:44). The narrative dynamic of Acts follows the spreading word of God, with thousands upon thousands embracing the Messiah and his teaching of the word of God as preached by followers like Peter and Paul, to both Jews and Gentiles.

As the gospel spreads, however, some of the "falling" within Israel are "filled with jealousy" and contradict Paul's message (13:45). But Paul's focus is clear. Along with his companion Barnabas, Paul speaks "boldly, saying, 'It was necessary that the word of God should be spoken first to you [Jews]. Since you reject it and judge yourselves to be unworthy of eternal life, we are now turning to the Gentiles'" (13:46). Paul never stops speaking to fellow Jews, but always with mixed results: some follow Jesus—the "rising"—while others spurn the gospel. The "falling" include the jealous leaders who hounded Jesus and who persecute his followers in Acts. In spite of adversity, Paul continues "proclaiming the good news" (14:3–7) of God's kingdom, which he demonstrates by healing the diseased (14:8–10).

The jealousy of the Jewish leaders continues, as Jews from neighboring cities stone Paul, leaving him for dead (14:19–20). But Paul survives and moves on with Barnabas. "After they had proclaimed the good news to that city and had made many disciples, they returned to Lystra, then on to Iconium and Antioch" (14:21). Here the two "strengthened the souls of the disciples and encouraged them to continue in the faith, saying, 'It is through many persecutions that we must enter the kingdom of God'" (14:22). From Antioch Paul and Barnabas travel down to Jerusalem to resolve the crisis of how Gentile believers are to be incorporated into the kingdom.

Joined by Luke, the author, Paul travels to Macedonia (16:10).[4] On the Sabbath he goes to where Jews are praying, and "a worshiper of God" has her heart opened; "she and her household" are baptized (16:9–15). We are frequently reminded that Paul's bringing God's word to his fellow Jews is effective, though often not—especially among Jewish leaders.

When Paul exorcizes a spirit of divining from a woman, her handlers are furious. Paul and his new companion Silas are thrown into prison—from which they and the other prisoners are freed by an earthquake. They assist the Gentile jailer, who embraces Jesus as his Lord; the jailer, in turn, feeds his new Jewish friends and dresses their wounds. Their mutual kindness is the briefest of the narrative snapshots of the kingdom's communal well-being in Acts (16:16–40).

Paul and Silas travel to Thessalonica, where, "as was his custom," Paul seeks out the synagogue leaders to explain the gospel. While some Jews and God-fearing Greeks are "persuaded," other Jews, again jealous leaders, drag the believers before the officials, accusing them of causing trouble all over the world (17:5–9). Under concealment of darkness, Paul and Silas escape to the next city, Beroea, where many Jews are receptive to the proclaimed word of God (17:10–12).

When, again, jealous Jewish leaders stir up trouble, however, the local believers escort Paul to Athens, where, as was his custom, be began teaching in the synagogue (17:13–17). Curious about Paul's teaching, some Greek philosophers bring Paul to a place of public debate and oratory called the Areopagus to see "what this new teaching . . . means" (17:19–20).

Paul's Only Speech to Gentiles (Acts 17:22–31)

What would you say to Gentiles if you had but one chance? Paul makes sure that all the essentials are included in this speech to non-Jews. He concludes with a challenge: "Repent, because . . . the world [will be] judged in righteousness by a man whom [God] has appointed" (17:30–31). Who is this man, they might be wondering, and what is his authority to judge?

One True God as Holy Spirit

Just as Stephen referred implicitly to the Holy Spirit as God's presence everywhere for the patriarchs—limited neither to tabernacle, temple, nor holy city—so too Paul suggests implicitly the *everywhere-to-anyone* presence of God as Holy Spirit. He compliments his Athenian audience for their religious seriousness and then announces the identity of their mysterious "unknown god," as inscribed on one of their altars (17:23). The "unknown god," says Paul, is the God of the Hebrew Scriptures who "made all nations" through one ancestor (17:26), a deity not confined to a temple or captured in an icon made of gold, silver, or stone. Indeed, Paul says, God made the world and all the nations "so that they would search for God and perhaps grope for him and find him—though indeed he is not far from each one of us" (17:27). The Spirit is just a turnaround-of-life away.

Repentance

Before the advent of Jesus, the world could claim ignorance of God, but "now he commands all people everywhere to repent" (17:30). Without turning away from wickedness toward God's way, there can be no salvation.

Resurrection, Authority—and Judgment

"Repent," Paul goes on, "because he has fixed a day on which he will have the world judged in righteousness by a man whom he has appointed, and of this he has given assurance to all by raising him from the dead" (17:30–31). Resurrection grounds the authority of Jesus, who will judge on the grounds of righteousness. You can be sure of this, Paul admonishes, because God raised him from death. Hearing of "the resurrection of the dead," some scoff; but others say, "We will hear you again about this" (17:32).

Given their lack of interest, Paul simply moves on.

Conclusion

From fellow Jews to Greek Gentiles, Paul emphasizes God's mercy in forgiving the sins of those turning from their wicked ways to God's way. Luke wants his audience to be clear and certain about the meaning of the events fulfilled: God raised Jesus from death as predicted in the Hebrew Scriptures, establishing his authority as Messiah and Teacher; the Holy Spirit poured out, as predicted in the Hebrew Scriptures, empowers the repentance necessary to enter the kingdom and keep to the clarified law; Israel becoming "servant Israel," taking God's blessing to all peoples.

Paul's first two speeches raise at least two problems in reading biblical narratives: first, readers can't easily hear the embedded hearing cues;
second, we read into the text our long-held theological views (often based
on other texts, like Galatians). Paul *in Acts* sees the resurrection, not the
crucifixion, as God's decisive act. *In Acts,* we aren't justified by the blood of
Jesus; rather, we are set free from the tyranny of sin by the power of God,
demonstrated by God's raising Jesus from death and effected through the
gift of the empowering Spirit. Further, Jesus will judge at the end of time
on the basis of one's righteousness, obtained through continuing repentance made possible through the empowering Holy Spirit. Thus released
from the human tendency to sin, the believer finds a new life, salvation,
within a righteous and inclusive community sustained by the Holy Spirit.

CHAPTER 22

Paul's Full Gospel: His Only Speech to Believers (Acts 20:18–35)

Proclaiming the Kingdom of God

Luke's narrative structure shows less interest in Paul's adventures than in his repeated proclamations and demonstrations of the good news of God's kingdom.[1] The linked hearing cues in Acts' eighteen speeches constitute the main thematic progression of Acts.

After the mixed reception in Athens to his only speech to Gentiles only, Paul visits Corinth, where he stays for a while making tents with a fellow Jew. *Jews and Gentiles (Greeks)* constitutes a refrain, a repeated motif. Early in his ministry, Paul went with Barnabas "into the Jewish synagogue and spoke in such a way that a great number of both Jews and Greeks became believers" (14:1).

In Corinth, when not making tents, "Paul was occupied with proclaiming the word, testifying to the Jews that the Messiah was Jesus. When they opposed and reviled him, in protest he shook the dust from his clothes and said to them, 'Your blood be on your own heads! I am innocent. From now on I will go to the Gentiles'" (18:5–6). Two verses later we hear that while Paul is staying with a Gentile believer next door to the synagogue, "Crispus, the official of the synagogue," becomes "a believer in the Lord, together with all his household"; and many other Corinthians become believers and are baptized (18:7–8). Jews and Gentiles. Some believe; some refuse the good news.

Paul leaves Corinth, traveling to Jerusalem by way of Ephesus, then back to Antioch. After staying there a while, he leaves and travels "from place to place through the region of Galatia and Phrygia, strengthening all the disciples" (18:22–23). There is little meaning in the journeying except that Paul gets around—with the word of God for both Jews and Gentiles, "strengthening all the disciples," both Jews and Greeks.

Paul then returns to Ephesus. "He entered the synagogue and for three months spoke out boldly, and argued persuasively about the kingdom of God. When some stubbornly refused to believe and spoke evil of the Way before the congregation, he left them, taking the disciples with him, and argued daily in the lecture hall of Tyrannus. This continued for two years, so that all the residents of Asia, both Jews and Greeks, heard the word of the Lord" (19:8–10). Both Jews and Greeks hear the word of the Lord.

For three months here and for two years there, Paul speaks "the word of the Lord," the word "about the kingdom of God." And "God did extraordinary miracles through Paul, so that when the handkerchiefs or aprons that had touched his skin were brought to the sick, their diseases left them, and the evil spirits came out of them" (19:11–12). Such summaries of action, peppered as they are with occasional healings, set the narrative stage for the major speeches that convey Paul's meaning about the kingdom of God—of inclusive and compassionate gatherings of captives released from disease and oppression.

Attempting to promote themselves, some Jewish charlatans, sons of a high priest, try exorcising in "the name of the Lord Jesus . . . whom Paul proclaims," but they are overpowered by the demons, fleeing the house naked and wounded. When news of this spreads to all residents of Ephesus, *both Jews and Greeks*, everyone is "awestruck; and the name of the Lord Jesus [is] praised" (19:13–17).

Once again, we hear: "The word of the Lord grew mightily and prevailed" (19:20).

Widespread following of the Way threatens the livelihood of makers and sellers of shrines of the goddess Artemis, and their protestations create confusion and chaos in the city. "After the uproar had ceased, Paul sent for the disciples; and after encouraging them and saying farewell, he left for Macedonia. When he had gone through those regions and had given the believers much encouragement, he came to Greece" (20:1–2).

Paul speaks so long one night that a young man falls asleep and out of a window, to his death (20:7–12). As with Jesus and Peter, Paul brings the dead back to life.

Paul goes through several more cities, four of them within two verses. He sends a message to Ephesus, asking the leaders of the assembly of believers in Ephesus to meet with him.[2] In his speech to Jewish and Gentile leaders of the Way, Paul refers to his testimony "to *both Jews and Greeks* about repentance toward God and faith toward our Lord Jesus" (20:21).

Paul's Third Speech, to Jewish and Gentile Followers (Acts 20:18–35)

Paul delivers a farewell speech to leaders of the followers in Ephesus, both Jew and Gentile.[3]

Like Jesus, he will embark on his final journey to Jerusalem, and for Paul, beyond Jerusalem to Rome. Paul speaks God's word to these believers—a complete version of the good news he has been proclaiming and demonstrating. His announcement of his journey is replete with overtones of danger and even death, suggesting to these believers what they might face themselves.

Repentance

Paul recounts his basic message. "I testified to both Jews and Greeks about repentance toward God, and faith toward our Lord Jesus" (20:21). While repentance involves a *turning away*, from normal but divisive self-interest, it also involves a *turning toward*—toward the "the Way" (9:2), "the way of God" (Luke 20:21). This way of God is the divine will for communal well-being of all peoples in God's kingdom on earth. "Faith toward our Lord Jesus" is the embrace of and allegiance to Jesus as Lord of God's way.

Resurrection

Although resurrection is not mentioned explicitly, "faith toward our Lord Jesus" is based on confidence in the authority of Jesus established by God's raising him from death. (The resurrection is mentioned four times by Paul in his first speech: 13:29–30, 32–33, 34, 36–37.)

The Holy Spirit

Paul's reflections on the Spirit, the empowering presence of God in believers' lives, are intensely personal: "As a captive to the Spirit, I am on my way to Jerusalem, not knowing what will happen to me there, except that the Holy Spirit testifies to me in every city that imprisonment and persecutions are waiting for me" (20:22–23). But the Spirit is needed not only for such extraordinary circumstances: believers need the empowerment of the Holy Spirit in their daily embracing of Jesus as Lord. Finally, Paul admonishes the leaders, "keep watch over yourselves and over all the flock, of which the Holy Spirit has made you overseers" (20:28).

Striving for the Kingdom

The fullness of the gospel is evident as Paul addresses the need to continually strive for the kingdom (in keeping with Luke 13:24–30; 9:51–19:44). He graphically warns followers and leaders alike of the price paid already on behalf of the kingdom and the price they may have to pay. Following is a key sequence containing three references to blood, in italics:

> Now, behold, I know that you all, among whom I went about preaching God's Kingdom, will see my face no more. Therefore I testify to you today that *I am clean from the blood of all men*, for I didn't shrink from declaring to you the whole counsel of God. Take heed, therefore, to yourselves, and to all the flock, in which the Holy Spirit has made you overseers, *to shepherd the assembly of the Lord and God which he purchased with his own blood*. For I know that after my departure, *vicious wolves will enter in among you, not sparing the flock*. Men will arise from among your own selves, speaking perverse things, to draw away the disciples after them. (20:25–30 World English Bible)

"I Am Clean from the Blood of All Men"

Paul begins by absolving himself of any responsibility for their blood: "for I did not shrink from declaring to you the whole purpose of God." You have been well warned of the consequences of following Jesus, Paul is, in effect, saying; the good news of God's kingdom requires taking up one's cross, which requires sacrificing self-interests and maybe even life itself.

"To Shepherd the Assembly of the Lord and God Which He Purchased with His Own Blood [Blood of His Own]"

Paul proceeds with a reminder that God has secured his assembly (gathered people) through "the blood of his own." The phrase, which can be translated in more than one way, likely refers to the blood of the prophets—God's own—who were killed on God's behalf.[4] *God's own*, then, includes John who was beheaded, Jesus who was crucified, and Stephen who was stoned.

"Vicious Wolves Will Enter in Among You, Not Sparing the Flock"

Figuratively or literally, the blood of God's own will also include some in his audience. "I know that after I have gone," Paul adds, "savage wolves will come in among you, not sparing the flock." *God's own* now extends to all those who pick up their crosses daily to follow Jesus (Luke 9:23; 14:27). We have heard Paul say, "It is through many persecutions that we must enter the kingdom of God" (Acts 14:22). Paul is pleading, in concert with the teaching of Jesus, that these Ephesian leaders should be willing to relinquish even their own lifeblood for the kingdom—which Paul apparently expects for himself (20:25, 36–38a).

"I do not count my life of any value to myself," Paul says to his Ephesian friends, "if only I may finish my course and the ministry that I received from the Lord Jesus, to testify to the good news of God's grace" (20:24). He expects never again to visit face-to-face with these friends (20:38a).

"Then they brought him to the ship" (20:38b).

Conclusion

In his presentation of the gospel to the Greek Gentiles in Athens, Paul cites the key elements of the gospel message, *resurrection* and *repentance*. He repeats these same elements to the Ephesian believers, along with references to the empowering Spirit of God. He goes on to speak to his audience of believers, both Jew and Gentile, about the need to continue striving for the kingdom through suffering, persecution, and even death.

Paul will now move on to Jerusalem and then to Rome, where he faces his own death.

Paul's Three Speeches in Self-Defense before the Powers (Acts 22:1–21; 24:10–21; 26:1–23)

Paul Goes on the Offense

After his speech to Ephesian believers (20:18–35), Paul begins his momentous and dangerous journey to Jerusalem, where he will incur the wrath of Jewish leaders and their trumped-up charges.

As before, he travels to Jerusalem with a personal friend, presumably Luke, who narrates the action in his own voice. They travel by cargo boat from Miletus, on the west coast of modern-day Turkey, to Syria's Tyre. Their passage through five cities is covered in just four verses (21:1–4). While interesting things happen in this city or that, Luke's account is oriented more around what Paul says than what he does. Luke's Acts, then, is quite unlike an adventure story like Homer's *Odyssey*, in which various locales noted for this or that horror challenge the hero's physical and mental greatness. Acts is more about Jesus and his being raised by God and believers spreading the word of God than Paul's glorious conquests and vanquishing of foes. Civil unrest, arrests, and trials function more as narrative occasions for major speeches explaining the gospel of God than events with inherent dramatic interest. In this section of the narrative, three times before the Jewish powers, twice in collusion with Roman powers, Paul speaks eloquently in his own defense against false charges—managing all the while to spread the good news of God proclaimed and demonstrated by Jesus.

From Tyre, Paul and friends travel to Ptolemais, and then, after a day, on to Caesarea. Some disciples and other believers have misgivings: "Through the Spirit they told Paul not to go on to Jerusalem" (21:4). But Paul refuses to listen. "I am ready not only to be bound," he responds, "but even to die in Jerusalem for the name of the Lord Jesus" (21:13). He arrives in Jerusalem to warm greetings by fellow believers (21:17). These include "many thousands of believers . . . among the Jews, and they are all zealous for the law" (21:20). To ensure that other Jews understand that Paul still observes the law, the Jewish elders who follow Jesus urge Paul to go to the temple to take an oath of purification with four men, with Paul paying to have their heads shaved (21:22–26). However, some Jewish leaders—out-of-towners—are enraged. They seize Paul, shouting, "Fellow Israelites, help! This is the man who is teaching everyone everywhere against our people, our law, and this place" (21:28). As tumult ensues, Paul is dragged out of the temple to be beaten to death. A Roman commander intervenes to restore order. He takes Paul into custody, binding him in chains. When he asks the crowd who Paul is, the resulting cacophony prevents his hearing. Paul asks permission to speak (21:30–37).

Paul's following three speeches stress two common themes: resurrection and Paul's claim to be a Jew in good standing. In two of the three speeches, repentance is repeated in very personal terms, Paul's dramatic account of his own turnaround to God's way. His insistence on being an upright Jew serves Paul's purposes in defending himself before Jewish officials and serves Luke's purpose of explaining that by becoming a follower of Israel's Messiah, one is more fully an Israelite in God's sight, not less.

First Speech: Paul, before Roman Authority, Speaks to Jewish Leaders and Crowd (Acts 22:1–21)

The crowd of Jews, worked up by their leaders, shouted concerning Jesus, "Away with this fellow!" (Luke 23:18). Here the crowd of Jews, worked up by their leadership, shout concerning Paul, "Away with him!" (Acts 21:36). Rescued by Roman authorities from a brutal crowd of his own people, Paul begs for a chance to speak to the crowd. Permission granted, he speaks.

A Jew in Good Standing

"Brothers and fathers, listen to the defense that I now make before you," Paul begins. Luke adds, "When they heard him addressing them in Hebrew, they became even more quiet" (22:1–2). By addressing them in their own language, rather than in Greek,[1] Paul identifies himself with his Jewish audience, claiming that he is "zealous for God, just as all of you are today"—a really good Jew. As proof of his zeal Paul reminds them that he "persecuted this Way up to the point of death by binding both men and women [believers] and putting them in prison" (22:3–4). He then recounts his transformative encounter with the living Jesus on his way to persecuting believers in Damascus, an account we have already heard but from the perspective of Luke (Acts 9:3–20).

Repentance: Paul's Own Story

Paul tells how he was born in Tarsus but brought up in Jerusalem "at the feet of Gamaliel,[2] educated strictly according to our ancestral law, being zealous for God, just as all of you are today" (22:3). Paul, with the best rabbinic credentials, was a good and respected Jew.

He put his training to work as a defender of orthodoxy. "I went [to Damascus] in order to bind those [of the Way] who were there and to bring them back to Jerusalem for punishment" (22:5). But at noon he was blinded by a great light and heard a voice. "Saul, Saul, why are you persecuting me?" He knew it was the voice of "the Lord" and asked what he was to do. Go into Damascus, he was told, and you will find out (22:10–11).

Paul continues. "A certain Ananias, who was a devout man according to the law and well spoken of by all the Jews living there, came to me.... Then he said, 'The God of our ancestors has chosen you to know his will, to see the Righteous One and to hear his own voice; for you will be his witness to all the world of what you have seen and heard'" (22:12–15). Paul is seeking to assuage the fear that his repentance meant turning away from the law. Having self-identified as a pious Jew, here he recounts his assistance by Ananias, "a devout man according to the law," in turning to Jesus as Messiah. Ananias urged Paul to have his sins washed away in baptism (22:16), which Luke's audience knows is the symbol of repentance and new life.

Resurrection

Though he never encountered the earthly Jesus, Paul nonetheless saw and heard the risen Jesus. Later, he tells of a second visitation from the resurrected Messiah: "I had returned to Jerusalem and while I was praying in the temple, I fell into a trance and saw Jesus saying to me, 'Hurry and get out of Jerusalem quickly, because they will not accept your testimony about me'"

(22:17–18). Paul *saw Jesus saying*. Paul is saying, "I didn't just hear a mysterious voice speaking from who knows where; I saw Jesus, one long ago departed from earth, speaking!" Paul has *seen and heard* the risen Jesus.

Servant Israel to Gentiles

Paul concludes with his mission: "Then he [Jesus] said to me, 'Go, for I will send you far away to the Gentiles'" (22:21). Perhaps taking Paul's mission to the Gentiles as an insult, the audience of Jewish officials and people, we hear, listened to him "up to this point . . . but then they shouted, 'Away with such a fellow from the earth! For he should not be allowed to live'" (22:22).

The Roman tribune rescues Paul, putting him in a barracks for examination and flogging (22:23–24). Paul pleads his Roman citizenship to a centurion, who, with the tribune, ceases the harassment: a natural-born Roman has rights. Paul will be heard again. The tribune orders the Jewish leaders to meet with him about their accusations (22:25–30) and, with him, to hear further from Paul. Paul claims a clear conscience and, noticing some Sadducees, who do not believe in the resurrection, contends that he is "on trial concerning the hope of the resurrection of the dead" (23:6). When a dispute ensues between the Sadducees and their rivals, the Pharisees—a tiff surely anticipated by Paul—the tribune, afraid that they will "tear Paul to pieces," orders the soldiers to "go down, take him by force, and bring him into the barracks" (23:7–10). For the second time, Rome rescues Paul from his own people.

With the blessing of the Jewish leaders, forty zealous Jews take an oath of fasting until they have killed Paul. But when the Roman commander gets wind of their plot, he orders that Paul be taken at night to Felix, the Roman governor of Judea, whose residence is in the seacoast city of Caesarea, north of Jerusalem (23:12–31). For the third time, in close succession, Rome has rescued Paul from his own people. The repetition makes its point: the real enemies of the kingdom are not from outside Israel but from within.

Second Speech: Paul, to Jewish and Roman Authorities (Acts 24:10–21)

Five days after Paul's arrival in Caesarea, the high priest, Ananias, appears with an attorney, Tertullus, who accuses Paul before Felix of being "a pestilent fellow, an agitator among all the Jews throughout the world, and a ringleader of the sect of the Nazarenes. He even tried to profane the temple" (24:1–8). Felix motions for Paul to speak (24:10). Rome, wanting peace, protects Paul and seeks to defuse the agitation of the Jewish leaders.

A Jew in Good Standing

Paul reassures Felix that he is a faithful Jew and observer of the law: he is not an agitator. "As you can find out," Paul reassures the governor, "it is not more than twelve days since I went up to worship in Jerusalem. They did not find me disputing with anyone in the temple or stirring up a crowd either in the synagogues or throughout the city" (24:11–12).

Furthermore, Paul goes on, "I worship the God of our ancestors, believing everything laid down according to the law or written in the prophets"—albeit "according to the Way, which they call a sect" (24:14).

As to profaning the temple Paul says that he went to the temple "to bring alms to my nation and to offer sacrifices" and to complete "the rite of purification" (24:17–18). Paul argues that he is faithful to Israel in worship, words, and alms. Although the Way is taken by his accusers as blasphemy, Felix has heard enough of this Way to inquire of Paul further (24:22).

Resurrection

Paul contends that the fuss is over "this one sentence that I called out while standing before them, 'It is about the resurrection of the dead that I am on trial before you today'" (24:21). Paul appeals to a shared belief: "I have a hope in God—a hope that they themselves also accept—that there will be a resurrection of both the righteous and the unrighteous" (24:15). The opposition to Paul, of course, is not so much because of a shared belief in "the resurrection of the dead" but because of an unshared belief in Jesus's resurrection.

After hearing Paul speak, Felix adjourns for a few days. Accompanied by his Jewish wife, Drusilla, Felix later summons Paul and hears him "speak concerning faith in Christ Jesus." As Paul discusses justice, self-control, "and the coming judgment," Felix becomes frightened and says, "Go away for the present; when I have an opportunity, I will send for you" (24:24–25).

Paul's talk of resurrection has angered the Jewish leaders, while the threat of judgment, based on righteousness, has frightened a Roman leader.

At the end of the second year, with Paul still in custody, Felix is succeeded by Festus, who travels to Jerusalem to hear the charges against Paul by the Jewish religious leaders. They ask Festus to cooperate with them to have Paul transferred to Jerusalem so they can ambush and kill him. Festus resists their entreaties and invites a few of the Jewish agitators to Caesarea to make their case (25:3–5). To appease the Jews and also to protect Paul, Festus asks Paul if he would be willing to go to Jerusalem. Paul balks, appealing to the emperor, as is his right as a Roman citizen. Festus, whose hands are tied by law, says, "To the emperor you will go" (25:6–12).

The Rome-appointed King Agrippa (son of the struck-dead King Herod [12:23]) and his sister Bernice visit Caesarea and pay their respects to the newly appointed Festus. When Agrippa learns of Festus's dilemma with Paul and the Jews (25:14–21), he says, "I would like to hear the man myself" (25:22).

Third Speech: Paul, Again to Jewish and Roman Authorities (Acts 26:1–23)

"The next day Agrippa and Bernice came with great pomp, and they entered the audience hall with the military tribunes and the prominent men of the city. Then Festus gave the order and Paul was brought in" (25:23).

A Jew in Good Standing

Standing before both Roman and Jewish leaders, Paul thanks Agrippa for the opportunity to respond to the charges against him.

As in his prior two speeches of self-defense, Paul begins by affirming his status as an observant Jew. Everyone, says Paul, "know[s] my way of life from my youth, a life spent from the beginning among my own people and in Jerusalem. . . . I have belonged to the strictest sect of our religion and lived as a Pharisee" (26:4–5). Paul repeats what he said before: "I am a Pharisee" (23:6).[3] Paul is a transformed Pharisee, having turned away from the self-serving aspects of this sect to the way of God as taught by Jesus. Paul is a righteous rather than a hypocritical Jew.

Resurrection

As a faithful Jew, Paul affirms the promises of God: "And now I stand here on trial on account of my hope in the promise made by God to our ancestors, a promise that our twelve tribes hope to attain" (26:6–7). In the Luke-Acts context, *the promise made by God . . . that our twelve tribes hope to attain* is the restoration of Israel through a Messiah that God would raise from death. "It is for this hope, your Excellency, that I am accused by Jews!" Paul says. "Why is it thought incredible by any of you that God raises the dead?" (26:7–8).

Repentance: Paul's Own Story

For the third time in Acts, we hear Paul's story of his repentance, the second instance of his own telling. After recounting his active resistance to Jesus and his followers, he describes turning toward Jesus's way (26:9–18).

He concludes with Jesus's commissioning him to call others to repentance, "to open their eyes so that they may *turn from darkness to light and from the power of Satan to God*, so that they may receive forgiveness of sins and a place among those who are sanctified by faith in me" (26:18).

Repentance, then, is a transformation that initiates both forgiveness and entry into God's kingdom. Paul offers his own repentance as an example of such repentance (26:4–18). Paul goes on: "After that, King Agrippa, I was not disobedient to the heavenly vision, but declared first to those in Damascus, then in Jerusalem and throughout the countryside of Judea, and also to the Gentiles, that they should repent and turn to God and do deeds consistent with repentance" (26:19–20). "For this reason," Paul goes on to claim, "the Jews seized me in the temple and tried to kill me" (26:21).

Resurrection

Paul returns to his central claim, the one that has gotten him into so much trouble—the claim that God raised Jesus from the dead. "Why is it thought incredible by any of you that God raises the dead?" Paul asks (26:8). Downplaying his audience's skepticism, Paul concludes that the prophets had foretold the resurrection, guaranteeing a "message of light" for both Israel and the Gentiles (26:22–23). Thinking "dead" means dead, Festus declares that Paul is out of his mind (26:24). Paul, speaking "the sober truth," appeals to King Agrippa as a believer in the prophets (26:25–29). Paul is certain that the Jewish Agrippa has heard of Jesus's death and resurrection, because it "was not done in a corner." Agrippa replies, "Are you so quickly persuading me to become a Christian?" (26:28).

Whether Paul is deranged or delusional, the Roman leaders concur that "this man is doing nothing to deserve death or imprisonment" (26:30–31). But Paul has tied their hands: unfortunately, says King Agrippa, "this man could have been set free if he had not appealed to the emperor" (26:32). Paul must be sent to Rome (27:1–12).[4]

Conclusion

In these three speeches Paul insists on his standing as a faithful and observant Jew, one who respects the law. As a faithful Jew, then, Paul embraces Jesus as Israel's Messiah and as God's authoritative and definitive teacher of the law—"the way of God" (Luke 20:21; Acts 9:2). Regardless of the murderous slurs, Paul's plea is that he is a Pharisee in good standing with his own people and with God.

Luke's patterned hearing cues—repentance, resurrection, and the Holy Spirit, along with the "true Jew" and Paul's mission to the Gentiles— guide us into Luke's theological meaning.

- The true Jew: According to Paul, the Jesus movement, considered a "Jewish sect" (24:5, 14; 28:22), is the genuine "worship [of] the God of our ancestors," the fulfillment of "everything laid down according to the law or written in the prophets" (24:14). Jesus, Paul, and all followers of Jesus from within Israel are true Jews. This is what comprises the basis for the many rising within Israel, as shown by Acts.
- Repentance: Paul offers his own life as a model of the turnaround required to become a follower of Jesus (24:14). While repentance was required before the advent of Jesus, it now requires a turning away from self-assertion toward God's way as taught by Jesus (Luke 20:21).
- Resurrection: Paul's "hope in the promise made by God to our ancestors, a promise that our twelve tribes hope to attain," the restoration of Israel, is grounded in God's raising the dead (26:6–8). Jesus is Israel's Messiah, affirmed by his resurrection; therefore, *listen to him!* (Luke 9:35).

- Gentiles: Paul proclaims his Jesus-given mission to the Gentiles. He refers to the prophets, who declared "that the Messiah must suffer, and that, by being the first to rise from the dead, he would proclaim light both to our people and to the Gentiles" (Acts 26:22–23). Paul's mission to the Gentiles affirms, following Peter, that Israel would bring blessing to "all the families of the earth" (Acts 3:25; Gen. 12:3).

Luke's audience has already heard that God's salvation involves "a light for revelation to the Gentiles and for glory to your people Israel" (Luke 2:32). Paul's conversion, then, is microcosm to God's macrocosm, the blessing brought by Abraham's seed to the entire world. The light that blinded Paul will become the light that Paul bears to Gentiles—fulfilling God's choice of Israel and his promise to bless all the nations through Israel.

CHAPTER 24

Paul's Repentance, Three Versions
(Acts 9:3–19; 22:6–22; 26:1–23)

A Climactic Revelation

Biblical literary art includes much more than the major structuring device of hearing cues within overlapping patterns of repetition, though this artistic shaping is significant for determining message. It also includes the play of language, such as allusions, irony, metaphor, imagery, alliteration, and onomatopoeia (the sound of words suggesting their meaning).

Such playfulness can be serious, as in the linguistic play in the repetition in Paul's accounts of his turnaround. Serious religious probing is heard in these strikingly similar but distinctly differing accounts recalling his extraordinary turnaround from persecuting followers of Jesus to following Jesus. Progressing metaphors—hearing cues—of light and voice function with patterns used in each story of Paul's repentance. Through these three repeated scenarios, *seeing* the gospel's light and *hearing* its life-changing truth rise to a climactic revelation.

In each of the three versions of Paul's turnaround, we hear these shared details:

- Paul is journeying to Damascus to drag followers of Jesus from synagogues.
- He intends to bind them and haul them before the Jewish authorities in Jerusalem.
- His journey is interrupted by a light and voice from heaven.
- On the spot, he turns from persecuting "those who belonged to the Way" and joins them (9:2).

We slow down, now, to listen for the meaning in the stories' similarities and differences.

Voices

Consider first the use of *voice* in each version.

Voice, First Version (Acts 9:3–19)

- "[He] heard a voice saying to him, 'Saul, Saul [*Saulos*], why do you persecute me?'" (9:4; Paul's friends hear the voice).
- Paul asks, "Who are you, Lord?" (9:5).
- "I am Jesus, whom you are persecuting. But get up and enter the city, and you will be told what you are to do" (9:5–6).

Voice, Second Version (Acts 22:6–22)

- "[I] heard a voice saying to me, 'Saul, Saul [*Saulos*], why are you persecuting me?'" (22:7; Paul's friends do *not* hear the voice).
- Paul asks, "Who are you, Lord?" (22:8)
- "I am Jesus of Nazareth whom you are persecuting" (22:8).
- Paul asks, "What am I to do, Lord?"
- "The Lord said to me, 'Get up and go to Damascus; there you will be told everything that has been assigned to you to do'" (22:10)

Voice, Third Version (Acts 26:1–23)

- "I heard a voice saying to me in the Hebrew language, 'Saul, Saul [*Saoul*], why are you persecuting me? It hurts you to kick against the goads'" (26:14).
- Paul asks, "Who are you, Lord?" (26:15).
- "I am Jesus whom you are persecuting. Get up and stand on your feet; for I have appeared to you for this purpose, to appoint you to serve and testify to the things in which you have seen me and to those in which I will appear to you. I will rescue you from your people and from the Gentiles—to whom I am sending you to open their eyes so that they may turn from darkness to light and from the power of Satan to God, so that they may receive forgiveness of sins and a place among those who are sanctified by faith in me" (26:15–18).

Note indications of the growing knowledge and increasing intimacy between Jesus and Paul as the versions progress:

- In Luke's version (the first), the voice identifies itself as "Jesus," but in the second version, Paul's, the voice is more specific: "I am Jesus *of Nazareth*"[1] (22:8).

- In the second version, Jesus speaks only to Saul (and not his friends), indicating a greater intimacy.
- In the third version, the heavenly voice speaks to Paul in his own language: Hebrew (not Greek or Aramaic, the lingua franca).[2]
- In the third version, "Saul" (Greek, *Saulos*) becomes the Hebrew *Saoul*, a further sign of the increasing intimacy between Jesus and Paul, both Hebrews.
- In the third account, the voice spells out the full vision of Paul's mission—the global offering of God's salvation. Previously Ananias had instructed Paul. Now it's Jesus himself, at great length and with greater power of metaphoric language.

Light

Now consider the use of *light* in each version.

Light, First Version (Acts 9:3–19)
- A "light from heaven" flashes around Paul (9:3), throwing him to the ground; when he gets up, though his eyes are open, he can't see anything (9:8).
- A "disciple" in Damascus, Ananias, is approached by the Lord and instructed to find Saul. When Ananias obeys and lays his hands on Saul, "something like scales [fall] from his eyes" (9:18).

Light, Second Version (Acts 22:6–22)
- Paul sees "a *great* light" (22:6).
- His companions see the light (26:9).
- Paul cannot see "because of the brightness of that light" (22:11).
- "A certain Ananias . . . came to me; . . . he said, 'Brother Saul, regain your sight!' In that very hour I regained my sight and saw him. Then he said, 'The God of our ancestors has chosen you to know his will, to see the Righteous One and to hear his own voice'" (22:12–14).

Light, Third Version (Acts 26:1–23)
- Paul sees a light "brighter than the sun" (26:13).
- The light knocks Paul and his companions to the ground (26:12–14).
- Light is used metaphorically to indicate a global understanding of the gospel: "I will rescue you from your people and from the Gentiles—to

whom I am sending you to open their eyes so that they may turn from darkness to light and from the power of Satan to God" (26:17–18).

The light increasingly strengthens to the point of outshining the sun itself; by knocking Paul *and* his companions to the ground, it has become all-encompassing in appearance and impact, just as the light of Paul's message will become all-encompassing—the light of God brought to Israel and, through Israel, to the world (26:17–18; Gen. 12:3). Paul, then, is God's solution to what Peter sees as Israel's covenantal challenge (Acts 3:25) of bringing "a light for revelation to the Gentiles" (Luke 2:32)—the blessing of God's kingdom to the entire world.

The opening of Paul's eyes to the light of his Messiah becomes the light that Paul will bring to the Gentiles, so that their eyes too can and will be opened.

By the third version the voice has become more intimate and more fully instructive, while the light has become "brighter than the sun"; all peoples of the world are to be given the chance, through Paul, to be illumined with the life-giving rays of God's gospel light. Just as Paul had the scales of darkness lifted off of his eyes, he will open Gentile eyes, as Jesus says, "I am sending you *to open their eyes so that they may turn from darkness to light* and from the power of Satan to God, so that they may receive forgiveness of sins and a place among those who are sanctified by faith in me" (26:15–18). The light of Paul's message, gleaned from "the things in which you have seen," is his light to the Gentiles so that they, like him, "may turn from darkness to light and from the power of Satan to God."

Luke's careful arrangement of sound and sight and voice and light highlights Paul's dramatic turnaround from ordinary hearing and seeing—a state of deafness and blindness—toward the hearing and seeing that reveals God's truth, God's kingdom way. Paul will offer what he now hears and sees about God's kingdom way to the world beyond Israel. He will offer all people what he himself has experienced in turning "from darkness to light and from the power of Satan to God."

Through the progression of the three accounts of Paul's turning, the voice of Jesus, speaking from heaven, becomes more focused on Paul and more intimate. The light progresses also, becoming brighter than the sun; the light becomes, by the third account, the light that shines through redeemed Israel to the entire world. Luke is also offering Paul's story as a paradigm for everyone. The voice speaking to Paul is the voice that speaks to everyone who encounters Jesus. As the voice intimately zeroes in on Paul, so too the text intimately zeroes in on everyone listening. The light that overcomes the darkness of Satan and his deeds becomes the light that shines on believers all over the world.

Hearing Cues That Echo Luke

Throughout Luke-Acts we have encountered the hearing cues of eyes and ears, seeing and hearing. Luke has prepared his listening audience for the voice that Paul hears and the light that Paul sees.

Words, the Word, and Listening

Luke warns of hearing without listening: "Let anyone with ears to hear listen," says Jesus (Luke 8:8; 14:35). Listening to Jesus as the clarifier of the law and Lord to be obeyed is essential to salvation. "Listen to him!" God said to Peter, James, and John (Luke 9:35). "Listen to whatever he tells you," Peter says, in reference to the new prophet, Jesus (Acts 3:22).

Luke begins his story with Mary listening to the word come from God, ready to do whatever God wishes; Zechariah hears similarly but doesn't listen with ears informed by a heart of trust; in doubt, he asks for further signs. Zechariah hears but doesn't act on what he has heard (Luke 1). This theme is reinforced by a story Jesus tells at the end of his poem on the plain:

> I will show you what someone is like
> who comes to me, hears my words, and acts on them.
> That one is like a man building a house,
> who dug deeply and laid the foundation on rock;
> when a flood arose, the river burst against that house
> but could not shake it because it had been well built.
> But the one who hears and does not act
> is like a man who built a house on the ground without a foundation.
> When the river burst against it,
> immediately it fell,
> and great was the ruin of that house. (6:46–49)[3]

Earlier in the sermon Jesus offered the most revolutionary of all challenges: "I say to you that listen, Love your enemies, do good to those who hate you" (Luke 6:27). Hear, listen, and then act.

Regarding the establishment of a new leadership of redeemed Israel (Luke 22:30), Jesus says, "Whoever listens to you [the twelve disciples] listens to me, and whoever rejects you rejects me, and whoever rejects me rejects the one who sent me" (Luke 10:16). Acts records many who heard the twelve but did not listen—the falling in Israel—along with the many thousands rising in Israel who did listen and became part of God's kingdom (9:2).

Light and Seeing

The light that blinded Paul into seeing Jesus and his way morphs from physical light to the metaphorical light of God's good news, the message that can turn his listeners from darkness to light (Acts 26:18). Such light and seeing echo themes in Luke.

Jesus is coming, we hear, "to give light to those who sit in darkness and in the shadow of death" and "to guide our feet into the way of peace" (Luke 1:79). As Simeon puts it, holding the baby Jesus, Israel's Messiah will be "a light for revelation to the Gentiles and for glory to your people Israel" (Luke 2:32). As he holds the infant Jesus, Simeon exclaims to God, "Master, now you are dismissing your servant in peace, according to your word; for my eyes have seen your salvation, which you have prepared in the presence of all peoples" (Luke 2:29–31).

We soon hear an echo in John the Baptist's claim that in Jesus "all flesh shall *see* the salvation of God" (Luke 3:6). Jesus unites both seeing and hearing imagery: "Blessed are the eyes that see what you see! For I tell you that many prophets and kings desired to see what you see, but did not see it, and to hear what you hear, but did not hear it" (Luke 10:23–24).

By the time we encounter the light in the third version of Paul's repentance, we hear that it has come to shine with the greatest scope, metaphorically illuminating the entire world, Jew and Gentile alike. Consider how the light transformed Paul: the light that blinded Paul exposed Paul to his blind way of life, walking in darkness and in death. And his temporary plunge into darkness was prelude to his seeing the light of God's truth: "Scales fell from his eyes, and his sight was restored. Then he got up and was baptized" (Acts 9:18). Baptism, then, represents rising up to light and life from the symbolic plunge into the dark waters of sin and death. Those who follow the way of God taught by Jesus (Luke 20:21) are called by Jesus "children of light" (Luke 16:8).

Conclusion

Paul's turnaround—from zealous, status-seeking Pharisee to zealous pro-claimer of the gospel—is Luke's most dramatic and paradigmatic example of repentance. In Acts we see Paul's heart transformed from normal selfish and tribal and cultural values—social climbing, status, wealth, power—to the other-regarding orientations of those within God's inclusive and com-passionate kingdom. Striving to hear the voice of God and to see by way of God's light, captured in the carefully shaped writing of Luke, transforms the heart required of those who enter God's kingdom (Luke 13:23–30). Believers are blessed—saved—within this community of radically trans-formed hearts (Gen. 12:1–3). This "blessing"—envisioned by the writer of Genesis, affirmed and expanded and clarified by Jesus in Luke (4:18–19), and reaffirmed by Peter (Acts 3:25)—is the blessing of God's kingdom peace offered to all peoples of the world through servant Israel.

CHAPTER 25

Paul's Farewell Speech to Jews:
The Focus Now Shifts to Gentiles (Acts 27:1–28:31)

The Kingdom, Promise and Reality

After Paul's third speech in his own defense before Jewish and Roman
leaders, King Agrippa muses, "This man is doing nothing to deserve death
or imprisonment." Later, alone with Festus the governor, the king comments, "This man could have been set free if he had not appealed to the
emperor" (Acts 26:31–32).

"We put to sea" (27:2). Paul journeys, under Roman escort, for his
requested hearing before the emperor. After several months of unfavorable
winds, treacherous seas, starvation, shipwreck, and poisonous snakes, we
hear, "And so we came to Rome" (28:14).

The narrative stage is set for Paul's last of seven major speeches, a
farewell to fellow Jews visiting him in his residence where he is being held
under house arrest (28:25–28). "They came to him at his lodgings in great
numbers. From morning until evening he explained the matter to them,
testifying to the kingdom of God and trying to convince them about Jesus
both from the law of Moses and from the prophets" (28:23). For two years
Paul boldly proclaims the kingdom without any interference from the Roman government (28:30–31). The result? "Some were convinced by what
he had said, while others refused to believe" (28:24).

Paul began his first speech to fellow Jews with "Listen!" (13:16). In his
final speech he addresses fellow Jews again. Their lack of listening is an issue.

The Holy Spirit was right in saying to your ancestors through the
prophet Isaiah,

"Go to this people and say,
You will indeed listen, but never understand;
you will indeed look, but never perceive.

262

> For this people's heart has grown dull;
>> their ears are hard of hearing;
>>> and they have shut their eyes
>>>> so that they might not look with their eyes,
>>> and listen with their ears,
>> and understand with their heart and turn—
>> and I would heal them."

Let it be known to you then that this salvation of God has been sent to the Gentiles; they will listen. (28:25–28)

Since so many fellow Jews have failed to *listen*, the salvation of God is going to the Gentiles who will *listen*. It is time for servant Israel to focus its kingdom expansion efforts on the Gentiles: "This salvation of God," Paul concludes, "has been sent to the Gentiles; they will listen."

Servant Israel will continue to bring the light of Jesus to Jews but will shift its focus to Gentiles, echoing Simeon's vision of the "light [brought] to the Gentiles" (Luke 2:30–32). Paul, under house arrest and apparently consigned to death, has already been a far-reaching witness—out of Jerusalem, all the way to Rome—of the teaching of Jesus about the gospel of God's kingdom.

The hearing cues build like a musical motif that runs the length of a symphony: from the "*light* to those who sit in darkness" (Luke 1:79) and the *light* of "glory to your people Israel" (Luke 2:32) to the *light* seen by Paul in the sky and the resurrected Jesus proclaiming "*light* both to our people and to the Gentiles" (Acts 26:23). The same applies to hearing cues like *voice* and *listen*, present from the opening of Luke through the end of Acts in the repeated accounts of Paul's repentance and in Paul's final speech: *listen* to the *voice* of Jesus and then *live* in the *light* of God's way in God's kingdom come to earth.

To the very end, in a home open to fellow Jews, Paul is "proclaiming the kingdom of God and teaching about the Lord Jesus Christ" (28:31). God's kingdom promised in Luke (e.g., 2:44–47; 4:32–37) has become a reality in Acts. But the gospel of God proclaimed in Luke's first volume—with stories of miraculous release (Luke 4–9), offering glimpses of the "year of the Lord's favor" (Luke 4:18–19)—seems far from fulfilled. Without Acts, the kingdom would seem insignificant, ephemeral, and unattainable. Acts delivers what Luke promises: the mustard plant of Luke, though the tiniest of seeds (Luke 13:19; 17:21), begins to bloom in Acts.

Events Fulfilled among Us: The Unity and Vision of Luke-Acts

Luke's promise of "an orderly account of the events that have been fulfilled among us" is the "exact truth" of the promise and challenge of God's kingdom come to earth. We catch glimpses of the kingdom in Luke, vignettes of the compassionate Jesus releasing the oppressed and possessed—from outcasts to the demon-possessed to the unclean to children—from their prisons. Alienated and oppressed and dispossessed "little ones" are released from their social or cosmic "demons" and made whole within God's compassionate and inclusive kingdom. But to try to understand Luke without its second volume, Acts, is like trying to grasp the meaning of Charles Dickens's *Great Expectations* halfway through. Likewise the attempt to comprehend the scope of Luke-Acts without the prior "chapters" of the Hebrew Scriptures is doomed.

As Zechariah looked into Israel's future, he returned to Israel's past where he first heard God's covenant promise to bless humanity. This future, God's promise fulfilled, is the story told by Luke: "The Lord God of Israel . . . has looked favorably on his people and redeemed them, rais[ing] up a mighty savior for us in the house of his servant David" so that "we would be saved from our enemies and from the hand of all who hate us" (1:68–71). Saved not through military force and political ascendancy but through a God who "has remembered his holy covenant, the oath that he swore to our ancestor Abraham, to grant us that we, being rescued from the hands of our enemies, might serve him without fear, in holiness and righteousness before him all our days" (1:72–75).

In Luke-Acts being saved means to live within God's kingdom of compassion and justice and peace. Members of God's kingdom are saved—rescued—from sin and Satan, from alienation and ostracism, from dis-ease and disease, from power and pride, from greed and idolatry, and from shame and humiliation. In God's kingdom they are welcomed, respected, fed, included, clothed, valued, housed, employed, and loved; and they have so reoriented their lives that they, in turn, welcome, respect, feed, include, clothe, value, house, employ, and love everyone in the kingdom (from the little ones to the enemy). To be saved, then, is to flourish in God's kingdom, "in holiness and righteousness before him all our days."

In Acts, Peter likewise connects his message with the Hebrew Scriptures; when speaking of Jesus, he cites Moses: "The Lord your God will raise up for you from your own people a prophet like me. You must listen to whatever he tells you. And it will be that everyone who does not listen to that prophet will be utterly rooted out of the people [Israel]" (3:22–24). All the prophets, Peter goes on, have "predicted these days" that are now coming to pass: "You are the descendants of the prophets and of the covenant that God gave to your ancestors, saying to Abraham, 'And in your descendants all the families of the earth shall be blessed.' When God raised up his servant, he sent him first to you, to bless you by turning each of you from your wicked ways" (Acts 3:25–26). As the Scriptures foretold and Luke told, Jesus, God's servant, is turning us from our wicked ways and returning and reorienting us to God's covenant.

How then does one obtain God's blessing? How does one enter into God's compassionate kingdom? Many listeners, compelled by one of Peter's powerful speeches, asked, "Brothers, what shall we do?" Peter answered, "Repent, and be baptized every one of you in the name of Jesus Christ so that your sins may be forgiven; and you will receive the gift of the Holy Spirit." "Those who welcomed his message" and repented—who turned their lives from cultural to kingdom values—"were baptized, and that day about three thousand persons [those repenting] were added" to God's kingdom (2:37–41).

Again, living among those mutually devoted to kingdom values is our salvation, our rescue from the dizzying and deadly competition of ordinary selfish and social life. These first believers, following the kingdom mandates, "devoted themselves to the apostles' teaching and fellowship, to the breaking of bread and the prayers" (2:42). And we hear: "Awe came upon everyone, because many wonders and signs were being done by the apostles. All who believed were together and had all things in common; they would sell their possessions and goods and distribute the proceeds to all, as any had need. Day by day, as they spent much time together in the temple, they broke bread at home and ate their food with glad and generous hearts, praising God and having the goodwill of all the people" (2:43–47; for the second picture, see 4:32–37).

Following the kingdom "way," in God's compassionate and inclusive community, involves the holding of possessions in common in order to share according to need. According to the teachings of Jesus (specifically, Luke 12:13–34; 16:1–31) and under the presiding Spirit of God, everyone's needs are anticipated and met. In this breathtaking kingdom paradigm, compassionate and just attitudes and actions unite for the mutual satisfaction of human needs. Luke's promise of the kingdom is manifested in these motley and joyous gatherings of believers: Jews and Gentiles, Roman officials and crippled beggars, Ethiopians and Egyptians, Cretans and Arabs, rich and poor, privileged and destitute, honored and shamed, "clean" and "unclean"—united as one by God's impartial love.

Luke is equally keen to communicate the kingdom's challenges. The disciples' repeated insistence on repentance echoes Jesus's demand to sacrifice self and possibly even life itself for the good of the kingdom. Entrance into God's kingdom requires repentance—a complete turnaround from our ordinary social and selfish ways to the radically compassionate and inclusive way of the kingdom. But the kingdom's gentle but decisive assault on earthly authority and power and honor will be met with resistance: John the Baptist was beheaded and Jesus was crucified. Jesus's disciples are asked to take up their crosses and follow Jesus.

Yet the persecution of believers in Jerusalem produces a good result— it forces the gospel out of the "holy" land to the world, in fulfillment of God's covenant with Abraham that through servant Israel all the world will be blessed. The kingdom persecuted, as foretold, is also the kingdom thriving and growing and spreading God's blessing to all the nations. Everyone in the entire world will hear God's gracious offer to enter into his compassionate and inclusive kingdom in which they mutually flourish among deeply other-regarding believers.

The extent to which this kingdom of radical inclusivity and sacrificial compassion played out as reality into the late second century and beyond is a matter of historical debate, but the kingdom's radical vision and its astonishing first steps were clear to Luke's audience.

Attention to the patterns of hearing cues, in both Luke and Acts, yields an increasingly concrete vision of God's blessing spreading throughout the world; all peoples of the world, we hear, will come to hear God's gracious offer of his compassionate and inclusive kingdom. Jesus's gracious gift of the Spirit empowers both the repentance required to enter the kingdom and the striving required to maintain it. The announcement by Jesus of the kingdom age, "the year of the Lord's favor" (Luke 4:19), when allied with Paul's farewell speech in Rome, portends the continued spread of God's word and the growth of God's kingdom come to earth.

PART FIVE

The Gospel of John

CHAPTER 26

The New Creation, Now (John 1:1–51)

The Work of Jesus, the Work of Believers

John's major theme, stated in his brief poetic preface (1:1–18), is that "to all who received him, who believed in his name, he gave power to become children of God" (1:12). But believe what exactly about Jesus? According to John, the work of Jesus is to perform miracles that explain and encourage belief in the intimacy between the Son and his Father, revealing the Father (5:36). The corresponding "work" of mortals is to believe in this intimacy between Son and Father (6:28–29).

Throughout John's Gospel we hear echoes that explain and elaborate: believers never die (6:50); they become, at the point of believing, immortals—eternal children of God (11:26), divine siblings of Jesus, who breathes God's Holy Spirit into them (20:17–22).

Jesus, co-creator of the world, creates a new "world" for God's new family beyond this world of sin and death. In this new world, believers are rescued from their slavery to sin (8:34) and the children of God live within the divine family, eternally abiding in Jesus, who abides in God. This eternal, divine life does not begin in the distant postmortem future; life in God's family is now, at the very point of believing.

This chapter covers John's introduction, which consists of a prefatory poem that encapsulates the whole story of John (1:1–18), the story of belief that generates eternity in God.

The Preface (John 1:1–18)

The work of Israel's Messiah and the work of those wishing the Messiah's deliverance are both captured in a dazzling preface that opens the story. In just eighteen verses, John offers a poetic gem that unpacks the heart of his gospel. Five major themes echo each other in reverse order. A sixth theme stands alone at the poem's center point. One can easily "hear" the connection between a theme's first statement and its subsequent echo and elaboration. In this "ring composition" we find John's major theme in the dead center of the ring, emphasized in the following chart illustrating how each idea is repeated, creating the "ring" (1 echoed by 1', 2 echoed by 2', and so on). The entire contents of John are here:

1 In the beginning was the Word, who was with God and was God (1:1–2)
   2 All things came into being through him (life and light) (1:3–5)
      3 John came to testify to that light (1:6–9)
         4 Though the world existed because of him, the world rejected him (1:10–11)
            5 To all receiving him, believing in his name (1:12a)
               6 Power given (for believers) to become children of God (1:12b)
            5' Those receiving him are born not of flesh but of God's will (1:13)
         4' The Word entered the world, accepted by those who saw his glory (1:14)
      3' John testified that Jesus is greater than he is (1:15)
   2' Jesus Christ gives the grace and truth for new life (1:16–17)
1' God the only Son, close to the Father's heart, has made the Father known (1:18)

The pattern's center point is the narrative's main point, that "to all who received him, who believed in his name, he gave power to become children of God" (1:12b).

We slow down now, as all such ancient literary masterpieces invite us to do. Think about the first theme, for example (1:1–2), and its parallel echo at the poem's conclusion (1:18):

Theme 1: "In the beginning was the Word, and the Word was with God, and the Word was God. He was in the beginning with God."

Theme 1': "No one has ever seen God. It is God the only Son, who is close to the Father's heart, who has made him known."

The divine unity is introduced first as abstract truth: the images of the Word (*logos*) and God (*theos*) are intimately related as powerful co-creators of the world. But then, in the poem's conclusion, this divine unity is pictured in personal and concrete imagery: *logos* (1:1) becomes the Son (1:18), and *God* (1:1) becomes the Father (1:18).

The entire poem is arranged with similar precision. A second related theme follows the first; then, second to last, the related theme echoes and elaborates (2 and 2'); similarly with the following (3 and 3', 4 and 4', 5 and 5'). Then at the center point of this ring composition we hear the grand revelation of the entire poem: *power is given to believers to become children of God* (1:12b).

John urges us to listen: *here is the first creation ("in the beginning") superseded by a new creation—a divine family consisting of Father, Son, and believers who become offspring of God; believers receive the power to become the children of God* (1:12b). According to John, no higher aspiration and longing can be experienced by humankind than the power to become a child in God's eternal family.

The story John tells offers increasing clarity about this intimacy between Father and Son, a familial union available to those who believe. The hard-to-picture, philosophically abstract Word (*logos*) becomes, by the end of this packed prefatory poem, the Word in human flesh, making the Father known. The movement of John's prefatory poem captures the larger movement of the entire story: what seems far out, difficult to comprehend in the poem's opening becomes near and comprehensible by the last line, which is itself a mini-poem:

No one has ever seen God.
    It is God the only Son,
        who is close to the Father's heart,
who has made him known. (1:18)[1]

The abstract language of *at the beginning, the Word was with God—and was God* becomes an intimate family portrait of *God-the-only-Son, who is close to the Father's heart*. The poem affirms that the Word who was with God *is* God and that the Son, "close to the Father's heart," is also God(-the-only-Son). To receive Jesus is to believe in this intimate union of God and Jesus, Father and Son.

But John is not so simple as might be suggested in our overview of this prefatory poem. Consider, for example, a second set of corresponding ideas in 5 and 5', above.

Theme 5: To all who receive him, believing in his name (1:12a)

Theme 5': Those receiving him do so not by human will, but God's (1:13)

Theme 5 speaks of human choice ("to all who received him, who believed in his name"); this idea is echoed and qualified by theme 5' with its emphasis on divine choice: those choosing to believe "were born not of blood or of the will of the flesh or of the will of man, but of God." On the human side, one believes in and embraces Jesus (1:12a); on the divine side, God wills the human choice and imparts the "power to become children of God" (1:12b–13). The parallelism of 5 and 5' provides the paradox of choice: believing is a *human choice*, which is the result of God's will, *God's choice*.[2]

John's story, filled with paradox, invites us to slow down and take our time to wrestle with understanding the belief that empowers us to become children of God. It takes time to make sure we hear correctly, for example, that the very human Jesus, God the Son, is the Word who was *with* God before creation and *was* God (1:1); that one becomes a child of God *by choosing Jesus*, though God chooses who believes (1:12–13).

Jesus's Titles and the Expectations of Israel (John 1:19–51)

John's introduction concludes with a cluster of titles for Jesus that place him within Israel's history. Clusters function, for the preliterate listener, as loose patterns—easier to understand and memorize than titles randomly scattered throughout the narrative.

John the Baptist is the object of speculation following the prefatory poem, in which he appears briefly as witness to the light, Jesus (1:6–9).

Messiah

When asked by the Jewish leaders who he is, John replies, "I am not the Messiah." So they ask him if he is Elijah or a prophet. Again, he says, "No" (1:19–22). As great as John may be, he is insignificant compared to the one who is coming, the Messiah (which John is not).

Lord

Who then is John? He himself answers, "I am the voice of one crying out in the wilderness, / 'Make straight the way of the Lord,'" quoting the prophet Isaiah (1:23). "I baptize with water," he goes on. "Among you stands one whom you do not know, the one who is coming after me; I am not worthy to untie the thong of his sandal" (1:26–27).

This buzz created by John the baptizer, coupled with the suggestiveness of the prefatory poem by John the author, sets the stage for the narrative entrance of Jesus.

Lamb of God

The next day John sees "Jesus coming toward him and declare[s], 'Here is the Lamb of God who takes away the sin of the world!'" (1:29).

Not even the prefatory poem could prepare us for this breathtaking claim—the Lamb of God who takes away or conquers (*airō*) sin, the evil of the world.[3] How does the Lamb of God conquer sin? This implicit question, buried in this cryptic reference to the Lamb of God, will be answered later in the text.

Rabbi, Son of God, King of Israel

Future followers of Jesus, disciples, begin to gather around him; some drop everything and follow (1:35–51). When Philip is summoned, he seeks Nathanael and says to him, "We have found him about whom Moses in the law and also the prophets wrote, Jesus son of Joseph from Nazareth" (1:45).

A bit later, Jesus sees Nathanael coming toward him and says of him, "Here is truly an Israelite in whom there is no deceit!"

Nathanael asks him, "Where did you get to know me?"

Jesus answers, "I saw you under the fig tree before Philip called you."

Nathanael replies, "Rabbi, you are the Son of God! You are the King of Israel!" (1:47–49). In a single sentence, Nathanael identifies Jesus with three titles culled from the Hebrew Scriptures, each designation indicating deliverance from grievous circumstances.

Son of Man

After Nathanael expresses his surprise that Jesus knows him so intimately, Jesus replies, "You will see greater things than these." Of those greater things, Jesus goes on, "you will see heaven opened and the angels of God ascending and descending upon the Son of Man" (1:50–51). In the second half of John's introduction, we find the seven designations for Jesus that indicate Israel's expectation of deliverance:

1. Messiah/Deliverer ("Anointed") (1:20)
2. Lord (1:23)
3. Lamb of God (1:29)
4. Rabbi/Teacher (1:49)
5. Son of God (1:49)
6. King of Israel (1:49)
7. Son of Man[4] (1:51)

Each designation would have excited the Jewish audience, fueling expectancy.

The first half of John is taken up with miracles serving as signs to the spirit realm—the opened heaven and the relationship between the Son on earth and the Father in heaven. John's audience, along with Nathanael, will figuratively hear/see heaven opened—and staying open. With the allusion to the "ladder" connecting heaven and earth in Jacob's dream, they, along with Nathanael, will understand Jesus as the link between heaven and earth revealing the divine reality above.

Conclusion

In his introductory chapter, John has offered a superb outline to guide his audience through the very rich narrative that follows. We glimpse Jesus from above, as the Word who was with God and was God, and from below, as Word made flesh. The remainder of John's Gospel—the greater things we will see—gives us more than a glimpse of the Messiah within the context of Israel's history and Israel's grandest of expectations.

The greater things to be seen, for example, are seven miracle-signs that both confirm and explain Jesus's titles. Making up the first half of John, the so-called Book of Signs, these miracles are symbols that point beyond the material world to the world of spirit. They increasingly focus on the intimacy between Son and Father and the everlasting life available to those who believe in this intimacy. The relationship between Son and Father is seen through Jesus, the "ladder" between heaven and earth. Reflecting later on these miracles, Jesus says to his Father, "I glorified you on earth by finishing the work that you gave me to do" (17:4; see also 5:36).

God sends Jesus into the world to accomplish this crucial work. God is glorified by Jesus in his doing the work of miracles that signify their intimacy as God and the Word (1:1–2), Father and Son (1:18). The miraculous transformations effected by the miracles are, in turn, signs of the believer's transformation from mortal to child of God (1:12). Performing and explaining these miracle-signs is the "work" that God sent Jesus to do. This, according to John, is why the Word became flesh.

CHAPTER 27

Water to Wine: A Sign Pointing to Transformation, Living Water (John 2:1–4:42)

John's Miracle-Signs

John divides his narrative into two major parts, a "book of miracle-signs" (chaps. 1–11) and a "book of the hour" (chaps. 13–19), which speaks of his departure to his Father and preparation of the disciples for his coming glory. Beginning with the changing of water into wine, each miracle is, in John's words, a "sign" urging belief in the intimacy between Jesus and the Father (20:30–31). Each sign points to and explains the eternal, spiritual life of a child in the divine family. By spiritual life, John means a life in the spirit realm, even as the believer continues to live on in the physical realm. Each miracle-sign follows a pattern with significant features: (1) the need miraculously met; (2) the prior positive disposition of the recipient; (3) responses to the miracle; and, most importantly, (4) the miracle's symbolic meaning.

In this chapter we examine the first sign, the transformation of water into wine and the three following sequences that elaborate on the symbol of water, indicating the possibilities of human spiritual transformation.

First Sign: "The Steward Tasted the Water That Had Become Wine" (John 2:1–11)

At a wedding, the stores of wine are running dry. But there is a good supply of water. Begrudgingly, Jesus transforms it into wine.

Need Miraculously Met

The wedding has run out of wine, Jesus's mother informs him. Jesus tells the servants to bring six large water jars intended "for the Jewish rites of purification," to fill them with water, and to "draw some out, and take it to the chief steward." The steward, unaware of the miracle, commends the bridegroom for saving the best wine until last (2:6–10).

Prior Positive Disposition

Mary ignores her son's reluctance to help with the shortage of wedding wine. Though rebuffed by Jesus, she nevertheless tells the servants, "Do whatever he tells you" (2:5).

Response

The disciples, having seen the glory of Jesus revealed, "believed in him" (2:11).

Symbolic Meaning

The changing of purification water into superior wine is symbolic of spiritual transformation, explained in three successive episodes following the miracle: the purging of the temple (2:13–22); Nicodemus and birth from above (3:1–21); and the Samaritan woman and living water (4:4–42).

The audience is assured that these three episodes belong together by the technique of *inclusio*—bookending, or using similar language at the beginning and the end of a section of literature; the middle of the two bookends supports or explains the words. The bookends of John's inclusio are "Cana in Galilee." The transformation of water into wine occurs in Cana (2:1, 10); immediately following the Samaritan woman episode, "[Jesus] came again to Cana in Galilee where he had changed the water into wine" (4:46). These parallel bookends frame the significance of the miracle of water in Cana in Galilee.

What, then, does the miraculous transformation of water into wine mean? The answer, spelled out in the following episodes, points to the great transformation of those who believe from mere mortal to immortal, from mere flesh and blood to spirit-being, from one who dies to one who lives forever ("Everyone who lives and believes in me will never die" [11:26]), and finally, from one burdened by sin to one who is freed from sin (for the believer, Jesus is "the Lamb of God who takes away the sin of the world!" [1:29]). John weaves together the following three episodes as an introduction to this great transformation, not the pedestrian one of water into wine, but the astounding one of mortal into immortal.

The Purging/Purification of the Temple (John 2:13–22)

Jesus enters the temple, purging it with "a whip of cords," driving out the moneymakers and their goods. The jars of water for the Jewish rites of purification have been transformed into wine, portending Jesus's purifying of the temple. God's sacred temple is being profaned by crass and selfish business interests. Jesus exclaims to the polluters, "Stop making my Father's house a marketplace!" (2:16).

The distraught temple merchants demand a sign of authority from Jesus that would warrant his overturning of their livelihoods. Jesus replies with a prophecy: "Destroy this temple, and in three days I will raise it up" (2:19). The temple lords are puzzled, not understanding that "he [is] speaking of the temple of his body" (2:20–21). Jesus will become the believers' temple, the locus of worship and praise for those who believe and abide in Jesus, who abides in God. Believers will abide in Jesus, the replacement temple. Jesus, we hear, is "speaking of the temple of his body. After he was raised from the dead, his disciples remembered that he had said this; and they believed the scripture and the word that Jesus had spoken" (2:18–22).

The transformation of water into wine symbolizes the transformation of the temple, upon its destruction, into the person of Jesus, the eternal, spiritual temple beyond all temporal and earthly temples.

Nicodemus: Birth from Above (John 3:1–21)

"I tell you," says Jesus to an inquisitive religious leader, "no one can enter the kingdom of God without being born of water and Spirit" (3:5; see also 18:36). While many scholars often claim that "born of water" means baptism, the context suggests that it means physical birth; believers who have been born as flesh, from the waters of the womb, are reborn as spirit, that is, "born from above."[1] This sort of transformation is consistent throughout

John—the fleshy mortal who receives Jesus becomes (is reborn) a spiritual child of God (1:12). "What is born of the flesh is flesh and what is born of the Spirit is spirit," Jesus explains. So, Nicodemus, "do not be astonished that I said to you, 'You must be born from above'" (3:6–7).

In John's Gospel, God sends Jesus both to liberate us from sin (1:29) and to transform our mortal life into eternal life within the divine family. God, we hear, so loved the world that he sent his Son so that those who believe in him would never die (3:16). Believers escape condemnation, death, and the death-in-life of mundane living.

The change of water into wine, then, signifies the transformation of the believer's ordinary earthly life (symbolized by the water of birth) into the extraordinary spiritual realm above. Again, "to all who received him, who believed in his name, he gave power to become children of God, who were born, not of blood or of the will of the flesh . . . but of God" (1:12–13).

Samaritan Woman: Living Water (John 4:4–42)

Before he returns to Cana, Jesus stops at Jacob's well and asks a woman to draw him some water. "How is it that you, a Jew, ask a drink of me, a woman of Samaria?" the woman asks ("Jews do not share things in common with Samaritans," John explains parenthetically). Jesus then makes his symbolic point: I can give you "living water" (4:9–10). While the water from Jacob's well temporarily quenches thirst (allowing relief and a bit more earthly life), the water Jesus offers "will become in [believers] a spring of water gushing up to eternal life" (4:14).

After the woman denies being married, Jesus tells her that he knows that she has had five husbands and that she is now living with a man who is not her husband (4:16–18). She replies, "Sir, I see that you are a prophet. Our ancestors worshiped on this mountain, but you say that the place where people must worship is in Jerusalem" (4:19–20). But Jesus—recall that he is the new, spiritual temple—rejects worship in Jerusalem or any earthly location whatsoever: "God is spirit," Jesus says, "and those who worship him must worship in spirit and truth" (4:24). When the woman assures Jesus that she believes that the "Messiah is coming," he informs her that "I am he, the one who is speaking to you" (4:25–26). Excited but not fully persuaded, she rushes back to town and tells people of the one who knows everything about her and wonders if he might just be the Messiah (4:28–30).

Hearing cues come in words, phrases, parallel dramatic scenarios, and elaborate chiasms. Here we find, among other cues, *water*. Just as the ordinary water of the wedding feast has been transformed into wine, so too, through the ordinary water of this well "gushing up," the Samaritan woman has been transformed into eternal life.

Conclusion

The transformation of water into wine signifies more than a richer celebration of the earthly union of a man and a woman. It ultimately symbolizes the spiritual rebirth of believers into immortal children of God. While John baptizes with water, Jesus baptizes with the Holy Spirit (1:31–33), which transforms believers into members of the divine family, children of God the Father and God the only Son (20:17, 22).

Being children living within the divine family is a never-ceasing worship and intimacy, so Jesus replaces any earthly temples. "Believe me," Jesus says to the woman intrigued by water gushing up to eternal life, "the hour is coming when you will worship the Father neither on this mountain nor in Jerusalem" (4:21). The water of purification changed into wine is prefatory to the temple's purging and transformation from a locale within space and time into the eternal and spiritual Son.

The transformation from mortal to immortal is the first step in God's new creation, a new "In the beginning" (1:1)—the beginning of God's expanding family. While the first creation by God and the Word brought order to "a formless void and darkness" (Gen. 1:2), this new creation of Father and Son brings hope of overcoming the world and its sin with a new kind of living within the divine family above.

CHAPTER 28

Dying, Crippled, Hungry, Terrified: Four More Signs (John 4:46–6:21)

Transformation

In the first half of John (chaps. 2–12), we hear of profound physical needs miraculously met. A wedding runs out of wine, and Jesus transforms water into wine. But more important than the physical transformation is the transformation in the spiritual realm, as we saw in what followed the wine miracle: the cleansing of the temple points to Jesus as the new temple; ordinary water transformed points to "a spring of water gushing up to eternal life" (4:14); birth by water points to birth by spirit.

This first miracle-sign of water transformed into wine is followed by six more miracle-signs, each pointing to the transformation from life in the physical realm into true life in the realm of spirit:

- An official's son lies dying (4:46–54).
- An ignored and helpless man is ill for thirty-eight years (5:2–47).
- A crowd pursuing Jesus is hungry but without food (6:1–14 and 6:25–65).
- Caught in rough seas, the disciples are terrified by a man walking on water (6:16–21).

We find in these four miracle-signs the same succession of movements as in the first miracle: (1) meeting of pressing need; (2) prior positive disposition of parties involved; (3) responses to the miracle; and, most crucially, (4) what the miracle-sign points to, its symbolic meaning.

Second Sign: "Sir, Come Down before My Little Boy Dies" (John 4:46–54)

"Then he came again to Cana in Galilee where he had changed the water into wine. Now there was a royal official whose son lay ill in Capernaum. When he heard that Jesus had come from Judea to Galilee, he went and begged him to come down and heal his son, for he was at the point of death" (4:46–47).

Need Miraculously Met

The royal official pleads for Jesus to heal his sick son. Jesus heeds his plea, and the son is healed.

Prior Positive Disposition

The royal official's initial belief in the power of Jesus is shown both in his twenty-some-mile walk from Capernaum to Cana and in his passionate insistence that Jesus heal his son. Though Jesus seems to berate him for needing "signs and wonders" to bolster his belief, the official is undeterred: "Sir, come down before my little boy dies." Jesus replies, "Go; your son will live" (4:48–50a).

Response

"The man believed the word that Jesus spoke to him and started on his way" (4:50b). The official's initial and desperate belief in the possibility of Jesus as healer allows him, at the word of Jesus which he believes, to return home—without Jesus.

Symbolic Meaning

The deepening of the official's belief from desperate hope to trust to unwavering and wholehearted commitment is the symbolic significance of the healing. While the father exhibits belief of some sort by making the long trek from Capernaum to Cana, such belief can mean simply "mental assent." But on his way home he is met by servants who proclaim his son's health—and at the very hour Jesus spoke the word. The father returns home in confidence, trusting in "the word that Jesus spoke to him." Finally, back home with his healed son, he commits his whole life and entire family to God: "he himself believed, along with his whole household" (4:53). The significance of this second miracle-sign is its model of the growth of belief from hopeful venturing forth to seek Jesus, to believing the word of Jesus, to faithful commitment to Jesus. "Now this was the second sign that Jesus did after coming from Judea to Galilee"—a reminder of why Jesus performs miracles, according to John, as signs pointing to truth in the realm of spirit (4:54).

Third Sign: "Take Your Mat and Walk" (John 5:2–47)

The next miracle occurs at "a festival of the Jews" attended by Jesus (5:1).

Need Miraculously Met

Jesus finds a man who has been lame for thirty-eight years sitting next to "healing waters" but with no one to help him get into the pool. Jesus heals him, but without the water.

Prior Positive Disposition

The lame man wants help, a point underscored by John's inclusion of a rhetorical question from Jesus, "Do you want to be made well?" Has the man given up hope entirely? "Sir," the man answers, "I have no one to put me into the pool when the water is stirred up; and while I am making my way, someone else steps down ahead of me." Jesus apparently takes this as a yes to his prior question; he says to the lame man, "Stand up, take your mat and walk" (5:2–8).

Response

The man obeys. Standing, he takes up his mat and walks. In the prior two miracles, the responses from all the characters were uniformly positive.

Here, however, we find some negative responses mixed in. The Jewish leaders, enemies of Jesus, ask the cured man the healer's identity. On first inquiry, the man does not know. But later, Jesus reveals himself to the man in the temple, who then tells the leaders it was Jesus. The Jewish leaders then start to persecute Jesus for breaking Sabbath rules. Jesus responds, "My Father is still working, and I also am working" (5:17). On hearing him identify himself with the Father, which is blasphemous, they seek to kill Jesus (5:15–18).

Symbolic Meaning

While there has been healing of the body, the potential for truly significant healing is found elsewhere: "Do not sin anymore," Jesus tells the healed man (5:14). Only by believing in Jesus can this man not sin anymore (Jesus, the Lamb of God, as we have seen, conquers the tyranny of sin [1:29]). The severely ill man is given a transformed physical life, which symbolizes the transformation of the believer's mortal life into a child of God in the realm of spirit—free from the tyranny of sin that rules life below. When the irate religious leaders protest Jesus's arrogation of divine power, he replies, "Just as the Father raises the dead and gives them life, so also the Son gives life to whomever he wishes. . . . Anyone who hears my word and believes him who sent me has eternal life, and does not come under judgment, but has passed from death to life" (5:21, 24). The miracle of a new physical life, though, pales in comparison to life in the realm of spirit where sin is taken away. The lame man walks, and as a child of God. The incensed leaders, however, choose darkness: "You refuse to come to me to have life," Jesus says to them (5:40).

Fourth Sign (a): "But What Are They among So Many People?" (John 6:1–14)

We have moved from water to life-saved to walking and now to bread—all staples of human life. While water and bread along with health and ambulation are essential for a good earthly life, more importantly they symbolize life above, in the realm of spirit.

Need Miraculously Met

A large crowd has been following Jesus "because they saw the signs that he was doing for the sick." As they grow hungry, a small portion of bread and fish are miraculously multiplied and distributed (6:1–11).

Prior Positive Disposition

Jesus sees the crowd but, "to test" his disciples, asks how so many people can be fed. In so doing, he is asking how much the disciples really believe. Philip answers him, "Six months' wages would not buy enough bread for each of them to get a little." Andrew counters Philip's cynicism by saying that there is "a boy . . . who has five barley loaves and two fish." No great faith here, as Andrew goes on to wonder, "But what are they among so many people?" With no food in sight, the crowd nevertheless responds positively to the disciples' command to sit down (6:5–10).

Response

After seeing "the sign that [Jesus] had done" in feeding them all, the crowd begin to say, "This is indeed the prophet who is to come into the world."[1] Later, after Jesus has explained the significance of this sign, the people think him a prophet and want to make him king (6:14–15).

Symbolic Meaning

The explanation of this bread miracle (6:25–71) is interrupted by a very brief miracle dealing with fear at sea. John's purpose for this interruption between the food multiplication miracle and its symbolic meaning—both lengthy and complicated—will be explored in a moment.

Fifth Sign: "It Is I; Do Not Be Afraid" (John 6:16–21)

After Jesus's bread miracle, the people begin to say, "This is indeed the prophet who is to come into the world." They are about to "take him by force to make him king" when Jesus escapes, going off "again to the mountain by himself" (6:14–15). People living in fear of oppression by their enemies want a Messiah, a deliverer, a king. Here, they think, he is! Fear is the focal point of the shortest of these miracle accounts, which intervenes between the bread miracle and its meaning.

Need Miraculously Met

At nightfall, with Jesus gone, the disciples get into a boat and head for the coastal town of Capernaum. With a strong wind blowing, the sea becomes rough. After three or four miles of rowing, they see Jesus walking on the sea toward them, and they are "terrified." Upon taking him into the boat, they find themselves safe on shore (6:16–21—the shortest miracle-sign of all).

Prior Positive Disposition

While the disciples are believers (2:11), they are nonetheless terrified at the sight of Jesus walking on the very seas that threaten them—and yet "they [are] willing to receive Him into the boat" (6:21 NASB).

Response

When the believing disciples are terrified at the sight of Jesus, he says to them, "It is I [*I am*]; do not be afraid" (6:20). Their response, in the face of the precarious situation, is eager: they willingly take on board that which had moments before terrified them. "And immediately the boat reached the land toward which they were going."

Symbolic Meaning

This miracle points to the source of comfort and peace, Jesus, the *I Am*, the always-present God. "It is I" echoes God's response to Moses's request for God's name: tell Pharaoh, says God, "I Am" sent you (Exod. 3:14).[2] What Jesus says here, we will hear again: *"I am"* (John 8:58). This brief miracle account introduces fear, a concern that looms in the chapters that follow. For the fearful disciples, the presence of Jesus as the great *I Am* overcomes both the threat of the sea and of a person who walks on that sea.

This episode of believers taking Jesus into their boat is followed immediately by an explanation of the symbolic meaning of the bread miracle in which believers take Jesus, the bread of heaven, into their being: they eat his flesh and thereby abide in him. The symbolic significance of these two interconnected miracles is suggested in the parallel intimacies of (1) welcoming Jesus into their storm-tossed boat and (2) taking Jesus into one's own body.

Fourth Sign (b): Symbolic Meaning of Feeding Miracle (John 6:25-26)

From the miracle at sea we return to land and to the bread miracle. "When [the people wanting to make Jesus king] found him on the other side of the sea, they said to him, 'Rabbi, when did you come here?' Jesus answered them, 'Very truly, I tell you, you are looking for me, not because you saw signs, but because you ate your fill of the loaves'" (6:25-26).

"Do not work for the food that perishes," Jesus continues, "but for the food that endures for eternal life, which the Son of Man will give you—for it is on him that God the Father has set his seal" (6:27). *Son of Man*[3] indicates authority, understood by the audience as divinely authorized and underscored by God the Father's seal. But what kind of *food* is Jesus talking about? The answer is not immediately forthcoming.

Meanwhile, when the people ask, "What must we do to perform the works of God?" Jesus answers, "This is the work of God, that you believe in him whom he has sent" (6:28-29). Doing the work of God is to believe in Jesus—the Son, intimately related with the Father. They ask him, "What *sign* are you going to give us then, so that we may see it and *believe* you? What *work* are you performing? Our ancestors ate the manna in the wilderness; as it is written, 'He gave them *bread from heaven* to eat'" (6:30-31). The symbolic meaning of the multiplied bread is suggested by the four key points emphasized in this question: *sign*, *believe*, *work*, and *bread from heaven*. These are spelled out throughout John:

1. The *signs* given are the seven miracle-signs that point to the transformation of the mortal into an immortal child of God.

2. Believing, aided by these miracle-signs, is the only work required by humans for salvation, *believing* in the intimacy of Father and Son.

3. "What *work* are you performing?" The answer is the signs, the miracles that he is performing and explaining (4:34; see also 17:4; the *work* of followers is to believe, 6:29).

4. The *bread from heaven* is Jesus, his body and blood: when eaten and drunk, mortals are transformed into immortal children in the divine family.

The remaining conversation elaborates on this last point. "Sir, give us this bread always," the audience responds (6:34).

A hearing cue guides those listening to John's story: "Sir," the thirsty woman asks, "give me this water, so that I may never be thirsty or have to keep coming here to draw water" (4:14–15). The woman at the well is promised "a spring of water gushing up to eternal life," while the hungry crowd wants the bread of heaven *always*. Believing, they will have it always just as the woman, believing, will have the water of eternal life always. "I am the bread of life," Jesus says. "Whoever comes to me will never be hungry, and whoever believes in me will never be thirsty" (6:35).

In these miracles, hunger and thirst, along with the desires of the diseased, signify our deepest spiritual longings, desires that find fulfillment once and for all beyond anything the physical world can offer. "I am the living bread that came down from heaven," claims Jesus. "Whoever eats of this bread will live forever" (6:50–51). *I am the bread of heaven; feast on me.* Then Jesus says, more graphically, "Those who eat my flesh and drink my blood abide (*menō*, "dwell") in me, and I in them" (6:56). The metaphor of eating Jesus, "bread of heaven," is as outlandish as what it signifies: that ordinary mortals become, while still on earth, immortals; such transformed mortals abide in Jesus, who abides in his Father (14:20; 15:4).

Cannibalism is, to most cultures, an abomination, and from Genesis 9:4 and throughout the Hebrew Scriptures, drinking blood from any source was forbidden. So why are we told to feast on Jesus and to drink his blood? What can he be saying?

Eating Jesus, in John's Gospel, is a graphic image of abiding in Jesus. The ordinary pleasure of appetitive fulfillment is but a faint image of abiding in him as he abides in the Father (1:18).

To preclude any implications of cannibalism or religious blood rites—including symbolic substitutes for flesh and blood[4]—John includes a postscript where Jesus clarifies that eating the bread of heaven and drinking

Jesus's blood are symbolic—that he is speaking of the spirit, after all, not of his body: "It is the spirit that gives life; the flesh is useless" (6:63a).

The bread of heaven has nothing to do with Jesus's dead body or spilt blood; rather, it has to do with his spoken words, revealing the Father. He says plainly that "the words that I have spoken to you are spirit and life" (6:63b). Ingest and digest these words, and live. Drink this water, Jesus has told the thirsty woman, and you will live truly, eternally. Immortal life, the life of a transformed child of God, is found by ingesting Jesus's life-giving words.

Of all the symbolic meanings offered for the seven miracles, this is the most complex. Its difficulty drove early disciples away. "Do you also wish to go away?" Jesus asks the twelve. Peter replies, "Lord, to whom can we go? You have the words of eternal life. We have come to believe and know that you are the Holy One of God" (6:67–69). Peter's short but revealing reply indicates his comprehension: How can we leave the only food that sustains, your "words of eternal life"? To ingest the flesh and blood is to ingest, take deep within oneself, *the words of eternal life.*

Words. Multiple meanings and interplays of Word and word abound in John's Gospel. John began with the Word who was with God and was God (1:1). This Word (*logos*) brings light to the darkness and order to the primeval chaos (Gen. 1:1–19). The Word takes on flesh—"the light of all people" who live in the chaotic darkness of sin (John 1:4a). The Word appears as light, "shines in the darkness, and the darkness did not overcome it" (1:4b–5). The fleshed Word, Jesus, did miracles that required explanation, words—"words of eternal life."

In the middle of his symbolic teaching about being the bread from heaven, Jesus quotes Scripture regarding this present time, that the people "shall all be taught by God" (6:45). Jesus has been recognized by a Jewish leader, Nicodemus, as the "teacher who has come from God"—in both his words and in "these signs that you do," which no one can do "apart from the presence of God" (3:2). We hear an echoing in what Jesus says here, that "everyone who has heard and learned from the Father comes to me" and "whoever believes has eternal life. I am the bread of life. Your ancestors ate the manna in the wilderness, and they died. This is the bread that comes down from heaven, so that one may eat of it and not die. . . . Whoever eats of this bread will live forever" (6:47–51).

Eating the flesh and drinking the blood of Jesus means taking in and believing the words of life spoken by the Word. Peter understands: "*You have the words of eternal life. We have come to believe and know that you are the Holy One of God."* To eat his flesh and drink his blood is to believe in the Word and his words that offer "eternal life," and so to abide in Jesus as Jesus abides in the Father (1:18). These words, Jesus tells us, are spirit and life.

Conclusion

The point of patterns of repeated hearing cues in ancient literature is to shape the narrative in such a way as to embed meaning. What, in John, does this pattern of seven miracles point to? Are there differing truths, a string of wise sayings? Or is there a unifying thread? Consider:

- A desperate father travels far to implore Jesus on behalf of his dying son; his son's miraculous revival leads to trusting commitment in Jesus by the father and his entire household.
- A man sick for thirty-eight years is released from his crippling illness and, in believing, released from the tyranny of sin.
- Terrified disciples on rough seas take Jesus into their boat; Jesus gives them peace.
- A hungry crowd is miraculously fed, pointing to the transformation of the person who ingests Jesus, the bread come down from heaven; the believer thereby lives a life eternal in the divine family.

Each miracle points to, is a sign of, the reality of miraculous transformation in the realm of spirit.

The father of the dying son and his entire household come to belief in Jesus, which inducts them into the family of God, who is spirit (1:12). The desperately sick man, lame for thirty-eight years, is offered spiritual life with the challenge from Jesus not to sin, an impossibility without belief in the Lamb of God who takes away the tyranny of sin (1:29). The terrified but believing disciples deepen their life in the realm of spirit by receiving the *I Am* of the universe into their boat. Those who have eaten the miraculously multiplied bread are offered a life of "abiding" in Jesus by eating him, the bread from heaven—the enfleshed Word eaten by feasting on his words in order to secure life eternal within the divine family: "It is the spirit that gives life; the flesh is useless. The words that I have spoken to you are spirit and life" (6:63).

CHAPTER 29

True Seeing and Resurrection Life: Culminating Symbolic Truths (John 9:1–52; 8:12–11:57)

"Before Abraham Was, I Am"

In ancient narratives, a twist in the pattern of hearing cues indicates special meaning. In John's orchestration of seven miracle-signs, only one, the multiplication of bread, is interrupted by another, the terrified disciples receiving Jesus into their boat. What, then, is the special meaning of this conspicuous twist?

Fear is the central theme in the interrupting miracle at sea, and the presence of Jesus, the *I Am*, is fear's antidote. The granddaddy of all fears is death: bread sustains mortal life, but for only so long. Immortal bread from heaven, on the other hand, sustains unending life. John's audience, decades after the departure of Jesus, was facing circumstances fearful enough to threaten faith. So John's narrative faces death and its fears head-on. The twist accentuates the meaning of the two intertwined miracle-signs: belief in the intimacy of the Son and his Father produces life eternal, a life that is impervious to all earthly fears, removing the threat of the world's evil and sins (1:29).

The miracle-signs encourage belief in the face of these very real fears by affirming and explaining the abundant and eternal life of those abiding in Jesus. In a dramatic two-chapter break from John's miracle pattern, we hear of Jesus's forthcoming death. But John explains that what will happen to Jesus following his death will likewise happen to believers following theirs: translation into heaven.

In this sequence that interrupts the pattern of miracles, John offers a hearing cue that hearkens *back* to the first miracle's "spring of water gushing up to eternal life" (4:14) and *forward* to the imparting of the Spirit and living water: "On the last day of the festival . . . [Jesus] cried out, 'Let anyone who is thirsty come to me, and let the one who believes in me drink. As the scripture has said, "Out of the believer's heart shall flow rivers of living water."'"

Now he said this about the Spirit, which believers in him were to receive; for as yet there was no Spirit, because Jesus was not yet glorified" (7:37–39). John's insertion of the Spirit to come in the middle of dire threats is a reassurance that regardless of how grim the prospects, the believer has (a) flowing rivers of living water and (b) the comforting, guiding Spirit to come.

After the healing of the lame man, the tone has become decidedly dark with repeated references to threats of death. The audience is warned: Jewish leaders will resist, to the point of death, Jesus and his spiritual family:

- "For this reason the Jews were seeking all the more to kill him, because he was not only breaking the sabbath ["working" to heal the lame man], but was also calling God his own Father, thereby making himself equal to God" (5:18).
- "After this Jesus went about in Galilee. He did not wish to go about in Judea because the Jews [that is, their leaders] were looking for an opportunity to kill him" (7:1).
- "'Why are you looking for an opportunity to kill me?' The crowd answered, 'You have a demon! Who is trying to kill you?'" (7:19).
- "Now some of the people of Jerusalem were saying, 'Is not this the man whom they are trying to kill?'" (7:25).
- "Is he going to kill himself? Is that what he means by saying, 'Where I am going, you cannot come'?" (8:22).

Immediately preceding the sixth miracle, Jesus says to his opponents, "Very truly, I tell you, before Abraham was, I am" (8:58). The promise of life requires *believing*, and the content of that belief—Jesus is God (the *I Am*)—is considered blasphemous by the "pious" but envious Jewish leaders. So they angrily seek to stone him (8:59).

Unlike those in John's audience, Jesus is undeterred by the death threats. Indeed, he is all the more resolved to complete the work that God gave him to do. But his final two miracles, which enhance his claim to be God, only serve to increase the fury of his opponents.

Sixth Sign, True Seeing: "If This Man Were Not from God, He Could Do Nothing" (John 9:1–43)

Jesus has hidden himself after the threat of being stoned to death; later he is walking along and sees a man blind from birth (8:59–9:1).

Need Miraculously Met

A blind man sees.

Prior Positive Disposition

The blind man permits his eyes to be plastered by Jesus with saliva and mud; he complies when told to go to the pool at Siloam for washing (9:6–7).

Response

Although some can see that the blind man sees, most of his neighbors and the religious leaders don't or can't see that Jesus gave sight to the blind. While some neighbors affirm the healing, others suggest that the man claiming to be healed is an imposter: it is not him; "it is someone like him" (9:9a).

The blind man insists that he is the formerly blind man, attributing his healing to Jesus (9b–11).

Some of the skeptical Jewish leaders call the blind man's parents to them to prove that he had been, unequivocally, blind; his parents assure them that he was but, fearing repercussions from the Jewish leaders, they profess ignorance of his cure; they defer to their son. The Pharisees return to the man, claiming that Jesus is a sinner (9:18–24).

The cured blind man becomes a preacher (whose words sound like those of John himself): "I have told you already," the man responds, "and you would not listen. Why do you want to hear it again? Do you also want to become his disciples?" He pauses, letting the possibility sink in, then proceeds: "Here is an astonishing thing! You do not know where he comes from, and yet he opened my eyes. We know that God does not listen to sinners, but he does listen to one who worships him and obeys his will." *Listen, worship, obey*—the preacher's three inevitable points. "Never since the world began," the witness for Jesus concludes, "has it been heard that anyone opened the eyes of a person born blind. If this man were not from God, he could do nothing" (9:25–33).

"Are you trying to teach us?" the indignant leaders exclaim. And they force him out (9:34).

Symbolic Meaning

We have just heard of a host of sighted people who cannot see Jesus as healer. But the symbolic meaning is more about spiritual seeing. Jesus finds the cured man and asks, "Do you believe in the Son of Man?" The man asks, And who is that? "Jesus said to him, 'You have seen him, and the one speaking with you is he.' He said, 'Lord, I believe.' And he worshiped him"—a belief that embraces (9:35–38). The transformation of physical blindness to sight is a sign pointing to the transformation of those who are spiritually blind to those who, in the realm of spirit, see and believe and live (9:39; 1:12).

The purpose of John's selection and arrangement of miracles is less to show the compassion of Jesus and more, as the writer himself explains, "that you may come to believe that Jesus is the Messiah, the Son of God, and that through believing you may have life in his name" (20:31). That is, the miracles are signs prompting belief—as the prologue to this miracle-sign suggests: "[Jesus] saw a man blind from birth. His disciples asked him, 'Rabbi, who sinned, this man or his parents, that he was born blind?' Jesus answered, 'Neither this man nor his parents sinned; *he was born blind so that God's works might be revealed in him*'" (9:1–3). The meaning of the miracle is in its symbolic meaning—the transformation from physical blindness to physical sight, a prelude to transformation from spiritual blindness to a spiritual seeing and membership in the divine family of Father and Son.

Seventh Sign, Resurrection Life: "I Am the Resurrection and the Life" (John 11:1–53)

While Jesus offers eternal life within God's family to those who believe— that Jesus is the Messiah, the Son of Man, the *I Am*, and that Jesus and the Father are intimately related one—we hear of unbelief, resistance, and even threats of violence (John 10). To those who believe that Jesus and the Father are one, Jesus will give eternal life; they will never perish (10:28–30). Those who don't believe, who are stuck in their captivity to the world and its sin, are denied eternal life.

John's narrative takes a dramatic shift from belief and unbelief, and their respective consequences, to Jesus's mixed feelings about the death of his dear friend Lazarus. Jesus could have prevented the death, but allows it to happen in order to manifest God's glory for the purpose of engendering belief.

Need Miraculously Met

Jesus raises Lazarus from death.

Prior Positive Disposition

Lazarus's distressed sisters, Mary and Martha, send a message to Jesus: "Lord, he whom you love is ill." Jesus delays his coming, and Lazarus dies. When Martha meets Jesus, she is upset, telling him that if he had been there, Lazarus would have lived. Nonetheless, she believes that "God will give you [Jesus] whatever you ask of him." But when Jesus reassures her that her brother will rise again, Martha believes only that he will rise again "on the last day" (11:1–24). But Jesus wants more *content* to the belief, more even than what Martha confesses, that Jesus is "the Messiah, the Son of God, the one coming into the world." Jesus wants another kind of believing: that he himself is "the resurrection and the life"—and that "those who believe in me, even though they die, will live," and that "everyone who lives and believes in me will never die." Believers at their "death," like Jesus will be at his, will simply slip from their mortal flesh and continue in their immortal spiritual status as offspring of God (11:25–27).

Sister Mary likewise is upset at the delay of Jesus—that, had he chosen to arrive on time, Lazarus would have been healed (11:32). True, as Jesus will explain.

When Jesus commands those near Lazarus's tomb to "take away the stone," they do (though Martha fears the stench of four days' putrefaction). The prior disposition of the sisters is a mix of rather generic belief (Lazarus will rise on the last day of judgement) and unbelief (because Jesus arrived too late, Lazarus is beyond help).

Response

After seeing the raising of Lazarus, many Jews believe in Jesus, but the jealous and fearful Jewish leaders plot to kill him: "The chief priests and the Pharisees [call] a meeting of the council, and [say], 'What are we to do? This man is performing many signs. If we let him go on like this, everyone will believe in him, and the Romans will come and destroy both our holy place and our nation.'" Caiaphas, the high priest, defends the sacrifice of Jesus for the good of the whole nation (11:44–53).

Symbolic Meaning

In the previous chapters, Jesus has spoken, on the one hand, a great and disturbing deal about death—his impending death—no doubt to the consternation of his followers; on the other hand, he has said a lot about life—everlasting life—for all who believe. John unites these two themes in a dramatic crescendo: the resurrection of Lazarus in which Jesus reassures believers that he, indeed, is the resurrection and that believers need not fear death because, along with sin, death and its stench are conquered. So Jesus prays for the proper response to and understanding of this miracle: "Father, I thank you for having heard me. I knew that you always hear me, but I have said this for the sake of the crowd standing here, so that they may believe that you sent me" (11:41–42).

Jesus has intentionally delayed coming to the home of Lazarus and his sisters, allowing his dear friend Lazarus to die so that the miracle might be seen as a sign of God's providing eternal life for believers—that they might "see the glory of God" (11:40–42). John surely anticipated the shock of including this detail of allowing death in order to demonstrate, as Jesus puts it, the glory of God. As with the blind man, some problems are permitted so that believers will "see the glory of God"—not when they die, but now. Jesus will later commend "those who have not seen and yet have come to believe" (20:29).

In response to Martha's generic but dismissive claim that, yes, of course Lazarus will rise again on the last day (like everyone else), Jesus makes the astonishing claim, *I am the resurrection*, identifying himself as the source of eternal life: "Those who believe in me, even though they die, will live, and everyone who lives and believes in me will never die"

(11:25–26). Through belief in Jesus, all believers, like Lazarus, are transformed into never-dying children of God. This final miracle dramatically demonstrates the symbolic meaning of all the miracles, first heard in Jesus's retort to the Samaritan woman: "The water that I will give will become in them a spring of water gushing up to eternal life" (4:14). Drinking that water transforms the believer from mortal to immortal, in eternal union with the Father and Son (1:12).

Conclusion to the Book of Signs (John 2–11)

The miracles of Jesus that occur in the realm of the material world are signs of the realm of spirit—that is, signs of life in the realm above as God's children (1:12; 20:17). John's artful arrangement of the seven signs in the first half embeds his theological perspective: the miraculous transformations occurring in the material world point to the more important transformation in the spiritual world where the believer is transformed from mortal to immortal, from child born of human parents to child of God, abiding eternally and intimately in the divine family of Father and Son. One either lives and dies, or lives eternally now and forever in the joy of the divine family, death a mere leave-taking of pure spirit from the body.

The fourfold arrangement of need met, prior disposition, proper response, and symbolic meaning are far from mere formalities repeated precisely. In them is meaning that, working in concert, is compelling.

Need Miraculously Met

Each need arises in ordinary life, the realm of the physical. Meeting this need speaks of the believer's extraordinary transformation into the realm of spirit, explained by Jesus or by John the author.

Prior Disposition

The mother of Jesus tenaciously pursues her reluctant son to use his transformative powers. The official with an ill son tenaciously believes in Jesus, the healer, traveling miles to see him and then returning with only a promise of healing.

The disposition of others, however, is ambivalence or negativity. When Nicodemus comes to Jesus by night, Jesus says that "those who believe in [Jesus] are not condemned" but that "those who do not believe are condemned already, because they have not believed in the name of the only Son of God" (3:18). What is the cause of belief and unbelief? Unbelief, in John, results from a negative prior disposition: "the light has come into the world, [but] people loved darkness rather than light because their deeds were evil" (3:19). As Jesus says to those disposed to darkness: "You are from your father the devil and you choose to do your father's desires. He was a murderer from the beginning and does not stand in the truth, because there is no truth in him. When he lies, he speaks according to his own nature, for he is a liar and the father of lies. But because I tell the truth, you do not believe me" (8:44–45). Since those whose "father" is the great Liar are not disposed to the truth, they cannot believe the truth offered by Jesus. Those accustomed to doing evil "hate the light and do not come to the light," while "those who do what is true come to the light" (3:20–21). Already loving darkness precludes one's perception of the light.

Response

Response to the miracle-signs reinforces the importance of prior dispositions. Jesus's first sign in Cana, water transformed into wine, "revealed his glory; and his disciples believed in him" (2:11). Prior disposition—they had been following Jesus—leads to belief. The royal official believes enough to make a difficult journey; he believes more deeply when, hearing from Jesus that his son will live but without Jesus going to his home, he "believe[s] the word" spoken by Jesus; finally, he believes with the belief bringing eternal life in the divine family when hearing—while not quite home—of his son's healing: "So he himself believed, along with his whole household" (4:50–53). Moreover, while Mary and Martha consent, their consent falls shy of believing that Jesus *is* the resurrection, just as he is the temple. This is difficult believing—that the one who reveals the Father is also the resurrection itself. "This is the bread that comes down from heaven," Jesus has explained, "so that one may eat of it and not die" (6:50).

Believing, then, is both complete enough to immediately engender eternal life and a process through which one grows in understanding.

Symbolic Meaning

The entire point of the seven signs, escalating in complexity and significance, is clear from the beginning, at the heart of the chiastic preface: "To all who received him, who believed in his name, he gave power to become children of God, who were born, not of blood or of the will of the flesh or of the will of man, but of God" (1:12–13). The complexity of this ultimate significance is underscored by its the poetic arrangement:

- "To all who received him, who believed in his name [human choice],
    - he gave power to become children of God,

- who were born, not of blood or of the will of the flesh or of the will of man, but of God [God's choice]."

On the one hand, believers choose God, and, on the other hand, God chooses them (instilling in them a positive prior disposition). Put succinctly, you must choose, but you can't choose unless God has already chosen you.

The narrative tension between (a) a God-instilled prior disposition and (b) responsibility for choice runs through the narrative. "No one can come to me," says Jesus after the bread miracle, "unless drawn by the Father who sent me" (6:44). Jesus later says, "I, when I am lifted up from the earth, will draw all people to myself" (12:32). At first it seems that some do not come to Jesus because they are not drawn by the Father; then Jesus says he will draw all persons to himself, period. Perhaps the tension here is resolved by the simple truths (1) that no one comes to the Father unless they are drawn, though some refuse; and (2) that those who receive him, believing in his name, have been "born" as children of God because it is God's will that such choice be honored. In any case, the entire purpose of John is to show how the "work" of Jesus (17:4) is performing miracle-signs to prompt the choice of believing (20:30–31).

But this first half of John is more than a simple pattern of repeated miracle-signs. There appear, as in all the great literary art of this time and place, twists in the pattern, a narrative way of underlining or qualifying or elaborating something critical to the embedded meaning. For example, the miracles proceed successively except in the case of the bread and sea miracles: the latter interrupts the former, as we have seen. Jesus multiplies the bread, but before the symbolic meaning is explained, another miracle of Jesus walking on water and dealing with terrified disciples interrupts. Why?

Recall that, caught in a turbulent sea, the disciples are terrified at the sight of Jesus walking toward them. "It is I," Jesus says; "do not be afraid" (6:18–20). The experience of God, the *I Am*, in the person of Jesus, received into their boat, anticipates the explanation by Jesus of the bread miracle: Jesus is the bread of heaven, and to eat him is to receive Jesus into one's being, becoming an immortal child of God. Ingesting the eternal Word, the *I Am*, is to abide in Jesus who abides in God, all in a divine family in the realm of "spirit and life" (6:63). To have the *I Am* in one's boat indicates a certain intimacy with God, but to ingest the *I Am* into one's body raises the image of intimacy to heights well beyond the ability of words to convey.

This first half of John, often referred to as "The Book of Signs," is no mere listing of miracles that prove Jesus to be God's Son. Rather, the miracles all point to the claim that belief in Jesus, the resurrection and the life, is to live forever—starting now, at belief—in the divine family. Jesus doesn't merely provide resurrection from death: he *is* the resurrection. Jesus doesn't merely provide release from hunger, disease, and deprivation: he *is* the way, the truth, and the life (14:6); he himself *is* the bread of heaven and the eternal water. He *is* the temple—the place and object of worship. As resurrection, he is the antidote to death, the one through whom the believer passes, in the moment of death, into the world of resurrection and pure spirit. Death becomes an entrance rather than an exit—a more complete enjoyment of the heavenly abode without the encumbrance of the physical body. Resurrection conquers death—which, for the believer, ceases to exist. Jesus's work, miracles-signs which encourage the transforming power of belief, are explained with Jesus's words: "I tell you, anyone who hears my word [*logos*] and believes him who sent me has eternal life" (5:24). This echoes the Word (*logos*) who was with God and was God, the Word who became flesh in order to demonstrate God's glory in the transformation of death into life.

CHAPTER 30

The Book of the Hour, Phase One: "The Hour Has Come" (John 13–17)

What Is the Hour?

While Jesus repeatedly speaks of his death, it is, in the first twelve chapters, off in the future. His hour, which we learn is simultaneously and curiously the hour of both his death and his glorification, has not yet come (12:23; 12:27). The hearing cue *hour* is crucial. Initially we hear:

- "And Jesus said to [his mother], 'Woman, what concern [shortage of wine] is that to you and to me? *My hour has not yet come*'" (2:4).
- "Then they tried to arrest him, but no one laid hands on him, because *his hour had not yet come*" (7:30).
- "He spoke these words while he was teaching in the treasury of the temple, but no one arrested him, because *his hour had not yet come*" (8:20).

The repetition in chapter 12 further highlights the importance of the hour:

- "Jesus answered them, '*The hour has come for the Son of Man to be glorified*'" (12:23).
- "Now my soul is troubled. And what should I say—'Father, *save me from this hour*'? No, it is for this reason that *I have come to this hour*'" (12:27).

And then we hear: "Jesus knew that *his hour had come* to depart from this world and go to the Father" (13:1). The hour that had not yet come has come. The hour—of plotting and betrayal and arrest and trial and death and departure and glorification—has finally arrived. "Father, *the hour has come*," Jesus will pray; "glorify your Son so that the Son may glorify you" (17:1).

What *is* this hour? Why does John organize the entire second half of his story around it, with hearing cues judiciously placed in the first half? The hour is, first, that of dying in which Jesus-as-Word returns to his Father. John introduces this hour as "his hour . . . to depart from this world and go to the Father" (13:1). Second, for Jesus, reunited with the Father, it is the hour of glorification (12:23); and yet it is the hour from which Jesus wants, in part, to be saved (12:27). Jesus's final hour, then, is an hour of both gloom and glory: Jesus will suffer horribly and, upon "death," leave his friends. When the hour is finished, he leaves his friends and departs from this world to return as promised in "a little while" to his followers (16:16).

At the precise moment that the hour is fulfilled, the dying Jesus says, "It is finished." The hour finished, he bows his head and gives up (*para-didōmi*, "delivers up, entrusts, conveys") his spirit to the Father (19:30). When Jesus and the Father are reunited as the One portrayed in John's prefatory poem, Jesus is glorified and glorifies his Father (17:1): the Word with God *and* God the Son in the bosom of the Father (1:1, 18). Jesus has successfully completed his work, and the Word who was God and was with God is, once again, with God. Their shared glory, then, is the glory of their restored primal union, God the Son reunited with the Father (minus the body he took on as the Word become flesh; 1:1, 14, 18). The glory of the unified God/Word in their first creation is restored and fulfilled in the glory of the reunified Father/Son upon completion of the new creation.

Prior to finishing this hour, Jesus shares his pleasure at having finished his assigned task of performing the miracle-signs: "I glorified you on earth by finishing the work that you gave me to do," he says in prayer with his Father (17:4; see 10:25, 37; 14:10–12). Lying ahead is the hour that must be finished. Chapter 12 transitions between the work of miracles that is finished (chaps. 2–11) and the so-called Book of the Hour (chaps. 13–19). We slow down, now, to explore John's transition between the Book of Signs and the Book of the Hour (chap. 12); Jesus's preparation of his disciples for the coming hour (chaps. 13–16); and Jesus's own preparation for the hour (chap. 17).

Between Miracle-Signs and the Hour: "The Hour Has Come for the Son of Man to Be Glorified" (John 12)

John 12 looks both backward and forward—backward to Lazarus raised from death (12:1–8) and forward to the hour of Jesus's glorification (12:23;

12:32). This transitional chapter moves quickly from Jesus acclaimed to Jesus deeply troubled (12:27).

Jesus praises Mary for anointing his feet with precious oil for his coming burial; a crowd sings Hosanna as he approaches Jerusalem; testimony about the raising of Lazarus continues to annoy religious leaders; and Jesus snubs some Greeks[1] because "the hour has come for the Son of Man to be glorified" (12:20–23). His glorification will come at the point of death, after trial and suffering, and so he speaks of his soul being "troubled" about the hour ahead (12:27).

But Jesus realizes that, in being lifted up on the cross, he "will draw all people to [himself]" (12:32). Not all who are drawn will come to believe. "While you have the light," Jesus urges, "believe in the light, so that you may become children of light" (12:36). Many who have experienced this light, who have witnessed the many signs done in their presence, do "not believe in him" (12:35–36). Then again, "many, even of the authorities," believe, but some refuse for "fear that they [will] be put out of the synagogue" (12:42). At the heart of the fear is their love for "human glory"—status and power—rather than "the glory that comes from God" (12:43). *Glory* is a key hearing cue in John. Glory, sharing in the intimate relationship of the Son with the Father, is neither understood nor sought by those imprisoned in the world and its evil. Instead, they seek worldly glory, clinging to self-importance and self-aggrandizement, hoping to be honored by others.

John 12 ends with Jesus crying aloud, "Whoever believes in me believes not in me but in him who sent me. And whoever sees me sees him who sent me. . . . I speak just as the Father has told me" (12:44–45, 50). From here on out, Jesus focuses on his preparation for the hour ahead of those who have seen and heard and believed (chaps. 13–17). He offers his disciples the kind of assurance that they need to face both the departure of Jesus and their own hour of suffering and death.

Jesus Prepares the Disciples for the Hour (John 13–16)

Jesus and his disciples remain in the same room together for five chapters. The last (chap. 17) focuses exclusively on Jesus in prayer with his Father. Only Judas interrupts the scene by leaving (13:30) to betray Jesus (13:2).

"Now before the festival of the Passover, Jesus knew that his hour had come to depart from this world and go to the Father" (13:1). This verse marks the beginning of the second half of John, the so-called Book of the Hour. Jesus and his disciples are indoors, sitting around a table. The narrative spotlight shifts from the showy outside events of the miracles section to an inside scene with the intimate dialogue it permits. This narrative structure reflects the meaning: Jesus is inviting the few true believers from the big outside world of external and fleeting concerns into the interior realm of spirit. Jesus is, in a sense, preparing his disciple for the intimate life in the divine family (14:1–3).

Time slows down here, and space shrinks to a room with just the twelve and Jesus. The audience leans in, trying to hear more clearly the sometimes-hushed tones of this intimate dialogue.

"Unless I Wash You, You Have No Share with Me" (John 13:1–20)

It is just before the Passover festival. Jesus and his disciples are seated at a table. Jesus gets up, takes off his robe, ties a towel around his waist, pours water into a basin and stoops before each disciple, washing and drying their feet.

When Peter objects to having his feet washed by his Messiah and Lord, Jesus answers, "Unless I wash you, you have no share with me" (13:8). To have a "share" is to be a part or have a portion of a whole. The "whole," here, is the union of Son and Father. Jesus, then, is pointing symbolically to the intimacy of having a share with Jesus himself, who abides in his Father. The foot washing represents a sharing in divinity with Jesus.[2]

When Peter hears that unless he submits to the foot washing, he can have no share with Jesus, he insists on being washed all over, not just his feet. But Jesus clarifies: "One who has bathed does not need to wash, except for the feet, but is entirely clean. And you are clean—though not all of you." He is referring to Judas, who will betray him (13:9–11). To have a share with Jesus requires one to be "entirely clean," which comes by virtue of believing (as all the disciples but one do).

Such an intimate sharing inspires a new commandment for members of God's family, to love one another as Jesus has loved them, to serve others as Jesus has served them. By lovingly washing the feet of others, the disciples offer a symbolic reminder of their being made clean by their believing, thus initiating them into their own intimate union with Jesus (13:34).

"Where I Am Going . . . You Will Follow Afterward"
(John 13:21–14:31)

Jesus, "troubled in spirit," gives a piece of bread, dipped in a dish, to his betrayer Judas—who disappears into the night (13:21–30).[3] "Little children," he says to the remaining eleven, "I am with you only a little longer. You will look for me; and as I said to the Jews so now I say to you, 'Where I am going, you cannot come'" (13:33). Peter wonders where, to which Jesus responds, "Where I am going, you cannot follow me now; but you will follow afterward" (13:36). The mystery is slowly clearing up, but only for those who listen with care.

Anticipating his disciples' fears about his forthcoming departure, Jesus offers them words of profound and much-needed assurance: "Do not let your hearts be troubled. In my Father's house there are many dwelling places." Where is Jesus going? The answer comes: "I go to prepare a place for you. . . . I will come again and will take you to myself, so that where I am, there you may be also" (14:1–3). Will come again—but when? And where? Thomas asks him, "Lord, we do not know where you are going. How can we know the way?" Jesus replies, "I am the way, and the truth, and the life. . . . If you know me, you will know my Father also" (14:5–7). Just as Jesus is the resurrection, so too Jesus is the way to the Father's eternal house (not a "way" as in a path on which one journeys to a destination, but a "way" as in *I Am*, so that one who believes is immediately present with the Father).

In the meantime, Jesus goes on, you need not be troubled. "I will not leave you orphaned," Jesus says. "I am coming to you. In a little while the world will no longer see me, but you will see me" (14:18–19). I am returning, Jesus says, and I will be with you. He has promised to return and "to take you to myself" (14:3), and he will share with them a helper, God's own Spirit (14:15–17, 26).[4]

John's story at this point progresses along these lines of mystery and confusion by explaining more and more as this section unfolds. Along with the disciples, John's listeners will indeed come to see and know.

"Abide in Me": "I Am the Vine, You Are the Branches" (John 15:1–17)

Believers, we've heard, abide in Jesus by eating his flesh (6:56), the metaphoric language of intimate union with God. "Abide in me as I abide in you," says Jesus here (15:4). He offers a different, more organic metaphor of *abiding in*: "Just as the branch cannot bear fruit by itself unless it abides in the vine, neither can you unless you abide in me. I am the vine, you are the branches. Those who abide in me and I in them bear much fruit, because apart from me you can do nothing" (15:4–5). This metaphor symbolizes a deeply intimate love flowing within the divine family: "As the Father has loved me, so I have loved you; abide in my love" and "love one another as I have loved you" (15:9, 12). It also symbolizes God's joy flowing within and through God's children: "If you abide in me, and my words abide in you," all will be done for you and "my joy" will be in you so that "your joy may be complete" (15:7, 10–11). Finally, the vine metaphor suggests that God's goodness and love will flow into the believer and out to the world: "Those who abide in me and I in them bear much fruit" (15:5).

"They Will Put You out of the Synagogues . . . [and] Kill You" (John 15:18–16:4a)

Since such communal intimacy is an offense to cultural normalcy, Jesus warns of opposition: "If the world hates you, be aware that it hated me before it hated you" (15:18).

So Jesus prepares his disciples for the hour ahead by talking directly about the troubles to come—they will be hated, persecuted, expelled from the synagogues, and even killed. Jesus thinks forewarned is forearmed: "I have said these things to you so that when their hour comes you may remember that I told you about them" (16:4; see also 15:18–25). Most importantly, Jesus promises he will send a divine helper, "the Advocate, . . . the Spirit of truth who comes from the Father [who] will testify on my behalf" (15:26). Recall the miracle at sea in which the disciples' terror was relieved when the *I Am* entered into their boat. So too the Advocate, who comes from the Father, will abide with them in their hour of darkness, thus relieving and overcoming their deepest fears.

"A Little While, and You Will No Longer See Me, and Again a Little While, and You Will See Me" (John 16:4b–33)

John returns to the mystery of Jesus departing in a little while and returning to his friends in a little while. Jesus continues to comfort his discouraged and confused disciples who are facing both his absence and their own hour of suffering and death. "Sorrow," he says, "has filled your hearts" (16:6). But only by his leaving can the Advocate come, who will confirm Jesus's teachings, give the disciples the words they need to say, share God's glory with them, and give what is God's to them. He will, in short, turn their pain into joy. This joy, Jesus repeats several times, will be theirs in "a little while." But the disciples are understandably wary and fearful.

> "A little while, and you will no longer see me, and again a little while, and you will see me." Then some of his disciples said to one another, "What does he mean by saying to us, 'A little while, and you will no longer see me, and again a little while, and you will see me'; and 'Because I am going to the Father'?" They said, "What does he mean by this 'a little while'? We do not know what he is talking about." Jesus knew that they wanted to ask him, so he said to them, "Are you discussing among yourselves what I meant when I said, 'A little while, and you will no longer see me, and again a little while, and you will see me'?" (16:16–19)

What they don't know at this point is that the Advocate or Comforter (*parakletos*), also called the Spirit of truth (15:26), will be brought to them in person, breathed into them by Jesus in his promised return (20:22).

But just "a little while"? What could Jesus mean? Jesus does, of course, return in a matter of days. Upon departing to his Father, then, Jesus prepares the divine household as promised and returns as promised, in a little while: "If I go and prepare a place for you, I will come again and will take you to myself" (14:3). And then, shortly thereafter, he inaugurates them into the divine family when he breathes into them the Advocate, the promised Spirit of truth, and they become divine "brothers" in God's family (20:17).

Of course, they will also be without Jesus in the not-too-distant future after they see Jesus for the last time: they will face their own suffering. Your hour is coming, he tells the disciples (16:32). Jesus has offered an analogy to help them understand: "When a woman is in labor, she has pain, because her hour has come. But when her child is born, she no longer remembers the anguish because of the joy of having brought a human being into the world. So you have pain now; but I will see you again, and your hearts will rejoice, and no one will take your joy from you" (16:21–22). The joy of having her child in her arms overwhelms the mother's memory of suffering. Whether an hour or two or even more than a few, the joy of her child makes every mother think her suffering took just a little while. So too with the disciples: in a little while they will experience pain and sorrow *and* in a little while there will be joy in their new life. The joy of rejoining Jesus will so overwhelm the suffering that it will be thought to have taken "a little while." So looking retrospectively, in the mirror as it were while sitting in a seat of glory, one's previous suffering seems like nothing.

"I came from the Father and have come into the world [as flesh]," Jesus explains; "again, I am leaving the world and am going to the Father [as Spirit]" (16:28; see 19:30). Just as Jesus is returning to the Father after his hour of darkness, so too will the disciples rejoin him in abiding with the Father after their own dark hour of labor pains. Then, looking forward to his ultimate leave-taking, having brought them into the divine family with his God breath, Jesus adds: "In the world you face persecution. But take courage; I have conquered the world!" (16:33)—just as he has conquered the evil and sin of this world for believers (1:29).

Jesus Prepares Himself for the Hour (John 17:1–25)

"After Jesus had spoken these words [preparing his disciples for the hour], he looked up to heaven and said, 'Father, the hour has come; glorify your Son so that the Son may glorify you'" (17:1). Having spoken to his followers about their coming suffering, Jesus now speaks directly to his Father in preparation for his own hour of suffering. The two hours are intertwined: the believers' hour of grief at the departure of Jesus, for however little a while, will intersect and commence with the close of Jesus's hour, his death and departure to the Father. The hour of Jesus, with flesh flogged and crucifixion, is finished upon death, allowing his spirit to be yielded up to the Father. He returns to the Father as before creation (13:1).

Even in these quiet last moments before the playing out of the torturous yet crowning moment of his time on earth in the flesh, Jesus expresses his concern to the Father. "Now I am coming to you, and I speak these things in the world so that they may have my joy made complete in themselves." The completion will come upon his return, with the in-breathing of the divine spirit. Meanwhile, "I have given them your word, and the world has hated them because they do not belong to the world, just as I do not belong to the world. I am not asking you to take them out of the world, but I ask you to protect them from the evil one" (17:13–15).

Jesus delivers his final prayer of protection for the disciples from eternity ("Now I am no longer in the world" [17:11]) but also in time ("I speak these things in the world" [17:13]). Jesus existed in and with God before creation and has already completed his work of miracle-signs on earth (though his hour is not yet done); he will reclaim his pre-creation glory when he departs this world to return to the Father. So he prays, "Father, the hour has come; glorify your Son so that the Son may glorify you" (17:1).[5] In being lifted up and drawing to himself all who would be drawn, Jesus sees what John wants his audience to see, that the moment of death, for Son and Father, is the moment of glory.

Jesus uses this prayer as a summary of all that he lived and taught. In it we find answers to the questions, Why did the Word take on mortal flesh? What was the purpose of the life and death of Jesus? John's entire narrative has been aiming at the answer: "The glory that you have given me," Jesus says to his Father, "I have given them, so that they may be one, as we are one, I in them and you in me, that they may become completely one" (17:22–23). Believers abide in Jesus and the Son abides in the Father; they abide in each other as members of the divine family.

Perhaps the believer's relationship to space-time is not unlike Jesus's: believers abide eternally in God from the moment of belief and yet continue to live on this very temporal earthly plane until, like Jesus, they shed their flesh. As Jesus says in his prayer, "They do not belong to the world, just as I do not belong to the world" (17:16). And yet, like Jesus, they remain in the world. "As you have sent me into the world," Jesus adds, "so I have sent them into the world" (17:18). In the world, they will, again like Jesus, bring others to believe and become members of God's joyful, glorious, and eternal family.

Conclusion

Jesus prays in and about his "hour" within space and time all the while pointing to his departure from space and time when the Word returns to the eternal realm with the Father. His family is also expanding to include mortals transformed into immortal children of God. Jesus's mortal hour ends in his eternal glorification, one shared with all believers (17:22). Jesus prepares his disciples for their hour of glorification by, of all things, washing their feet. He then prepares them for their hour of darkness by reassuring them that he is returning (in "a little while") to the Father to prepare a "place" in which they will (in "a little while") dwell together; there they will become one with Jesus who is one with God (like branches abiding in their vine). Jesus reassures his anxious disciples that in "a little while" they will see him again, and that they will be given the Spirit of God. Their joyous life of sharing in the divine glory will begin soon, upon his return, and it will continue forever upon the shucking off of their mortal and sinful flesh.

The Book of the Hour, Phase Two: "It Is Finished," the Hour Fulfilled (John 18–19)

Three Finishings

The final words of Jesus to his Father, as he prepares for death, express God's desired intimacy of the divine family that includes the Son and Father and also God's children, mortals transformed into immortals. Jesus prays that "they may be one, as we are one" and that "those also, whom you have given me, may be with me where I am, to see my glory" (17:22, 24). How can they—believers, Son and Father—be one, with Jesus soon to reside above with the Father while the believers remain below? How can they *be with me where I am, seeing my glory*?

The answers come in John's carefully choreographed explanation of God's new creation. Within John's story of this new creation, John includes three *finishings* (accomplishments or completions):

- Finished work: "I glorified you on earth by finishing the work [miracle-signs] that you gave me to do," Jesus says to his Father (17:4).
- Finished hour: "'It is finished.' Then he bowed his head and gave up [or *yielded*] his spirit" (19:30).
- Finished creation: Returning from his Father in the little while promised to his followers, Jesus breathes into them the divine life of the Spirit, the *Ruah* of God (20:22), making them children of God (1:12; 20:17).

We have already discussed the work that God gave Jesus to do—the miracle-signs and their explanations. Here we explore the second finishing, Jesus's hour that has come and soon will be finished.

Having concluded his preparatory prayer to his Father (chap. 17), Jesus, accompanied by his disciples, goes out across the Kidron Valley and enters a garden (18:1). Listeners to John's story are taken from the garden through the corridors of the world and its human power and its exercise of ultimate evil—death by crucifixion. Judas brings the religious leaders to the garden, and Jesus is arrested. During the arrest he chastises Peter for cutting off the high priest's slave's ear. "Put your sword back into its sheath," Jesus commands. "Am I not to drink the cup that the Father has given me?" (18:11). The "cup" is the dark side of the coming ordeal. In John, the finished hour includes both the gloom of harassment, suffering, and dying and the glory of Jesus's return to the Father. The gloom also includes flogging by the opposition and the betrayal and denial by both Judas and Peter (18:25; 19:1).

John prepares his audience to reconcile gloom and glory by indicating the divine plan behind the shocking events. The structure of John's narrative of the humiliating death of Jesus suggests that, despite appearances to the contrary, Jesus is King. Despite appearances, the powers and potentates characterizing the world are trumped by a dying king who, returning from the realm of spirit and the source of all that is, reappears in glory to his followers—reappearing *with* glory for his brothers and sisters.

Two patterns of repeated hearing cues take the listener through the events leading to the death of Jesus. We follow their lead.

Two Telltale Patterns: King of the Jews and According to Scripture

John provides two clusters of material that are crucial in recognizing who Jesus is beyond what has already been established. John reinforces and reassures his audience with the historical-religious context for determining who Jesus is.

"King of the Jews"

An ancient lector reading John to a listening audience would emphasize various patterns of hearing cues. For example, when reading Nathanael's announcement of Jesus as "King of Israel" (1:49), the lector may have paused dramatically, bowing slightly with arms outstretched just prior to the grand pronouncement. In the sequence covering the finishing of Jesus's hour, an ancient lector might have again emphasized *king*—sometimes with respect, sometimes quizzically, and sometimes in derision:

- "Blessed is the one who comes in the name of the Lord—the *King of Israel!*" (12:13).
- "*Your king* is coming, sitting on a donkey's colt!" (12:15).
- "Are you *the King of the Jews*?" the Roman official Pilate asks (18:33).
- "So you are *a king*?" Pilate asks, repeating himself (18:37).
- "Do you want me to release for you the *King of the Jews*?" asks Pilate (18:39).
- "Hail, *King of the Jews!*" shout the soldiers (19:3).
- "Here is *your King!*" Pilate says. The crowd shouts, "Crucify him!" (19:14–15a).
- "Shall I crucify *your King*?" asks Pilate (19:15b).
- "Jesus of Nazareth, *the King of the Jews*," reads the inscription on the cross (19:19).

When quizzed by Pilate about being King of the Jews, Jesus expresses himself very carefully, affirming only the possibility that he is "a king"—but not of Israel as a political entity. "My kingdom," he says, "is not from this world." If it were, Jesus adds, "my followers would be fighting to keep me from being handed over to the Jews." So as it stands, Jesus explains, "my kingdom is not from here" (18:36). Pilate rephrases his question: "So you are a king?" Jesus's reply, "You say that I am a king," suggests that Pilate is right but perhaps not completely right (18:37). Jesus, as we've heard in the entirety of John's narrative, is not a king in this world, though the king of the world, king over all creation (1:1–2). He is, moreover, king of a new creation, God's heavenly family. *Jesus of Nazareth*—the lector thinks to himself—*King of the World*. The Roman prefect Pilate comes to his own conclusion, which John's audience hears as the headpiece Pilate insists be placed on the cross: "Jesus of Nazareth, the King of the Jews" (19:19).

To be sure, Jesus is no ordinary king, and he's not the king many Jews were hoping for. He is not offering deliverance from Israel's tyrannical oppressors. He does not carry a sword and a shield. He is not asserting his military might or political power. For John, King Jesus delivers believers instead from the vastly worse tyrannies of sin and death. Jesus reigns, then, as the "Lamb of God who takes away"—conquers—"the sin of the world!" (1:29). Jesus is, again ironically, the powerful Lamb, able to destroy in one fell swoop the sorrow and strife caused by sin's domination of the world. The people had wanted to make Jesus king after their own fashion of royalty (6:15), but God makes Jesus king as the conquering Lamb removing evil from the life of the believer. As a result, believers—released from the grip of sin—reside above sin's sorrow and strife.

"So That the Scripture Might Be Fulfilled"

From the pattern of the repeated cue *King of the Jews*, John moves to another meaning-filled pattern with the hearing cue *fulfilled*. None of this, John is saying, is mere happenstance; all of it is planned.

While Jesus's arrest may look like a cacophony of humanly orchestrated events, from the betrayal of Judas to soldiers carrying torches and weapons, John portrays God as in control of the drama of Jesus's death. Jesus appears kingly. We hear, for example, that Jesus knows "all that [is] to happen to him" (18:4). When Peter lops off the ear of a servant, Jesus tells Peter to sheath his sword because he must drink the cup that the Father has given him. John intertwines these hearing cues pointing to divine control with further cues citing fulfillment of ancient and authoritative scripture that foretells the unfolding story:

- "Although he had performed so many signs in their presence, they did not believe in him. *This was to fulfill the word spoken by the prophet Isaiah*" (12:37–38).
- "While I was with them," Jesus tells his Father, "I protected them. . . . I guarded them, and not one of them was lost except the one [Judas] destined to be lost, *so that the scripture might be fulfilled*" (17:12).
- Soldiers prize Jesus's tunic. "So they said to one another, 'Let us not tear it, but cast lots for it to see who will get it.' *This was to fulfill what the scripture says*, 'They divided my clothes among themselves, and for my clothing they cast lots'" (19:24).
- "[Jesus] said (*in order to fulfill the scripture*), 'I am thirsty'" (19:28).
- "These things occurred *so that the scripture might be fulfilled*, 'None of his bones shall be broken'" (19:36).
- "*And again another passage of scripture says*, 'They will look on the one whom they have pierced'" (19:37).

John's citations of fulfilled scripture would have reassured his listening audiences. Fulfilled scriptures, like the multiple miracle-signs, were intended to instill and encourage belief (20:30–31). They would have heard that the Father and his Son, even at history's darkest hour, are in control.

John is saying—when the small hints of Jesus's control are magnified by the big picture to show divine control exemplified in the fulfillment of Holy Writ—that Jesus *is* King, as seen in the context of scripture and its present fulfillment.

The Hour Finished

The greatest irony[1] in John is that the hour of Jesus's death is not his hour of humiliation and defeat; it is, rather, the hour of glory, of being at once with his Father upon yielding up his spirit. Rather than the glory of a returning and victorious king, the returning Jesus shares in the glory of his Father as he had when, as Word, he was with God and was God (1:1). Such glory far outshines any glory known on earth. And Jesus promises this same glory to his believers.

On the cross, having received the requested wine to quench his thirst ("in order to fulfill the scripture"), Jesus says, "It is finished" (19:28–30). And so we come to the second of three finishings, that of *the hour*. For the listener attentive to hearing cues, there is little doubt as to the antecedent of *it* in these last words of Jesus in the moment of his dying. "It is finished." Surely the lector speaks here in tremulous tones, then pauses—perhaps dropping his head for a long moment before slowly lifting his gaze as if to the heavens. The dramatic pause yields a final description of the finishing: "He bowed his head . . . and yielded up his spirit" (19:30). His flesh had expired, been shucked off, his spirit at that very moment yielded up to his Father. As declared at the beginning of this last half of John, "Jesus knew that his hour had come to depart from this world and go to the Father" (13:1).

Conclusion

The hour that had not yet come (first half of John) has now come (beginning of second half of John, 12:23 and 13:1). And now it is finished. It is the hour of death, departure, and, finally, glory. Without Jesus's death and departure, he couldn't return to breathe the divine Spirit into believers— and so, no life in God's family. But believers, according to John, are given "power to become the children of God" (1:12).

To a wary religious leader, Jesus has tried to explain: "What is born of the flesh is flesh, and what is born of the Spirit is spirit. Do not be astonished that I said to you, 'You must be born from above'" (3:6–8). John's narrative aims at encouraging belief in Jesus as God, transforming the believer from a sinful mortal to an immortal child of God. As a result, the believer—released from the grip of sin (1:29)—resides, above sin's sorrow and strife, in the glory of the family of the Father and of the Son. The hour is finished.

CHAPTER 32

"He Breathed on Them and Said to Them, 'Receive the Holy Spirit'" (John 20–21)

Finishings

Upon dying, Jesus departs and is glorified with the glory that he had when he was with God "before the world existed" (17:5). He then returns to his disciples in the "little while" that he promised (14:19) in order to breathe into them the divine Spirit, completing God's new creation (20:17, 22). This new creation, hinted at in the opening words of John's preface, replicates the opening words of Genesis, "In the beginning . . ." (Gen. 1:1; John 1:1). This new creation for John is the divine family, incorporating believers transformed from mortals into eternal children of God (John 1:12). Human beings on earth are fully incorporated into, abiding in, the divine family above.

The first creation peaked on day six with God breathing life into their inert human clay form. But from John's perspective, the first humans are mortal, with a breath that ties them inexorably to the earth and its evil. Release from the earth and evil—even from death itself—comes when Jesus breathes God's breath into believers, transforming them into immortals living in union with the divine family in the spirit realm above (20:22). The work of the new creation is completed.

The architecture of John's Gospel is structured, as noted, by patterns of repetition oriented around three successive "finishings": finished work (of miracle-signs), finished hour, and the finished new creation. In this chapter we explore the finished new creation—the inauguration of God's new creation in which believers become children of God by receiving the Holy Spirit.

The last section of John (chaps. 20–21) focuses on the four postmortem appearances of Jesus. Jesus returns from the Father—as promised—not in the physical form assumed by the eternal Word but as the Word in spiritual form, released from the trappings of flesh. Subtly embedded in John's pattern of repeated appearances is the culmination of meaning in John:

the new creation in which the believer's life in the spirit realm has likewise triumphed over flesh and matter, evil and sin—and even death itself.

First Appearance: "Do Not Insist on Touching Me" (John 20:1-18)

"While it [is] still dark," early in the morning just days later after the crucifixion, Mary Magdalene sees that the stone has been removed from Jesus's tomb. She runs to Peter "and the other disciple, the one whom Jesus loved" (the so-called beloved disciple),[1] to report the theft of Jesus's body. Peter and the beloved disciple run to the tomb, the latter arriving first; he sees "the linen wrappings lying there," but he does not enter. When Peter arrives, he enters and sees "the cloth that had been on Jesus's head, not lying with the linen wrappings but rolled up in a place by itself" (20:1-7).[2] Although they are mentioned twice, John doesn't explicitly explain the meaning of Jesus's corpse wrappings. Heard within the context of John's entire narrative, the meaning slowly emerges.

When the beloved disciple finally enters the tomb, he sees and believes (20:8). He sees what Peter sees and he believes, while Peter, like the other disciples, is befuddled—"for as yet they did not understand the scripture, that he must rise from the dead" (20:9). Only the beloved disciple understands that Jesus could not be contained by death. The beloved disciple, who "saw and believed," would become a model for future listeners who "see" through the eyes of faith: "Have you believed because you have seen me?" asks Jesus in his second appearance. "Blessed are those who have not seen and yet have come to believe" (20:29).

Jesus's exit from his wrappings and his fastidious attention to his head cloth suggest his unimpeded exit from his linens. While Lazarus required human assistance to get out of his burial bindings, the resurrected Jesus exited his clothes unaided. John seems to imply that the smooth exit of Jesus from his burial clothes mirrors Jesus's instantaneous exit from his flesh-and-blood body at its expiration.

Mary, John's narrative proceeds, returns to the burial site and stands "weeping outside the tomb" (20:11). She sees someone she takes to be a gardener and says, "Sir, if you have carried him away, tell me where you have laid him, and I will take him away." When Jesus speaks her name, she cries out in recognition, "Rabbouni!" (20:15-16). The Teacher has returned. Jesus says to her, "Do not insist on touching me because I have not yet ascended to the Father" (20:17a).[3] Then he commissions her as the story's first evangelist: "Go to my brothers and say to them, 'I am ascending to my Father and your Father, to my God and your God.'" Only now, after his return from the Father, does Jesus address his disciples as "brothers," members of his family. "Brothers" suggests that these believers are kin of Jesus in the divine family: as brothers, the distinction between Jesus and his disciples, mere mortals, has been abolished. Jesus is saying to Mary, *The time of the gathering of the divine family is now; go and tell my brothers.* "Mary Magdalene went and announced to the disciples, 'I have seen the Lord'" (20:17b–18).

Since John's account includes neither a resurrected body of flesh nor an ascension, we don't know what it means for Jesus to "ascend" to the realm of eternal spirit. In John, there is no record of a body lifting off earth and moving upward to the heavenly Father. But the important point is not the precise nature of Jesus's final return to the Father; it is, instead, that he is *on his way* to the Father. And, by way of the Spirit of God, believers, "my brothers," are also on *their* way to the Father. Jesus, recall, is the way (14:6). Jesus thus commences God's new creation of his divine family *within* and *beyond* the realm of flesh in the realm of spirit. Jesus had said to his disciples, "If I go and prepare a place for you, I will come again and will take you to myself, so that where I am, there you may be also" (14:3). This has come true. He has come again and is now able, with the inbreathing of the divine Spirit, to take believers to himself, so that where he is, there they are, too.

Second Appearance: Jesus Came through Locked Doors and Stood among Them (John 20:19–31)

That very day, in the evening, "the doors of the house where the disciples had met were locked for fear of the Jews, [and] Jesus came and stood among them and said, 'Peace be with you'" (20:19). Through doors locked against fear of the Jewish leaders, Jesus appears and offers peace. The disciples rejoice (20:20).

Jesus's resurrected body is no ordinary body. There is no indication that his body is anything like the human flesh that Jesus had assumed as Word, and every indication to think otherwise. And when he returns from the Father to induct his brothers and sisters into the divine family, he breathes on them and says, "Receive the Holy Spirit" (20:22). This breath is not from a body in the realm of flesh; it is God's "breath" from the realm of spirit. In the first creation, God breathed mortal life to inert creatures of clay. In his new creation, when the Spirit breathes the life of the Father, life eternal, the mortal is transformed into an eternal child of God.

Only now does John mention the forgiveness of sins: "If you forgive the sins of any," says Jesus to his brothers, "they are forgiven them; if you retain the sins of any, they are retained" (20:23). This reference is to be understood in the context of the whole story. Earlier, Jesus said to unbelievers, "You will die in your sins unless you believe that I am he" (8:24).[4] According to John, the Lamb of God conquers sin by liberating the believer from slavery to sin.[5] The role of Jesus in John, then, is to provide escape from the tyranny of sin (1:29), not to forgive sins. Believers escape the "sin of the world" and thus death itself (1:29). We hear Jesus say again, "Peace be with you. As the Father has sent me, so I send you" (20:21). The disciples are sent into the world as Jesus has been sent into the world, as witnesses to the unity of Father and Son and to the efficacy of the Lamb to conquer sin.

Third Appearance: Again through Locked Doors (John 20:24–29)

John prepares his audiences for a strange turn in the story: "Thomas (who was called the Twin), one of the twelve, was not with them when Jesus came" (20:24). Told of the meeting between his disciple friends and Jesus, Thomas says, "Unless I see the mark of the nails in his hands, and put my finger in the mark of the nails and my hand in his side, I will not believe" (20:25). A week later the believers gather in the same house, this time with Thomas. And again, "although the doors were shut, Jesus came and stood among them" (20:26). Jesus then says to Thomas, *Touch and see, and believe.* Without any record of touching, Thomas believes, exclaiming, "My Lord and my God!"

With an eye to his own audience decades later, John uses the story of Thomas to encourage life-giving belief in future generations: "Have you believed because you have seen me?" Jesus asks. "Blessed are those [John's audience] who have not seen and yet have come to believe" (20:29). This question by Jesus, and praise for those coming later who believe without having to see, or touch, is likely the last action or dialogue of the original version of John. It concludes with a summary statement by John: "Now

Jesus did many other signs in the presence of his disciples, which are not written in this book. But these are written so that you may come to believe that Jesus is the Messiah, the Son of God, and that through believing you may have life in his name" (20:30–31). And so, very likely, the Gospel according to John has concluded. A fitting ending indeed.

Fourth Appearance: "A Last Meal" (John 21)

Most Bibles include John 21 as John's final chapter, although it is likely a later add-on, perhaps tacked on as an epilogue. Let's assume, though, for the sake of taking the whole as a coherent unity, that this is the intended ending.[6]

Here we find a final appearance of Jesus: "After these things Jesus showed himself again to the disciples by the Sea of Tiberias" (21:1).

Several disciples have gone fishing, but with no luck. Jesus stands on the shore, but none of the disciples recognize him (21:4).

"Children, you have no fish, have you?" the unrecognized Jesus asks. He then tells them of a good fishing spot (21:5–6). When they fish as instructed, they find immediate and abundant success—"a hundred fifty-three" fish. Only then does the "disciple whom Jesus loved" recognize Jesus, shouting, "It is the Lord!" (21:5–7). The load of fish is dragged to shore, where they find charcoal-broiled fish and bread awaiting them (21:9).

"Come and have breakfast," Jesus says. It is their last meal together. In John, there is no mention of the "last supper," with broken bread representing the body of Jesus and wine representing his blood. John, however, narrates a last meal in which Jesus serves grilled fish. The story, echoing the washing of their feet and the feeding of the hungry crowd, is followed by the command to feed Jesus's lambs. Jesus is modeling, once again, the works of self-sacrificial love that the disciples must continue toward one another in his absence (21:15–17).

The disciples have been, of all things, fishing—a noble vocation, for sure, but not *their* vocation. After all, they had just been commissioned and empowered to complete Jesus's work of peace (20:21–23). Perhaps they need one more concrete reminder of the focus and demands of their life on earth before their release from flesh upon death. So the eternal, risen Word serves bread and fish to his disciples.

Jesus reminds them of their vocation, emphatically urging Peter, three times, to manifest his love of Jesus by caring for his lambs:

- "Feed my lambs" (21:15).
- "Tend my sheep" (21:16).
- "Feed my sheep" (21:17).

We hear echoes, of course, of Peter denying Jesus three times. But, empowered by the Spirit, Peter does indeed love Jesus in Jesus's radically self-sacrificial feed-my-sheep way. Recall the "new" commandment—the only commandment we find in John—"love one another as I have loved you" (13:34; 15:12). Peter, we now hear, finally gets it: he will self-sacrificially love as Jesus loved, to the point of death (21:18–19). And just as Peter previously denied Jesus in order to avoid death, he now sincerely affirms his willingness to follow Jesus to his death, which many in John's audience would know to be the case. Peter's inquisitiveness, however, is a distraction from single-mindedly following Jesus (and loving as Jesus loved): he wants to know both the identity of Jesus's betrayer and the destiny of the beloved disciple. Jesus says in effect, "That is no business of yours. Here, one last and emphatic time, is your business: 'Follow me!'"[7]

There is, of course, much more that John could have written; so many miracle-signs, so many astounding teachings, and so many models of self-sacrificial love. But enough is enough, so John concludes: "This is the disciple who is testifying to these things and has written them, and we know that his testimony is true. But there are also many other things that Jesus did; if every one of them were written down, I suppose that the world itself could not contain the books that would be written" (21:24–25). Enough said. Believe, receive the in-breathing of God's Spirit, live in the new creation as God's own children; abide in Jesus as he abides in the Father; love one another as he loved you.

Conclusion

By the end of John's twenty-one chapters, John's audience has learned that they should not take God's miracles and deeds at face value. Bread, after all, represents the bread of heaven, and water, the spring of eternal life. The fish—"a hundred fifty-three of them" (21:11)[8]—represent the "sheep" the disciples are to nourish. Indeed, the miracles are not so much about alleviating human pain and physical suffering as about pointing symbolically to a spiritual reality beyond our very mundane flesh-and-blood world.

John's Gospel, then, concerns the spiritual realm and how believers attain to it. And John has prepared his listeners to hear his summative message in his final two chapters. Let us gather, then, into one theological basket all of John's hearing cues.

Consider how the four appearances of Jesus after his death address the nature of the spiritual Jesus. John has taken care to present the physical reality of Jesus after death as very different from the human flesh taken on by the Word. Jesus's body has not been resurrected like that of Lazarus. After all, his "body" twice passes through locked doors. And he can't or shouldn't be touched or clung to. Mary is told to stop trying to hold onto Jesus; Thomas, demanding proof, does not touch Jesus's wounds. And while Jesus cooks and serves food to his disciples, we don't see him ingesting it. Jesus's death, John is saying, was a release from his taken-on flesh. Just as Jesus slipped from his corpse wrappings in the tomb, he has sloughed off once and for all, on the cross, material flesh and blood. He returns to his disciples as promised, not in the same flesh that the Word once donned, but in an untouchable, immaterial, life-giving, Spirit-breathing spirit-body.

Believers in the intimacy of this Spirit-breathing Jesus and the Father whose breath he imparts become members in full standing of the divine family, joining in the intimacy of Father and Son. How can John get these profound meanings across, with mere words, with metaphor and symbol? He has succeeded, albeit only to those ears willing to listen carefully. Just as Jesus is "ascending to [his] Father and [their] Father," so believers now inhabit flesh of no consequence, mere vessels of the inbreathed Spirit. They temporarily inhabit flesh to be shucked off at death—in effect, not dying at all: "everyone who lives and believes in me will never die" (11:26). For John, the believer already, as brother or sister, shares the nature of the post-death, spiritual Jesus.

In John, then, there is no earthly kingdom in which one seeks and finds peace, communal flourishing. Instead, the peace that Jesus offers is the believer's release from the burden of flesh and the tyranny of sin (1:29). Eternal life is here, now, abiding in Jesus who abides in God: to abide in the presence of God is to abide in the family dwellings prepared by Jesus (14:1–3). While still on earth, the believer finds her peace above. Jesus, the Lamb of God, conquered the sin that plagues ordinary flesh, effecting liberation and peace—an entirely new creation. Because Jesus has conquered the world (16:33), the believer finds the otherworldly peace of God that transcends earthly troubles, persecutions, and fears (14:27;

20:19, 26). The disciples, in these final chapters, are commissioned by Jesus to share *this* message of peace: "As the Father has sent me, so I send you" (17:18).

The Father sent Jesus, we heard, out of love to encourage transforming belief (3:16). And the disciples are commissioned to love *like Jesus*. This raises two questions: How did Jesus love? And what did he require by way of belief? Jesus, the eternal Word, temporarily donned human flesh to empower believers to become children of God (1:1–18). The Word temporarily became flesh to verify and explain, through various miracle-signs, believers' transformation from mortal to eternal children of God. When Jesus tells Peter to care for his sheep, John's audience will recall the "new" commandment (13:34)—the *only* commandment offered in John—"that you love one another as I have loved you" (15:12). Again, how has Jesus loved? By temporarily housing the Light within flesh, Jesus manifests and explains love as intimate union, barely explicable—as in the eating of another's flesh, the bread of heaven. The words of eternal life offered by Jesus, ingested and digested, transform believers into children of God and draw them into the intimacy within the divine family—abiding in each other. "The spirit . . . gives life; the flesh is useless. The words that I have spoken to you are spirit and life" (6:63).

What, finally, must one believe to inherit everlasting life? After all, John wrote his gospel so that we might "believe that Jesus is the Messiah, the Son of God, and that through believing . . . have life in his name" (20:31). Belief, not action, lies at the heart of John's message. Contrary to the demands of kingdom life in the Synoptic Gospels, John's Gospel cares very little for the law: "The law indeed was given through Moses; grace and truth came through Jesus Christ" (1:17). As noted, Jesus asks us to believe in him and to love one another. That's it. Indeed, *doing good*, in John, is to believe in the intimate union of Father and Son: "This is the work of God, that you believe in him whom he has sent" (6:29). *Doing evil*, then, is refusal to believe. What, then, does John require by way of belief?

John's required belief is at once more intellectual and metaphysical than one might expect given inherited Christian tradition.[9] According to John, by believing in the unity and intimacy between the eternal Word and the Creator God on the one hand and Jesus and his Father on the other, the believer can enter into this creatively powerful yet deeply intimate divine unity. Believers are transformed, by the power of God, from sinful mortals to immortals; they become, like the Son, members of God's eternal family (1:12).

What began with the original creation, "in the beginning," concludes with God's new creation: believers who abide, with and in each other, in the divine family. John's narrative has moved from the promise of God's family (1:12) to its realization through the divine Spirit breathed into mortal flesh (20:17–22). At the point of believing, even before death, the believer is transported from flesh and blood to her eternal spiritual family. The post-death appearances of Jesus confirm the believer's transformation from mortal sinner to immortal child of God, abiding in Jesus who abides in God, a life both eternal and now.

Notes

CHAPTER 1

1. N. T. Wright, *How God Became King: The Forgotten Story of the Gospels* (New York: HarperOne, 2012). His follow-up study focuses on what the gospels actually say about the meaning of the crucifixion, as indicated by the book's subtitle: N. T. Wright, *The Day the Revolution Began: Reconsidering the Meaning of Jesus's Crucifixion* (San Francisco: HarperOne, 2016).

2. While we recognize the very difficult task of determing the authorship of the gospels, we prescind from questions of authorship. We will simply refer to the authors of each text by their traditional name—Matthew, Mark, Luke, or John.

3. Mark 1:14–15; Matt. 4:23; Luke 4:43; Acts 1:3; Gen. 12:1–3.

4. John 1:1–18. You will note that John has quite different answers than those offered by Matthew, Mark, and Luke-Acts—more like the wrong answers coauthor Borgman used to offer, which he had assumed were true for each gospel. John does not use the term *gospel*.

5. "To repent" (*metanoeō*) means a change of mind or reorientation of life. "To believe" (*pisteuō*) signifies trust, confidence, or affirmation (Matt. 5:20; Mark 9:47; 10:14; Luke 13:23–30).

6. Mark 1:1; 14–15; Matt. 4:17, 23; Luke 4:43; 8:1; Matt. 26:28; Mark 14:24; Luke 22:20; Acts 3:25 (Gen. 12:1–3).

7. John 1:29.

8. Walter Ong, *Orality and Literacy* (New York: Methuen, 1988). Working with other scholars of oral-derived literature, Ong reinforces the point that for the ancient storyteller, "thought [came] into being in heavily rhythmic, balanced patterns, in repetitions or antitheses. . . . Serious thought [was] intertwined with memory systems" (34). Literary scholars of biblical narrative have built on the insights of Ong and others in the field of oral storytelling: Robert Alter, *The Art of Biblical Narrative* (New York: Basic Books, 1981), to whose work we will soon turn. Meir Sternberg, *The Poetics of Biblical Narrative: Ideological Literature and the Drama of Reading* (Bloomington: Indiana University Press, 1985). Sternberg talks about the silences, or gaps, that typically appear where we might expect an explanatory transition from

one narrative unit to another, an important feature we will be dealing with below. These are intentional, a "strategy [that] cannot have been less than deliberate. Far more eloquent than the recourse to particular forms [with no "gaps"] is the particularity for complex formation in the teeth of constraints [the "gaps"] that would dictate ready intelligibility" (42). Moshe Garsiel, *First Book of Samuel: A Literary Study of Comparative Structures, Analogies, and Parallels* (Israel: Revivim, 1985). In his literary analysis, Garsiel focuses on what this guide in part proposes, to uncover repetition in the form of "comparative structures, analogies, and parallels" (his subtitle). J. P. Fokkelman, *Narrative Art and Poetry in the Books of Samuel,* vol. 1, *King David* (Dover, NH: Van Gorcum, 1981). Martin Buber, "Abraham the Seer," in *On the Bible: Eighteen Studies,* ed. Nahum N. Glatzer (Israel: Schocken, 1982), 22–43. Jacob Licht, *Storytelling in the Bible* (Jerusalem: The Magnes Press, 1986). Cedric H. Whitman, *Homer and the Heroic Tradition* (Cambridge, MA: Harvard University Press, 1958). Whitman outlines a rather complex pattern of repetition, a chiasm that shapes the entire twenty-four books of *The Iliad.*

9. Alter, *Art of Biblical Narrative,* 93. The present work stands on the shoulders of and benefits from the work of others. These include R. Alan Culpepper, *Anatomy of the Fourth Gospel: A Study in Literary Design* (Minneapolis: Fortress Press, 1987); Mark Allen Powell, *What Is Narrative Criticism?* (Minneapolis: Fortress, 1990); Mark W. G. Stibbe, *John as Storyteller: Narrative Criticism and the Fourth Gospel* (Cambridge: Cambridge University Press, 1992); James L. Resseguie, *Narrative Criticism and the New Testament: An Introduction* (Grand Rapids: Baker Academic), 2005; David M. Rhoads, Joanna Dewey, and Donald Michie, *Mark as Story: An Introduction to the Narrative of a Gospel,* 3rd ed. (Minneapolis: Fortress, 2012); Jonathan T. Pennington, *Reading the Gospels Wisely: A Narrative and Theological Introduction* (Grand Rapids: Baker, 2012).

10. The contrasting approaches to the two distinct creation stories that begin Genesis illustrate the point. Alter notes that traditional biblical scholarship has been busy—and successful—in locating strands of oral tradition with differing writers, while the literary scholar explores the "composite artistry" that reflects the unity of the two in a literary whole—a singular hand that makes of the two accounts one unified and compelling picture of creation. Alter, *Art of Biblical Narrative,* 19, 132, 154.

11. Alter, *Art of Biblical Narrative,* 95.

12. Like the two distinct creation stories that begin Genesis.

13. Before any of the four gospels appeared in written form, a version of the gospel appeared in written letters, from Paul. Its gospel was mostly different from what became John on the one hand and from the Synoptic Gospels on the other. This gospel began appearing in the fifth decade of the first century, at least two decades earlier than any of the written gospels. Paul himself considered *his* version the true gospel and was upset at the other versions (still in unwritten oral traditions), which he considered "different" and perverted. "I am astonished," Paul writes his converts in Galatia, "that you are so quickly deserting the one who called you in the grace of

Christ and are turning to a different gospel—not that there is another gospel, but there are some who are confusing you and want to pervert the gospel of Christ" (Gal. 1:6–7). He goes on in the rest of Galatians to articulate more fully his version of a gospel (especially in chapter 3). Its fundamental vision—all are equal in being sinful and candidates for grace—allows for no boasting; it is a vision yielding fruits of the Spirit (rather than dead works of the Law): "the fruit of the Spirit is love, joy, peace, patience, kindness, generosity, faithfulness, gentleness, and self-control" (Gal. 5:22–23). The issue of the relationship of Paul's understanding of the gospel to the understandings of Matthew, Mark, Luke, and John is beyond the scope of our attempt to hear attentively and accurately the voice and message of each of the New Testament gospels.

CHAPTER 2

1. The verses following 16:8a are from a later manuscript, a clear addition by a later and possibly nervous scribe—as most commentators agree. Decades later, as the majority of scholars agree, two additional "conclusions" were added: 16:8b and 16:9–20, marked in most Bibles in brackets.

2. Jesus curiously commands the demons to keep silent about his identity. These silenced minions of Satan seem to know too much while the disciples, as we will see, know too little. Both disciples and demons are silenced. The matter of Jesus wishing to keep his identity secret, in Jewish territory, will come up again: it is likely that fixating on Jesus's power would reinforce expectations for a political champion while ignoring the importance of the suffering "Son of Man" whose good news is of a kingdom whose rule and manner of life subverts all known political systems. Mark emphasizes the strategic importance of Jesus wishing his identity to be kept secret among the Jews.

3. We hear that people had come to Jesus "in great numbers from Judea, Jerusalem, Idumea, beyond the Jordan, and the region around Tyre and Sidon" (3:7–8)—that is, from far and wide. The sick are healed, and "whenever the unclean spirits saw him, they fell down before him and shouted, 'You are the Son of God!'" (about which Jesus wants no broadcasting [3:11–12]).

4. Later we hear, "Truly I tell you, there is no one who has left house or brothers or sisters or mother or father or children or fields, for my sake and for the sake of the good news, who will not receive a hundredfold now in this age—houses, brothers and sisters, mothers and children, and fields, with persecutions—and in the age to come eternal life. But many who are first will be last, and the last will be first" (10:29–31).

5. See the insightful treatment of this idea in Ched Myers, *Binding the Strong Man: A Political Reading of Mark's Story of Jesus* (Maryknoll, NY: Orbis Books, 1988).

6. The other substantial teaching is in chap. 13. Because Mark repeatedly refers to

Jesus as one who teaches, the listening audience will be able to pick up on the many small teachings, like the one on nuclear family being trumped by God's kingdom family, almost always in a context of show-and-tell—as we will see more clearly in the following chapters.

7. Mark's audience will know, of course, that the disciples became receptive of the gospel of Jesus. But in this story the crowds turn murderous, following their toxic leaders, and the disciples deny and desert Jesus.

8. Differing scholarly opinions can be found on the meaning here. This guide will attempt to place this foreknowledge of Jesus, as in Matthew and Luke as well, within the narrative as a whole and coherent unity.

CHAPTER 3

1. In the Hebrew Scriptures, the sea often represents chaos held in check by God (Job 7:12; Ps. 74:13; Isa. 27:1). Just as the Creator God of Genesis spoke order in dividing the originally chaotic waters (1:6–8), Jesus speaks calm to the stormy sea.

2. *Awe* (crowd, 9:15); *astonishment* (crowd, 1:22; 6:2; 7:37); *amazement* (crowd, 1:27; 2:12; 5:20; 12:11, 17; disciples, 10:32; Pilate, 15:5).

3. Allusions for "seven" are uncertain. Perhaps it is meant to recall the seven fruitful years in Egypt, during which time Joseph stored extra food in order to have enough for Egypt and even "all the earth" during the seven lean years ahead (Gen. 41:26–36, 56–57). Perhaps it points forward to the period of the early believing community, wherein there were appointed "seven men of good standing, full of the Spirit and of wisdom" in order to distribute food to the Hellenist widows who "were being neglected in the daily distribution of food" (Acts 6:1, 3). Further, we note that "the twelve called together the whole community" with their judgment that they "select from among [themselves] seven men of good standing, full of the Spirit and of wisdom, whom [the twelve] may appoint to this task" (Acts 6:2–3).

4. Those who have responded in awe or astonishment suggest a lack of initial faith; on the other hand, those who have begged for help and have approached Jesus in faith are not described as being astonished or surprised.

5. Biblical scholars call this intertwining/interruption *intercalation*.

6. Within scholarly circles, the so-called Messianic Secret has been widely explored. Viewed within the interlocking patterns of repetition, the need for secrecy becomes clear: since no one understands the nature and mission of Jesus in bringing the good news of God, broadcasting his astonishing power would mislead, disastrously.

7. Mark appears to assume what Jesus himself assumes, that there is no hope for the world outside Israel without Israel itself first coming to their Messiah.

CHAPTER 4

1. Common in orally derived literature like the gospels, this type of framing is an example of *inclusio*, a literary device that parallels thematic hearing cues in forming a beginning and a circling conclusion to a particular section or even a whole story.

2. In the thinking of Jesus, false honor is all the world knows. Ancient codes of honor centered on defending family and tribe against attack, whether physical or verbal. Such a sense of honor and glory is approvingly manifest in Homer's epics, *The Iliad* and *The Odyssey*. Homer's epics were the Greek bible in the centuries up to the time of Jesus. Bloodshed was a common ingredient in this code of honor. Jesus's teaching turns such thinking upside-down: those who embrace the good news of God must be willing to suffer the loss of honor, to embrace shame, ridicule, even the shedding of one's blood for the sake of others—even those outside of family and tribe. The ancient code of honor, adhered to apparently by the disciples, is a powerfully exclusive and parochial force, while the honor and glory accruing to Jesus, exemplified by the ridicule and shame he suffers for the well-being of others, is a powerfully inclusive force, a spreading out of well-being to the world.

3. For all the differing theological takes on what *ransom* means, however, most scholars agree that the disciples, like the Messiah, must be willing to suffer radical loss in service to others. "If any want to become my followers," Jesus has warned, "let them deny themselves and take up their cross and follow me" (8:34). This cross demands a daily dying to self-interest. Becoming another's servant for the sake of the kingdom, Jesus says, comes at the cost of one's own honor and possibly of life itself.

4. John Drury, "Mark," in *The Literary Guide to the Bible*, ed. Robert Alter and Frank Kermode (Cambridge, MA: Harvard University Press, 1987), 404–5.

CHAPTER 5

1. Jesus and the Pharisees, competing religious authorities, are in the synagogue along with others, including a man with a withered hand. The established authorities "watched him to see whether he would cure him on the sabbath, so that they might accuse him" (3:1–2). Jesus calls to the deformed man and then confronts the religious leaders: "Is it lawful to do good or to do harm on the sabbath, to save life or to kill?" They are silent, and Jesus is angry, grieving "at their hardness of heart." Jesus restores the man's hand, and "the Pharisees went out and immediately conspired with the Herodians against him, how to destroy him" (3:3–6).

2. This is the only reference of the seven to the coming glory of the Son of Man. "Those who are ashamed of me and of my words in this adulterous and sinful gener-

ation, of them the Son of Man will also be ashamed when he comes in the glory of his Father with the holy angels" (8:38).

3. The text continues, "he will send out the angels, and gather his elect from the four winds, from the ends of the earth to the ends of heaven" (13:27).

CHAPTER 6

1. Rather than encouraging worship, the leaders oppress the would-be worshipers. They sell sacrifices to all, including the poor—and perhaps at inflated prices.

2. See Isa. 56:7 and Jer. 7:11.

3. Authority and response: from the very beginning of Mark, the religious powers, who have felt their authority threatened by that of Jesus, want to destroy him (3:6).

4. A man plants a vineyard, appoints overseers, and goes to another country. He sends emissaries at harvest time to collect his share, but the tenants beat these slaves and send them away empty-handed. A second try, and this time the tenants kill the master's slave. A third try, then "many others" (12:5). The master of the vineyard knows what will work—or thinks he does: "He had still one other, a beloved son. Finally he sent him to them, saying, 'They will respect my son.' But those tenants said to one another, 'This is the heir; come, let us kill him, and the inheritance will be ours.' So they seized him, killed him, and threw him out of the vineyard" (12:6–8). The owner will come back, however, "destroy the tenants and give the vineyard to others" (12:9).

5. The "things that are the emperor's" would have been suspect for the audience, most especially the Roman poll tax which so burdened poor Jews.

6. Jesus adds to this identification with "Son of Man," as we saw in the prior chapter: "And you will see the Son of Man / seated at the right hand of the Power,' / and 'coming with the clouds of heaven.'"

7. Early in the story we found, similarly, that the crowds were "astounded at his teaching, for he taught them as one having authority, and not as the scribes" (1:22).

8. It is possible that there are two distinct "crowds" in this section of Mark. The "crowd" that hailed Jesus coming into Jerusalem is the same crowd that the religious leaders fear. The "crowd" that screams for Pilate to crucify Jesus might be a new crowd, introduced in the garden scene (14:43). Since arrest to crucifixion took about twelve hours, the crowd that came out with swords and clubs to arrest Jesus is likely the crowd in Pilate's courtyard demanding him to free Barabbas (15:11–13). It seems unlikely that Mark would have conflated these groups, and thought that all of a sudden the crowd who loved Jesus and hailed him as king was now, in a few short hours, screaming for his crucifixion. On the other hand, perhaps "the crowd" is meant to be amorphous and Mark is making a comment on the fickleness of fame and popular opinion, undermining those pursuits and demonstrating his point about

what true service, true leadership, true "messiahship" are all about and what they require of followers (rejection by the fickle masses).

9. "At the festival [Pilate] used to release a prisoner for them, anyone for whom they asked. Now a man called Barabbas was in prison with the rebels who had committed murder during the insurrection. So the crowd came and began to ask Pilate to do for them according to his custom. Then he answered them, 'Do you want me to release for you the King of the Jews?' For he realized that it was out of jealousy that the chief priests had handed him over. But the chief priests stirred up the crowd to have him release Barabbas for them instead'" (15:6–11).

10. Perhaps for the crowd the picture of a humiliated Jesus did not fit with their understanding of the "coming kingdom of our ancestor David," as they had earlier shouted in praise of Jesus (11:9–10).

11. The teaching is less about the future than it is a warning about response for those listening in the present. Whatever was happening in the future has presumably happened, since for Mark the listening generation has experienced the beginning of God's kingdom on earth (9:1).

12. This perspective is arguable. Those who are listening to Mark are more likely to face suffering and even death at the hands of fellow Jews than from Roman persecution, which was isolated and rare in the first century. "Brothers" and family members at odds would suggest the extreme discipline and possible death that believers faced from fellow Jews.

13. "You do not know what you are asking," Jesus responds to his disciples' overriding concern for their own status and honor (10:35–37, 41). They prove reluctant to wrap their minds and hearts around the unlikely association of suffering and power. Jesus invites the disciples to share in his "cup" of suffering, in his role as one who ransoms others in need. "Are you able to drink the cup that I drink, or be baptized with the baptism that I am baptized with?" he asks them (10:38). His rhetorical question contains its answer: not yet. The kingdom's strange power is connected, in this context, with the cup of suffering that accompanies the commitment to serve. "The Son of Man came not to be served but to serve, and to give his life a ransom for many" (10:45). So, too, the disciples, but not yet: "The cup that I drink you will drink," says Jesus; "with the baptism with which I am baptized, you will be baptized" (10:39). This fulfillment is realized after the ending of Mark's text.

14. In Mark, this covenant is not a "new" covenant (as it is only in Luke of the four narratives about Jesus) but rather an extension and fulfillment of "the covenant." The story of Mark, then, flows on from the longer story of the covenant told in the Hebrew Scriptures. The initial sealing of the covenant between God and God's people involved Moses and the pouring out of sacrificial blood on both the altar and the people. "Moses came and told the people all the words of the LORD and all the ordinances; and all the people answered with one voice, and said, 'All the words that the LORD has spoken we will do.' And Moses wrote down all the words of the LORD [the covenant words]. He rose early in the morning, and built an altar at the foot of

the mountain, and set up twelve pillars, corresponding to the twelve tribes of Israel. . . . Moses took half of the blood and put it in basins, and half of the blood he dashed against the altar. Then he took the book of the covenant, and read it in the hearing of the people; and they said, 'All that the LORD has spoken we will do, and we will be obedient.' Moses took the blood and dashed it on the people, and said, 'See the blood of the covenant that the LORD has made with you in accordance with all these words'" (Exod 24:3–4, 6–8).

15. Some interpretations of the last supper in Mark, and in particular the pouring out of blood for many, suggest that Jesus's dying on the cross was to effect forgiveness of sins for those who believe—that salvation depends on Jesus's dying on the cross for their sins. Such a view reflects more the thought of Paul (in, say, Galatians) and also the two thousand years of theological and liturgical tradition than what Mark indicates by reference to the covenant.

16. This suffering includes the emotional upheaval of experiencing ridicule and the loss of honor, which should be expected of any servant coming to the rescue and providing ransom for others seeking communal well-being.

17. In the courtyard, Peter denies knowing Jesus three times—as foretold by Jesus (14:66–72). Just before, immediately following the betrayal of Jesus by Judas, we hear that "all of them [the disciples] deserted him and fled" (14:50).

CHAPTER 7

1. Only the epoch beginning with David measures fourteen generations, the other two thirteen each. Beyond the seven-day creation, consider also that David is the odd brother out of his circle of seven older brothers: God alone can upset the perfection of seven by choosing the eighth and youngest, an outsider, to rule over Israel as its ideal king. The possibility of the latter would emphasize the extent of divine providence in moving from King David to King Jesus (25:34, 40; 27:11). In any case, the numerical precision and repetition, in itself, implies the magisterial hand of God in the history of Israel and its three major ages past, and in the fourth, which begins now.

2. From David Bentley Hart's splendid translation of the New Testament, *The New Testament: A Translation* (New Haven: Yale University Press, 2017).

3. Hart rejects "repent" as the appropriate translation of *metanoia* given its pedestrian usage for merely saying sorry. We will follow him in using the phrase "change of heart" instead.

CHAPTER 8

1. Each discourse is clearly marked by formulaic indicators: at the beginning we hear, "Now Jesus began to teach, saying . . ." while at the end we hear, "When Jesus had finished teaching . . ." The first and last discourses serve as bookends to the other three, offering Matthew's most systematic analysis of the superior righteousness required for entry to the kingdom (as well as the kind of behavior that disqualifies entry to the kingdom).

2. See the section on the Abraham saga in Paul Borgman, *Genesis: The Story We Haven't Heard* (Downers Grove, IL: InterVarsity, 2001). Mary Douglas, anthropologist and critic of ancient literature and culture, describes her experience as a reader and scholar of Numbers: "I first read the book of Numbers in 1987, and was surprised to find that it has been much depreciated by commentators for disorderly writing. I later found that it is not disorderly but well organized as an elegant ring. After seeing how badly that great book has fared at the hands of qualified commentators, I could not get the topic off my mind." *Thinking in Circles: An Essay on Ring Composition* (New Haven: Yale University Press, 2007), ix. She goes on, "Friends ask me, what does it matter? Why is it important to know the construction? This leads to another point: in a ring composition the meaning is located in the middle. A reader who reads a ring as if it were a straight linear composition will miss the meaning. Surely that matters! The text is seriously misunderstood, the composition is classed as lacking in syntax, and the author dismissed with disdain. Surely, misinterpretation does matter." She has also heard this from colleagues: "'Ring composition is a loose and fuzzy concept. Mary will always be able to find a ring form if she looks hard enough, in a laundry list, sports news, or whatever. Rings are everywhere.' This lethal criticism I must rebut. Fear of it was one of the reasons why I was not too disappointed to find that Leviticus is not an example of construction in a ring" (x). But Numbers is just such a sweeping chiasm, which Douglas demonstrates masterfully.

3. The first book parallels book 24, book 2 parallels book 23, and so on, to the center point of books 12 and 13; see Cedric H. Whitman, *Homer and the Heroic Tradition* (Cambridge, MA: Harvard University Press, 1958). At the back of this volume Whitman has a chart that illustrates chiastic structure within individual chapters as well—book 22, for example:

appeal of Priam
　　appeal of Hecuba
　　　　soliloquy of Hector
　　　　　　chase around Troy
　　　　　　　　duel
　　　　　　dragging of body around Troy
　　　　lament of Priam
　　lament of Hecuba
lament of Andromache

4. For a helpful overview, see David C. Sim, *Apocalyptic Eschatology in the Gospel of Matthew* (Cambridge: Cambridge University Press, 1996).

5. "Pray then in this way: Our Father in heaven, hallowed be your name. Your kingdom come. Your will be done, on earth as it is in heaven" (6:9–10).

6. Matthew portrays the beginning of the kingdom age but with an eye toward "the end of the age"—the day of judgment.

7. Commentators acknowledge the ambiguity of this section concerning the days ahead before "the end [that] will come" (24:14), specifically on what it is that the disciples will experience before the end and what generations of believers to follow will experience before perhaps the final end of the age marked by judgment and eschaton. The polemical point, however, is clear: disciples are to beware, to be wary, on guard, awake; they are to be prepared for trials, betrayal, and even death (24:9).

CHAPTER 9

1. But in the scripture quoted (Isa. 6:9–10), it's not the people's heart that has grown dull and stopped ears from hearing, but the divine will! "Make the mind of this people dull," says God through Isaiah,

stop their ears,
shut their eyes,
so that they may not look with their eyes,
listen with their ears,
comprehend with their minds,
turn and be healed. (Isa. 6:9–10)

2. Throughout Matthew, the righteous one is "the one who hears the word and understands it, who indeed bears fruit" (13:23), an echo of the ending of discourse one: "Everyone then who hears these words of mine and acts on them will be like a wise man who built his house on rock.... And everyone who hears these words of mine and does not act on them will be like a foolish man who built his house on sand" (7:24–26).

CHAPTER 10

1. A stone is *like* a rock but is not a rock. "Peter" is *Petros* (stone), not *petra* (bedrock or massive rock formations). There is scholarly debate about whether the people assembled by God in the kingdom come to earth is founded on Peter (a stone, *petros*) or his acknowledgment (rock, *petra*) of Jesus as the Christ.

2. Peter is given the keys to *the kingdom*, not to the *ekklēsia*, usually translated as "church." Jesus requires workers in the kingdom come to earth, of whom Peter is foremost.

3. See the remarks concerning "ransom" in the section "Movement Three (Mark 10:32–45)" in chap. 4 and in the section "Blood of the Covenant Poured Out for Many" (Mark 14:24) in chap. 6. Matthew's use is similar in wording and meaning to Mark's.

4. In fulfillment of "what had been spoken through the prophet" (21:4), Jesus rides on a lowly beast: he is "mounted on a donkey," "on a colt, the foal of a donkey" (21:5; cf. Zech. 9:9 and the Septuagint version of Isa. 62:11).

CHAPTER 11

1. Matt. 17:9, 12, 22; 20:18, 28. Twice more Jesus talks to his disciples about his coming betrayal and death (26:24, 45). The triumph of God over Satan and the kingdoms of this world will not come without the extreme suffering of Jesus and of his disciples, as Jesus has warned in the two parallel discourses addressed only to his followers.

2. It is possible that the listening audience would hear an echo of the anointing associated with Israel's kings. As Son of Man, Jesus accepts and confirms the anointing and its honor. See 1 Sam. 10:1; 1 Kings 1:39; 2 Kings 9:12. Matthew's references and imagery of royalty are certainly compatible with suggestions of kingly demeanor—and what will be revealed—in the stately manner of Jesus's death.

3. "This assertion Moses then confirms, for as he dashes the remaining blood upon the people, he reminds them that the covenant, contracted with Yahweh, has been solemnized in blood, having been made clear to the people by the words that Yahweh has spoken." John I. Durham, *Exodus*, Word Biblical Commentary 3 (Grand Rapids: Thomas Nelson/Zondervan, 1987), 344; emphasis added.

4. E. P. Sanders attempts an explanation of "covenant" in the Hebrew Scriptures that remains true in the New Testament. Covenant refers to "the view that one's place in God's plan is established on the basis of the covenant and that the covenant requires as the proper response of man his obedience to its commandments, while providing means of atonement for transgression." And, "The overall pattern of Rabbinic religion as it applied to Israelites . . . is this: God has chosen Israel and Israel has accepted the election. . . . As long as he [the Israelite] maintains his desire to stay in the covenant, he has a share in God's covenantal promises, including life in the world to come. The intention and effort to be obedient constitutes the *condition for remaining in the covenant*, but they do not *earn* it." *Paul and Palestinian Judaism: A Comparison of Patterns of Religion* (Minneapolis: Fortress, 1977), 75, 180.

5. Especially in the narrative segues connecting the discourses, Jesus demonstrates his ransoming of those in bondage: he intimates the parallel need for his disciples to sufferingly serve others even to the point of death. They must be willing, as he himself is, to relinquish even their lives as "a ransom for many" (20:20–28). In the Hebrew Scriptures, the idea of ransom was, essentially, a putting-forth of oneself and one's re-

sources to provide rescue for someone in need (see Exod. 21:30; Hos. 13:14; Job 33:24). See the discussion in the section "Movement Three (Mark 10:32–45)" in chap. 4 and the section "The Death of Jesus: Blood of the Covenant Poured Out for Many" in chap. 6.

6. "You will become deserters," Jesus had announced to his disciples just prior—a fulfillment of Scripture and a repetitive reminder that God is in control (Zech. 13:7–9). No, says Peter, I'll not desert. Jesus responds, this very night "you will deny me three times" (26:33–34). No, Peter responds, "'even though I must die with you, I will not deny you.' And so said all the disciples" (26:35). But they are all far from able to drink the cup Jesus must drink.

7. "Go into the city to a certain man," Jesus commands his disciples, "and say to him, 'The Teacher says, My time is near; I will keep the Passover at your house with my disciples.'"

8. Only the Persian king Cyrus is called "Messiah" in the Hebrew Scriptures; he is the "anointed" one who delivers Israel out of exile back to Jerusalem (Isa. 44:28; 45:1, 13)

9. Donald Hagner, *Matthew 1–13*, Word Biblical Commentary 33A (Dallas: Word, 1993), 59.

10. Three times Jesus uses "you have said so" (to a betrayer, a Jewish high priest, and a Roman governor) as a way of forcing the questioner to answer his own question in the affirmative (26:24–25; 26:63–64; 27:17).

11. The chief priests and scribes tell King Herod something he must have found especially unnerving, that Jesus's birth has the authority and validity of the Hebrew Scriptures, "for so it has been written by the prophet:

'And you, Bethlehem, in the land of Judah,
    are by no means least among the rulers of Judah;
for from you shall come a ruler
    who is to shepherd my people Israel.'" (2:5–6)

King Jesus is "ruler" and "shepherd," just as David was shepherd and ruler. But now, in Jesus, Israel and the world have an ultimate deliverer, a king who ushers in God's kingdom.

12. There are these additional citations of fulfillment: 8:17; 11:10; 12:17; 13:14, 35; 21:4.

CHAPTER 12

1. See the section "The Lost Message of the Gospels" in chap. 1.

2. We do not know whether Theophilus is an actual person or a clever use by Luke of a name, "lover of God" in the Greek, suggesting an ideal audience for his narrative.

3. David Moessner suggests that "Luke does not explicitly challenge another account; yet the consistent linkage of scope and sequence, the author's credentials, and

the impact on the reader . . . indicates that in Luke's mind all is not well with the 'many's' accounts." Moessner, "The Appeal and Power of Poetics (Luke 1:1–4): Luke's Superior Credentials (παρηκολουθηκότι), Narrative Sequence (καθεξῆζ), and Firmness of Understanding (η ασφάλεια) for the Reader," in *Jesus and the Heritage of Israel*, ed. Moessner (Harrisburg: Trinity Press International, 1999), 92–93. "By Papias's time," Moessner goes on, "the appeal and power of Luke's poetic claims were indeed provoking a 'firmer grasp of the true significance of the tradition which you have been taught'" (119).

4. There would have been both oral and written sources for stories about Jesus, short of the final form of the texts we have in the New Testament.

5. A brief word is in order here about our goal of recovering the lost gospels, nowhere more evident than in the case of Luke-Acts—on two counts. First, Israel is promised deliverance and salvation in volume one, Luke, and that promise is fulfilled in volume two, Acts. Second, the kingdom's coming is promised in Luke, and that promise is fulfilled in Acts. By the third century and continuing on into our own time, Israel has been thought of as not delivered, and the kingdom has been thought of as passé, having morphed into "the church." While Luke-Acts may not comport with Christian history, it deserves a hearing on its own account.

6. Of all forms of language, poetry offers maximum content per formal composition. It is the most economical way of expressing meaning in a language form. Most translations have Gabriel's words as prose; the parallel lines suggest otherwise. The reader can easily "translate" the prose into balanced parallel lines.

7. Robert Alter, *The Art of Biblical Narrative* (New York: Basic Books, 1981), 91.

8. This, one of several central themes, will be spelled out ahead: see Luke 13:18–30; see also 1:47–49; 8:15; 8:21; 11:28; Acts 2:37; 10:44; 15:7; 28:27.

9. While most translations render this extraordinary poem in ordinary prose, the parallelism of lines indicates the author's intentional line breaks.

10. It is likely that the author echoes Hannah, mother of Samuel. Each woman's poem has an emphasis on the reversals characterizing God's kind of kingdom wherein can be found a most unusual justice. The justice begins with the reversal of favor and fortune for this woman and that, this social outsider and that. Who was Hannah to be singled out by God? And who is Mary to be so blessed and favored? Why, in fact, has Israel as a people been favored, this people whom God "has helped"? Luke will answer these questions, whether or not the audience has been sufficiently alert to ask them. As another mother with a peculiar story regarding conception, Hannah gives miraculous birth to a great word-bearer from God (1 Sam. 2:1–10). She praises God in poetry:

My heart exults in the LORD;
my strength is exalted in my God. (1 Sam. 2:1)

"The Lord" is "*my* God," says Hannah; Mary's "Lord" is "God *my* Savior." In Jesus, the Most High who rules God's kingdom on earth is also *my* Savior.

11. "My eyes have seen your salvation," says Simeon, holding the infant Jesus,

"which you have prepared in the presence of all peoples, a light for revelation to the Gentiles and for glory to your people Israel" (Luke 2:30–32).

12. The audience would have been identified as a Jewish sect embracing Jesus as their Messiah (Acts 24:14). As we will see, the term *Christian* in Acts is used twice, negatively, as what others called followers of Jesus. *Christian* meant something like "fanatic for Jesus," a Christ-crazy. If we date the writing of Luke-Acts into the early second century, then *Christian* as a self-referential term is possible.

CHAPTER 13

1. In line for purification are both mother (Lev. 12:6–13) and her firstborn male (Exod. 13:2, 12, 15; Num. 18:15).

2. Again, the reader can translate the prose into the poetry of balanced lines; only a portion of this poem is rendered as such by most modern translations.

3. *Tribal* here is any community beyond family that commands similar loyalty as family. Family members love you; members of your tribe (community) benefit you (do good to you). Members of your community do work that you don't want to or can't do. So you pay them for their labors. You don't want to or can't raise crops, repair your automobile, or add an addition to your home. So you pay a farmer, mechanic, or carpenter. Likewise, you have goods and services they need. Your "love" of community members is little more than economic transaction. Even sinners "love" those who "love" them (those who benefit them). Tit for tat is the guiding principle of loving those who do good to us (and if they stop doing good to us, we stop doing good to them).

4. We certainly love our children, and we "love" members of our community (where "love" means "do good to those who benefit us as long as they benefit us"). Such loves are kinds of selfishness, within the purview of sinners. Our kin, especially our children, are extended selves (our children carry half of our genes). In a sense, in benefiting our children, we are benefiting ourselves. In fact, we get a great deal of reflected honor and shame from the good and bad actions of our children. The economic calculation that underlies exchanges with members of our community is little more than enlightened self-interest. As soon as we feel we are getting a bad deal, we stop "loving" (benefiting) other non-kin members of our community. If enough of us get a bad enough deal, we put them in prison, ostracize them, or even kill them.

5. At the conclusion of ten chapters of teaching by Jesus in the central section of Luke, we find Jesus approaching Jerusalem. It comes into view, and Jesus breaks down in tears. To no one in particular, Jesus expresses the heart of his distress: "If you, even you [Israel], had only recognized on this day the things that make for peace!" (19:42). Acts will demonstrate a reversal of what makes Jesus weep—when God sends the Holy Spirit and thousands upon thousands upon thousands from Israel turn to their prince of peace.

CHAPTER 14

1. "You divided the sea by your might," sings the psalmist; "you broke the heads of the dragons in the waters" (Ps. 74:13). "Am I the Sea, or the Dragon," asks a distressed Job, "that you set a guard over me?" (Job 7:12). In creation, God brings order to the chaotic void by separating the waters above, in the sky, from the waters below—and then further brings creation orderliness by separating the land from the seas (Gen. 1:1–10). Ancient Jewish thought, along with other ancient cultures, saw the seas as potentially violent, ruled by demonic forces and offended gods.

2. Jews hired by Rome to collect taxes from other Jews were despised.

3. Jesus, in turn, rebukes his host, a Pharisee, who is appalled that Jesus consorts with a sinner. "I entered your house," Jesus says to Simon; "you gave me no water for my feet.... You gave me no kiss, but from the time I came in she has not stopped kissing my feet. You did not anoint my head with oil, but she has anointed my feet with ointment" (7:44–46). Jesus lifts the woman that others look down on, pointing to her extraordinary love (7:36–50).

CHAPTER 15

1. On ring composition, see the section "The Five Teachings about Righteousness" in chap. 8.

2. Disciples, friends, and even enemies frequently refer to Jesus as "Teacher" (3:12; 7:40; 9:38; 10:25; 11:45; 18:18; 19:39; 20:21, 28, 39; 21:7).

3. The antipathy between Jews and Samaritans was intense.

4. Jesus thanks God for hiding such kingdom initiatives as communal peace and health from "the wise and intelligent" and revealing them to the childlike (10:21). The wise are among the power elite, for whom such initiatives are inimical to their rule.

5. A *how* to pray is added to the *what* to pray by way of a parable (11:5–8). A friend goes to another friend and begs for food because a guest has come unexpectedly and he has no food to give him. Only because of the petitioner friend's persistence does the friend with plenty accede to the request. Jesus goes on to say, "Ask, and it will be given you" (11:9). The point is elaborated in the concluding line of the section: "If you then, who are evil, know how to give good gifts to your children, how much more will the heavenly Father give the Holy Spirit to those who ask him!" (11:13).

6. The Pharisee, a religious leader, gives thanks to God that he is blessed—not destitute like so many others, such as that poor fellow on the other side of the temple beating his chest and crying out to God. The tax collector is a paradigmatic societal outcast pleading with God for grace. Of course, it is this disenfranchised person, recognizing dire personal need, who will receive grace.

7. By *little ones* "Jesus probably means the weak, the lowly, the vulnerable (see

at 7:28). Though otherwise unmentioned in the context, we are to understand that they are present as those drawn to Jesus. To cause one of these little ones to stumble morally or spiritually is to get oneself into a worse predicament than would be the case if one were to have been tossed into the sea with one's head poking through the center hole of a millstone that had been firmly secured as a kind of bizarre necklace." John Nolland, *Luke 9:21–18:34*, Word Biblical Commentary 35B (Waco, TX: Word, 1993), 838.

8. The audience has just heard a tale about a beggar who is overlooked by a rich man. As a consequence, the beggar stumbles his way through life but is then rewarded in the next. The rich man dies and is tormented in Hades (16:19–31). The "little ones" in Luke-Acts are like this beggar, disenfranchised: women, little children, the diseased, and those forced to beg. Here the antecedent for "little ones" recalls the immediately preceding story of the despised beggar. We recall that one of the chain of five clustered failures of the disciples in Luke 9 was their failure to heal a little boy, because, as Jesus says, they participate in a "faithless and perverse generation" (9:41). "Whoever welcomes this child in my name welcomes me," Jesus says shortly after (9:48). In the echo section 5', we find a sequence (17:1–19) that poses faith as the antidote to the potential hypocrisy of claiming to follow Jesus while ignoring the little ones for whom the kingdom is intended (9:46–48).

CHAPTER 16

1. Jesus will pour out his blood for this covenant (1:72; 22:20).

2. See theme 5' (Luke 17:1–19).

3. Jesus tells his followers to expect division in their nuclear families, "three against two and two against three; they will be divided: father against son and son against father, mother against daughter and daughter against mother, mother-in-law against her daughter-in-law and daughter-in-law against mother-in-law" (12:52–53). Jesus follows this with talk of counting the cost of following him (14:27–35).

4. "Hate" (*miseō*) has a range of meaning in the Greek, from "detest" and "regard with ill-will" to "to be disinclined toward, *disfavor, disregard* in contrast to preferential treatment."

5. The alternation of woman healed / man healed fits Luke's pattern of alternation between male and female—the good Samaritan followed by the good Jewish woman Mary; the testy lawyer followed by the anxious Martha; news of miraculous conception first to an aging priest, then to a young virgin.

6. Failed Jerusalem may represent any typical kingdom of this world, ruled over by leadership concerned not with justice and mercy but with a show of power and prestige. It's the kingdom of God (13:18–21) versus a merely earthly kingdom masquerading as a religious powerhouse.

7. Even Jesus's adversaries recognize this teaching as "the way of God" (20:21).

CHAPTER 17

1. Relying on the prophetic visions of Isaiah (2:2–22) and Joel (2:31), Jesus alludes briefly to the end of history as marked by the transitional "day of the Lord," a time of judgment on all nations and peoples. Separation of the good from evil, the wheat from the tares (the tares will be burned) gives way to prophesied peace among all humans, among all animals, and between humans and animals. This transitional day of the Lord occurs at the point of kingdom fulfillment, an apocalyptic havoc that will yield to the never-ending eschatological parousia, with Jesus as King.

> The sun shall be turned to darkness, and the moon to blood, before the great and terrible day of the LORD comes. (Joel 2:31)

> There will be signs in the sun, the moon, and the stars, and on the earth distress among nations confused by the roaring of the sea and the waves. People will faint [or die] from fear and foreboding of what is coming upon the world, for the powers of the heavens will be shaken. Then they will see "the Son of Man coming in a cloud" with power and great glory. (Luke 21:25–27)

> The sun shall be turned to darkness and the moon to blood, before the coming of the Lord's great and glorious day. (Acts 2:20)

2. Jesus points to the temple's proper function as a "house of prayer," citing the authority of Scripture (19:45–46; see Isa. 56:7; Jer. 7:11).

3. What do you think about the Baptist's authority? asks Jesus. Did his salvation "come from heaven, or was it of human origin?" (20:4). If the religious leaders question John's revered authority, then the people will be after them, but if they declare John's authority to be based in heaven, then Jesus will answer, "Why did you not believe him?" (20:5–6). We do not know about John's authority, the leaders answer. And so Jesus refuses to answer their questions about his own authority (20:7–8).

4. They kill the owner's "beloved son" (20:13), implying that Jesus himself, as that son, is "the stone that the builders rejected [that] has become the cornerstone," and that "everyone who falls on that stone will be broken to pieces" (20:17–18; see Ps. 118:22–23; Isa. 8:14–15).

5. Jesus, interpreting Ps. 110, quotes David as saying, "The Lord [God] said to my (David's) Lord, 'Sit at my right hand, until I make your enemies your footstool.' David thus calls him Lord; so how can he be his son?" (20:42–44). Jesus points out from Scripture his adversaries' mistaken views concerning the Messiah: surely, they argue, the Messiah must be a son of David (20:41). While not denying this, Jesus says the Messiah is more: "the Lord" is Israel's future king-deliverer (Messiah) about whom God the Lord says (to David's Lord) that his enemies will be his footstool.

6. There is a difference of opinion regarding "this generation" among scholars. "This generation" has already appeared in Luke as a description of corrupt cultures every-

where at all times, going back to Jonah. The mayhem in the heavens and on earth and distress among nations will be seen and suffered by "this generation." Jesus implies that the ancient Ninevites were a wicked generation—a *this* generation—that repented: "When the crowds were increasing, he began to say, 'This generation is an evil generation; it asks for a sign, but no sign will be given to it except the sign of Jonah. For just as Jonah became a sign to the people of Nineveh, so the Son of Man will be to this generation'" (11:29–30).

7. In a longer manuscript tradition, we find, "This cup that is poured out for you is the new covenant in my blood" (22:20). We, however, will follow the shorter, likely more reliable tradition.

8. When their times of trial come, upon the arrest, trial, and crucifixion of their Teacher and Lord, they fail. But many more such times of trial await these same disciples, trials met with stunning victory through the inward dwelling Spirit of God.

9. Jesus's self-reference, "Son of Man" (Dan. 7:13–14), echoes his authority established already in the temple. Judas has been a disciple, just like the people who have been following Jesus with enthusiasm.

10. Galilee at the time was considered a hotbed of revolutionary activities against the established authorities.

11. The audience may recall that Herod had previously wondered about Jesus: "John I beheaded; but who is this about whom I hear such things?" (9:9). Authority loves exhibitions of power, but Jesus doesn't respond to Herod's foolishness (23:11). Meanwhile, the Jewish leaders "stood by, vehemently accusing [Jesus]" (23:10).

12. Moreover, "that same day Herod and Pilate became friends with each other; before this they had been enemies" (23:12). Together, then, the two political leaders representing Rome face the ire of Israel's religious leaders against the supposed subversive, Jesus, for whom Roman authority is ultimately responsible.

13. In two other New Testament narratives a Roman centurion declares, "Truly this man was God's Son!" (Matt. 27:54; Mark 15:39).

14. In recognizing the innocence of Jesus and in honoring him in his death, these two outsiders offer an implicit verdict as to the authority question: Jesus is Israel's new authority in matters of law, covenant, and the coming kingdom, replacing the traditional leaders.

CHAPTER 18

1. Twice in Acts they are called by others, with snide intent, *Christians*: "It was in Antioch that the disciples were first called 'Christians'" (11:26); and Agrippa's question to Paul, "Are you so quickly persuading me to become a Christian?" (26:28). "Christian" would have meant something like *Christ-Crazies*.

2. Gentile worshipers of Israel's God.

3. This same Spirit descended on Jesus (Luke 3:32), empowering him as God's "holy servant" (Acts 4:27, 30). Redeemed Israel will be similarly empowered as

"servant Israel" (Luke 1:54). Just as God's holy servant Jesus was anointed and empowered by this Spirit to bring light and blessing of God's word to Israel, so too the leaders of God's servant Israel are empowered by the Spirit to bring the light and blessing of God's word and rule to all peoples.

4. See Ps. 16:8–11. When the resurrected Jesus opens the eyes of his disciples (Luke 24:44–47) and of the two who are traveling to Emmaus (Luke 24:25–27), the whole of what he claims the Scripture foretold about the Messiah was to be found in one thing, that he would be raised from death. According to Luke-Acts, scriptural prophecy of the Messiah concerns his suffering and God's raising him from death.

5. In Luke-Acts, we don't hear of the forgiveness of sins through the cross. Later, Philip will explain a passage from Isaiah about the Messiah suffering to an Ethiopian official, a eunuch. What he reads, significantly, omits the verses about this servant bearing the sins of all. See Acts 8:30–39; compare with Isa. 53:7–9. Conspicuously missing is Isaiah's reference in this passage to forgiveness of sins ("For he was cut off from the land of the living/ stricken for the transgression of my people" (Isa. 57:8b). There is in all of Luke-Acts no atoning sacrifice attached to the death of Jesus on a cross. Some scholars think that there may be two exceptions: one, the last supper in Luke, which we have already explored; the other, in Paul's speech to Ephesian believers, which we will see in the following chapter.

6. "Listen to him [Jesus]," God is quoted as saying to some of the disciples (Luke 9:35). Whose voice speaks for God is made clear to the disciples.

7. "Repent," as we learned in the teaching section of Luke, means a decisive turning around, a complete change of heart (Luke 9:51–19:44).

8. God's grace, as presented in Luke-Acts, is a major component of the text's theology. This grace consists primarily in the gift of the Messiah's clear teaching of what one needs to do for salvation, and his sending the Spirit to empower that doing. The empowering Spirit is pure grace—a "gift," as Peter puts it here.

9. See Deut. 18:15–10 and Lev. 23:29.

10. "Repent therefore," Peter says, "and turn to God so that your sins may be wiped out, so that times of refreshing may come from the presence of the Lord, and that he may send the Messiah appointed for you, that is, Jesus, who must remain in heaven until the time of universal restoration that God announced long ago through his holy prophets" (3:19–21). As Acts makes clear, Jesus is Messiah for those Jews embracing him as such—in the present. But the ultimate reign of God over all the earth, and Israel, awaits "the time of universal restoration."

11. Acts 16:5 reads, "The churches were strengthened in the faith and increased in numbers daily." As discussed, *ekklēsia* is consistently translated anachronistically as "church," whereas the literary context clearly indicates kingdom belonging, as in 9:2.

12. As we saw, the nine clustered poems in the first six chapters of Luke focus on salvation. Zechariah, for example, praises "the Lord God of Israel" who "has looked favorably on his people and redeemed them"—a faithful God who "has raised up

a mighty savior for us in the house of his servant David" (1:68–69). And Simeon praises God for preparing this salvation "in the presence of all peoples, a light for revelation to the Gentiles," bringing "glory to [God's] people Israel" (2:29–32). Jesus speaks of his mission to Israel as proclaiming release for all who are oppressed (4:18–19).

CHAPTER 19

1. Joseph illustrates Stephen's point: God's presence everywhere and at all times. And as Joseph was rejected by his brothers, so was Jesus by Stephen's audience, Israel's traditional leaders.

2. Moses was abandoned as an infant by his family and then, as an adult, was "pushed aside" (7:27) by his countrymen; later, his kinfolk again "pushed him aside" (7:39). This repetition, however, emphasizes the presence of God even in times of estrangement from home and family.

3. Moses was "instructed in all the wisdom of the Egyptians" and became "powerful in his words and deeds," a person "beautiful before God" (7:20–22). For Jesus, see Luke 4:22.

4. "Now when forty years had passed, an angel appeared to him in the wilderness of Mount Sinai, in the flame of a burning bush. When Moses saw it, he was amazed at the sight; and as he approached to look, there came the voice of the Lord: 'I am the God of your ancestors, the God of Abraham, Isaac, and Jacob.' Moses began to tremble and did not dare to look. Then the Lord said to him, 'Take off the sandals from your feet, for the place where you are standing is holy ground'" (7:30–33).

5. We translate *ekklēsia* in Acts as "gathering." There was no organized "church" at this point, a fact noted by David Bentley Hart throughout his translation of the New Testament. Hart renders *ekklēsia* as "assembly" in Acts 8:3.

CHAPTER 20

1. According to Paul, Jesus has been appointed by God as a judge whose verdicts will be rendered on the basis of repentance and obedience to the word of God taught by Jesus (17:31).

2. While "Hellenists" often denotes Jews of the diaspora in Acts, the context here demands that we read "Greek Gentiles," not "Greek Jews." Scholars agree that the original text is a muddle here.

3. F. F. Bruce, *The Book of Acts*, New International Commentary on the New Testament (Grand Rapids: Eerdmans, 1988), 292.

4. Amos 9:11–12; Jer. 12:15; Isa. 45:21.

CHAPTER 21

1. See especially the first chapter of Galatians and the view of Israel's status in Romans. Subsequent teaching within church tradition has, perhaps unwittingly, widened the gap between Luke's presentation of Paul's thinking and Paul's vision as expressed in his letters.

2. This verse is not in all ancient manuscripts, but parallelism between Luke and Acts suggests its reliability.

3. God-fearers, as we have seen, are non-Jews like the Ethiopian eunuch (8:27–40) who have adopted, to the extent allowed them, the religious culture of the Jews.

4. The switch from third-person narration ("they" and "she") to first-person ("we") presumes an author entering the text as a character, one who is now doing the storytelling. "When he had seen the vision," the narrator comments, "we immediately tried to cross over to Macedonia, being convinced that God had called us to proclaim the good news to them" (16:10). The first-person-plural point of view continues through 16:17 and then resumes at 20:5, including Paul's momentous journey to Jerusalem ("When we arrived in Jerusalem, the brothers welcomed us warmly"; 21:17) and his arrival in Rome ("When we came into Rome, Paul was allowed to live by himself, with the soldier who was guarding him"; 28:16). At this point the narration switches back to the third-person: Paul has his last meeting and speech with Jews (28:17–31). We think that the best explanation of the shifting in narration is the added authority it gives the author for knowing firsthand what was happening with Paul in the latter part of his ministry.

CHAPTER 22

1. There are three discrete "missionary" journeys: 13:1–14:28; 15:36–18:22; and 18:23–21:16 (which does not include his last journey to Rome, as a prisoner). This last journey is filled with rapid-paced adventures at sea and on land.

2. Just as in the life of synagogues, leaders within individual and local gatherings emerged.

3. While not specified, the mixture of Jew and Gentile in the assembly at Ephesus can be assumed by the literary context in which Jews and Gentiles are consistently turning to Jesus as Messiah (Jews) and Lord (Gentiles).

4. Paul may intend to single out Jesus as the one providing the purchase price for securing God's people. However, this is the one phrase in all of Luke-Acts to assign such a meaning to the death of Jesus alone, and not the death of other true prophets for the sake of God's people. Jesus self-consciously aligns himself with the prophets whose blood was shed for the sake of God's people. Jesus says, "I must be on my way, because it is impossible for a prophet to be killed outside of Jerusalem."

He continues, "Jerusalem, Jerusalem, the city that kills the prophets and stones those who are sent to it!" (Luke 13:33–34).

CHAPTER 23

1. "Hebrew" can mean Aramaic here, the common language of Jews in and around Jerusalem. Those Jews dispersed from Jerusalem and its environs would have adopted the common language of Greek.

2. Gamaliel, himself a student of the influential Hillel, was a Pharisaic teacher of the Law.

3. In Luke, Jesus did not come to condemn Pharisees, but to raise them—as Pharisees—to life in the resurrected Messiah and his kingdom.

4. If not sent to Rome, Paul would be living with the daily threat of being killed by Jewish leaders.

CHAPTER 24

1. In identifying himself as "Jesus *of Nazareth* whom you are persecuting," the heavenly Jesus might be signifying for Paul's primarily Jewish audience (and for Luke's audience as well) an ironic tragedy shared by both Jesus and Paul with regard to their reception among their own. Jesus is rejected in his hometown of Nazareth (Luke 4:16, 24), while Paul, too, is being vilified by his fellow Israelites in their shared religious home, Jerusalem.

2. The dramatic effect of hearing that the heavenly voice speaks in Hebrew would parallel Paul's use of Hebrew when addressing the Jewish leadership and imperial powers in his first defense speech: "When they heard him addressing them in Hebrew, they became even more quiet" (22:2).

3. Recall that poetry rendered as prose in the NRSV has been transposed here and throughout as poetry.

CHAPTER 26

1. The last verse (1:18) is a poem in itself. No one has ever seen God (line 1), but now God can be seen (line 4)—through God-the-only-Son (line 2) who is ever at the Father's side (line 3).

2. While Jesus says that he will draw all people to himself when lifted up from earth (12:32), we also hear that no one can come to Jesus "unless drawn by the Father" (6:44); moreover, it seems in John that very few are drawn to Jesus.

3. "The truth will make you free," says Jesus, who goes on to speak of everyone who sins as being "a slave to sin." We also hear that "if the Son makes you free, you will be free indeed" (8:32, 36). The powerful Lamb will conquer sin by vanquishing the tyranny of sin.

4. Jesus affirms his authoritative and close relationship to God by referring to himself as the Son of Man (1:51), a familiar term at the time of Jesus, reflecting Daniel's son of man ("one like a human being," 7:13–14): "As I watched in the night visions, I saw *one like a human being* coming with the clouds of heaven. And he came to the Ancient One and was presented before him. To him was given dominion and glory and kingship, that all peoples, nations, and languages should serve him."

CHAPTER 27

1. "Born of water" could simply mean birth as a mortal from within the waters of the womb, and "born of Spirit" could mean that the believing mortal is transformed by the Spirit into an eternal child of God.

CHAPTER 28

1. Messianic expectations were mixed with expectations of a return of "the prophet"—Elijah, perhaps, or Moses.

2. In only one other of two instances where "I am" stands alone, Jesus's equation of himself with God is clear: "before Abraham was born, I am" (8:58; possibly 18:5, 6, 8). In other instances, Jesus uses "I am" to indicate metaphoric identities, as in *I am ... the bread of life; the light of the world* (8:12); *the gate for the sheep* (10:7, 9); *the good shepherd* (10:11, 14); *the resurrection and the life* (11:25); *the way* and *the truth* and *the life* (14:6); and *the true vine* (15:1, 5). Jesus also uses it with an *implied predicate*: "I am [he]," "I am [the one]," indicating he is the Messiah (4:26; 8:24, 28; 13:19), and "It is [I]" and "I am [he]" simply to identify himself (6:20; 18:8; and possibly 18:5, 6, 8), as did the man born blind (9:9). Here in the fifth miracle-sign, "It is I" can be taken to mean simply a statement of ordinary identification (as in 4:26; 6:20; 18:8, and possibly 18:5, 6, 8), or as the "I AM" signifying God. "Say to the Israelites," God had challenged Moses, "'I AM has sent me to you'" (Exod. 3:14). In either case, the miracle stands as a miracle pointing not only to control over nature but to the miracle of allaying fear.

3. See chap. 5 on Mark's understanding of Jesus as Son of Man (Mark 4).

4. As we have noted, and will see ahead in John, all religious rites and sacred places are replaced entirely by the person of Jesus.

CHAPTER 30

1. These are Greeks who have come to worship at Passover and want to see Jesus. He apparently refuses them as "outsiders" for now: he must first die and then will bear much fruit (12:24). "And I, when I am lifted up from the earth," Jesus says, "will draw all people to myself" (12:32; see 8:28). *All people*, given the context, probably include these Greeks.

2. Scholars have puzzled over the meaning here. Some suggest the foot washing relates to baptism, or to purification rites beyond baptism, or to the "cleansing of sins" achieved at the cross. What Jesus will go on to explain about being clean already, however, would seem to trump any meaning other than the one most explicit: *You disciples are already "clean,"* says Jesus (13:10); *by this act I am offering you a share with me, as you have already heard of abiding in me. Before any foot washing, you were clean, purified, because "you have already been cleansed by the word that I have spoken to you"* (15:3), *abiding in me with my words abiding in you* (15:7). The disciples will replicate what Jesus is doing—"later," Jesus says, "you will understand" (13:7): "Whoever receives one whom I send [disciple, believer] receives me [has a share with me], and whoever receives me [abides in me] receives him who sent me [abides in God the Father]" (13:20).

3. This is not a "Passover meal," of which there is no trace in John. The celebratory Passover meal for Jews (as in Matthew, Mark, and Luke) occurs after the slaying of the paschal lambs; this meal occurs many hours before. In John, Jesus will be slain at the same hour as the paschal lambs. Jesus the paschal lamb, as with the blood of the paschal lamb poured out by Moses, signals deliverance from evil—in this case, not Egypt but the tyranny of sin.

4. "And I will ask the Father, and he will give you another Advocate, to be with you forever" (14:16); "But the Advocate, the Holy Spirit, whom the Father will send in my name, will teach you everything, and remind you of all that I have said to you" (14:26); "When the Advocate comes, whom I will send to you from the Father, the Spirit of truth who comes from the Father, he will testify on my behalf" (15:26); "Nevertheless I tell you the truth: it is to your advantage that I go away, for if I do not go away, the Advocate will not come to you; but if I go, I will send him to you" (16:7); "When the Spirit of truth comes, he will guide you into all the truth; for he will not speak on his own, but will speak whatever he hears, and he will declare to you the things that are to come" (16:13).

5. It does not appear that the disciples are privy to this prayer—it is not for them or to them, but for and to the Father. Yet this prayer of Jesus to his Father would offer reassurance to the listening audience who, decades after the departure of Jesus, have to face *their* hour.

CHAPTER 31

1. Irony is employed by the author throughout this story, as frequently noted by scholars. Most "literary" approaches to John, and indeed to the other New Testament narratives about Jesus, focus on such literary elements as irony, imagery, foreshadowing, character, and plot but without recognizing the patterns of repetition wherein the entire narrative, including the above elements, finds its meaning. That is, we get literary details but not a literary interpretation of the whole, which explains these details.

CHAPTER 32

1. As some scholarly discussion now suggests, this disciple, the "beloved disciple," was probably Lazarus, not John. Note these texts: "So the sisters sent a message to Jesus, 'Lord, he whom you love is ill'" (11:3); "Accordingly, though Jesus loved Martha and her sister and Lazarus . . ." (11:5); "So the Jews said, 'See how he loved him!'" (11:36).

2. It has been suggested, Colin G. Kruse points out, "but cannot be proved, that Jesus' resurrected body simply passed through the linen strips, leaving them still in the shape of his body, though somewhat collapsed. Perhaps attentive readers of John are meant to note the difference between Lazarus' restoration to life and Jesus' resurrection. Lazarus emerged from the tomb still 'wrapped with strips of linen, and a cloth around his face' and he had to be released by others (11:44), whereas in the case of Jesus the linen strips and burial cloth were simply left behind when he rose from the dead." *The Gospel according to St. John*, Tyndale (Downers Grove, IL: IVP, 1988, 2017), 371–72. This is one way of expressing the transformation of Jesus's ordinary body into the strangely different body in which he appeared to believers after his death.

3. George R. Beasley-Murray cites this translation by M. J. Lagrange approvingly. Beasley-Murray, *John*, rev. ed., Word Biblical Commentary (Grand Rapids: Zondervan, 1999), 377.

4. With no sense of forgiving this sin or that; the only other places in John where the problem of sin is mentioned (rarely in terms of forgiveness) are 9:41; 15:22, 24; 16:8–9; 19:11; and 20:23.

5. See John 8:34, where Jesus contrasts being a slave to sin with a believer's freedom. Jesus then says, "If the Son makes you free, you will be free indeed" (8:36).

6. There are, however, some discontinuities with previous chapters: some of the disciples, for example, do not recognize Jesus just after recognizing him—in spite of the fact that he speaks to them. And, as noted, the stated purpose of John, offered in the conclusion of the prior chapter, sounds like a conclusion to the entire book, not a transition to its final chapter.

7. Jesus responds to Peter's ungenerous curiosity about *who* by saying, "If it is my will that he remain until I come, what is that to you? Follow me!" (21:22–23). This is the single mention of a "second coming," which, given the status of a later addition to John, may reflect more the growing consensus, based on texts other than John, that there would be a second (and soon) return of Jesus. Of such there is no evidence in John.

8. As our readers might guess, much scholarly effort has been exercised on figuring out the symbolic significance of 153 caught fish.

9. A focus on this verse or that, so often the case with John, illustrates the importance of an advisory note pleading a thorough reading of John as a unified literary whole. For example, understanding "For God so loved the world that he gave his only Son, so that everyone who believes in him may not perish but may have eternal life" (3:16) requires a complete context to understand what it means to "believe in him." John's story as a whole is a profound exploration of believing in Jesus and why that matters to one seeking the way, the truth, and the life.

Bibliography

Alter, Robert. *The Art of Biblical Narrative*. New York: Basic Books, 1981.

Beasley-Murray, George R. *John*. Rev. ed. Word Biblical Commentary. Grand Rapids: Zondervan, 1999.

Borgman, Paul. *Genesis: The Story We Haven't Heard*. Downers Grove, IL: InterVarsity Press, 2001.

Bruce, F. F. *The Book of Acts*. New International Commentary on the New Testament. Grand Rapids: Eerdmans, 1988.

Buber, Martin. "Abraham the Seer." Pages 22–43 in *On the Bible: Eighteen Studies*. Edited by Nahum N. Glatzer. New York: Schocken, 1982.

Culpepper, R. Alan. *Anatomy of the Fourth Gospel: A Study in Literary Design*. Minneapolis: Fortress, 1987.

Douglas, Mary. *Thinking in Circles: An Essay on Ring Composition*. New Haven: Yale University Press, 2007.

Drury, John. "Mark." Page 404–5 in *The Literary Guide to the Bible*. Edited by Robert Alter and Frank Kermode. Cambridge, MA: Harvard University Press, 1987.

Durham, John I. *Exodus*. Word Biblical Commentary 3. Grand Rapids: Thomas Nelson/Zondervan, 1987.

Fokkelman, J. P. *Narrative Art and Poetry in the Books of Samuel*. Vol. 1, *King David*. Dover, NH: Van Gorcum, 1981.

Garsiel, Moshe. *First Book of Samuel: Comparative Structures, Analogies, and Parallels*. Israel: Revivim, 1985.

Hagner, Donald. *Matthew 1–13*. Word Biblical Commentary 33A. Dallas: Word, 1993.

Hart, David Bentley. *The New Testament: A Translation*. New Haven: Yale University Press, 2017.

Kruse, Colin G. *The Gospel according to St. John*. Tyndale. Downers Grove, IL: IVP, 1988, 2017.

Licht, Jacob. *Storytelling in the Bible*. Jerusalem: Magnes Press, 1986.

Moessner, David. "The Appeal and Power of Poetics (Luke 1:1–4): Luke's Superior Credentials (παρηκολουθηκότι), Narrative Sequence (καθεξῆς), and Firmness of Understanding (η ασφάλεια) for the Reader." In *Jesus and the Heritage of Israel*, ed. David Moessner. Harrisburg: Trinity Press International, 1999.

Myers, Ched. *Binding the Strong Man: A Political Reading of Mark's Story of Jesus.* Maryknoll, NY: Orbis Books, 1988.

Nolland, John. *Luke 9:21–18:34.* Word Biblical Commentary 35B. Waco, TX: Word, 1993.

Ong, Walter. *Orality and Literacy.* New York: Methuen, 1988.

Pennington, Jonathan T. *Reading the Gospels Wisely: A Narrative and Theological Introduction.* Grand Rapids: Baker Academic, 2012.

Powell, Mark Allen. *What Is Narrative Criticism?* Minneapolis: Fortress, 1990.

Resseguie, James L. *Narrative Criticism and the New Testament: An Introduction.* Grand Rapids: Baker Academic, 2005.

Rhoads, David M., Joanna Dewey, and Donald Michie, *Mark as Story: An Introduction to the Narrative of a Gospel.* 3rd ed. Minneapolis: Fortress, 2012.

Sanders, E. P. *Paul and Palestinian Judaism: A Comparison of Patterns of Religion.* Minneapolis: Fortress, 1977.

Sim, David C. *Apocalyptic Eschatology in the Gospel of Matthew.* Cambridge: Cambridge University Press, 1996.

Sternberg, Meir. *The Poetics of Biblical Narrative: Ideological Literature and the Drama of Reading.* Bloomington: Indiana University Press, 1985.

Stibbe, Mark W. G. *John as Storyteller: Narrative Criticism and the Fourth Gospel.* Cambridge: Cambridge University Press, 1992.

Whitman, Cedric H. *Homer and the Heroic Tradition.* Cambridge, MA: Harvard University Press, 1958.

Wright, N. T. *The Day the Revolution Began: Reconsidering the Meaning of Jesus's Crucifixion.* San Francisco: HarperOne, 2016.

———. *How God Became King: The Forgotten Story of the Gospels.* New York: HarperOne, 2012.

———. *The Kingdom New Testament: A Contemporary Translation.* New York: HarperOne, 2011.

Index of Names and Subjects

Index of Scripture References